D0638199

THE SOCIAL MESSAGE
OF THE EARLY
CHURCH FATHERS

The SOCIAL MESSAGE of the EARLY CHURCH FATHERS

IGINO GIORDANI

TRANSLATED BY ALBA I. ZIZZAMIA, D. LITT. (ROM.)

ST. PAUL
EDITIONS

IMPRIMATUR:

✠ Humberto Cardinal Medeiros
Archbishop of Boston

TRANSLATOR'S NOTE: The present volume is the third in a history of early Christian social thought, which the author intends to trace up to the period of Gregory the Great. It appears before the second volume because it is to be used as a text book of Patristic-Homiletics in the School of Theology of The Catholic University of America, and it was produced at the request of the Right Reverend Monsignor Francesco Lardone, Director of Ecclesiastical Studies at the same university. The first volume of the series, *The Social Message of Jesus*, was published in English in 1943; the second, *The Social Message of the Apostles*, is in the process of translation.

All quotations from the Old Testament in the present translation are from the Douay version; those from the New Testament, with one or two exceptions, are from the Confraternity of Christian Doctrine revision (1941, St. Anthony Guild Press).

I am deeply indebted to the Rev. Dr. Patrick W. Skehan of The Catholic University of America for his extremely generous and painstaking assistance with the quotations from the Fathers and for his suggestions regarding the translation; and to Miss Ellen A. Ganey for her careful reading of the manuscript.

Alba I. Zizzamia, D. Litt. (Rom.).

Library of Congress Cataloging in Publication Data

Giordani, Igino, 1894-
    The social message of the early church fathers.

    Translation of Il messaggio sociale dei primi
padri della chiesa.
    Reprint of the 1944 ed. published by St. Anthony
Guild Press, Paterson, N.J.
    Bibliography: p.
    Includes index.
    1. Sociology, Christian—Early church, ca.
30-600.   2. Fathers of the church.   I. Title.
BR166.G5613   1977   261.8   77-4935

Quotations from the revised New Testament, copyright 1941 by Confraternity of Christian Doctrine, are used with its permission.

Copyright, © 1977, by the Daughters of St. Paul

Printed in U.S.A. by the Daughters of St. Paul
50 St. Paul's Ave., Boston, Ma. 02130

The Daughters of St. Paul are an international religious congregation serving the Church with the communications media.

NOTE ON THE AUTHOR

Igino Giordani, who has had a long and successful career as teacher, journalist, and writer, is at present associated with the Vatican Library. For the *Social Message of Jesus* and the *Social Message of the Apostles*, Mr. Giordani received the *Premio Savoia-Brabante* for excellence in the field of history. With regard to this award, the Vatican newspaper, *L'Osservatore Romano* (Feb. 27-28, 1939) says: "These two works, which complement each other, together evidence the loftiness of the theme and the author's skill in overcoming its inherent difficulties. They indeed represent a weighty contribution to social and historical research with regard to early Christianity, based as they are on a wide knowledge and understanding of the field, such as we might expect of one who for long years has completely dedicated himself to these studies . . . examining with patient research (as his careful bibliography attests) the sources available in this field . . . of every nation and time."

TABLE OF CONTENTS

CHAPTER IV

THE ATTEMPT AT RECONCILIATION WITH THE STATE

CHAPTER V

THE "IUS CHRISTI"

CHAPTER VI

THE CITY OF GOD

CHAPTER VII

THE NEW CIVIC CONSCIENCE

CHAPTER VIII

RATIONAL EDUCATION

CHAPTER IX

SOCIAL RELATIONS

CHAPTER X

WEALTH: ITS VALUE AND USE

CHAPTER XI

LABOR

CHAPTER XII

SOLIDARITY

CHAPTER XIII

HERETICAL DISTORTIONS OF SOCIAL THOUGHT

CHAPTER I

CHURCH AND EMPIRE
IN THE SECOND CENTURY

THE FIRST ANTONINES

AFTER Domitian had been killed, the senatorial party recovered from the nightmare of terrorism which had divested it of its authority and cut down its best men; and it succeeded once again in getting the upper hand in the government by electing an emperor from its own ranks, the aged NERVA (96 A. D.), under whose rule, according to Tacitus, liberty (that is, senatorial authority and privileges) and the ruling power were able to live happily together.

Nerva begins the line of Caesars who take their name from the most humane of them all, Antoninus Pius, and their period marks the most enlightened administration in the Empire's history. Each of them, before dying, chose as his successor the senator he thought most fit for the office; and this criterion was the one desired and blessed by the philosophers, Stoics and Cynics, who formed the opposition and who demanded that the sovereign power (βασιλεία) be conferred on the best citizen, not as a pleasure and privilege (ἡδονή), but as a ministry assigned to him by God and ordained for the service of his subjects, so that before their ruler they would not be slaves but free men. The standard of choice was good; substantially it was in harmony with the Christian standard. We are in a period in which philosophy rises to power; the learned

1

Christians considered themselves philosophers — the true philosophers — and as such they conversed and argued with the "other" philosophers. And though they certainly had no part in nominating this or that emperor, they did spread and popularize those theories which the Stoics were disseminating only in restricted intellectual circles.

Cocceius Nerva, who reigned for only two years (96-98), appointed TRAJAN (98-117) as his successor. He reorganized the army and waged war against the Parthians, from whom he took Mesopotamia, and against the Dacians, whose territory, the modern Rumania, he subjected and converted into a province. Though the purpose of these wars was to seek new markets, to relieve the border provinces of constant pressure and danger from the barbarians, and to make Italy once more the economic center of the Mediterranean, they drained huge sums from the public treasury and as a result the economic situation only grew worse, for in those poor and distant lands the legions could not be supported by the war itself as they had been in the rich and nearby countries of the Greek Orient or Gaul. From then on, Rome's wars became an expense instead of a source of booty, but on the other hand, because of her mentality and her traditions as well as for reasons of defense and honor, she could no longer do without them.

As far as Italy's major exports, wine and oil, were concerned, the provinces had already become economically independent of her. Greece, Asia Minor, Africa, Gaul and Spain offered her ruinous competition, so that though Domitian had limited vine-growing, Trajan quite uselessly induced the senators, now drawn for the most part from the municipal centers in the Romanized provinces, to invest capital in land in Italy. The investors then rented these lands to farmers, who for lack of a market, suspended certain crops altogether and converted their fields into pastures; the result was an increase in great landed estates.

Trajan's successor, HADRIAN (117-138) gave up the attempt to restore the economic conditions that had been Italy's in the first century, abandoned Mesopotamia and found peaceful settlements for the frontier difficulties, his aim being the internal reorganization of the Empire. With this in view, he traveled far and wide about the Empire, and, with the slightly bizarre taste of the artist but with the mind of a ruler, he more consciously and with more deliberate intent assumed the role of sovereign of a Graeco-Roman state, in which the more the Latin-Roman privileges of the Peninsula lost their importance, the better grew the condition of the provinces. He built cities to stimulate a more intense economic life in the rural districts, from which he drew the flower of his army and many of the officials in his administration. Imperial bureaucracy was growing constantly, taking one function after another from the senate and the equestrians, especially after the distinction between the possessions of the emperor and the possessions of the state became so slight as finally to disappear altogether. This last greatly benefited the ruler's finances and also provided a temporary relief for the tax-payers, since the direct and better controlled provincial administration of the imperial officials eliminated in good measure that horde of governors and tax-farmers who had been having their own hateful and arbitrary way with them.

Hadrian's dream of peace was disturbed by various revolts, the most violent of which was that of the Jews. During Trajan's reign they had risen in revolt in Egypt, Cyprus and Palestine; now they rebelled again when Hadrian became emperor. Their resistance was nourished by the messianic ideal kept burning, as in a citadel, by the rabbinical school of Jamnia with a tenacity all the more desperate as the economic condition of the people became more wretched after the disastrous uprising of 70. In 129 an earthquake destroyed Caesarea, the seat of the legate, and Emmaus Nicopolis. With his passion for public works, Hadrian wished to rebuild Jerusalem, in which only a few edifices had remained standing, just as he was constructing new urban centers everywhere else. He proposed to call the city Elia Capitolina from his own name and that of the Roman Jupiter, to whom he began to erect a temple on the site of the old Temple of Solomon and Herod.

But Rabbi Aqiba's preaching had fanned to flame again that nationalistic pride of the Jews, who believed themselves the people of God destined to overthrow the pagans. Under the scourging blow of this last outrage, which placed the seal of idolatry on the ruins of Israel and reduced their holy city to a Roman colony and the site of their Temple to an altar of the most hated of the pagan gods, they revolted and acclaimed as their general and messias a certain Bar-Cosiba, whom the aged Aqiba rechristened Bar-Kokba, which means "Son of the star."

For two years he was the personification of the religious nationalism and exasperation of his race. He fell upon some Roman garrisons and destroyed them. Hadrian had to send the legate Tineius Rufus with a few legions against him, and then his best general, Julius Severus, recalled from Britain. One by one, the latter took about a thousand villages and towns of the enemy either by assault or by starving them out, and he shut Bar-Kokba and his best troops up in the citadel of Bether, which he took by storm in 135 or 136, burying in its ruins the leaders of the revolt and also the last sparks of resistance on the part of the chosen people. About half a million Jews were put to the sword and a lesser number sold into slavery; the country was depopulated and circumcision and proselytizing were forbidden.

The Christians, whom Bar-Kokba had also harassed and killed during the rebellion, now had one enemy less, at least in Palestine. Their controversy with Judaism gradually died out and they remained alone to uphold against imperial universalism, not the particularism of one race, but spiritual universality.

Hadrian was succeeded by the upright ANTONINUS PIUS (138-161) and he, in turn, by MARCUS AURELIUS (161-181), who, despite his talents and his virtues, made the mistake of disregarding the rule of succession adopted by his predecessors in order to raise his son COMMODUS (180-192) to the throne. In the latter's reign all the horrors and lunacies of Nero and Domitian came to life again. The Senate was tyrannized and the administration of the government handed over to parasites. Like Domitian, he was killed by a dagger-thrust, and his death marked the beginning of a period of disorganization in which general decadence marched along at a swift pace. One evidence of it was the financial crisis, which hinged on the intrinsic value of gold coin, the *denarius aureus*. Up to Nero it had contained seven percent alloy, under Antoninus twenty-five percent, under Marcus Aurelius thirty percent, and under Septimius Severus this leaped to fifty percent. This was a kind of inflation indicative of the progressive economic disorganization of the state.

THE SECOND ANTONINES

After the death of Commodus, the succession to the throne was contested by candidates from the senate and the army: Helvius, Pertinax, Pescennius Niger, Clodius Albinus, Didius Julianus. It was won by a general, SEPTIMIUS SEVERUS (193-211). He began, or rather, carried on a war of extermination against the senate and gave new impetus to the social betterment of the soldiers, who were recruited from among the peasants in the provinces. Their entrance into government offices altered the Roman character of the governmental policies in general and barbarized the administration. On the other hand, since he did not wish to give up the prestige attached to the name of the Antonines, Septimius Severus fashioned for himself a kind of adoption by Marcus Aurelius and placed his two sons in that line of succession. For his own political purposes he intensified the emperor-worship.

Thus the age of Greek philosophers under the first Antonines gave way, under these second, semi-barbarous Antonines, to that of the Latin jurists, Papinian, Ulpian, Paul, who sought to mold the new legislation with the spirit of Stoicism derived

from those who had been the wise men of the preceding era:
Seneca, Epictetus, Marcus Aurelius, Plutarch. Similarly, in the
Christian camp, the period of philosopher-apologists, Justin,
Athenagoras, Tatian, who wrote in Greek, is followed by that
of the lawyers armed with jurisprudence, Minucius Felix and
Tertullian. These write in Latin, while the authors of Egypt
and Asia continue to write in Greek. The plunder and confiscation which punished cities and individuals who had supported rival candidates, continual warfare abroad and Commodus' bad government only served to deplete further the resources of the Empire. The emperor did relieve the lot of the
lowliest workers and favored the corporations, binding them
more closely to the state, but by imposing state and municipal
burdens on the middle classes, he reduced them to a poverty
which was on its way to match that of the *tenuiores.* Not only
Italy but the provinces in general grew poorer, for the fiscal
system was like a vast series of cupping-glasses through which
the state drained the bulk of their revenues to maintain its
cumbersome bureaucracy and its huge military system and to
line the private coffers of the emperor without producing or
stimulating any new sources of wealth. Strikes increased, that
is, the worker abandoned either his labor or the place of his
labor. Banditry appeared again, while spying and political
persecution were rampant so that "thousands of people, both
guilty and innocent," were forced "to flee from their homes.
The chief evil, however, was the enormous number of government agents, mostly soldiers performing the duties of police-
men — the *frumentarii, stationarii* and *colletiones* — who, in
their pursuit of political 'criminals' penetrated into all the
cities and villages and searched private houses, and who were,
of course, accessible to bribes. Still more serious were the
exactions of these same agents in connection with the frequent
military expeditions of the emperor . . . ; "[1] taxes which were

---

1. Rostovtzeff, *The Social and Economic History of the Roman Empire,*
p. 363; by permission of the Oxford University Press.

collected by violence from poor and hostile people and generally ended in ruinous plunder.

This wretched populace, sometimes mad and unjust, which saw itself beggared by a succession of civil wars, reverses of fortune, the perversity of the weather, the brutal confiscation of its holdings and excessive taxation of one sort or another, exploded its wrath against the Christians, for it interpreted its own misfortunes as a punishment of the gods for the Christians' desertion of their worship. All these difficulties and obstacles led farmers and townsmen to abandon their fields and their cities, and over one and the other there slowly gathered a deadly solitude. Rome, at the head of them all, was falling into decay, while round her stretched the everwidening circle of abandoned farms and the increasing scarcity of provisions.

The Carthaginian priest, Tertullian, could not explain why, despite all progress, human living seemed about to be paralyzed by a crisis, which he attributed to excessive population. And like his contemporaries, he yielded to the general sense of uneasiness for the morrow and also of economic insecurity which weighed, as it always does in periods of transition, on those minds who felt, most of them without realizing it, the slow, almost irresistible process of decay and collapse. And he wrote:

"Certainly, the world itself, as it appears to our eyes, becomes more refined and progresses from day to day. Now all lands are accessible, all are explored, all are opened to traffic; ill-famed deserts have been invaded by pleasing, smiling fields; forests have been conquered by farms; flocks and herds have taken their lairs from the wild beasts; today we sow where once was sand; the rocks are covered with vegetation; swamps are dried; there are now more cities than there once were houses. The islands no longer frighten us; nor are cliffs terrifying; everywhere there are habitations, people, a state, life. And the most important evidence that the population is so great is that we are now a burden on the world, there are barely enough of the essentials for us, our needs have become more acute, and there is a cry of complaint on the lips of all men, for nature can no longer sustain us."[2]

And thinking, like his fellows, that there was need of a different economic set-up, he arrived at the conclusion that one remedy was "epidemics, famines, wars, and the earth's opening to swallow whole cities"[3] — a pruning of this growing human race. And this was the most banal solution of all.

Of the two sons of Septimius Severus who succeeded him, Geta was assassinated (212) and CARACALLA carried to more severe extremes his father's policy of repressing the upper classes while dignifying the army which was drawn from the lower classes, and of using the various police agencies to spy upon real or supposed conspirators. An example of that policy of repression, carried on by excessive increase in taxation and also in crime, is to be found in the treacherous destruction of the youth of Alexandria.

Among his reforms are some legislative measures dealing with better treatment for slaves, the punishment of adultery and the guardianship of minors, but the most famous of them all is the so-called "Antonine Constitution" or Edict of Caracalla, in 212, which extended Roman citizenship to all *peregrini*. Its purpose was probably to humiliate the upper classes, widen the sources of revenue and level all members of the Empire. This was in accordance with a traditional imperial policy, furthered by the Severi, which tended to extend the foundations of Caesar's authority out toward the frontiers, where, in the *castella* (fortified villages) the bravest troops were conscripted. There were, however, some rural or barbarous or military groups to whom citizenship was not extended. The gesture had no great social effect. Social differences remained, but the number of taxable citizens increased. Politically speaking, the Empire ceased to be a possession of the city of Rome. All its citizens became Romans when Roman citizenship had ceased to constitute a privilege.

---

2. *De Anima*, XXX, P. L. II, 700.
3. *Ib.*

Caracalla was killed in 217 at the instigation of OPELLIUS MACRINUS, who succeeded him and was quickly overthrown in his turn by HELIOGABALUS, priest of the god of the same name of Emesa. His government is noteworthy for its attempt to impose a universal state religion at the apex of which was a god whose name he bore and whose incarnation he seemed to be. Because of his crimes and his shameful life he was assassinated along with his mother.

ALEXANDER SEVERUS had a longer reign (222-235). Despite his excellent intention of reviving the enlightened regime of the Antonines, he was really a slave to the army and still more to the growing economic distress of his day, and so he could not help subjecting private enterprise and property more completely to the needs of the state. As these became constantly more pressing due to the threats from the Parthians in the east and the Germans in the north, he went so far as to make private citizens and then their cities responsible for levies imposed in increasing measure.

In 235 he too was assassinated, and there followed a disastrous period of military anarchy ended only by Diocletian some fifty years later. In that period Rome's frontiers were pushed back in several places because of the lack of discipline and efficiency in the army, whose claims had produced anarchy in the government and had forced the various emperors who followed each other in a rapid succession of crime to repress the "haves," to impoverish the greater part of the bourgeoisie and to pillage public property such as temples and monuments, in short, to plunder the Empire as if it were a conquered land. Even the intellectuals were harassed, so that the surest safeguard was to be or to seem poor and uneducated. Naturally, this is true only in a general way.

THE APOSTOLIC FATHERS

The Church traveled through these difficulties strengthening her organization. The work of the Apostles had been mainly directed to the diffusion of the Gospel through the founding of churches. The following period, which takes its name from the Apostolic Fathers, is marked by the work of organization which was to secure for the new society a solid disciplinary structure at once hierarchical and united.

The writings of the period, therefore, reflect this organizing activity and also a constant solicitude that this communal activity of the Christians might not congeal into factions and that the teachings of the Gospel might not disintegrate in gnostic speculations.

The name Apostolic Fathers is given to writers of the third generation after Jesus who were or were believed to have been disciples of the Apostles. In a broader sense it is given to almost all the authors who wrote between 90 and 155 (or 156), the year of the death of Polycarp, who was the last disciple of the Apostle John. They are followed by a series of more highly educated and ingenious writers who show the influence of Greek sophistry and introduce into the simple, colloquial language of these writings with its Hebrew flavor, a philosophic and legalistic technique and mode of thought. These latter go to meet the Graeco-Roman world in the field of speculation and law and they inaugurate the process of incorporating into Christian thought the best fruits of Greek philosophy, both Stoic and Platonic, seeking to break through the rampart of prejudice which the ruling and the educated classes (and under the Antonines these were one and the same for the most part) had raised against the new religion. Their work is directed outside the Church and seeks the first road to reconciliation between faith and learning, between the Church and the law, between the barbarians, as they said, and the Greeks.

Subapostolic literature, generally speaking, comprises the following writings, arranged in their probable chronological order:

1. The *Didache* (80-90)
2. The so-called *Letter of Barnabas* (96-98)
3. *The Epistle of Clement to the Corinthians* (95-98)

4. The letters of St. Ignatius (107-110)
5. The homily called the *Second Epistle of Clement to the Corinthians* (120-140)
6. Papias and the presbyters quoted by Irenaeus (about 150)
7. The *Epistle to Diognetus*
8. *The Shepherd* of Hermas (140-155)
9. The letter of Polycarp (135-155)
10. The *Acts of the Martyrdom of Polycarp* (156-157)

For the most part we shall not search these documents for sociological teaching. We must content ourselves with finding in them maxims which are mainly moralizing and pedagogical, dictated by common sense and broadened in their application by love. They are really variations on the teachings of Jesus and the Apostles as applied to specific cases.

The *Didache* (Διδαχὴ τῶν δώδεκα ἀποστόλων — Teaching of the Twelve Apostles) is a little treatise which marks the beginning of ecclesiastical law. It contains rules for the organization and good management of the churches, for the instruction of converts, baptism, fasting, prayers, the Eucharist, relations with and conduct toward the members of the hierarchy, etc. At the same time it sketches the model Christian in a summary of evangelical ethics.

Composed, according to Funk, between 80 and 90 in Syria or Palestine, it enjoyed great prestige, almost as if it were a canonical work; and it gives us a lively picture of the background against which the Apostles worked.[4]

Neither do we know the author of the letter which legend attributes to St. Barnabas, the companion of St. Paul. Its allegorical interpretation of the Old Testament suggests the place where allegory blossomed exuberantly among both Jews and Christians, Alexandria. It may perhaps be assigned to

---

4. The Greek text was discovered by the metropolitan Philotheos Bryennios in a manuscript in Constantinople (*Codex Hierosolymitanus,* which has been in Jerusalem since 1887) and published in 1883.

the reign of Nerva, in whom some have seen the eleventh king of Daniel's prophecy.

The second, or, as most think, the third successor to St. Peter in the bishopric of Rome was CLEMENT, called ROMANUS. He was perhaps related, as a freedman or son of freedmen, to the younger branch of the Flavian family, which gave some of its members to the Church. He had heard one and probably both Apostles, Peter and Paul, and he governed the Roman church during Domitian's persecution, between 92 and 101. His personality, expressed in the *Epistle,* the only authentic one extant, which was sent to the church of Corinth to settle the disturbance caused by a pair of daring schismatics, had such great influence that legends flowered around it, attributing to his sanctity a series of romantic adventures that ended in martyrdom, and crediting his learning with the production of numerous writings: eight epistles, among which is a second one to Corinth, two on virginity, two to James the cousin of Jesus, and three included in the false Decretals.

We include the second epistle to the Corinthians here among the writings which interest us, because it is really a homily, that is, a lecture given in a period — between 120 and 140 — when "sophistic" lectures were all the rage. Harnack thought he found in it the letter with which the Bishop of Rome, Soter, sent financial assistance to the church of Corinth, but there is no foundation for this supposition.

The second successor to St. Peter in the bishopric of Antioch was the martyr IGNATIUS, called also Theophorus, a convert from paganism. Under Trajan a sudden and apparently rather short-lived persecution struck at that famous center of nascent Christianity and the bishop was the most illustrious victim. He was condemned to be led to Rome in chains, "spiritual pearls," to be, "like the grain of God, ground by the teeth of wild beasts and thus become the immaculate bread of Christ," as he wrote in the highly figurative language of the Oriental. During his journey, which reminds us a little of

St. Paul's, he wrote seven letters to various churches. He was martyred about 107 or a little later.

In his letters, except for the one to the Romans, Ignatius aims at strengthening the hierarchical unity of the churches in their bishop, who is assisted by the presbyters and deacons, and he tries also to combat the disruptive influence of Judaizing and Gnostic-Docetic tendencies.

The third Apostolic Father whose personality history has preserved for us is ST. POLYCARP, bishop of Smyrna, who helped St. Ignatius when he passed through that city. He with Papias was the disciple of John the Evangelist. He became bishop while still a young man and governed the church of Smyrna for at least fifty years. Among his disciples were Irenaeus, the defender of the orthodox faith against Gnosticism, and Florinus, who himself became a Gnostic.

In 154 St. Polycarp went to Rome to settle with Pope Anicetus the controversy regarding Easter, which the Orientals wanted to celebrate on the fourteenth day of Nisan while the Romans wanted it to be a movable feast celebrated on a Sunday. The two bishops failed to reach any agreement but parted from each other with great charity, and out of deference, the Bishop of Smyrna was invited to celebrate the Eucharist during his visit. A year or two later, upon his return to Smyrna, Polycarp was burned alive in the Circus for his faith. Of his two letters, we have the one to the Philippians, written on the occasion of Ignatius' journey. We have also preserved to us the *Acts* of his martyrdom.

PAPIAS, bishop of Hierapolis, in Phrygia, had also, according to Irenaeus, listened to the Apostle (others say the presbyter) John. He wrote a mediocre work entitled *Explanation of the Sayings of the Lord* in which he introduced chiliastic ideas. Irenaeus also speaks of *presbyters* (elders) who were disciples of the Apostles or belonged to the generation immediately following them and who wrote or handed down maxims, the greater part of which have been lost.

We know nothing about the sender of the *Epistle to Diognetus*. Diognetus was a pagan who had made various objections to Christianity. From the literary standpoint this is one of the most beautiful documents of Christianity in its restraint, the lofty serenity of its thought and its grace of style. In the past it was attributed to Justin, who could not, however, have put that charm and order into his writing. Because it is apologetic in character it stands between the apostolic writings and the real apologias.

The *Shepherd* of Hermas is in a class by itself. Origen identified this Hermas with the Hermas to whom St. Paul sends his greeting in his Epistle to the Romans, but it is more likely that he is the brother of Pius, the Bishop of Rome (c. 140-155) as the Muratorian Canon says he is. It is a treatise on ascetics and morals made up of a series of revelations, frequently very ingenuous (five *Visions,* twelve *Commands,* ten *Similitudes*), in which the Church first, appearing as a woman, and then the angel of penance, appearing as a shepherd, instruct Hermas and through him his rather lax community with regard to their duties and the performance and fruits of penance. They teach also, in a series of precepts, the exercise of the other virtues. Although this little treatise does not bear the mark of any great intellect or of any culture or education whatever (Hermas was a slave freed by a good matron named Rhode) and although it is badly written, it had very great, almost canonical authority in the first centuries because of its prophetic tone and its sound good sense.

CHAPTER II

THE ATTEMPT AT RECONCILIATION WITH CLASSICAL THOUGHT

THE APOLOGISTS

NOW that order was established within her house and her dogma and hierarchy were sufficiently defined and organized to preserve the deposit of Faith in its integrity and to withstand competition and the early heresies, the Church felt the need of defending herself abroad against the growing tide of popular hatred, with its attendant influence on the political and legislative activity of the authorities. The task was gladly assumed by the Christians, and even by laymen, who, since they came from environments in which that hatred was seething, were better able to judge its unreasonableness and combat its outbursts.

Under the Antonines, the password in the world of thought and government was philosophy, a word rich in significance, which clothed the noblest and most ambitious aspirations of intellectual speculation, cultural refinement and patriotism. It was a kind of illuminism which inspired some of the most notable administrative and legislative reforms of the period.

Almost as if to realize the ideal republic of Plato, intellectuals sat at the table of government, and the title they most desired was precisely that of philosopher. Their language was Greek, the language of the educated, spoken also at Rome and in the Church. Philosophers and magistrates who wanted to be philosophers were called to fill the highest public offices. Lecturers and rhetoricians, called sophists, lived in this period their golden age. The masses could no longer have any interest in politics, and so these lecturers supplied them instead with a literary-philosophical interest, and the people waxed as enthusiastic as they would at a sleight-of-hand performance. Dion Chrysostom, Florus, Favorinus, Artemidorus of Ephesus, a historian and dream-theorist, the wealthy Herod Atticus, Aelius Aristides, who consented to let the emperor listen to him provided applause was permitted, Polaemon, Apuleius, Fronto, etc. — these were the idols of the day. Cities vied with one another in raising them statues and decreeing them triumphs, and the emperor frequently elevated them to the highest honors.[1]

People said philosophy in those days just as they said "Reason" in the eighteenth century and "Progress" in the nineteenth. And that philosophy invaded theology, that is, it claimed it could lead to the knowledge, in fact to the contemplation of God. Now Christianity did lead to this contemplation and also claimed to be a philosophy, and therefore it drew the attention of Platonism and at the same time was attracted by it. That is why Christianity had its philosophers too, and the exigencies of the time required the first of these to vindicate in the eyes of the learned, who were also the powerful, a faith that had sprung up among a barbarous people and was set forth in uncouth language.

These Christian philosophers were the apologists, called so because they undertook the *apologia,* the defense, of Christianity. At that time the African Apuleius was writing an apologia, glittering with literary conceits, assonances, rhymes, witticisms and puns, to defend himself against the charge of magic, that is, to defend the patrimony that had come to him through his marriage to a wealthy widow. The defense, in his hands, became a literary composition sparkling with rhetorical ornaments, of which he was a tireless inventor. The Christians, who usually came from the same schools and had the same literary taste, defended their new patrimony of Christian ideas in apologias which brought them not triumphant acquittals but more

---

1. Tatian wrote that some philosophers wangled "from the emperor a salary of six-hundred *aurei* a year, for no other reason but that they might not even wear their beards gratis" (*Orat.,* XIX, 1).

probably the sentence of death. And yet they forced upon the learned world a critical examination of the claims and the reasonableness of Christianity.

After the downfall of the Antonines, when philosophy lost its political prestige, the world of culture turned with new vigor to the study of law. Teachers of Roman law flourished, and so did the first Christian jurists. They were apologists who transferred the defense from the field of reason to that of law, or better, who used the law to defend the Christians — the faith brought to trial — before magistrates and advocates.

At the end of the century the greatest apologists do not show the influence of Greek sophistry but of Latin jurisprudence, though they have attended the schools of rhetoric. They are the African lawyers, Minucius Felix and Tertullian. We cannot and must not, however, draw a definite line of demarcation between one and the other group of apologists, since there was a gradual development of their thought and approach determined by the conditions of the times. The first Greek apologists, for instance, appealed to the law on behalf of the Christians, rejecting the special legislation passed against them as unreasonable and unjust, while the Latin apologists also draw arguments, and sometimes very fortunate ones, from philosophy.

This transfer of doctrinal activity to the world outside the Church is of immense value, because for the first time men are able to test the consistency of the Christian moral and theological system with the touchstone of rational speculation; and the problem of the relationship between faith and reason is consciously settled for the first time although the immediate purpose of the apologists is to solve the relationship between the Church and state by abolishing the law of persecution.

Naturally, all this was necessary after Christianity had transferred its headquarters from Palestine and entered the Graeco-Roman world. Contemporary with the murmurings and outbursts of the populace and the official acts of the magistrates, the intellectuals also quickly turned their attention to the new phenomenon, studying it under its social as well as its rational aspects. The philosophy of the time was convinced, or at least pretended to be convinced, that its own foundations were essentially rational, and whoever attempted to shake them was guilty of offense against the community and against rationality.

Various sophists must have given lectures on the barbarism — the obscurantism — of Christianity. The cynic Crescentius was engaging in public debate with the Christian Platonist Justin. The Epicurean Celsus, who leaned toward Platonism, was gathering into a compact charge all the accusations brought against the Church on patriotic and philosophic grounds. Fronto and Aelius Aristides were presenting elaborate memoranda to the emperor to exterminate this outrage to knowledge, this enemy of the nation.

In the teachings of the New Testament there were passages through which some fundamental idea of ancient philosophy might enter. St. Paul had asserted the rationality of the moral law and St. John had identified the Logos, which is Reason and the Word, with Jesus. From these concepts and under the influence of Platonic and Stoic ideas grew the corollary that all that was rational was Christian, that philosophy, therefore, belonged to Christianity just as revelation did, for they were both ways, one indirect, the other direct, of arriving at the knowledge (gnosis) of God. This knowledge was imperfect because philosophy had been frequently clouded by errors and spurious elements while revelation had been frequently made through mysteries, symbols and circumlocutions not always capable of consistent explanation, until finally with the Incarnation of the Logos, Jesus, who had already enlightened philosophers and inspired prophets, all rationality was made manifest as in the noonday sun and the knowledge of God was complete.

Therefore, since they possess this complete knowledge without shadow or imperfection, the Christians are the true, the perfect philosophers (gnostics, as Clement of Alexandria said) ; Christianity is the complete and conclusive philosophy (gnosis) and hence a completely rational system of life in which all the thought and speculation of the pre-Christian era find their resolution and conclusion.

It was thus that a common meeting-ground was found for the Bible and philosophy, for the new religion and ancient thought, for Moses and Plato, for Socrates, the victim of his belief in the rationality of religion, and the martyrs, victims of the irrationality of public hatred.[2] In fact, going back to the origin of those points of contact, to the one source from which the two currents had flowed, the Christian apologists followed the example of those Jews of Alexandria who first attempted to reconcile the two "philosophies" and supposedly discovered that Plato, by virtue of his direct knowledge of the Egyptians, had plagiarized the books of the Bible. Plato's thought approached that of Moses because he had copied Moses. (Tatian said Homer instead of Plato in order to go back to the original ancestor of the pagan "poets and historians" and thus despoil the Greeks of any vestige of originality.)

The charge of plagiarism was an expedient the apologists used, frequently without discretion or method, to support their other principle of the original unity, the monogenesis, of reasoned and revealed truth identified with the Logos. Modern criticism finds such a mode of reasoning arbitrary, but ancient criticism did not. Celsus reversed the argument; he did not deny the plagiary but contended that the Jews and Christians had plagiarized Plato, Heraclitus and the other philosophers. He attempted to deny any merit of originality to Christianity to present it as a hodge-podge of Greek and Jewish ideas. Historical criticism at that time usually went no further than that.

In a related field, Julius Africanus (died after 240) tried to find a kind of historical basis of agreement by synchronizing events in sacred and pagan history. He was the Christian archi-

---

2. *Apud vestros quoque sapientes* ΛΟΓΟΝ, *id est sermonem atque Rationem, constat artificem videri universitatis* (Tertullian, *Apol.*, XXI, 10).

tect of a pagan emperor and tried hard to build bridges from one shore to the other.

Now this contamination of the Christian world with the pagan world in matters philosophical was not unaccompanied by grave dangers and serious protests. The Gnostics, or rather the pseudo-gnostics, the exponents of a false gnosis (knowledge) as Clement of Alexandria and Irenaeus branded them, overestimated the value of knowledge and confused it with faith. They lost the boundaries between reason and dogma (supra-rationality); frequently substituting the imaginative for the gnostical process, they used material borrowed from Greek philosophy and the Oriental religions as well as from Judaism and Christianity to build fantastic and complicated cosmogonies from which they sometimes deduced ethical-social standards contrary to the teachings of the New Testament. The most dangerous development was their progress from the dualism of divine principles in their cosmogony to the deduction that there was a dualism between morality and action, between body and spirit, and this led to amoral aberrations. Thus Gnosticism became a dangerous threat to orthodoxy, and the Church was forced to defend herself in all her communities, beginning at Rome, by defining the Canon of the Scriptures and the creed, by strengthening her discipline and mobilizing her writers — Miltiades, Aristides "the philosopher," Justin, Athenagoras, Clement of Alexandria, Irenaeus, Tertullian, Origen — and especially by obliging the hierarchy to guard the great body of uneducated faithful within the fold of tradition, whose limits and vicissitudes her scholars were studying with infinite care.

In addition, all this dialectic activity threatened to scandalize the illiterate, the humble little people of the lower classes who formed the majority of the Church's members. Not only did the Gnostics stand aloof, through their ambition to possess a superior knowledge, and thus inject into Christian equality the distinctions which rabbinical pride had already introduced into the synagogues; they also introduced heterogeneous dogmas and particular rites (special baptismal ceremonies in the nuptial chamber, etc.). At the same time it was feared that the orthodox Christian scholars, the true gnostics according to Clement of Alexandria, might come to form a kind of aristocracy of the "elect" which, socially speaking, would upset the original simplicity of Christian brotherhood. Certainly in the beginning all the Christians, and even the lowly, must have felt admiration and gratitude toward these grammarians, rhetoricians, and lawyers who with so much eloquence and logic undertook the defense of the beliefs and the members of the Christian communities. But as Christian thought passed from defensive to autonomous activities they also felt instinctively that something was entering their creed which their minds did not quite grasp. And probably there were not lacking teachers — especially the most mediocre ones — who made the weight of their superiority felt. Actually the type of *gnostic* outlined by the author of the *Stromata,* with his well-balanced bundle of virtues, and the *gnostic* set up by Origen as a perfect Christian superior to the Christians who had only faith, was an elevated being who started a new social and religious class not a little reminiscent of the Greek intellectual *élite.* The *simpliciores,* therefore, were scandalized; and Tertullian, who goes looking more for differences rather than points of contact between pagan and Christian thought and who is partial to the proletarian and ascetic element, rejects all possibility of agreement between faith and philosophy at the very moment when in Africa, in Alexandria, the very center of Hellenism, Clement was translating Christian dogma and particularly Christian ethics into terms of Greek philosophy, and bolstering Moses and the Apostles with Plato and the writers of comedy. The great Origen often reveals his anxiety to justify and therefore excuse deep philosophical speculation in the eyes of the less educated. After all, the latter were a useful foil for him too.

Thus the new society is stirred by a new leaven, by which it feels enriched but at the same time fears to be adulterated. It is up to the leaders, the bishops, who usually remain hidden in the shadows, to preserve its unity by coördinating its many tendencies, giving due consideration to the exigencies of charity and culture, of thought and action, and working out their mutual integration. The bishops' prudence brought new social and spiritual influences into play which, without causing any appreciable harm, produced immeasurable good.[3]

It is sufficient here to mention thus in passing this contact between the Christian and the pagan worlds in learned discussions that follow to a certain extent St. Paul's sermon on the Areopagus. Elsewhere and more at length we shall speak of the Christian teachers and the more complex relationship between faith and culture.

JUSTIN

In defending their correligionists, the apologists at first appeal directly to the emperor with great confidence in his discretion, reasonableness and impartiality. The Antonines, who were trying to effect an enlightened rule, insisted on being completely informed about everything, on not taking action except in the light of sound reason. So, imitating the example of Antoninus Pius, they listened to anyone who had something to propose that was of use or interest to the state. In addition, with the progressive concentration of all political and administrative activity in the hands of the emperor, every enterprise or activity turned for support, justification or sanction to the head of the government, the Court, the central administration.

Thus the Athenian Quadratus presented, it seems, a defense of the Christians to Hadrian; Miltiades and Marcianus Aristides each presented one to Antoninus; Justin to Antoninus, Marcus

---

3. Cyprian also writes: *Nos autem qui philosophi non verbis sed factis sumus* (*De bono patientiae,* III), but he is closer to St. Paul and does not name any pagan philosophers; he is very suspicious of the "false" wisdom they display. Hippolytus gives us a long criticism of it in his so-called *Philosophoumena.* Irenaeus also makes some mention of Greek philosophy, but he says that Plato was more religious than the heretics (*Adv. haer.,* III, 25, 5), who, according to Tertullian, made the mistake of following the philosophers more than the prophets.

Aurelius and Verus; Melito of Sardis and Claudius Apollinaris to Marcus Aurelius. When the succeeding tyrannical and semi-barbarous dynasty revived the old law of persecution with new edicts, showing that no attention had been paid to Christian apologetics, then the ecclesiastical writers no longer appealed to the emperors.

JUSTIN is not content to defend Christianity on the basis of morals, pointing out the upright life of the Christians. He must defend it also on the basis of philosophy, demonstrating the rationality of their faith. His intransigence in matters of fundamental dogma is unshakable; and his strength of character, with its deep speculative strain, makes him resemble Socrates as well as the most intrepid Christian martyrs. He knows the world of Greek philosophy, and after his baptism he has remained a philosopher, a sophist, as the old man laden with years calls him in the *Dialogue*. With these qualifications he undertakes to reconcile Christianity and Hellenism with a success the true value of which has not been appreciated. He approaches the problem in two ways, first seeking out the analogies between the two systems of thought and secondly seeking a common origin for both of them in the Logos, the Word.

In minds educated in Greek philosophy and Roman Stoicism, those neatly defined dogmas imposed on one's faith and not deduced from reason, and expressed besides in a language bristling with solecisms, excited only a feeling of repugnance, as if they were a plague, a loathsome expression of barbarism. Now Justin is a philosopher who walks about dressed in the pallium, conducts public discussions like the Cynics and Stoics and teaches in the manner of the Sophists; and he tries to cut a breach through that repugnance by showing that the distances between the two systems of thought are not so great as they seem. With regard to the life of Christ, he demonstrates that the virgin birth, the death on the cross and the resurrection should not be repellent to the pagan mind since mythology offers fables that are analogous and have been recounted by poets and believed by the people. As for Christian teaching, Justin takes from the introduction to the fourth Gospel the original idea of the Logos, which in the Greek sense of the term is the Word, Reason — Christ — and he places it where Hebrew revelation and Greek philosophy meet in order to make it the source of inspiration for both. All that the prophets had revealed, all the truth that the philosophers had perceived came from the Logos, which in the former was the Word that dictated and in the latter was the Reason that speculated. In essentials, Moses and Plato, the Sibyl and Socrates prepared the way for Christ.[4]

All that is certain in the one, all that is rational in the other belongs to the Logos, that is, to Christ. And in drawing his conclusions, Justin, who is Palestinian by birth and Greek by education, incorporates into Christianity as its precursors the fruits both of revelation and speculation, insofar as they are universal and certain. Abraham, Ananias, Mishael and Elias on the one hand, Socrates, Heraclitus, Musonius Rufus, etc. (who also were accused of atheism) on the other, were all Christians. In order not to recognize any debt at all to profane wisdom, Tertullian, with even greater boldness, carries the idea to its very limits and asserts that the soul is Christian by nature.

The difference between ancient thought and the new thought of the Gospel is this: on the Hebrews and pagans shone only glimmerings of the eternal Reason; on the Christians shone the full glory of Reason in its entirety incarnate in Christ. The Gospel puts an end to speculation and revelation so far as eternal truths are concerned because all of Truth has been made manifest.

It does not concern us here to discover how much of Justin's thought derives from Philo and from the works of the Jews in the Alexandrian Diaspora. His delightful merit consists in the fact that he drew the greatest advantage and benefit from

---

4. In the *Cohortatio ad Graecos* also the Sibyl is called upon to confirm Christianity.

the word Logos, which occurs in both the Gospel and philosophy even though with widely different meanings, and that he called Christianity to the attention of philosophers. His is the first attempt to rationalize the faith and it is therefore not well-organized or complete; but he intended that it should force the rulers, philosophers who boasted that they were disciples of Reason, to re-examine a religion which claimed to be a perfect creation of Reason and which rejected as irrational all anti-Christian elements, including the hostility of the populace and the trials to which the Christians were subjected. This matter of placing Socrates and the victims of the despotism of Nero and Domitian in the same Christian ranks was a happy thought which has also a slightly political flavor. In fact, the state religion had accused Socrates and the others of being politically subversive and had killed them as *molitores rerum novarum,* enemies of the state, just as it did the Christians, while actually they had been only austere disciples of Reason just as the Christians were.

In any case, with these ideas Justin opened new roads of communication between the two worlds and engaged in discussion with the learned pagans. He thus inaugurated a greater and swifter conquest of intellectual circles at the same time that he began to organize the simple Christian thought in philosophic form. In a certain sense this transfer of religion to philosophy met the movement started by Epictetus and other philosophers to transfer philosophy to religion. And they met on the common ground of moral ideas and especially of terminology. When Justin asks the philosopher-emperors not to allow themselves to be dominated by false opinions, he is stating the moral postulate of Epictetus and Marcus Aurelius.

Socially speaking, Justin's apologetics did immeasurable good in drawing two worlds, two mentalities closer together, in placing Oriental monotheism and Occidental polytheism, barbarian civilization and Graeco-Roman civilization in contact with one another. It broke down the last vestiges of resistance on the part of Judaizing Christians (it is not without reason that Justin's greatest work is an anti-Jewish polemic dialogue) and introduces Christian influence into what had seemed the impregnable fortress of culture at the very moment when the latter was beginning to launch against Christianity its most fearsome attacks and the most insidious reactions of philosophico-religious syncretism.

Justin accomplishes his work in a spirit of the most ardent faith. Since the Jews have drawn apart and since political and military disasters have forced them to close their schools in the desert and reduce their proselytizing activities, he and his companions take from St. Paul the message of the vocation of the Gentiles, claiming for them the benefits of the ancient prophecies and presenting them as the true Israel, the authentic, predestined chosen people. Thus they go to meet St. Paul's appeal for universality with confident gratitude, and in a certain sense they annex, as it were, the values of Judaism as if by a legitimate, divinely ordained act of possession. Christ fulfils the hopes and longings of the nations, and not merely those of the Jews locked within the walls of their exclusivism. The breach is open and it is wide, and the Gentiles walk through it as though it were an arch of triumph.

ATHENAGORAS, TATIAN, THEOPHILUS

ATHENAGORAS shows the same tendencies as Justin. Tradition says that he came from Athens, but we know very little about him. Between 176 and 178 he addressed an apologia of the Christians to Marcus Aurelius and Commodus in the manner of a philosopher speaking to philosophers. He is moderate in argument and courteous in expression, so much so that he refrains (chap. XVIII) from condemning idols. His style is correct and he aims to present the new faith in the light of reason in order to break down the barrier of prejudices which the intellectuals were constantly raising with a tenacity that persisted even under the Christian emperors, like a last line of defense of classical paganism.

TATIAN, a disciple of "that most admirable man," Justin, was an "Assyrian." He had received a Greek education, had embarked upon the career of sophist with all the eagerness of the provincial who lives furthest away from those centers where one may earn the most fame and wealth, and had pursued his ambition across the Empire. The teachings and virtues of the Christians converted him. But he remained an Oriental at heart and had a kind of spiteful grudge against Greek thought (though he used its rhetorical aids in his *Discourse to the Greeks*), Roman imperialism and the social-ethical equilibrium toward which Catholic teaching was tending. His own lack of moderation led him, a few years after the martyrdom of Justin, to found in 172 a Gnostic sect called Encratites, who condemned matrimony and the use of meats and wine. They were forerunners of the modern "drys" or prohibitionists of latter day America who cannot forgive Jesus for the miracle of Cana and the Eucharistic wine. In fact, Tatian's sect used water instead of wine in Holy Communion and thus earned for its members the nickname *Aquarii* (*hydroparastatae*).

THEOPHILUS was a convert from paganism like the other apologists. His exceptional qualities won him the episcopacy and he became the sixth bishop of Antioch, the see of St. Ignatius, where the term "Christian" arose. We have extant only three of his books, "three elementary works" addressed to Autolycus. They are polemical and apologetic treatises probably written at different times and with different aims. The third was not composed before 181 since he speaks of the death of Marcus Aurelius, and so he probably was bishop from 169 to some time later than 181.

Autolycus is the Diognetus of Antioch. In other words he is the personification of the official and cultured pagan world with its pride, its prejudices and its lack of comprehension of the new faith. The answers addressed to him in these books were supposed to represent the calm reconsideration of discussions and rebuttals that had already taken place orally, in conversations that were friendly but concerned with the conflict of opinion frankly expressed by both parties.

This polemic is like Justin's, or, looking at it from the other point of view, we may say it is of the Antonine type. We find the usual accusations, and the answers generally do not go beyond the scope we have undertaken to describe here. What is different is the personal note, the character of the man himself, who as bishop is always restrained in his expression and conservative in matters of principle. There is a certain nobility and clarity in his writing which render quite persuasive his exposition of a loftier morality in accord with a more evident rationality. He too bears the marks of the age in which he lived, so that his demonstrations are sometimes artificial and forced, or better, they seem so to the modern critic. But probably for ears accustomed to sophistic conceits, his arbitrary interpretations, forced parallels and specious etymology must have had an attractive brilliance.

Although he is deeply grounded in classical culture — as his age understood it and its limitations permitted — he is fundamentally at variance with Graeco-Roman thought. He does not bother to seek out analogies between it and Christianity, nor to imagine instances where it plagiarized Christian thought or showed some inspired influence of the latter, nor to take exception to any part of it even briefly. He stands solidly on the Scriptures and does not need any philosophical support. If he does quote some maxim from the Greek writers he does so to corroborate his thesis of the freedom of the will, which, in a Stoic world brushed by Asiatic influences, was assuming a definite importance.

While he rejects and speaks with horror of philosophers, historians and poets, he never has a word of blame for the Hebrews, although, living in contact with many of them as he did, he must have been aware of their antagonism to Christianity. But at the end of the second century, Hebrew pride had been somewhat blunted by political disasters, and the hatred of the Jews for Christianity was being tucked away in the intransigence of rabbinical teaching. The separation between the two religions was now clearly defined since there was no longer a Jewish-Christian compromise. Hence the danger to the Christian faith and its field for conversions as well were more than ever to be found in the pagan world which was daily mustering its forces against Christianity and at the same time was daily giving ground.

A great deal of water had passed under the bridge since Justin made his last attempt to persuade the Jews to disentangle the new religion from their materialistic interpretations. Theophilus can, with complete indifference toward rabbinical exegesis, indulge in the most innocent and fantastic symbolism to explain Genesis to his opponent. There are historical reasons for this attitude but it can be explained also by the gentle nature of the author who is never sharp really, not even with heretics. All he says is that heresies are rocks on which boats are shattered.

This Autolycus, like the Caecilius Natalis of the *Octavius* advances arguments against monotheism and against Christ and his moral teaching, and he makes fun of the name Christian. Theophilus' reply is polite, friendly, straightforward.[5] When, however, he takes up the charge of immorality, his language becomes stronger and bolder. He reverses the accusation just as Justin, Tatian and Tertullian did.

It was your philosophers and poets, he says, who preached atheism, taught adultery, waxed lyrical over rape and presented Thyestean cannibalism on the stage. Plato himself in Book V of the *Republic* advocates sharing women in common, and the Epicureans and Stoics agree with him. Such teachings are opposed to the austere standard of the Ten Commandments, to the commandments of justice, chastity, love of one's enemies, continence carried to the point of monogamy, truth, grace, indeed the whole body of virtues which have their origin in man's relationship with his God. You accuse the Christians of im-

---

5. Cf. I. Giordani, *La prima polemica cristiana*, Turin, 1930, pp. 136-138.

morality when for them the simple desire for a woman is equivalent to adultery; and you accuse them of Thyestean banquets when they are forbidden to attend the gladiatorial games where men are murdered, or the theatres where the erotic and obscene adventures of the gods are represented (who had human flesh, the members of their own family served to them to eat), and where the vicissitudes of Thyestes and Thereus are acted out.

With this argument, set forth along with a list of Christian virtues rather than a picture of their exemplary life, he certainly put his finger on the contrast between pagan and Christian morality — a contrast to which the pagans, year by year, were becoming more and more sensible, so much so that the Oriental religions and philosophism itself were working out an ascetics of their own to compete, at least exteriorly, with Christianity.

Theophilus gives special attention to one charge which is touched on implicitly by the other apologists, especially the author of the *Epistle to Diognetus,* and which is explicitly made by Celsus. The Christians were challenged with, "What are your dates?" Victor Hugo scornfully asked Catholics the same thing in order to deride them as antiquated. Instead the pagans derided their lack of age, of titles of nobility, of spiritual ancestry to compare with the ancient and therefore venerable wisdom of Greece and Rome. And Theophilus turns the argument about. — You are recent, you are of yesterday. We are *ab antiquo.* The Bible is ours, and since its authors, and Moses first of all, are older and more venerable than the most ancient authors who wrote the genealogy of your gods "it follows that our doctrine is neither recent nor mythical, but historical and more ancient" than yours.

The question of antiquity was of no little importance, especially if we remember that the religio-philosophy of the time tended to trace its origin to Egyptian and Hindu thought. There was real competition in claiming the greatest antiquity. Theophilus, child of his age, makes wide use of the numerology then in vogue for sacred symbolism, and indulges in a detailed and meticulous calculation of years and months to establish Moses' chronological priority over Homer. And his skill must have made some impression on the thought of his time. Borrowing from Manetho the Egyptian, Menander of Ephesus and Flavius Josephus, he demonstrates that in the history of humanity, the course of which from the creation of the world to the death of Marcus Aurelius could be computed as 5965 years, the biblical Exodus took place 393 years before Danaus migrated to Argos, that is, nine hundred to one thousand years before the Trojan War. Moses precedes Homer then by at least a thousand years. Thus Christian teaching is "most ancient and most true." And if this is not sufficient, then compare the two accounts of the flood, the Greek account based on contradictory versions, the Biblical account logical and consistent. From the latter does the myth of Deucalion derive thanks to one of those little errors common to the plagiarism of the pagans who took his name from the first two words of Noah's invitation: Δεῦτε, καλεῖ ὑμὰς . . . !

But the Greeks, either because their civilization is more recent or because the myths have given them a blind spot, do not appreciate the Christian title to nobility; they do not know the true God and curse him, and consequently they have persecuted and do still persecute his worshippers. And while they fasten prizes and praises on the actors who solemnize indecency on the stage, they stone, kill and torture the Christians because they are guilty of pursuing "a holy life." For such wickedness, however, they have been punished with the loss of the knowledge of God and of truth.[6]

The minor apologists writing in Greek who have left us some fragment of their works or some meagre record of themselves are MELITO OF SARDIS, a "philosopher" also called MELITO, CLAUDIUS APOLLINARIS, bishop of Hierapolis, HERMIAS

---

6. Cf. I. Giordani, *op. cit.,* pp. 140-142.

who caricatured pagan philosophy, and one or two others. Of the Christian martyr APOLLONIUS we have extant the "rational defense" which he delivered, it seems, before the senate in the reign of Commodus (185). In it he sets forth very persuasively the main themes in the apologetics of his day. He was a man of high social rank, probably senatorial.

IRENAEUS AND CLEMENT OF ALEXANDRIA

IRENAEUS has a place apart because he wrote principally against heresy. He was from Smyrna, a disciple of Polycarp and the "presbyters" of Asia, and he went to Lyons, perhaps with a group of emigrants. In 177, the martyrs imprisoned in Lyons sent him, as a priest, to Rome with a letter on Montanism. They were killed in that year and the story of their glorious end has come down to us in the authentic *Acts* recorded by the churches of Lyons and Vienna, perhaps by Irenaeus himself. He was made bishop and in that capacity bent his energies to the conversion of the countryside about Lyons. He wrote a treatise to refute false gnosis (*Adversus haereses*) as well as exegetical and hortatory works. He died, probably a martyr, in 202-203. As a bishop he did not accept the theories about the Logos but intelligently followed tradition and strove to protect it from contamination with heresy.

Another philosopher converted to Christianity was Clement, perhaps of Athenian origin. He is known as CLEMENT OF ALEXANDRIA because his longest and most noteworthy activity occurred during a period after 180 A. D., when, as disciple and successor of Pantaenus, he graced the catechetical school in Alexandria until Septimius Severus closed it in A. D. 203.

Alexandria was an active commercial center and also a center of intellectual life in the Mediterranean because of its museum and library, its pagan teachers such as Ammonius Sacca and Longinus and its schools like that of Philo among the Jews, who comprised one third of the city's population. Origen, the great Christian exegete, and Platinus, the founder of Neo-Platonism, had attended the school of Ammonius Sacca. Toward the end of the second century, through the work of Clement and other scholars, among whom were the Gnostics Valentinus, Carpocrates and Basilides, Alexandria quickly became a bright intellectual center of Christianity also. She formed the genius of Origen and molded an original (more allegorical) method of interpreting the Scriptures in contrast to that (more literal) of Antioch. Due to her long tradition of Hellenized Jews Alexandria was the best place to attempt a wide absorption of Hellenistic into Christian thought, to use and at the same time reconcile with Christianity the pagan authors and therefore classical culture. Clement was one of the most noteworthy writers in this daring activity, aided as he was by his great faith in knowledge and nourished by an extremely vast learning in things sacred and profane. But the *simpliciores* were scandalized at the relations he established between faith and gnosis, for they were "afraid of Greek philosophy as children fear ghosts";[7] and if they could no longer stop the movement they at least acted as a check on the deviations resulting from it.

In his attempt to weld the Hellenistic world to the Christian world, Clement, like Justin and Theophilus, also sometimes used the concept of the Logos as the wellspring from which all the little rivulets of truth were made to flow into the Logos, Christ, as into their sea. And since he found that Aratus and Hesiod had also formulated correct notions of God, he was led to consider that "the Greeks, having received some sparks of the divine Logos, expressed some elements of truth."[8] But more often he used the simple expedient of charging the pagans with plagiarism, and in reality he Hellenized Christianity more than he Christianized Hellenism.

It is very rarely that we catch him at any flagrant adulteration of the original thought of the Gospel, but this is partly

---

7. *Strom.*, VI, 80, 5.
8. *Protrept.*, VII, 74, 7.

because we do not possess the writings on which Photius based his charge of impiety against the pious and gentle Clement.

He had, however, to avoid offending to any great extent the refined and cultured mind of his public, which included both the aristocrats and the burghers of paganism, and at the same time he had to introduce the faith to them as a nobler philosophy — in fact, as an eclectic compendium of all the best findings of ancient ethics. Therefore he no doubt felt obliged to soften some of the characteristics of the Gospel teaching and reinterpret the Apostles, comparing them to the various philosophers, poets and prose-writers of Greece, while he gave their thought a new twist so that perhaps not rarely he indirectly altered its meaning or at least gave it a forced explanation. We can see that his was a constant anxious striving to reconcile the old ethical system with the new, pointing out that the new system was in accord with the old since it was the quintessence of rationality. And he piles up quotation after quotation. In fact, his prose is a succession of quotations from sacred and profane writings woven together in argument which is persuasive, ingenious and sincere. And in his effort to give a Greek cast to the formulae of religion, he presents as the model of Christian life the wise man—the Gnostic—who combined not only all the Christian virtues but Platonic, Stoic, and Pythagorean features as well. Certainly that huge mass of Christian and pagan material, thus juxtaposed, fused and compared, served admirably to attract the Greek bourgeoisie to the Church, to lure philosophic thought to the faith of the Gospel. And just when Clement himself seemed to be submerged by it all, he would recognize that there was a boundary line between the two worlds and that it was called the Cross. When his listeners heard him declare with Philo and the Stoics and Plutarch, etc., that philosophy is "the study of wisdom, and wisdom is the knowledge of things divine and human, and their causes"[9]

---

9. *Strom.*, I, 30, 1.

(even though he did compare it to Hagar, that useful concubine and handmaid of Sara, the faith) and when they heard him say that before the advent of Christ philosophy had been necessary to the Greeks for justice and that now it was useful to religion in all its aspects, then they must have agreed that a noble office was reserved for speculation in the new religion and that the latter received with honor the fathers of ancient philosophy though it did subordinate them to a religious goal. Nor did they find this absurd or hostile in an age when all philosophy was veering toward theosophic ground.

Clement assured the *simpliciores* that philosophy was, in a certain sense, the work of Divine Providence, a divine gift (not a diabolical intrusion) bestowed upon the Greeks, and that therefore it was not to be rejected but vindicated as an ally of the faith while remaining subordinate to it.[10]

It would have impoverished and adulterated Christianity to reduce it to simple gnosis or gnostic ethics as the Alexandrian seems to do at times; but it would have impoverished it as much and would have been a great error besides to consider it opposed to learning and philosophy as certain of the rigorists tried to do. With Origen, Clement has the merit of securing Christian citizenship for good gnosis and taking out of the hands of Christianity's adversaries such a formidable argument as the conflict between learning and faith.

Through the efforts of these thinkers, writers and teachers, Christian thought became an object of study and a force of spiritual regeneration among the upper classes; while the moral conduct of the more humble Christians and their polemics, carried on even in the palace of the Caesars and in the prisons, diffused throughout the whole social organism the revolutionary leaven of the Gospel.

Clement died between 211 and 216. Of his writings we have extant three intimately related works, the *Protrepticus,*

---

10. Cf. *Strom.,* I, 18, 1-20, 3.

the *Paedagogus* and the *Stromata,* a kind of unorganized summary of moral theology and apologetics; a work in biblical exegesis, *Hypotyposis;* a homily, *Quis dives salvetur,* which is a study of wealth in relation to the Christian's aim in life; and various fragments.

ORIGEN

In ORIGEN, the successor of Clement as teacher in the *Didaskaleion* in Alexandria, we find the greatest attempt to rationalize the faith, to believe rationally, as he used to say,[11] or to reconcile Plato with the introduction to the fourth Gospel — an attempt so bold that the boundaries between the two sometimes disappeared from sight.

He was the son of a martyr, and his was the ardent faith of martyrdom, so much so that he was called Adamantius (man of steel). But he was at the same time eager for critical study and information and so he went rummaging through all the learning of the period, both sacred and profane. He became the instructor of martyrs and teachers, among whom was St. Gregory Thaumaturgus. During the persecution of Decius (250-251) he hoped to give his life for the faith, but although he was imprisoned and tortured, he did not die until three or four years later, at the age of sixty-nine, in the city of Tyre where he had taken refuge.

He wrote or dictated an extraordinary number of works in a rather colorless style. There were no less than two thousand separate items dealing with the Scriptures, theology, ascetics, some polemics and apologetics, and among them a huge mass of homilies and letters. A great part of this work has been lost. For several years he shone from Egypt and Palestine as a beacon light for the Mediterranean countries. Around him there rose controversies and heresies, but above all he sowed a crop of fertile ideas which impressed even pagan culture. It

---

11. *C. Cels.,* III, 16.

is through his work especially that Christianity as a system of thought — as a complete embodiment of Reason — is placed aloft on the lamp-stand so that its light pierces through the breaches which, in the name of Plato, using his ideas and vocabulary, Origen has opened in the pagan wall. With its schools and its libraries, Alexandria, peopled with scholars and teachers, was at that time the busiest and most brilliant center of pagan culture. To non-Christians, this Christian culture seemed an agglomeration of barbarous formulae, reserved to workingmen and women; Origen takes it and gives it its most powerful exposition. He strives to achieve a grandiose synthesis of revelation and speculation concerning Christ, who is the divine apex of a hierarchy of inspired or enlightened searchers after truth, namely, the prophets and, just below them, the philosophers.

But since Christ is the source of knowledge as of all things, philosophy is subordinate to revelation — we should say to theology. In fact, it is partial truth because it is natural, while revelation is complete truth because it is supernatural. Plato had some "sublime and admirable" intuitions like that in the *Timaeus,* which had impressed other Greek Christian thinkers: "The Father and Maker of the universe is difficult to discover, and once discovered it is difficult to explain him to all." Hence Christian thought is superior because it reveals clearly and completely the fatherhood of God.[12]

Natural law — already mentioned by St. Paul — derives from the same rational source. In it Origen finds another point of universal contact among all men because it is common to and innate in all mankind. Though it cannot be compared to the law of faith and cannot be justified without the grace of faith it too is a law of God.

Therefore in Origen there is no *a priori* opposition to the non-Christian world, but rather a process of rational discrimina-

---

12. *C. Cels.,* VII, 42. Cf. Justin, *Ap.,* XLVI; Clem. of Alex., *Strom.,* V, 78, 1.

tion whereby some of its elements are absorbed (and vindicated) and others are rejected as spurious. "For philosophy is not in all things contrary to the law of God, nor is it in all things consonant with it."[13] Echoing Justin and Clement, Origen, in his controversy with the pagan Celsus, also writes: "We try not to oppose whatever good has been formulated by authors even though foreign to our faith, not to argue with or overthrow what is right."[14] And this criterion, which finally prevailed especially in the Occident, gave the Christian revolution a character all its own. It was more constructive, almost recapitulatory, than destructive.

Conversely, in so far as they make profession of knowledge and exhort men to virtue, the Christians resemble the best philosophers (Jesus himself in his betrayal and death resembles those philosophers who were betrayed by their disciples, and Socrates who was condemned to death). They surpass them in the social field in so far as they do not restrict their lessons to the educated but offer them to all classes. In short, here we have the two worlds reconciled as much as possible, but the old is subordinate to the new.[15]

MINUCIUS AND TERTULLIAN

Under the Empire, Latin North Africa developed a vigorous social life. The Church stimulated its native genius, which the decadence of secular literature had enmeshed in pointless rhetoric, and took from it some of the greatest thinkers and writers of the new Christian literature: Minucius, Tertullian, Cyprian, Augustine.

Critics have long disputed as to which one of the first two famous Latin apologists, Minucius Felix or Tertullian is influenced by the other, since there is an evident relation between the concepts expressed in the *Octavius* and the *Apologeticus*.

---

13. *In Gen.*, hom. XIV, 3.
14. *C. Cels.*, VII, 46.
15. *C. Cels.*, II, 12 and 17; III, 51; VII, 49.

Since one undeniably borrowed from the other, we might consider that the borrower was the one who presented the greater number of arguments; and Tertullian presents an array of legal arguments which is lacking in Minucius. If the latter, a lawyer, had had the *Apologeticus* before him when he wrote, he would have used the strongest and most original part of Tertullian's work. The critics list other reasons to prove that Minucius came first.

MINUCIUS' defense is classic. It is patterned after the dialogue of the great authors, being a discussion between Caecilius Natalis and Octavius. Caecilius is a typical exponent of conservative paganism, hostile to the Christian religion because it is an absurd innovation introduced by an illegal, immoral, proletarian society which is an enemy of Roman society. Octavius is the exponent of rational Christianity, sound and uncompromising when it comes to essential dogmas but conciliatory and tactful in his exposition. The result is a logical, concise and convincing defense of Christianity such as could appeal to the refined world of secular culture.

Stronger and more vehement is the defense of Quintus Septimius Florens TERTULLIANUS, who marched to the counter-attack with formidable vigor. It was as if he gathered to himself the bitter cries of thousands of oppressed Christians to hurl them impetuously into the face of a hostile world, now to challenge, now to persuade. Like the other apologists he was a convert from paganism. But he left paganism with such a feeling of revulsion for it that any reconciliation between it and Christianity, even a mere philosophical one, seemed impossible to him.

He belonged to the military bourgeoisie. He was born about 160 and was the son of a centurion in the proconsular cohort stationed in Carthage, which had become again a flourishing economic and intellectual center. Here he attended the best schools and studied the Greek and Latin languages and literatures so that he could write fluently in both. In his youth and while still a pagan he led a dissolute life. He studied law with great profit and some have identified him with the jurist Tertullian. He was converted when he was between thirty and forty years old, during a period of Christian persecution. To defend the persecuted he attacked paganism in the *Ad Nationes* and took up identical arguments in his *Apologeticus,* composed in the same year, 197. In 200 he was ordained a priest. He was already married at that time. He continued to engage in controversy with the pagans, to refute the heretics and to exhort the Christians. The bitterness of his criticism, his ascetical austerity and his uncompromising attitude on dogma grew harsher year by year, until his unyielding rigorism led him out of the Catholic Church, which seemed to him to have become too lax. He went over to the Montanists, troubled by supposed prophetic charisms, and then he broke with them to form a sect called the Tertullianists.

In the field of controversy his most noteworthy writings, besides the *Apologeticus,* are the *Ad Martyres,* an inspired exhortation to some Christians imprisoned for their faith, the *De testimonio animae,* a philosophico-theological treatise, and the *Ad Scapulam,* a threatening letter to the proconsul Scapula who was persecuting the faithful about 212. His works against heresy include *De Praescriptione haereticorum, Adversus Marcionem* (208-211), *Adversus Hermogenem, Adversus Valentinianos* (208-211), *Adversus Praxean* (213-217). Works of dogmatical catechesis are *De baptismo, De carne Christi* (208-211), *De resurrectione carnis,* written shortly afterwards, and *De anima.* Works on morals and discipline are *De oratione* (200-206); *De poenitentia; De pudicitia,* the subject matter of which is Montanist and is directed against a measure of one of the popes (perhaps Callixtus) which granted pardon to adulterers after a period of penance; *De cultu feminarum,* on women's dress; *De velandis virginibus, Ad uxorem, De exhortatione castitatis* and *De monogamia,* in which he begins by arguing against second marriages and ends up by declaring that they are illicit, contrary to the views of the Catholics (*psychici*); *De patientia, De spectaculis, De ieiunio, De pallio, De corona,* etc., etc.

Even after he became involved in heresy, the Church recognized Tertullian, because of the greater part of his very numerous writings, as one of her most courageous defenders and most original writers.

CHAPTER III

CULTURE, ART, SPECTACLES

LEARNING AND FAITH

G IVEN these men and these principles, we can readily understand what must have been the attitude toward the arts and culture in general.

There were two dangers to be avoided: on the one hand, the danger of superficial individuals like Hermias, who quite banally made fun of philosophy because he did not know it,[1] and of bigoted rigorists, like Tatian, who rejected philosophy although they did know it and used it; and on the other hand, the danger of reabsorbing religion in philosophy, faith in gnosis, as the Gnostics had done. These two dangers flowed together into extreme currents of Christian thought which more or less rapidly became heretical. After he accepted Montanism, Tertullian could assert that there was a cleavage between philosophy and religion, and, conversely, label the Gnostic Hermogenes a heretic because "from the Christians he had gone over to the philosophers, from the Church to the Academy and the Portico. . . . "[2] Clement of Alexandria and his disciple Origen border on heresy and sometimes involuntarily fall into it when they exaggerate the importance of learning for the attainment of salvation and actually divide Christianity into two classes, a lower class composed of the unlearned (the simple) and a higher class composed of the learned (gnostics), who alone enjoy perfection by virtue of their knowledge of the

---

1. In the work Διασυρμὸς τῶν ἔξω φιλοσόφων (*The Mockery of Heathen Philosophers*), which is a kind of satire.
2. *Adv. Hermog.*, I.

mysteries. Thus, socially speaking, they are in danger of splitting Christian unity and creating a caste system.[3]

The middle course between these two, which was the wavering result of long and sometimes dramatic conflicts, helped admirably to diffuse Christianity throughout the Empire.[4]

In an age when the mastery was held by erudite sophists and philosophers who dabbled in theology, culture, become a faithful handmaid, helped to attack Christianity's most dangerous adversary, which, entrenched among the ruling classes, had by now linked its secular arm in that of the government police. At the same time the principles which inspired this culture opened wide roads of communication between the two worlds thus preventing Christianity from locking itself up in any jealous particularism of its own, which would certainly have been of great harm to the Apostolate itself.

There was a distinction, though not always a clear one, between sacred and profane culture, between the science of the first causes and that of the second. For the first time men started from the premise, Christ is the *Logos* and also *Sophia* (wisdom),[5] that is, the source and synthesis of all knowledge and therefore of all the truths discovered by non-Christian peoples as well. Through the illumination of the Word, even though sporadic, all peoples had arrived at a wisdom of their own but had intermixed it with spurious elements. The Incarnation had served to divide the true from the false in this pagan wisdom, and this — according to Origen — caused the reaction of the princes of this world.[6]

---

3. Cf. Origen, *In Ioann.*, I, 7, 43; XIX, 31, 16, *passim*.
4. Clement of Alexandria used to say that if philosophy had been necessary to the Greeks before Christ for justice, now it was useful for religion (πρὸς θεοσέβειαν) (*Strom.*, I, 5).
5. *Unigenitus Filius Dei qui erat Verbum et sapientia Patris* (Origen, *Peri Archon*, III, 5, 6; cf. also II, 9, 4). It derives from the Scriptures: "How great are thy works, O Lord! thou hast made all things in wisdom ..." (Ps. 103:24); and, similarly, Col. 1:15-20: "He [Christ] is the image of the invisible God. ... For in him were created all things ... and he is before all. ... For it has pleased God the Father that in him all his fullness should dwell, and that through him he should reconcile to himself all things. ..."
6. *Peri Archon*, III, 3, 2, with a reference to Ps. 2:2.

The principle formulated by Justin begins for the first time to be widely applied, sometimes too widely; for we find Clement of Alexandria and the author of the *Cohortatio ad Graecos* helping themselves generously not only from the Scriptures but also from the writers of comedy and the poets, assembling rather than assimilating.[7] In them and in the others there is a lively sense of the conflict between monotheism and polytheism, and especially between good morals and corrupt ones. But monotheism itself and rectitude in particular had been preached — as the Alexandrian perceived — by the best Greek philosophy too, being natural products of the human spirit illumined by reason.[8]

This moved the poles of the controversy; it was no longer between Christianity and Hellenism but between all rationality (Christian, Hebrew, Graeco-Roman, etc.) and irrationality. The dialectic position of the Church became broader. There was danger that it might also become weaker.

In this field the Christians repeat the attempts to break the dikes that separated the wonderful stream of Hellenic learning from barbarian thought and especially from the Hebrews, after whom the Christians patterned themselves through the Scriptures; attempts which, by dint of the chronological reconstructions they were able to make in those days, went so far as to claim priority for the barbarians (Hebrews) in the invention of the arts and sciences and to state that the Hellenes, therefore, had derived their learning from the Hebrews, perhaps by plagiary (or outright theft).[9]

Other Christians reasoned that since all truth was to be found in the Bible, all other books were to be discarded as

---

7. In the *De Monarchia*, once attributed to Justin, we find Aeschylus, Sophocles, Menander and Plato quoted, but Christ never.

8. The rational Christian perceived the irrationality of punishments inflicted on the flesh, and he said to his judge (Demetrian): *Quid te ad infirmitatem corporis vertis? quid cum terrenae carnis imbecillitate contendis? Cum animi vigore congredere, virtutem mentis infringe, fidem destrue, disceptatione si potes, vince: vince ratione* (Cyprian, *Ad Demetr.*, XIII).

9. Cf. Clem. of Alexandria, *Strom.*, I, 15-16; II, 5.

superfluous. And here pious solicitude might easily be the ally of intellectual laziness, always a fertile soil for excuses to dispense with study. Even to learned men like Theophilus and Tertullian, secular learning[10] seemed stupid, in fact, harmful, and therefore to be rejected. And their intransigence was effectively stiffened by pagan scholars who showered either their silence or their arrogant insults upon a community recruited from among the illiterate and the ignorant and founded upon documents written or translated in a Greek and Latin that were frequently enough to make one shudder.

Learning is light, and the source of light is Christ. This idea goes from the manuals of Christian pedagogy to the art and epigraphy of the catacombs. It had immeasurable consequences for civilization, because it was Christ, the principle of universal conciliation, who preserved in ecclesiastical libraries — the only ones in the Middle Ages — so many masterpieces of classical art and speculation, which would have been burned along with the idols had the intransigent point of view prevailed. But that it might not prevail, prudent resistance and often stormy battles were necessary.[11]

THE USE OF PROFANE KNOWLEDGE

" . . . the Greeks look for 'wisdom,' " St. Paul had pointed out (1 Cor. 1:22-25), "but we, for our part, preach a crucified Christ — to the Jews indeed a stumbling block, and to the Gentiles foolishness; but to those who are called, both Jews and Greeks, Christ, the power of God and the wisdom of God. For the foolishness of God is wiser than men."

These words irritated not a few learned men, who, because of them, kept away from Christianity. Origen, noticing this phenomenon, points out that they do not at all imply a condemnation of culture. He declares that "culture is not an evil, in fact, it is a road to virtue. . . . It is no hindrance to the knowl-

---

10. *Doctrina saecularis litteraturae* (*De spectaculis*, XVIII).
11. A historical summary of this debate may be found in P. de Labriolle, *Hist. de la litt. lat. chrét.*, Intro. V-X.

edge of God," rather it favors it.[12] Therefore, "those Christians are to be reproved who take their ease in their ignorance."[13]

In reality, St. Paul — according to a comment of Irenaeus[14] — is criticizing false wisdom, the pride which has risen above wisdom, that wisdom which became prostitute to idolatry, confusing divinity with man-made objects, and which therefore is true ignorance. The Church was criticized because it was composed of the ignorant masses, but they knew the noblest truths concerning God and were therefore learned.[15] Thus the tables were completely turned.

"True wisdom does not err, but ignorance. The only stable thing among all existing things is knowledge and truth, and one and the other proceed from wisdom."[16]

Such an enthusiastic profession of faith in knowledge does not mean that all Christians are intelligent; not at all. There are also the dull and the slow-witted but they do not form the backbone of the new society; and in any case Origen prefers the "more intelligent and keen-minded" who love to plumb the mysteries of the Scriptures and search deeply into the enigmas of faith.[17] In such effort as this, learning, which is synonymous with wisdom, rises to a communion with the unknown; speculation becomes associated with dogma.[18]

To suppress this desire to know is against nature because it is a desire innate in man: "as the eye of its own nature seeks light and sight, and as the body of its nature desires food and drink, just so the mind has its own natural desire to know the

---

12. *C. Cels.*, III, 47, 49.

13. *Ib.*, III, 44.

14. In commenting on the statement in 1 Cor., 8:1, "Knowledge puffs up, but charity edifies," Irenaeus wrote: *Non quia veram scientiam de Deo culparet, alioquin seipsum primum accusaret; sed quia sciebat quosdam sub occasione scientiae elatos excidere a dilectione Dei, et ob hoc opinari seipsos esse perfectos.* ... In such a case it is better to be ignorant and love God than to be wise and not love him. (*Adv. Haer.*, II, 26, 1.)

15. *C. Cels.*, VI, 14.

16. *Ib.*, III, 72.

17. *Ib.*, III, 74.

18. Origen asserts a κοινωνίαν σοφίας ἐν μυστηρίῳ (*C. Cels.*, III, 61).

truth of God and to seek out the causes of things: a desire which comes from God."[19]

Toward the profane branches of learning, the Christians displayed a legitimate diffidence because of the schools in which they were taught, pagan schools where they were closely interwoven with idolatry. Hence they hesitated to encourage young men to embark upon an intellectual career. Origen knows that Gregory can become "an excellent Roman jurisconsult" or "a Greek philosopher"; but he exhorts him to take Christian doctrine as his goal, and to that end to make use of "those teachings of Greek philosophy, which, almost as auxiliaries, can be useful to Christianity; and that is, the doctrines of general erudition or the propaedeutics to Christianity"; that is, in interpreting the Scriptures, to make use of profane learning too, such as geometry, astronomy, etc.[20]

While still a pagan, Gregory Thaumaturgus learned in the school of Origen that knowledge leads to faith, and ignorance to blindness, that he who does not study philosophy cannot be pious.[21] Attracted by such a profession of faith in philosophy, Gregory and his brother Athenodorus became Christians, conquered for Christ by the learning of their teacher. He directed his students to the knowledge of the theories of the Greek philosophers, whatever they might be, excluding only atheistic doctrines. He did not permit his pupils to remain unaware of all that human thought had worked out in every age, but, good teacher that he was, he guided them through the dense and thorny wood, pointing out the true from the false.[22]

---

19. *Peri Archon*, II, 11, 4.
20. *Ep. ad Greg.*, I. Cf. Origen, *Peri Archon*, II, 11, 4, 6 (*P. G.*, XI, 243, 246).
21. *Paneg.*, VI, 14.
22. "Origen bade us study philosophy in such manner that when we had gathered together all the writings which remain of the ancient philosophers and poets, we were to throw none away and reject none (and on the other hand we were not able to discriminate among them) except the works of the atheists, who, abandoning man's common sense, deny the existence of God and of Providence.... And he bade us read all those other writings in such manner as not to give preference to one type or one book or one discourse more than another, and not to reject any author whether Greek or barbarian, but to listen to them all" (Greg. Thaum., *Paneg.*, XIII).

It is permissible, therefore, to use profane subjects (literature, grammar, geometry, arithmetic, dialectics) to further sacred learning, but these must be subordinate to theology. It is permissible if and insofar as good may come of it for the "true philosophy of Christ."[23] In this opinion, we find as always the absolute rule that everything must be directed to our final end, that every aspect of life must be convoyed by the general teleology which has its culmination in God. For the Divine Logos does not desire earthly things. He does not look for strength, or physical beauty, or nobility of birth, but for holy souls and godlike actions; and so he does not make poets, or philosophers, or formidable rhetoricians and rich men. Yet in recompense he gives immortality. In this sense, Christianity is a philosophy.[24]

Some heretics did not always bear this ultimate goal in mind, for to impress the pagans, with whom they sought to be reconciled even at the expense of faith, they gave learning an excessively cumbersome place. And still others, when they compared the mediocre culture of Christian society with that of imperial society, abandoned the Church on the pretext of knowledge. But probably this pretext cloaked ambitions for a career and very mundane interests.[25] Culture, since it comes from God, must lead to God.

In short, the essential thing is sanctity; the essential thing is the knowledge of God. Culture is necessary if it helps one to a knowledge of things divine. To attain eternal salvation, all other culture may be useful but it is not indispensable. The important and vital thing is that knowledge must not be bought at the price of faith.

As for faith, it is admitted that study is important for the Christians in order to plumb the divine mysteries, and for the

23. Origen, *In Gen.*, hom. XI (*P. G.*, XII, 222 and ff.).
24. This is the thought in the anonymous *Oratio ad Graecos.*
25. "Those who abandon the teaching of the Church put forth as an excuse the ignorance of the holy priests, not considering of how much more worth is a simple religious than a blasphemous and impudent sophist" (Irenaeus, *Adv. Haer.*, V, 20, 2).

pagans that they may appraise the true value of Christianity; for truth demands that it be not condemned when it is not known.[26]

STYLE

Intimately associated with culture is the art of writing or style. This creates an ethical problem for the conscience of the Christian, who appreciates the full and true value of the word (Christ is the Word!) but fears that the study of style may hide a siren decoy and work to the detriment of the naked truth. — Let your speech be yea, yea, and no, no, the Master had said. And St. Paul had affirmed the word of wisdom against the wisdom of the word; and in addition, the Bible, brimming with so much wisdom, was written in a barbaric style.[27]

Not a few Christian writers had been converted after they had already acquired the use and enjoyed the pleasures of fine style, to which the schools attached all the more importance the more empty their thought became. Truly form had grown in importance to the detriment of content and had come actually to take its place. Thus the Christians often found themselves faced by a dilemma: whether to disdain the art of writing and thus sacrifice a precious means of introduction into the learned world, of gaining readers and listeners by persuading them of the thing they affirmed by the very elegance of their style; or to run the risk of adulterating the genuine simplicity of the Gospels and the crude conciseness of the Prophets. Between the two horns of the dilemma, the greater number continued to write as they had written up to the time of their conversion or else quite unconsciously became entangled in a kind of compromise, so that while they might in word disdain

---

26. Tertullian, *Apol.*, I, 2.
27. Origen did not accept this opinion, too often expressed, concerning the style of the Scriptures; he thought them written not "in an unrefined and crude language, but according to a rule befitting divine learning," aiming, that is, to give the mystical meaning rather than the historical one (*In Gen.*, hom. XV, 1).

literary artifice, in practice they sought with great care after rhetorical effect. Typical of this last is Tertullian, who inveighs against stylistic conceits and then displays great ability in all the rhetorical art of his time. Style, even when it was not considered a value in itself, was conceived of not as something intrinsic in the creating spirit but as a more or less beautiful garment hung upon a more or less interesting thought. And the Christians shared this conception of form and content with their contemporaries. Clement of Alexandria, whose own style was graceful and polished, was convinced of it. And only under the influence of the asceticism of style implicit in the Christian precept did he declare that if diction is a dress then we must pay little heed to it but rather should we take heed for the flesh and the sinews, that is, we must take care to express ourselves clearly rather than elegantly. An excessively polished style is like a luxurious garment, and this is blameworthy from the point of view of ascetics. It is enervating and treacherous like effeminate garments. The word must not give delight at the expense of its aim, which is to be useful.[28]

These rules of aesthetics, however disputable they may be, were in large measure responsible for correcting the tendency of the time to dissolve the word in music.

As usually happens, these theories and stylistic anxieties had little influence on the art of these same writers. That is, those who were artists wrote artistically and those who were not could not give to their writing what they did not have. The style of Justin and Origen is hodgepodge and quite unadorned. They are teachers who dictate with the sole purpose of explaining something. The writing of Minucius and Tertullian is that of two cultured intellects to whom the efficacy of fine style is not unknown. Commodianus writes like a self-taught rustic because his education is elementary. In Cyprian, the ex-rhetorician is somewhat modified but not entirely destroyed by his pastoral cares.

---

28. *Strom.*, I, 10.

In the final analysis, in the majority of Christian writers, their love for the faith and for souls corrects the extravagances of a rhetoric which finds an end in itself, in its own music and formal conceits. The majority were powerfully influenced by their duty to illumine their brothers, even the most lowly of them, and therefore to be intelligible even at the sacrifice of a beautiful figure of speech or an ingeniously artful construction. As Origen pointed out, the crude narrative of Matthew, intelligible to all its readers, is more useful to life than the elegant *Criton* of Plato, which only a few learned men understand.[29]

In the matter of style as well as culture, Origen was disentangling a Christian social concern, the anxiety that style, by its very elegance, might ultimately restrict learning to the minority who could understand it; for this was what had happened in the case of the classical style of Plato and the other philosophers who behaved in the manner of physicians to noble families and denied their services to the great mass of the poor and the ignorant. But it was for these last, however, that the Apostles and prophets had written in an everyday style.[30]

Naturally, even though it was his aim, Origen did not always succeed in being intelligible to the lowly; for the difficulty more often lay, as it had for Plato, not in the style, which was simple, but in the thought, which was difficult.

In any case, the fact that so many at least were aiming at simplicity, was an antidote for the bombastic rhetoric of the sophist Greek and Latin lecturers.

ART

What has been said for the art of writing goes for all art in general. Christians feared that it might be mere tinsel draped over the naked beauty of a sentiment or an idea, especially since in the first centuries art is almost universally idola-

---

29. Origen was referring specifically to Matthew, 5:39-40 (*C. Cels.,* VII, 61).
30. *C. Cels.,* VII, 59-60.

trous and amoral. As Origen said of pagan poetry, it is the golden cup of which Jeremiah speaks. The eloquence and elegance of the poets are the gilt on a cup full of the poison of idolatry, foul language, ruinous opinions and false knowledge.[31]

When Christians could have places in which to worship, they naturally felt the need of adorning them, of honoring God with art. A church whose walls are covered with reminders of the precepts and episodes in the Gospels has an atmosphere more conducive to prayer than does a bare room.

Little of this early art has come down to us. At Dura Europos there have been unearthed some examples of it as it was used in a Christian church; and in Egypt a papyrus was found containing a Christian hymn with the music.[32] We know too that the Egyptian bishop Nepos composed numerous hymns and psalms which the faithful still sang with "delight" at the time of Dionysius of Alexandria (c. 190 - c. 265). We are in the third century, when the Church, taking advantage of the long rests between persecutions, is organizing and strengthening herself.

But because of the circumstances in which the early Church finds herself, her art grows up mostly about the tombs where persecution is less likely to reach it, and it lingers preferably about the memories of the martyrs.

Painting, sculpture and architecture create their first noteworthy works, which, in the first generations, do not have the characteristics of the art contemporary with them. In the Cemetery of Domitilla at Rome, are to be found paintings as early as the first century,[33] and this proves that though their religion was born of Judaism, the early Christians were not hostile to art. If anything, because they were descendants of Judaism and because of the nature of their faith and the clandestine conditions in which painting and sculpture more or

31. Origen, *In Jer.*, hom. XXXVIII, 7. He is alluding to Jer. 51:7.
32. *P. Oxy.*, 1786.
33. In the Gallery of the Flavii.

less began to grow, these arts tended prevalently toward symbolic and allegoric decoration. Images of historical personages are not lacking. First of all there is Jesus Christ, whose image frequently appears in the catacombs as early as the first century, either a child in his mother's arms or receiving the homage of the three Magi, or a grown man as teacher, judge, wonderworker, etc.[34] Christ, Moses, Isaias, Peter, the Madonna and Child, Daniel among the lions, Jonah and the whale are all there, while around the allegoric figure of the Good Shepherd, so dear to the Christians converted from paganism, and that of the "Orante" there gathered a goodly company of dolphins, doves, flowers, vases, birds, the pail of milk, the fish and the phoenix, anchors and tridents.

In the third century other elements appear to illustrate the profession of the deceased — little scenes from life such as selling vegetables or unloading wheat at a bakery; coopers carrying a barrel; boatmen, vine-growers and hucksters plying their trades; and then the tools of labor, such as pincers, combs, mallets, books.

Among them might be found also a few pagan subjects which had become very common decorative elements and had lost their original idolatrous meaning, as in the case of the myth of Orpheus. Toward the third century when the artistic conscience was better informed, it excluded such decorations.[35]

All those symbols, so dear to the Christians and so deeply venerated, were an expression of their love for Christ and his mother, for Peter and the Apostles and the prophets, for the Church and for the sacraments entrusted to her safekeeping.

Side by side with the decorative arts, epigraphy also developed, simple and to the point at first and then enriched by symbols.[36] In this class we might put the famous epitaph of Abercius.

34. Wilpert, *Le pitture delle catacombe*, p. 172.
35. Cf. *ib.*, p. 173 etc. and De Rossi, *Roma sotterranea*, II, 169, 1, 99 etc.
36. Cf. Grossi Gondi, *Trattato d'epigrafia cristiana*, Rome, 1920.

PUBLIC GAMES AND SPECTACLES

The Gospel teaching demanded that Christians stay away from all those places and exhibitions of one sort or another in which monotheism, or Christ as God, or his moral law might be offended.

Therefore they stayed away from religious festivals, they did not go to the temples, adorn their houses with garlands on the festival days, light torches, or wear wreaths upon their heads, etc. They continued to frequent the baths, the basilicas and the forums in the daily round of business but they did so with a feeling of revulsion, and they kept away from those places too as much as possible because of the records of idolatry, the exhibitions of corruption and the fraudulent transactions they were bound to run into when they entered them. The baths, for example, had in a great number of cases become real brothels and the attendants acted, even legally, as procurers.[37]

In some Christians this attitude developed into a morbid ascetic disdain even for those objects used in the idolatrous festivals, such as flowers. These were extreme cases, however, for the great mass of Christians continued to view and love flowers as graceful creations of Divine Art. Only they did not wreathe their heads with them after the fashion of the pagans. "Anything born as an inviolable gift of God cannot be adulterated by any human act," not even by an idolatrous rite; "however, we abstain that no one may believe we are surrendering to the devils to whom libation is made or that we are ashamed of our religion. Certainly the flowers of spring are pleasing to us, for we choose the rose of spring, the lily and whatever other flowers have the most pleasing color and fragrance; and we use them either singly and strewn about or woven into wreaths with which we adorn our necks," and this is a great advantage to the sense of smell, for the nose re-

---

37. Digest. Justin. III, 2, *de his qui notantur infamia*, 2 (Ulpian), 5.

ceives more fragrance from the blossoms beneath it than from those which bind the head.[38]

The central concept in Christian ethics is this: let beautiful things be beautiful, and let their beauty possess something divine because it has been fashioned by God; but let their use be regulated. Thus, as we shall see, even the dour Tertullian does not condemn the beauty of woman; he merely does not wish it to be a source of corruption.

This standard really derives from the general Christian concept of the things of this world, namely, that they are all good in themselves, even the stones of the amphitheatres, the voice of the singer, the sword, and herbs; the use made of them for indecent spectacles, obscene songs, to kill and to poison — that is evil.[39]

Usually associated with the religious festivals were the public spectacles and games in the theatre or the circus.[40] The people throughout the whole empire took a passionate and morbid delight in them, finding an outlet in them now that political strife had ceased. The ruins of theatres and circuses which keep coming to the surface of modern civilization to reveal to us a characteristic aspect of ancient civilization prove how central a place the spectacles had in public life. Cities, colonies, provinces and private citizens vied with one another to offer the richest and most sumptuous for the delectation of the populace. And the emperor could bestow no gift more acceptable to the descendants of Romulus than that indicated by the wonderful phrase *panem et circenses*. Sometimes the bread was lacking, and at the end of the second century the task of distributing provisions was becoming both difficult and dangerous. But the mob was just as likely to riot if there were not

---

38. Minucius, *Oct.*, XXXVIII, 2. Cf. Tertullian, *De corona;* and Clement of Alexandria, *Paed.*, II, 8 (*P. G.*, VIII, 484): "Those educated by the Logos abstain from wearing wreaths; they do not believe it is necessary to bind the reason, which is in the head; not because the wreath is the symbol of wild conviviality, but because it is related to idolatry."

39. Tertullian, *De spectaculis*, 1.

40. Vitruvius, V., 3: "Games are celebrated on the festival days of the immortal gods."

spectacles enough or if they did not receive free tickets to attend them. In the fourth century, in the very midst of a social-economic crisis, the Circus Maximus at Rome had been enlarged to accommodate more than 400,000 spectators.

The imposing ruins of the Colosseum, which could seat more than eighty thousand, are an eloquent reminder of the passion even the most upright emperors had for these violent spectacles, in which the military virtues of the Quirites seemed to have buried themselves. In the architecture of the amphitheatres, throughout the Empire as well as in Rome, we see in every stone and column and arch the effort to attain the most vigorous beauty and at the same time give concrete expression to the imposing grandeur of the Empire; for the stadia, theatres and amphitheatres were the expression of its wealth, its power and its very vitality. Within their marble-covered walls, adorned with records of national glory, the atomic multitude, which no longer heard the call to assemblies of war, were in a new way recomposed into a people and thus regained the consciousness* of their social unity. But with what a conscience!*

Once when Septimius Severus wished to give Abgar IX evidence of his favor, he had a hippodrome built for him at Edessa. It was a kingly gift and the seal of western civilization, which the people of Edessa were desirous of assimilating.

To ask Christians not to attend the public games was like forbidding our little boys to take part in any sports at all. It meant the same sacrifice; it meant depriving them of the surest, noisiest and most popular collective entertainment that life in those days afforded. Yet the Church demanded this sacrifice for the twofold reason that the games were usually given to celebrate some idolatrous feast-day and that they were licentious, degrading and cruel. Under Commodus, who had appeared before his subjects in the rôle of a charioteer and a gladiator, the amphitheatre had assumed an abnormal and grossly orgiastic character.

---

*The Italian has *coscienza* [Trans.].

With the growth of Christianity, not a few of the faithful must have lapsed on this point and yielded to the general passion, for in the second half of the second century we find ecclesiastical writers inveighing angrily against the corruption in the theatre, the circus and the amphitheatre, places where the soul of the people was being brutally miseducated.

In the theatre, the actors and mimes frequently played lewd scenes for the amusement of an audience that went wild, took sides for this or that "divo" of the stage and even came to blows over him.[41] And since the subject of the presentation was often taken from mythology, they made a shambles of the very idea of divinity in the adventures of gods who were adulterers, seducers of virgins, effeminate, incestuous. And the people were moved to tears by the erotic plots and wept over the fictitious adventures just as elsewhere they went mad with excitement and delight over the real murders of the *retiari* and *mirmillones*.

Even in the circus or stadium where gymnastic or athletic contests took place but where the special offering was the chariot-races, the crowd split into factions and sometimes engaged in real battles for the colors of this or that stable.[42] And this passion was so contagious that, despite the exhortations and punishments of the Church, it infected the Christians too, especially those of Asia Minor, Syria and the Bosphorus, on whom even the eloquent complaints of Chrysostom had little effect.

But the most savage amusements of all were those in the amphitheatre, a typically Roman and imperial institution where in bloody combats between gladiators and wild beasts real murders and legal massacres were perpetrated.[43] The Church's opposition to them from the very beginning was resolute and aggressive. She remained intransigent and forbade the Chris-

41. Minucius, *Oct.*, XXXVII, 12.
42. *Ib.*
43. *Ib.*, 11.

tians to attend such spectacles, for she considered watching the murder of a man for pleasure almost the same as killing him.[44] And since she wished not only to avoid the murders as such but also to restore his original dignity to man, whose blood was being shed to feed evil passions, she fought against the gladiatorial games until she finally ended them at Rome with the last voluntary sacrifice of a monk. *THEODORET, HIST. ECC. 5.26*

The gladiatorial games — school of most savage cruelty — born as they were of acts of cruelty (according to Tertullian they grew out of the practice of human sacrifices to placate the dead[45]), perished through the action of charity.

GAMES AND SPECTACLES IN THE LIGHT OF CHRISTIAN ETHICS

All the Church Fathers, especially the most rigorous moralists, thunder against the games, and first among them we find Tatian and Tertullian, who assail them with sarcasm and moral and aesthetic arguments.

Tatian has it in for the jugglers, magicians, contortionists, mimes and comedians who act out the adventures of Aphrodite and Apollo, as well as for the mob which applauds their parodies of the gods and heroes, and their actions inciting to vice and crime. Disfiguring and masking the person are merely the mendacious aspect of the inner lie. They offend the Creator because they alter that human body which has been fashióned after the divine image.

Some dance in chorus and twist their bodies; others "play the pipes with their noses and recite obscenities with shameless gestures," teaching adultery to the girls and boys who have been taken to such spectacles. No less scandalous are the declaimers and orators, who in the public halls boldly and freely recount scandalous things or recite scurrilous verses.[46]

---

44. Athenagoras, *Legatio,* XXXV.
45. *De spect.,* XII.
46. *Orat.,* XXII.

The theatres are schools of lust and pornography. Like the stadia they are chairs of pestilence, assemblies of confusion and disorder where men and women flock together mainly to exchange glances and kindle each other with desires nourished by the lascivious music.[47]

The stadium and the amphitheatre do not teach courage but violence and insolence. The fleshy, muscular athletes are the more esteemed the more blows they shower upon their adversaries. Some who boast that they do not work and aspire to a life of leisure sell themselves as gladiators to be killed. Whoever buys them knowingly buys assassins, public assassins whom the mob watches, without the least shudder of horror, in fact in ecstatic delight, as they kill and are killed. "Only the man prevented from assisting at the crime is grieved because he was not condemned to witness wicked and vicious exploits. You sacrifice animals to eat their flesh and you buy men to offer your spirit a cannibal repast, nourishing it with impious effusions of blood. The robber at least kills to rob: but the rich man who buys gladiators buys them to kill."[48]

Tertullian in his *Apologeticus* had already stigmatized the wicked frenzy of the games in words which echo those of Minucius' *Octavius*. But later, while still a Catholic, perhaps on the occasion of the reappearance of the games in the provinces to celebrate the victory of Severus over Albinus, he examined the whole fundamental question in a special treatise, *De Spectaculis*, which is the first exhaustive study of the prob-

---

47. Clem. Alex., *Paed.*, III, 11.
48. Tatian, *Orat.*, XXIII. The conscience of the most upright pagans had also felt the immorality of this murder and the pleasure derived from murder. Seneca wrote (*Ep.*, XCV, 33): *Homo, sacra res homini, iam per lusum ac iocum occiditur et quem erudiri ad inferenda accipiendaque vulnera nefas erat, is iam nudus inermisque producitur satisque spectaculi ex homine mors est.* Cyprian condemns all shedding of human blood, and therefore war and the gladiatorial games too, for which a man is fattened up so that he may be killed with more glory: *Homo occiditur in hominis voluptatem; et ut quis possit occidere peritia est, usus est, ars est. Scelus non tantum geritur, sed et docetur. Quid potest inhumanius, quid acerbius dici? Disciplina est ut perimere quis possit, et gloria est quod perimit* (*Ep.*, I, 7; *P. L.*, IV, 206).

lem of the theatre from the ethical point of view. And just as we might expect from the author's character, the result was a radical condemnation of all games and spectacles, theatrical, athletic and gladiatorial; but because the condemnation was too general the Church did not accept it as a rule. Being more realistic, she wished to christianize the theatre rather than suppress it. She forbade the obscene and the criminal, and substituted Bible stories for mythology. Entertainment, having once more become harmless, became also ethical. It is true that the Christian theatre does not derive from the ancient theatre by way of corrections and substitutions, but represents rather an indigenous growth.[49]

The apologist is examining a thesis formulated by the pagans themselves when they claimed that the spectacles did not offend God or morality since they entertained the bodily organs, such as the ear and the eye, without touching the moral consciousness of the honor and respect due to God. Even if this had been true the Christians would have kept away from them if only to train themselves for martyrdom by abstaining from entertainments and pleasures.

The fundamental elements of the theatre are not harmful in themselves; it is their actual use which is offensive. The games in the amphitheatre are all clearly against the law of God which has "destroyed every kind of murder with the one and fundamental precept: — Thou shalt not kill!"[50]

Man was made to the image and likeness of God in order to possess the universe and not to commit crimes.

---

49. In a treatise, *De spectaculis,* attributed (but perhaps wrongly) to Cyprian, we find the statement that in the beginning dances, musical instruments and other like things connected with the spectacles were holy and good. The obscenity of the Greek myth and the suggestive gestures had altered their nature making them subject to the idols, that is, to the devils (III). The spectacles are forbidden, therefore, because they are related to idolatry. *Idolatria ludorum omnium mater est* (IV).

50. "We did not receive our eyes for concupiscence, our tongue to speak evil or our ears to hear it, nor the appetite for gluttony, nor the belly in order to satisfy our gluttony, nor the genital organs to commit excesses of unchastity, nor our intelligence to meditate fraud" (*De spect.,* II).

The games are idolatrous in origin and in nature. And even though the other places which the Christian must frequent to carry on his business contain reminders of idolatry, let it be remembered that "the places in themselves do not contaminate us but that which is done in them."[51]

Now the theatre arose and remains a shrine to the wanton Venus, so much so that not even the ancient censors regarded it with a favorable eye.[52]

All the actions and deeds which are condemned outside the theatre are applauded on the stage, where the Atellan mime outrages chastity, and the pantomime, disfigured from boyhood, brings the brothel to the footlights and scandalizes even the women, from whose sight these things are ordinarily hidden. We cannot speak of these things; why should we be able to see them?[53]

Neither let it be said that the plays besiege only the organs of sight; rather they excite the nerves and the mind, which takes delight in them and is stimulated to repeat the vicious acts of licentiousness, envy, wrath. "The episodes excite the emotions."[54]

The games in the circus are conducive to anxiousness, hatred and violence, emotions which do not become Christians, who are "the priests of peace." And if they are condemned outside the circus they should also be condemned within it.[55]

---

51. *Ib.*, VIII.
52. *Ib.*, X.
53. *Ib.*, XVII.
54. On the stage parricide is extolled and incest is realistically portrayed *expressa ad imaginem veritatis actione* for fear that in the course of time those crimes might cease to be committed; it is a school of crime for all ages. The most ancient crimes never die out; they become examples. *Adulterium discitur dum videtur.* A matron who goes to such spectacles a modest woman returns a harlot. And the gods presented on the stage! A harlot Venus, an adulterous Mars, Jupiter, the prince of vices. . . . *Deos suos quos veneratur imitantur, fiunt miseris et religiosa delicta*, says Cyprian who censures the spectacles with such eloquence and imagination (*Ep.*, I, 8; cf. also Tert. *De spect.*, XVII).
55. Tertullian, *De spect.*, XVI. Cf. his scornful question to the follower of Marcion: *Quid non frequentas tam solemnes voluptates circi furentis, caveae saevientis, et scenae lascivientis? (Adv. Marc.*, 1, 27). Clem. of Alex., *Paed.*, III, 11 (*P. G.*, VIII, 656): "Let spectacles, therefore, and plays that are full of scurrility and abundant gossip, be forbidden."

THE SPECTACLES OF THE CHRISTIAN

Some lukewarm Christians used to justify their passion for the circus by quoting passages from the Bible that contained the word *stadium*. That is all very well, answers Tertullian, "but what goes on in the stadium is without doubt unfit to be seen: blows, kicks, slaps and violent play of the hands while the personality is attacked in all possible ways in its most human and therefore divine qualities."

Athletic contests are a violation of human nature. Therefore races, the javelin throw, the various jumps, the parade of physical strength and all the exercises which tend to give the human body a plasticity and mold different from that fashioned by the hands of the Creator are vain and blameworthy.

This is Tatian's argument further developed by Tertullian. And as often happens with these writers, it is sophistic argument based on the purely external aspect of things and therefore not a little specious. Nor, in fact, was it considered sufficient basis for condemning sports as an exercise to strengthen the body. More reasonable from the social point of view is Tertullian's exhortation to despise the idleness of the athletes, tended and fattened in Greece that they might develop strong and handsome physiques; and this is above all a moral and social condemnation of athleticism as an end in itself. He goes so far as to say that "the art of wrestling is a business of the devil."[56] This exaggeration flutters about a kernel of truth in so far as it condemns exhibiting man in a kind of act of public prostitution as a thing all lines and muscles only, when his essential duties are not the development of his muscles and the bravado of his blows but rather justice and charity. Man is not a horse to be shown in the market-place nor is he an exhibition piece. His dignity is far greater and nobler than that, and his worth does not reside in his hocks.

---

56. Tertullian, *De spect.*, XVIII. More reasonable is the opinion of Clement of Alexandria (see page 196) who approves of wrestling as a sport or exercise.

According to the same criterion, a mixture of ethical and purely external evaluations, Tertullian, along with Tatian, also condemns the make-up actors use on the stage, for with the razor and false beards they hide their own features to assume those of Saturn or Isis or Bacchus; or by using the tragic buskin they even make themselves taller when the Gospel has declared that no one can add a single cubit to his physical stature! (Lk. 12:25). "Such as these wish to make Christ out a liar." Masks and make-up are a deception; the Christian must be sincere and truthful with himself even with regard to physical things for the Author of truth does not love what is false (Exod. 20:16). He who condemns every hypocrisy cannot approve any disguise of the voice either, or false tears, pretended moans and feigned love or outbursts of anger. Deuteronomy condemns whoever dresses as a woman; therefore the pantomimes who do that are to be condemned. And boxers are to be condemned also because when they smash the eyes of their opponents with the cestus they deform one of God's creatures.[57] This external and literal interpretation of the Biblical text naturally had no effect.

More convincing and logical are the objections to the amphitheatre. We may attend it, he says, only when the moral law permits cruelty, impiety, savagery and the enjoyment of human blood. Christians shrink from using even the blood of animals as nourishment. A good man cannot enjoy the sight even of a criminal's death. How then can he enjoy the spectacle of the murder of innocent men like the gladiators who are sacrificed as "victims to the lust of the populace"?[58]

And here Tertullian scores a bull's eye.

The usual Christians who dangle between virtue and vice object that the sun, in fact God himself contemplates the spectacles from heaven without being contaminated. True — comes the dry and biting answer of the African — the sun sends its

---

57. Tertullian, *De spect.*, XXII-XXIII.
58. *Ib.*, XIX.

rays down upon the sewers too without being infected; and God contemplates thieves and adulterers, fraud and idolatry as well as the spectacles, but not as a spectator — as a judge. The true Christian does not go to see the spectacles in order not to be seen there by him who sees everything.[59]

On the whole, Tertullian's opinion on the ethics of the spectacles of his time derives from a strict harmony between morality and practice. He reasons thus: if the indecencies presented in the theatre cannot be permitted in everyday relationships and if no self-respecting father would repeat that gutter-talk in front of his daughter, why must young girls be taken to the theatre to hear it, and why do people go to see what they do not approve of? If two citizens are not permitted to fight in the public square why must one go to the stadium to see a pair of wrestlers give it to each other with quite different vehemence? And if one cannot look upon the corpse of one who has died a natural death, why must he go to feast his eyes on the spectacle of dead bodies that lie bleeding on the sand of the amphitheatre? How are those persons consistent who, while they profess to be friends of order and peace, when they attend the circus or amphitheatre, go mad with excitement and urge the wrestlers and gladiators on to combat and murder? And where is there any consistency in that society which condemns actors, theatre managers, charioteers, gladiators and the whole personnel of the circus to a *diminutio capitis,* excludes them from the curia, the court, the senate, the equestrian order and from any public office as being highly unworthy, and then in their own field of action offers them tribute of honor and applause while men and women (as Juvenal narrates) even shamefully prostitute themselves to them.

The theatre seemed, as it was, a blight upon the civic honor even in ancient society. But the latter did not have the courage to suppress or reform it, due to that mixture of good and evil, of true and false, so characteristic of pagan ethics and philoso-

59. *Ib.,* XX.

phy which Tertullian[60] pointed out in practical matters and
with Justin considered from the philosophical point of view.

But the Christian cannot hesitate in his choice. Since he
knows how to separate good from evil, he must separate the
theatre — the house of the devil — from Christian life, ruled
over by the Lord. One cannot serve two masters; "there can
be nothing in common between light and darkness, between
life and death."[61]

It is a radical ascetic norm with which the writer deepens
the chasm between the new society and the old, going so far
as to assert that the two are generally incompatible: "we cannot banquet with them, since neither may they with us. . . . We
weep when the pagans laugh."[62]

We must understand the writer's state of mind, verging on
fanatic rigorism, and also the time in which he wrote, when
all hope of living peacefully with the Empire was fast fading
and the Church was subjecting Christians to an energetic
prophylactic discipline of moral austerity in view of the im-
pending test of martyrdom.

The renunciation of the world made in baptism was carried to its furthest consequences. Yet all enjoyment is not dead
even for the austere Tertullian. Its source has been moved to
the opposite pole, to the spirit, that is all. Instead of the pleasures of the circus and the amphitheatre, the Christian enjoys
the insuperable pleasures of reconciliation with God the Father,
the revelation of the truth, the pardon of his sins, true liberty,
a sound conscience and a life sufficient unto itself, liberation
from every terror of death, the rejection of the gods, and
charisms such as the driving out of devils, the grace of healing
and the gift of prophecy: "these are the diversions, the holy,
eternal and gratuitous spectacles of the Christians; consider
these your circus games, contemplate therein the course of the
world and the flight of time, and count the laps of its race and

60. Tertullian, *De spect.*, XXI-XXII.
61. *Ib.*, XXVI.
62. *Ib.*, XXVIII.

look to the goal which is its consummation; defend the communities of the Church; rise at the signal of God; rise at the
trumpet-call of the angel; glory in the martyr's palm."[63]

All self-interest, all of life are transferred to the realm of
the absolute and there we find again the contests, the combats
and the victories.

These daily and particular spectacles will be succeeded in
the end by the vast, apocalyptic spectacle — against the dramatic background of light and darkness — of the triumphal
coming of Christ, midst the magnificent exultation of the
Angels and the laughing glory of the risen saints, to inaugurate — finally! — the rule of the just in the "new city," the
new state, of Jerusalem. His desire, brimming with hatred
for the pagan regime, kindles in his fancy the radiant vision
of the Last Judgment when all the insolent pride of the world
will crash fearsomely down into the fiery glow of flaming
craters, in which the works of centuries will crumble to ashes.
What a spectacle, what laughter then! What joy to see cast
out into the darkness and weeping so many false witnesses,
so many powerful kings, to whom the pagans paid tribute as
being assumed into heaven with Jupiter; to see the flames
devour the arrogant magistrates who had thought to destroy
the faith by burning the martyrs; to see trembling before the
sudden judgment seat of Christ all those rationalist and atheistic philosophers who had spat so much scorn and insolence
upon the modest Christians!

This will be a reversal of the usual spectacle; it will be
revenge! The actors who sneer now shall weep then over their
own wounds; and the charioteers now clothed in scarlet tunics
shall then be clothed in fire; and the actors and mimes and
lascivious dancers shall dance writhing among the flames.
And the spectators of tomorrow, seated upon elevated benches,
shall be those who are trampled upon today. The signal will
be given then by that Christ whom they struck and spat upon,

---

63. Tertullian, *De spect.*, XXIX.

to whom they gave gall to drink. And the Jews and pagans who smeared insinuations and slander over the honor of his Mother shall then see "who is son of the carpenter and the prostitute."[64]

Tertullian is carried away, quite overwhelmed and intoxicated by his vision of the judgment that will reverse the order of things, and he sadly confuses his notion of justice with his social and political antipathies.

Another Christian author, whose identity is unknown, devoted a lively little treatise to the game of dice, the most popular game in imperial society, played with the same morbid passion that characterizes games of chance today. To wean Christians away from it, the author of the treatise, *De aleatoribus,* unrolls before their eyes the picture of financial ruin and wasted estates, of savings gathered by the sweat of ancestors utterly dissipated, of imminent poverty and want.[65] It is a game invented by Satan and therefore incompatible with belonging to Christ. "Do not be a dice-thrower but a Christian: cast your money on the table of the Lord at which Christ presides and the spectators are angels and the martyrs are present; and the patrimony which you are about to squander with that ruinous passion divide instead among the poor: lose your wealth to Christ.... Play every day with the poor, visit the widows frequently; divert your income and your resources to the good of the Church."

Thus wealth, rescued from an immoral use, becomes no longer the source of ruination but a way to eternal salvation for its owner, and a means of economic relief for the needy. It destroys sins and poverty.[66] The game goes on, but with Christ, and the stake is eternity.

---

64. Tertullian, *De spect.,* XXIX.
65. *Nec lucrum confert, sed totum consumit. Hinc deinde pauperes fiunt, hinc opes suas perdunt, hinc iam consumptis omnibus rebus suis mutuis pecuniis se obruunt; hinc patrimonium sine ulla fori calumnia amittunt* (*De aleatoribus,* VII).
66. *Ib.,* XI.

CHAPTER IV

THE ATTEMPT AT RECONCILIATION WITH THE STATE

THE LAW AGAINST CHRISTIANS

"THE Roman Senate, successive emperors, the army, the people, the very kindred of the faithful, all conspired for the destruction of the Christians."[1]

The cessation of imperial persecution in the second century permitted the Church to develop so strongly that it was able to endure even the violent tempests that burst over it in the third. And then Origen, a martyr's son, could thus balance the accounts: "From the very beginning all men throughout the entire world opposed the dissemination of Christ's word: the sovereigns one after the other, generals and military officials, all those, it may be said, who held some public office, in addition to the heads of cities, the soldiers and the populace. Yet being the Word of God it conquered because its path could not be barred; in fact, it had been made more vigorous by this very opposition."[2] So that "the more the rulers and authorities and people in all stations afflicted the Christians, the more the latter increased in number and in power";[3] for, to use Tertullian's bold metaphor, the blood of martyrs had been the seed of Christians.[4]

At the end of the first century, Nerva recalled the political exiles and among them the Christians. This was a collective measure passed as a reaction against Domitian. But not even

---

1. Origen, *C. Cels.*, I, 3.
2. *Ib.*, I, 27.
3. *Ib.*, VII, 26.
4. *Apol.*, L, 13.

under the Antonines could Christianity hope for a peaceful existence. They were strict guardians of the state, champions of a conservative senate, and in their eyes the Christians still seemed subversive. Persecution began again, but because of the general character of the new regime, it was kept within bounds in the sense that the law against Christians was enforced with moderation and proper judiciary procedure and without any help, usually, from informers or the mob. The character of this branch of their administration is revealed in the exchange of letters in 112 between Pliny, legate to Bithynia, and Trajan. Pliny, without understanding very clearly what the crime of Christianity actually consisted in and knowing only that it was a crime, had put some Christians to death, and among them had been two deaconesses who were slaves. As such, he had subjected them to torture without, however, breaking their spirit, an indication that the faith had fashioned in them a great strength of character. Trajan answered that the Christians had to be punished; he had no doubts about that just as Pliny had none. There was the law, but he had regulated its enforcement by prohibiting anyone from deliberately seeking out those guilty of Christianity and by forbidding anonymous denunciations.[5] This temperance was dictated by political considerations, i. e., the preservation of order and peace.

Under Hadrian also, there were only sporadic persecutions. It is commonly held that in his reign the slave Mary (or Ariadne) was executed by burning, her faith having been discovered by the fact that she fasted on a day of family celebration. Episodes of this kind could not have been rare. Mary did not take part in the banquet of her masters because it was a day of fast for the Christians, and she refused to violate the Christian precept, courageously declaring to her mistress that she might command her body but not her soul. The magistrate,

---

5. Pliny, *Ep.*, X, 97-8.

whose mentality was characteristically pagan, asked her: "If you are a slave, why do you not follow the religion of your master?"[6]

In a rescript to Mucius Fundanus, proconsul of Asia, however, Hadrian insisted that in the case of accusations against the Christians there be due regularity in all the proceedings, that there be no use made of spies and no attention paid to the insistence or clamorings of the populace. He made the informers more cautious by threatening them, in the event that their accusations were not proved true, with penalties more severe than those that would have befallen the accused. The weak Christian could deny his faith, and his word alone was sufficient to free him from every imputation of guilt. The rescript bettered the lot of the faithful brought to trial and that is why Justin appealed to it, quoting it at the end of his first *Apologia*, as did Melito, writing from Asia. Perhaps because of it an unknown Christian poet about this time inserted a praise of Hadrian in the fifth book of the *Sibylline · Oracles*.[7]

Hadrian's successor, Antoninus Pius, followed his example. He forbade mob violence but allowed confessed Christians to be put to death. Proof of this are the apologias addressed to him by Christian writers.

Persecution grew more severe under Marcus Aurelius. He was a logician, and once it was established that Christianity constituted a danger for the state and that there was a law against it, he coldly deduced the inevitable consequences. Then there would pervade his soul a bitter sense of desolation. The Quadi and Marcomanni abroad, his son at home, economic unrest, a realization that the old Roman order was passing, all drew over his equanimity an ever deepening sense of sorrow,

---

6. Cf. Allard, P., *Histoire des Persécutions, I. Pendant les deux premières siècles,* 4 Paris, 1911, p. 243.
7. *Sibyll.* V, 46 ff. The text of the rescript is also given by Eusebius, *H.E., IV,* 13.

while, as a Stoic, he was caught up in the folds of fatalism. To escape he sought refuge in speculation and superstition, with which paganism was reviving old rites and oracles whose recrudescence threatened the one autonomous faith. And the twilight of the sovereign cast shadows streaked with blood over the Church too, for like Epictetus, he understood neither its essence nor its moral nature, the very courage of the Christians on the scaffold seeming to him no more than a theatrical pose. After his death, all illusions concerning a possible conciliation with the Empire grew definitely weaker. The Christians never rose up against the state, never; but deeper and stronger grew the realization of an ethical conflict between them and the Empire which only estranged them from it the more.

Among the victims of this period we find, at Rome, the noble lady Felicitas and her seven sons; Justin — a philosopher condemned to death by the philosopher Junius Rusticus, prefect of Rome, in the name of a philosopher-emperor — as well as several disciples and companions of this Christian teacher; and the martyrs of the church in Lyons. In 180 Africa offered her first known victims, the martyrs of Madaura and Scillium, and at Rome the Christian "senator" Apollonius met his death.

Persecution under Commodus was intermittent. He was not the conservative ruler, loyal to the senate, that his father had been. He could disregard, with complete indifference, even the law against the Christians, and so much the more so because he was under the influence of Marcia, a concubine "fearing God" and inclined to Christianity, and of various Christian functionaries, such as Carpophorus, Proxenetes and Hyacinthus. In fact it was to this last, a priest, that Marcia entrusted the mission of going into Sardinia and liberating the Christians condemned to the mines there under Marcus Aurelius. Armed with a letter from Commodus and a list of the prisoners from Pope Victor — the first Pope we know who approached the Palatine as head of the Church — Hyacinthus went to Sardinia and among others he also freed the future pope Callixtus, even though his name had been left off the list. It was the "first step toward the establishment of a *modus vivendi*."[8]

When Septimius Severus set about reorganizing the state, persecution began again with the edict of 200, which forbade both Jewish and Christian proselytizing. From then on, since the number of Christians had grown too great, persecution aimed particularly at striking down the leaders. Thus in Alexandria the *Didaskaleion*, the center of conversion among the learned element, was closed in 202. In the same year Felicitas and Perpetua along with their companions were led to martyrdom.

Meanwhile, side by side with Christianity, imitated with intelligent fervor by the Empress Julia Domna, and also in opposition to it, we find religious syncretism, with its scale of divinities (demons, minor deities) arranged about the sun-god, becoming better and better organized due to the need of a unity capable of reproducing the religious advantages of monotheism, or better, of divine monarchy, as it was then called; that is, one God in heaven and an emperor on earth who was his living image or incarnation. The syncretists also sought a prophet for the new religion, and, by a retroactive process, they found him in a certain Apollonius of Tyana, who lived in the first century. About his figure, Philostratus sketched an aureole of legendary miracles and wonders, so that he fashioned a kind of double of Jesus Christ, a herald of the syncretist gospel, a reformer of the ancient cults, the exponent of a philosophical religion spiritualized by an asceticism purged

---

8. Cf. Allard, *op. cit.,* I, 484. G. B. De Rossi compares the rescript of Marcus Aurelius and Commodus of 177 with the imperial order of persecution in the *Acts of St. Cecilia* and finds that both say substantially, "he who confesses being a Christian is to be punished; he who denies it is to be freed" (Cf. *Roma sotterranea,* II, page 150 ff.). The hypocritical Demas and Hermogenes suggest to Thamyris, the betrothed of Thecla, that he denounce Paul. "Say that he is a Christian and he will be lost" (*Acts of Paul,* XVI, 2nd century).

of superstition. The Neo-Platonists, Porphyry and Jamblicus, assigned a similar office to Pythagoras. All this was a sign that the influence of Christian teaching was being felt in high places and in low, forcing antagonistic thought to evolve in opposition and at the same time parallel to it. Numenius had already made an attempt at universal conciliation.

Syncretism became perverted when Heliogabalus, who at the age of thirteen had been appointed high priest of the temple of El-Gabal in Emesa, tried to impose the worship of the sun-god with obscene and orgiastic rites, the character of which could only cut more deeply into the Christians that feeling of incompatibility with a regime which expressed itself in such perverted and hostile ways. But syncretism itself benefited them under Alexander Severus (222-234), a gentle and religious prince, who in his private shrine offered indiscriminate worship to Abraham and Orpheus, to Christ and to Apollonius of Tyana. He was kindly disposed toward the Christians, and his mother, Mammea, was on friendly terms with Origen and Hippolytus, the two geniuses of intellectual Christianity at the time. Origen had friendly relations also with the Emperor Philip and his wife, Otacilia Severa, both originally from Arabia and both reputedly Christian.

After Alexander was assassinated, his violent and hostile successor, Maximinus, issued an edict against the heads of the Christian communities, and many churches were burned. At Rome, Pope Pontianus and the anti-pope Hippolytus were deported to Sardinia where it seems they were reconciled before they died for the faith.

Outside the Roman Empire things were very similar because of the universal concept of a deified state. Sapor I of Persia persecuted the Christians as deserters from the nation's laws, and his successors did the same thing.[9]

---

9. Ardashir had those who left the Mazdean religion imprisoned for one year and instructed by the Magi; if they did not retract they were condemned to death. That is how Manes was killed.

CHARGES AGAINST THE CHRISTIANS

The apologists of the period with one accord admit that the case against the Christians was based on their *name* and they contest the legality of an accusation that made a word a crime. They explained it was a word that in itself was neither good nor bad; in fact, according to its sound in Greek and the spelling, *Chrestianos,* with which it was often written, it connoted kindness, gentleness and also something useful.[10]

For the mob, it is true, that name implied a whole series of crimes, which might usually be summed up under three principal accusations:

1. Thyestean banquets (cannibalism)
2. Oedipean unions (incest)
3. Atheism

The judiciary authorities usually did not pay much attention to the first two of these accusations.[11] The third carried some weight because of its political implications.

In fact, dismissing the first two charges as unnatural, absurd and unproved, at least as far as the Church at large was concerned, the apologists went straight to the crux of the question. They knew very well that in the law the name *Christian* denoted a double crime: (1) irreligion, and (2) lese majesty — in other words, a crime of religious and civic apostasy. The second was much more serious than the first, as Ter-

---

10. Cf. Justin, *Ap.,* I, 4; Athenagoras, *Legatio,* II, 2; Tertullian, *Ap.,* III, 5.
11. In the trial of the martyrs of Lyons (177), the legate did not confine himself to condemning them on the simple fact of their *name* alone, but he tortured even the pagan slaves of the accused and learned from them (for in their terror they stated it almost at the dictation of their inquisitors) that the Christians committed "Thyestean banquets, Oedipean incest and other enormities, which it is not permissible to speak of nor to think of and which we did not believe could ever have been committed by men."
Other accusations were not lacking though they were less frequent — for example, that which declared the Christians (and the Hebrews) adored an ass (cf. Tertullian, *Apol.,* XVI); and we must remember also the caricature on the Palatine. In his *Metamorphoses.* (9, 14) Apuleius speaks of a lady, "an enemy of religion," and the devotee of a monotheistic "sacrilegious religion," who adored a she-ass.

tullian knew very well.[12] In fact it might well be said that the first, "the crime against the state religion and especially the Roman religion"[13] was contained in the second, since the emperor was the head of the state religion. And so it was. This was the core of the accusation; in fact, it was "the whole case."[14] It was in this regard that the Christians were classified as enemies of the state, and analyzed still further in common parlance as "enemies of the gods, rulers, laws, customs and all nature."[15] These were people who truly deserved to be banished.

More than a century later the charge not only had not been withdrawn but, if anything, had become more definite and more severe. The Christians offended Rome, the nation; they were not Romans but enemies of the Romans,[16] enemies of the rulers of the Romans.[17]

To the conservative, bureaucratic, learned pagans, Christianity represented a terrifying and mysterious peril. It threatened political, religious and moral revolution.[18] It was a spectacular upheaval gathering in the shadows and prepared by a ragged and desperate mob that was attacking their traditions, their privileges and their laws, attempting to impose on them barbarous and incestuous customs and displaying an obstinate and savage lawlessness that permitted even the slaughter of infants and cannibalism. Earth and heaven both were threatened with this cataclysm judging from all the apocalyptic prophecies of millennial reigns, world destructions and palingeneses, in which all social relations were to be reversed, the rich and powerful trod under foot and the beggars and slaves in

---

12. *Ap.*, XXVIII, 3.
13. *Ib.*, XXIV.
14. *Ib.*, X, 1.
15. *Ib.*, II, 16.
16. *Ib.*, XXIV, 9.
17. *Ib.*, XXXV, 5. That is why *nos nolunt Romanos haberi.*
18. The Christians seemed subversive, innovators. Celsus considered Jews and Christians seditious, for "out of desire for something new they rebelled against society" (Origen, *C. Cels.*, III, 5).

power. This danger was more ominous than that of the barbarians because it was teeming in the very bosom of the Empire, in its cities and families, on the Palatine itself.

This serious charge grieved most of the apologists because it meant that Christianity was outlawed from the Empire and that it was impossible for the Church to exist, and also because it was an insulting denial of their patriotism, or at least of their good citizenship, as well as a defamation of the upright moral conduct of the Christians in general. It was due to the Christian refusal to worship the national gods, especially the images of Caesar and of Rome, to participate with the other citizens in the festivals sacred to Caesar, to adorn their houses with laurel and with lamps, to banquet in the street, or to attend the amphitheatre, circus and hippodrome. And it was due also to their political "inertia," their reluctance to take part in political or administrative activities, while on the other hand they held secret meetings, formed illegal societies[19] in which — so it was said, at least — they committed crimes of incest and cannibalism.

National feeling in ancient times was expressed in the common worship of the gods of the nation;[20] the Christians did not accept the Roman religion, therefore (the pagans reasoned) they were not Roman.

The seven men and five women of Scillium were condemned to death by the proconsul of Asia because they refused to "return to Roman customs." The sentence of death read: "Since Speratus, Nartallus, Cittinus, Donata, Vestia and Secunda have confessed that they live *in the manner of the Christians* and since, when a reprieve was offered them if they would begin again to live *after the manner of the Romans,* they have persevered in their obstinacy, we condemn them to be put to the

---

19. *Illicitae factiones* (Tert., *Ap.,* XXXVIII, 1); *coitio Christianorum … illicita* (*ib.,* XXXIX, 20). Cf. Minucius, *Oct.,* VIII, 3: *Deploratae, inlicitae ac disperatae factionis.*

20. "They censure us because we do not recognize the gods which the City recognizes" (Athenagoras, *Legatio,* XIII).

sword."[21] Here we have the declaration of a conflict between Christian living and Roman living; Christian became synonymous with anti-Roman.

Ungrateful citizens were these "Palestinians" who denied the Roman gods, those gods who, according to the unanimous testimony of monuments, history and poetry, had built the grandeur of Rome and who now, conversely, heaped calamities upon the Empire to punish the continuous outrage offered them by Christian insolence. In this regard, Tertullian is the first to note the popular charge that the Christians were the cause of all the public woes. If the Tiber overflowed its banks, if the Nile did not rise, if there was no rain, or if there was an earthquake, or if famine and plague raged abroad, then immediately the mob yelled, "Throw the Christians to the lions!"[22] with the same desperate thoughtlessness with which the Milanese, harrowed by the plague, used to shout, "Kill the poisoner!" And the cry must have provoked extensive killings in the third century.

Here again patriotism was brought into play, with the same pretext which had condemned the Apostles. There were those who even went so far as to say that not only had the gods been responsible for the greatness of Rome, but that her conquests had not been military so much as religious undertakings in the sense that she had successively adopted the gods of the conquered peoples, so that while the Eleusinians adored Ceres, the Phrygians Cybele, the Epidaurians Aesculapius, the Syrians Astarte, etc., "the Romans adore them all." Hence "their warfare had been an exercise of religious devotion in the midst of war." "Thus, as they accepted one after another the various religions of all the other peoples, so did they deserve also to incorporate their nations."[23] So in reacting against Christianity, skeptics and atheists began to philosophize on the holy nature

---

21. *Act. Mart. Scill.*
22. *Ap.*, XL, 2.
23. Minucius, *Oct.*, VI, 1-2.

of the empire;[24] they turned religious out of hatred for the religion of Christ.

RELIGION THE CO-HELPER OF THE STATE

Out of his political-religious monism, Celsus produced a dilemma for the Christians which was typical of pre-Christian spiritual thought and feeling.

"One of these two: either they refuse to offer due sacrifices and to honor the authorities placed over them, and then let them cease to grow to manhood, take wives, beget children, and perform any other act relative to existence, and let them go hence in a body without leaving even their seed behind them, so that such a race will disappear completely from the earth; or else they wish to marry and have children and enjoy the fruits and works of life, enduring also its evils (for this is nature, to try men with calamities; since it is necessary that there be evil and there is no escape from it), and then they must pay due honor to those who have these things in their care and they must perform the duties relative to life until they are freed from such bonds, and this in order that they may not appear ungrateful to them: for it would be against justice to enjoy the benefits which they bestow and not render anything in return for them.

"To this dilemma, we (Christians) answer that for us there is no solution outside of religion and morality. But those to whom is attributed the power of judging us and who seem to have power over our lives place us in that dilemma, namely, whether to live violating the precepts of Jesus, or to die obedient to his teaching. Now, it was God who bade us take wives since it is not given to all to understand what is more fitting (Matt. 19:12), and that is absolute purity; and once married [he bade us] to nurture our children in all respects and not to kill the creatures given to us by Providence. These acts do not

---

24. *Ib.*, XXV, 1.

conflict with our duty to refuse obedience to the demons who rage over the earth; for, in fact, clothed in the armor of God we rise as soldiers of religion against the race of devils which conspires against us.

"Now then, although Celsus with arrogant vigor ejects us from life with his sophistries, proposing, as he says, to clean the earth of our race, we nevertheless intend to live among the sons of our Creator, obedient to his divine laws and refusing absolutely to subject ourselves to the laws of sin; we wed, if we like, and we educate our children, born of our lawful union; so long as it shall be necessary for us, we intend to participate in the activities relative to existence, enduring, as temptations to the soul, the evils which accompany it. . . . But we do not intend to pay the tribute of those honors which Celsus thinks are due to the idols as the supposed rulers of this world. We adore the Lord our God, and him alone do we worship, praying that we may become imitators of Christ. . . . No one can serve two masters; and we cannot serve God and Mammon, whether this word indicates one or more than one. But if a man, by violating a law, fails to honor the lawgiver, then to us it seems very clear that in the conflict between the two laws, that of God and that of Mammon, it is preferable not to honor Mammon by violating the law of Mammon, in order to honor God by observing the law of God, rather than not to honor God by violating the law of God, in order to honor Mammon by observing the law of Mammon."[25]

In this rather involved way, Origen sets forth the Christian theory of the right to life. Celsus, in the name of the pagan state, tells the Christians to destroy themselves if they are unwilling to live *more pagano;* Origen, in the name of Christian dogma, rejects the dilemma his antagonist has set before him and proposes another in its stead: either your law does not conflict with the law of God and we obey it; or it does con-

---

25. *C. Cels.,* VIII, 55-56.

flict and we oppose it. He vindicates the liberty of the children of God, who, since their life is from God, cannot acknowledge that it is from the state.

Celsus, who, in effect, deifies the state, is logical in demanding that the Christians serve it even with that supreme expression of service which is worship, or else destroy themselves. He does not see any other way out. The Christians, on the other hand, do not adore idols and neither do they destroy themselves because life does not depend on the idols (and therefore not even on the state), but on one superior to the state, and that is God. Having separated the state from idolatry and driven the idols into hell, they claim rights which existed before the state, the rights of the creatures of God. The conflict arises because the state, which is greedy (and therefore identified with Mammon) usurps divine rights for the gods of the city and thereby becomes diabolical, infernal.

If life comes from him who has created it, and if wedding, begetting children and educating them are faculties granted by him to individual men, the state cannot hinder either the free propagation and expansion of life nor any of the acts essential to it. To do so would be to oppose God, which is the true atheism so feared by Celsus.

In any case, the Christian refutation is a most important document of the reaction of the citizens who adopted the new religion to the treatment they received from the authorities.

Tertullian restricts his considerations of the charge to the field of law and views it in the light of the religious and moral autonomy claimed by Christianity. First of all he challenges the equity of the law against the Christians. In the first place, he reasons, a law cannot forbid anything except what is evil, and Christianity represents the most lofty morality and a patriotism above suspicion or reproach. In fact, the Christians pray for the emperors and their ministers and magistrates, for the preservation of the world, for the peace of the state:[26]

---

26. Tertullian, *Ap.*, XXXIX, 2.

"for we invoke the eternal God, the true God, the living God for the health of the emperors. . . . From him, who looks down upon us Christians with our hands outstretched, for we are innocent, and with our heads uncovered, for we need not blush, and finally without any prompter, for we pray from the heart, we beseech always for all the emperors a long life, a tranquil empire, a secure abode, strong armies, a loyal senate, a world at peace, and all that a man and a Caesar might desire."[27] This is complete loyalty then, to use the modern term, which perceives the most difficult aspects of an emperor's government threatened by conspiracies and disloyalty within and by powerful enemies abroad, and which goes so far as to pray for protection for his armies, for which the African personally could not have felt any too much sympathy. On the other hand, the Church might well wish for an Empire that was strong and at peace.[28]

The church in Carthage evidently prayed for its rulers then, in accordance, perhaps, with all the other churches[29] and especially with the church in Rome.

The latter, in its great liturgical prayer, sung perhaps by the whole congregation, made solemn and explicit mention of civic loyalty, which fulfilled an obligation left it by the Apostles, and discredited the public charge with facts:

---

27. *Ib.*, XXX, 1, 4. Other expressions: *Agnoscimus sane Romanam in Caesares fidem (Ad Nat.*, I, 17). The Christians had no part in the satires on the emperors and they did not hang accusing or satirical placards on the statues: while you pagans, *si non armis, saltem lingua semper rebelles estis (ib.*).

28. The martyr Apollonius was speaking the same language in the senate at that time. When asked to swear by the fortune of Commodus and to obey the "invincible laws," he replied: "I wish to swear indeed by the true God that we also love the emperor and pray for him." — "Every day," he also says, "by the just command of God who lives in heaven we pray for Commodus, who rules over this world, for we know full well that he reigns over the earth only by the will of God, who embraces all things" (*Acta Apoll.*, VI, 9 [*Analecta Bollandiana*, 14, 1895, 284-94]).

29. For example, that of Smyrna whose bishop exhorted the faithful with words consecrated by the New Testament: "Pray for the kings, for the magistrates and rulers, for those who persecute you and hate you, for the enemies of the cross: in such manner will your fruit be made manifest to the eyes of the world" (Polycarp, *Epist.*, XII, 3).

Grant harmony and peace
to us and all the inhabitants of the earth
as thou didst grant them to our fathers
when they invoked thee in holiness and faith and truth;
make us submissive
to thy omnipotent and glorious name
and to our rulers and governors on earth.

Thou, O Lord, didst grant them the authority to rule
through thy magnificent and ineffable power,
so that recognizing the glory and honor thou hast granted
      them
we might submit ourselves to them,
in no way setting ourselves against thy will:
grant them, O Lord, health, peace, concord, strength,
that they may exercise without offence
the authority which thou has accorded them.

For thou, O heavenly Lord, King of the ages,
dost give to the children of men glory, and honor
and power over the things of earth:

Thou, Lord, direct their counsel
according to "what is good and pleasing to thy sight"
                                          (Deut. 12:28)

in order that exercising in peace and in clemency, and
      in the fear of God,
the power that thou hast granted them,
they may encounter thy mercy.[30]

And this clear, compact prayer was composed before the end of the first century when a persecution had barely subsided. For it was a Christian duty to give good for evil; and it was certainly to the advantage of the Christians — the spiritual authorities were well aware of this — that the temporal authorities exercise their power in peace and justice according

---

30. St. Clement of Rome, *Ep. I ad Cor.*, LX-LXI.

to the law of God, which was not the law accepted by the deified state.

The Christians, with their universal point of view, did not separate themselves from the Roman State because of any racial prejudice as did the exclusivist Jews. They paid their taxes like good citizens. In fact, says Justin, "we make an effort to be the first to pay the taxes and the tribute to our officers everywhere: thus did he [Christ] teach us."[31] The martyr Speratus reasons in similar fashion with the proconsul Saturninus: "I am not guilty of any thefts. If I make a profit, I pay the taxes, for I know our Lord, who is King of kings and Master of all peoples."[32]

Even Tatian, who belongs to the minority opposed to political rule and reacts against pagan nationalism by asserting the merits of the barbarians, declares that he is ready and willing to pay the taxes levied by the emperor (we should say, the state).[33] This, then, was the most concrete and most onerous expression of their good citizenship. There were too many who sought to evade this civic duty, a burden so heavy that it not infrequently provoked revolt. But the Christians, accused of not fulfilling their duty not only with regard to the temple taxes but also the ordinary taxes, were instead vying with one another in punctuality of payment and did not make dishonest statements, thus balancing by the accuracy and honesty of their tax returns, the moral loss which the public institutions resented in their staying away from the games and from the religious and civil festivals.

Christian citizenship is not passive; it is active service in the functioning of the state. The Christians, as Justin explains, are the most precious collaborators and allies of the public authorities in the maintenance of order, for they insist that it is impossible for the evil-doer as well as the virtuous man to

---

31. *Ap.*, I, 17, 1.
32. *Act. Mart. Scill.*
33. Tatian, IV, 1.

escape the judgment of God since both are destined to receive an eternal sanction for their works. "If all men recognized this truth, no one would choose a short period of vice.... For evil-doers attempt to escape your punishments, not indeed because your laws are inadequate, but because they know when they perpetrate their misdeeds that there is a possibility of escaping from you, who are men. But if they had learned and believed that there is no possibility whatever of escaping from God, not only in their actions but even in their thoughts, if only for fear of the threatened sanctions, they would absolutely — you will agree — remain orderly men. But you [emperors] seem to fear that all men may behave justly so that you will no longer have anyone to punish; this is the sentiment of executioners, not of good rulers."[34] In other words, Christianity molds the best citizens. Theoretically, if all men were Christian — confirmed Christians — there would be no more evil-doers and therefore no more coercive bodies. The ideal state would be that composed of Christians. Plato had said of philosophers. And are not Christians real and true philosophers?

To Justin's theoretical conclusion, Tertullian adds a practical example. "Look at your prisons," he says, in effect. "They are overflowing with criminals, but they are pagan."[35] Only the Christians keep guiltless, because of the influence of the ethical teaching of the Gospel and because of their consciousness of an eternal sanction. For them it is not only noble, it is absolutely necessary to be free from guilt, to live, that is, according to the rule of righteousness taught by God, and therefore infallible and holy. But the pagans have been taught righteousness according to human notions, and therefore theirs is fallible and commanded by a transitory power such as the power of men, which is therefore neither feared nor venerated. This authority commands: Do not kill. But the other com-

34. Justin, *Apol.*, I, 12.
35. *Ib.*, XLIV. Cf. Minucius, *Oct.*, XXXV, 6. *De vestro numero carcer exaestuat; Christianus ibi nullus, nisi aut reus suae religionis, aut profugus.*

mands us not even to become angry. That is, it forestalls the very feeling of the mind from which comes the impulse to kill. One forbids adultery, but the other forbids the very glance of concupiscence. One does not permit injury; the other does not permit vengeance. In short, one punishes, when it succeeds, criminal actions; the other condemns the thoughts from which they germinate. "But what can be the authority of human laws when a man may succeed in eluding them, may very often remain undiscovered in his crimes, and may sometimes disregard the laws out of determination to violate them or through necessity, having in mind the brevity of any punishment, which cannot be extended beyond death. Epicurus, for example, scorns all torture and grief, for he says that it is either slight and therefore negligible, or it is great and therefore cannot last. We instead whose lives are scrutinized by an all-seeing God and who expect eternal punishment from him, rightly attend only to deeds of innocence, either because of the fullness of wisdom granted to us or because of the impossibility of hiding ourselves from him and the threat of punishments which are not long but eternal; for we fear a Being whom they also must fear who judge us fearing him, since we fear a God and not a proconsul."[36] According to this principle the state which kills its best citizens in the Christians harms itself.[37] In a certain sense, it commits suicide.

PATERNALISM AND DESPOTISM

Tertullian, hurling back the charge as usual, says that enemies of the state do exist, certainly, but they are the pagans themselves. Conspirators abound among the Romans (and

---

36. *Ap.*, XLV. Cf. Athenagoras, *Legatio*, XXXII, 2: "Our doctrine is not in the same situation as human laws, which the wicked may even evade ... it is taught us by God; but we have a law [divine?] which made us and our neighbor the measure of justice." The passage is not complete but we can gather from the context that Athenagoras bases the noblest civic and social morality on the divine and natural ethical law, which, acting on the spirit, is more binding than the positive laws, whose influence is external.

37. *Ap.*, XLIV.

therefore — he concludes ironically — not among Christians) and the greatest opposition to good government comes from the violent populace which, with riots and demonstrations, overrides the peaceful exercise of lawful authority.

The Christians take so little interest in public affairs that they are accused of inertia. Tertullian seems to point out that to a suspicious and totalitarian government such abstinence from public affairs should seem a merit rather than a demerit since it precludes any attempt at conspiracy against the emperor or at least against his political policies. It is not the Christians who are to blame for public disasters or calamities, which after all have always occurred. On the contrary it is the Christians who with their prayers delay the final catastrophe in view of the conversion of the Empire. The Empire has been willed by Divine Providence; therefore it is holy, but in a way quite different from the pagan concept. The emperors have been set at the head of their nation by God; their power is therefore sacred, but in a manner quite different from that taught by the defenders of despotism and imposed by its bureaucracy.[38] Far from rejecting the sovereign's authority, the apologist, while underlining constantly the differences and conflicts between the existing Roman order and the constitution and life of the Church, through the principle that power derives from God, actually justifies for Christianity the Roman Caesar, its persecutor. "The Emperor has been elected by Our Lord," not by your Jupiter; "so that it may rightly be said that Caesar rather is ours, since he has been established by our God."[39] Evidently these were not anti-Roman sentiments. They were simply anti-idolatrous sentiments. If Commodus had been

---

38. *Ap.*, XXXI. Cf. also XXXII and XXXIII.

39. *Ap.*, XXXIII, 1. Theophilus was saying the same thing in loyal Asia (*Ad Aut.*, I, 11) and so was the martyr Apollonius in Rome: "The Emperor was not instituted by others but by God, the only King, who holds all things in his hands" (*Act. Apoll.*, 9). And Athenagoras (*Legatio*, xviii): "To you (emperors), father and son, all has been given into your power, for you have received the Empire from above; for the soul of the king is in the hand of God, says the prophetic Spirit" (Prov. 21:1).

able to perceive that distinction, the young organic strength of Christianity would have been injected into the state one hundred and thirty years sooner. But such a principle, if it rendered imperial power holy and sacred, seemed also to diminish its importance (and from the despotic point of view it actually did diminish it). If Caesar derived from God he was therefore not a god himself. "Because of this is he great, that he is inferior to God. . . . As emperor he derives from him, from whom he has already derived as a man: his power comes to him whence comes also his life."[40]

Caesar from God, therefore, not the god-Caesar. He is a man, then, like any other. If he has any superior dignity, he has received it from God,[41] and to him, therefore, must he be subject as any other man. To the political theology of the time these statements were revolutionary and sacrilegious. Christian civic loyalty winds itself around Roman statism seeking to circumscribe it with conditions which reduce, "temper," the majesty of the sovereign. It puts him in the highest place, second only to God, but for that very reason it does not make him equal to God.[42] He may also be called "Lord" but *more communi,* when the use of that epithet as the equivalent of God[43] is not compulsory.

"What evil is there in saying, Lord Caesar?" ask the justice of the peace Herod and his father Nicetus of the aged Polycarp. But Polycarp finds there is evil in it because the only lord he recognizes in the religious sense of the word is he whose servant he has been for eighty-six years.[44] The sovereign should not be a despot, but something else. Conversely the citizen should not be a slave.

---

40. *Ap.,* XXX, 3.
41. *Per Deum tantus est (ib.,* XXXVI, 4). *Satis habeat appellari imperator; grande et hoc nomen est, quod a Deo traditur (ib.,* XXXIII, 3).
42. *Temperans maiestatem Caesaris infra Deum, magis illum commendo Deo, cui soli subicio; subicio autem cui non adaequo. Non enim deum imperatorem dicam . . . (ib.,* XXXIII, 2-3).
43. *Ib.,* XXXIV, 1.
44. *Mart. Pol.,* VIII, 2 and IX, 3: δουλεύω αὐτῷ.

Under Domitian, Dion Chrysostom, the first in the Empire to develop the Hellenistic-Oriental theory of monarchy founded on the grace of God, had wandered about in his exile preaching the Cynic-Stoic doctrine that the king received his authority from God but the tyrant did not, that he should not be a despot but the father and benefactor of his people, who should be allowed to retain their liberty. He had set forth these ideas in the presence of Trajan. It may very well be that Tertullian was familiar with them, as was Clement of Alexandria, who taught that "citizens have for good princes a fear mingled with veneration . . . but fear accompanied by hate is that of slaves toward their harsh masters,"[45] implying that there is a distinction between subjects and slaves, and similarly between sovereigns and masters. And in the function of the sovereign he recognized a "divine form: that which develops according to God and his holy Son," the Logos (Reason); and that is, briefly, according to reason, "since from them proceed all the goods of the earth and all external goods and perfect happiness." But the sovereigns who do not follow this "divine and rational form" of authority, "can follow either the second form, which is that based on the irascible element of the soul . . . ; or the third, which is that which aims only at victory and the extermination of enemies, like that of the Persians in Greece . . . ; or the fourth form, the worst of all, fashioned according to the passions, like that of Sardanapalus and of those others whose goal was to indulge their own lust as far as possible." The good "head of the state is the one who commands according to the laws and has the knowledge to command his subjects who adhere to him of their own free will"; that is, one who recognizes limits to his actions in the laws and in the consent of his subjects and models himself after the "Lord, who receives only persons who believe in him and through him," of their own will.[46]

---

45. *Paed.*, I, 9 (*P. G.*, VIII, 353).
46. *Strom.*, I, 24 (*P. G.*, VIII, 905, 908).

Tertullian was able to develop similar ideas on authority from statements in the New Testament and from Christian ethics in general in the light of his own Roman citizenship.

He also accepts the title of father for the ruler; however, "how can he who is the father of his nation be its master? But sweeter is the title of affection than that of power: the heads of families are also called father rather than master."[47] The word lord (master) implies that the children's relation is one of slavery and not sonship; it implies a state modeled more after the image of the galleys than of the family. For those times, a paternalistic concept of power was the most human and desirable.

"The Christian is the enemy of no one; much less of the head of the state. Knowing that the latter has been established by his God, he finds himself obliged to love, respect and honor him, to desire his well-being and that of the whole Roman Empire as long as the world shall last, for the Empire shall live as long as the world."

Here Tertullian contradicts some of his own sentiments, such as those expressed in the treatise De corona militis, in which he declares that there is an irremediable conflict between Christ and Caesar. But it is noteworthy that in speaking to the authorities, even as a Montanist, as he does in this writing of 212-213, he always repeats the principles which could be the only ones authorized by the Church. Not only is there a distinction between God and Caesar, but from it derive obligations toward Caesar once he is established in or invested with authority by God. And Tertullian goes even further. Like a good Roman he, with Horace, views the Empire as eternal. Once he has cleared his civic conscience in the eyes of the magistrate he goes on to remind him of the limits of political authority: "We therefore honor the emperor, as it is permitted us to honor him, and that is, as a man who is second after

---

47. *Ap.*, XXXIV, 2.

God. . . . "[48] The emperor then is the highest man, but a man after all, not God, and second to God.

But for a Roman, was not depriving an emperor thus of adoration the same as depriving him of power? Tertullian, becoming involved in the pentecostal rigorism of the Montanists, stops here.

FLIGHT FROM PERSECUTION

We may begin to note other differences of opinion in the Christian attitude toward the state, the most serious of which regard the matter of flight in time of persecution and that of military service.

When the threat of persecution looms ahead, most of the Christians move if they can. They do as Christ did to escape both Herods. Besides, he himself had advised the Apostles: "And when they persecute you in one town, flee to another" (Matt. 10:23). Polycarp and Cyprian flee although they are bishops; and Clement of Alexandria not only flees, like his intrepid pupil Origen, but also demonstrates the reasonableness of flight, which saves her sons for the Church and keeps that many more crimes from burdening the conscience of their persecutors. In making such statements he did not mean to recommend fear in the face of death nor to minimize the heroic beauty of martyrdom; but he does not want the Christians, so far as is possible, to be even indirectly accomplices in a crime like legal murder. He decisively condemns the rashness of those fanatics (belonging mostly to rigorist sects) who denounced themselves and provoked the magistrates in order to have the glory of martyrdom with the not infrequent danger of apostatizing under torture. They are like those stupid persons who provoke the wild beasts; they merit neither encouragement nor praise.[49] Perhaps Marcus Aurelius was thinking of them when he described the behavior of the martyrs as theatrical.

---

48. *Ad Scapulam*, 2.
49. *Strom.*, IV, 10 (*P. G.*, VIII, 1285 ff.).

Origen also advises those who do not feel sure of their own strength to flee in order not to give others a bad example of fear and cowardice.[50]

His own rigorist tendencies and the recrudescence of persecution in Africa had instead gradually led Tertullian to an extremist point of view opposed to that of the Alexandrian, so that he finally took his trenchant pen in hand to write a polemical treatise on the subject of flight. Some time before he too had maintained that it was reasonable not to expose oneself to death; he had said that it was better to flee than to deny the faith under torture.[51] But now, completely possessed by the Montanist idea of awaiting the advent of the Paraclete, he was led to hasten the coming of the kingdom of the Holy Spirit. Openly contradicting his own words, he declares it is not lawful for a Christian to flee, basing his statement on a strange deterministic principle, namely, that persecution, like everything else, comes from God, and therefore to evade it is to evade God. Justin, Athenagoras and Tertullian himself, while he was still a Catholic, had said that it came from the devil. But now Tertullian, the Montanist, replies that the devil is nothing but the instrument of the heroic perfection of death just as Judas had been the instrument of the Redemption. Christ's advice to the Apostles was restricted to that particular case, time and place (Judea), so much so that he himself went to meet his crucifixion though he could have avoided it, just as St. Paul went to face the persecution of the Sanhedrin though he had been forewarned against it. The Christian is a soldier in the service of his own general Christ, and he is armed by the Apostles; and when he hears the war-trumpet of persecution, he does not flee, but leaps to the fray. He must not fear; and in any case, during the worst lacerations of the flesh, the Paraclete is there to assist him. "How can you fear, you, O Christian, whom the angels themselves must fear because

---

50. *In Iudic.*, hom. IX, 1.
51. Cf. *Ad uxorem*, I, 3; and *De patientia*, XIII.

you are destined to judge them; and whom the devils must fear, since you have received power over them; and whom the universe itself must fear since in you the world is judged?"

If lay-people must not flee, much less should the heads of the churches, "the deacons, priests and bishops" take flight, for if the leader goes, the flock is scattered.

Paying ransom has the same results and is therefore equally condemned. In fact, it is perhaps better to flee than to make illicit, simoniacal traffic of the faith, bargaining with an informer or a soldier or with some "petty thief of a magistrate."[52]

From the definite stand Tertullian takes here, one might suppose him to be closer than the orthodox writers to that respect for law of which Plato speaks. But on the contrary his attitude is inspired solely by his religious views and is based on his profound contempt for the Roman magistracy, which persecuted the Christians and was considered the instrument of Satan, who is the direct antagonist of Christianity.

There is not much light on the problem, which after all does not concern us here, of how Tertullian, with such sentiments and writings to his credit, managed to pass unharmed through severe persecutions, during which no one whose activity was as truly subversive as his could have been unknown to the authorities. Certainly he must have been surrounded as a hare in the hunt.[53] But the hare is an animal notorious for fleeing.

THE CHRISTIAN REACTION TO THE LAW OF PERSECUTION

According to Tertullian's views regarding the legitimacy of laws, the anti-Christian law above all should never have been promulgated. Next, once having been promulgated through ignorance, error or some diabolical inspiration, then it should

---

52. *Furunculo praeside* (*De fuga*, XII).
53. *Nos ipsi ut lepores, destinata venatio, de longinquo obsidemur* (*Scorp.*, I). I point this out for anyone who may be studying this obscure phase of Tertullian's biography. Cf. my translation of Tertullian: *Seme di sangue,* Brescia, 1935, Intro., pp. 86-88.

be abrogated, for it is a duty to abrogate unjust laws, the work of fallible men. Since all the claims of the Christians were answered by the authority of the law (*dura lex, sed lex*), Tertullian goes back to the source and tries to show that the law in question, since it is contrary to right, is immoral and therefore abrogable. Were not the Papian law and that concerning debtors already suppressed? And had not many laws fallen into disuse? Unfortunately it was precisely the good laws which had fallen into disuse, like those regulating expenses and the theatres. All Nero's laws had been abrogated through hatred for their author; only this one provision had remained through hatred for the Christians.[54] Our man of law echoes not only Christian ideas but also the philosophical teaching of the Greeks, the influence of which was beginning to be felt in law-making, tending to make the juridical order correspond with the ethical order. He discusses the *institutum Neronianum* against the Christians, and from the very fact that his opponents refuse to accept such a discussion, he deduces that the law is basically unsound.[55] Proof of this, according to him, was the fact that the good rulers (the first Antonines) had not persecuted the Christians. This was stretching the point for the sake of argument and was only partially true, even though under Nero and Domitian — the worst Caesars — persecution had raged more fiercely than under the others.

To the conservatives like Celsus, discussions such as these spelled only insubordination. For them the citizens of a country must live according to the laws and customs of that country whatever they might be. The Christians are not a people, and therefore they are that much more in the wrong in deserting from the laws of their nation.

---

54. *Erasis omnibus hoc solum institutum Neronianum permansit* (*Ad Nat.*, I, 7).
55. *Christianum puniunt "leges...." Caeterum suspecta "lex" est, si probari se non vult* (*Ad nat.*, I, 6). For other sources see Allard, *op. cit.* For a complete historical-juridical treatment see vol. II of this series *Il messaggio sociale degli Apostoli*, p. 166, note (tr. in preparation).

Besides all this, in ancient thought law was the child of religion and therefore was also sacred. To protest against its enforcement was one way of rebelling against the gods of the fatherland and therefore its most sacred institutions.

Against this static concept of law, Origen sets the dynamism of reason, which had already caused various philosophers to abandon their country's institutions when they perceived them to be infected with superstitution; that is, when, in the light of reason, they seemed to err.

The law against the Christians has no foundation because the accusation that they are enemies of the state is not true. Not only is it not true as far as their daily lives and Christian teaching are concerned, but also with regard to all their temporal aspirations.

"You — contends Justin — hearing that we await a kingdom, have, without discernment, suspected that we allude to a human kingdom. But we mean the kingdom of God, as is proven by the fact that when you question us we confess that we are Christians although we know that death awaits whoever makes such confession. If, on the other hand, we were awaiting a human kingdom, we should deny it in order not to be killed, and we should have recourse to dissimulation to realize the object of our waiting."[56]

---

56. Justin is careful to distinguish between the kingdoms of this world and the eternal kingdom, of the other world, which is of Christ. But the distinction was not always clearly made because it was not clear to everybody. The author of the *Acts of Paul* (second century) records this dialogue between Nero and Patroclus, his slave who had been brought back to life by St. Paul:

"Who has brought you back to life?"

And the boy, carried away by the ardor of his faith, answered, "Jesus Christ, the king of eternity!"

Disturbed, Caesar replied: "Is this Jesus then to reign through all eternity and overthrow all other kingdoms?"

"Yes," answered Patroclus, "all the kingdoms, and he shall be the only king through all eternity, and no kingdom shall escape him!"

Nero struck him across the face and asked him: "Patroclus, are you also in the service of this king?"

"Yes, O Caesar," he answered, "since he has raised me from the dead." And Barsabas the Just, "of the broad feet," and Urion the Cappadocian, and Festus the Galatian, who were first among the slaves of Nero, exclaimed, "We too are in the service of the king of eternity!" And he had them chained, though he

And he adds, as if to seal the argument, "but since our hopes are not directed to the present life, we care nothing at all about the executioners: in any case, we must all die sooner or later," even the emperors.[57] This is the last, terrible resort, martyrdom; for the omnipotence of the state crashes against it only to discover its very impotence. In its struggle with free souls, it is defeated for it does not succeed in breaking them. And with keen psychological insight, Tertullian considers this a factor in the expansion of Christianity. "Ours is a real battle when we are dragged into the tribunals to battle for the truth against you under the pain of death. And victory is to obtain what you fight for. Such a victory carries with it the glory of pleasing God and the booty of eternal life. But — you say — we are overcome. True: but only after we have obtained what we wish. Therefore, we have conquered when we are killed, and we free ourselves at the moment when we are overcome. . . . So, come now, take heart, good magistrates! You are all the better in the judgment of the mob when you sacrifice the Christians to them. Martyr us, torture us, condemn us, crush us; the proof of our innocence is your very iniquity. . . . We increase in number every time we are mowed down by you: our blood is the seed of Christians. . . . By virtue of that conflict between the divine and the human, when you condemn us, then God absolves us."[58]

CHRISTIAN STRENGTH

This is a vehement cry of strength and also of challenge, the last supreme argument after all the numerous others uselessly cast on the ground of jurisprudence and logic.

It is a cry of freedom.

---

loved them much, and horribly tortured; and then he had the soldiers of this great king sought out (τοῦ μεγάλου βασιλέως) and issued a second edict saying that all who should be discovered Christians and soldiers of Christ should be killed (*Martyrdom of St. Paul*, II, ed. Vouaux, pp. 286-291).

57. *I Ap.*, XI.
58. *Ap.*, L.

When the prefect Urbicius had had the martyr Ptolemy put to death, a certain Lucius addressed him from among the mob: "And what has been your reason for this? A man who is not an adulterer, nor a male-prostitute, nor a murderer, nor a thief, nor a plunderer, guilty of absolutely nothing, only because he confesses to the name of Christian do you condemn him? You do not pass judgment, Urbicius, as the pious Emperor and the philosopher-son of Caesar and the sacred senate would have you judge!"

Here is that illusion common to many Christians in the second century that the emperors, because they are philosophers, followers of reason, cannot possibly be opposed to the Christians, who are exemplary citizens. This is civic loyalty carried to excess. When, however, Lucius was condemned to death in his turn merely and only because he was a Christian, he was able to complete his thought: if one has to live under a regime so iniquitous, it is better to die for a regime of complete justice. And he thanked the prefect, "saying that he was very grateful to him for having freed him from such a category of masters unworthy to approach the Father and King of heaven."[59] The King of heaven compensated for all that the kings on earth took away.

The apologists were expressing in the most searing terms a clear conviction of the early Christian conscience. Heroism was a common school. One arrived at it after a period of true training. And if some deserted under torture, they were considered inexperienced soldiers and wherever possible the others began again to reëducate them for martyrdom, as in the case of those who deserted at Lyons. We find expressed in the letter to Diognetus the certainty that martyrdom did not destroy but rather increased the number of Christians;[60] and Justin explained to the Jews, who were also as long as possible persecutors of the Christians and allies of their persecutors, how

---

59. Justin, *II Ap.*, 16 ff.
60. *Diogn.*, VII.

the Church, though its ranks might be decimated and cut to pieces, could yet grow more vigorous like a vine that has been pruned.[61]

The consciousness of this fact produced an independence of spirit in the face of the claims made by armed force; it established the power of the former against the impotence of the latter, which might kill but could not harm. The only thing that can harm man is moral guilt: "because we are of the opinion that we can receive harm of no one if we are not convicted of guilt or if we are not proved wicked. You may kill us, yes, but do us harm, no!"[62]

After all, if the Christians wished to gain any temporal power, they not only would not be so naïve as to confess to the magistrates, but they also would be so numerous and so well disciplined as to constitute a direct danger to the state and to be able to impose their will upon it by force. In the second century they are, in fact, the most compact and numerous body of citizens in the Empire with outposts even on the Palatine and in the army.

We know the warning, restrained, yet impressive and bristling with menace, which escapes from the review of Christian strength made by Tertullian, with a certain amount of exaggeration but also with much sense: "One night alone with a few little torches, would yield us abundant vengeance, if it were permitted to us to wipe out evil with evil.... If then we should wish to appear as declared enemies and not merely secret avengers, would we lack the force of numbers and strength? Do you think that the Moors and Marcomanni and the Parthians themselves or any race, whatever its size, which inhabits one country and lives within its own confines could be more numerous than a people that inhabits all the earth? We are of yesterday, and yet we have filled all that is yours, cities, islands, forts, towns, assemblies, the very camps, the

---

61. *Dial.*, CX, 4.
62. Justin, *I Ap.*, II.

tribes, the councils, the palace, the senate, the forum; we have left you nothing but the temples.[63] For what war would we not have been fit and ready, even though unequal in forces, we who so readily permit ourselves to be butchered, if it were not according to our teaching to be killed rather than to kill? Unarmed and without rebelling, merely by disagreeing with you, we should have been able to fight you with the invidiousness of our secession. And, in fact, if so great a body of persons as we had violently withdrawn from you to some remote corner of the earth, certainly the loss of so many citizens, of whatever sort, would have abashed your sovereignty, nay more, would have punished it by that very abandonment. Certainly you would have been frightened by your solitude, by the stoppage of business, and by the stunning effect of a deathlike world. And you would have asked yourselves whom you might yet command, and there would have remained to you more enemies than citizens. Now in fact you have fewer enemies by virtue of the multitude of Christians, since almost all the citizens you have in all your cities are Christians; but you have preferred to call them enemies of the human race rather than enemies of human error."[64]

From a political point of view, this was a formidable argument. The great body of Christians could constitute a threat. Before provoking it, the emperors had to proceed cautiously. Tertullian opportunely flavors it with the reminder of the many merits the Christians had chalked up in the eyes of the state by being an element of order in the midst of so many disorganic elements and real adversaries.

---

63. The early ecclesiastical writers take great satisfaction in the rapid diffusion of Christianity and use it as an apologetical argument. Justin considers it prophecied in the Bible: "There is absolutely no race of human beings, Greek or barbarous, whatever it may be called, not the cart-dwellers (Scythians), nor those without homes (the nomads), nor the shepherds that dwell in tents (the Arabs), from among whom prayers do not arise to the Father and Creator of the universe in the name of Jesus crucified" (*Dial.*, CXVII, 5). Cf. *Diogn.*, V, 4 and VI, 2; Hermas, *Past.* (Sim., 9, XVII, 4); Tertullian, *Adv. Marc.*, III, 20.

64. *Ap.*, XXXVII, 3-8.

A general secession would certainly have been difficult to manage, but the Christians actually never thought of it. In fact, the author of the *Epistle to Diognetus* and Tertullian himself were anxious — as St. Paul had been — that the Christians should not differentiate themselves socially, for the proselytism of the Church and the life or "trial" of the individual Christian had to take place within the great body of pagans.

CHAPTER V

THE "IUS CHRISTI"

THE AUTHORITY OF THE CHURCH

THE potential threat which the Christians constituted for the hostile state was repeated by Tertullian in 212 when he pointed out to the persecuting proconsul of Africa, Scapula, that the Christians now formed the majority of the population, so that to kill them would be the same as depopulating Carthage.

The Syrian Bardesanes, after listing the great variety of laws and customs of different peoples, says that the "new generation, of the Christians, built by Christ in every region" everywhere rejects laws and customs which are not compatible with the Gospel; and wherever they are, "the laws of those regions do not draw them away from the laws of Christ."[1]

Meanwhile the fact that they constituted a perfect society apart, the Church, detached the Christians in no small measure from the customs and legal institutions of Rome. We know, for example, that matrimony and therefore the family were governed by ecclesiastical laws, and the family was the nucleus of the state. Likewise, in the matter of disputes the Christian preferred to submit to the judgment of his bishop rather than that of the praetor. When an invasion of Goths and northern tribes poured into Pontus and Bithynia and brought the inhabitants, among other calamities, numerous changes in the ownership of property and various legal and social disarrangements, Gregory Thaumaturgus, the greatest evangelizer of the region, intervened with a series of dispositions to reëstablish the law as it was before the invasion. Here we have the canonical

---

1. *Liber legum regionum*, XLV (P. Syr., II, 602 ff.).

authority of the Church used to regulate social-economic difficulties. And the reëstablishment of the old order in those border territories must have seemed to the inhabitants not the least of the wonder-worker's miracles. Of course, there was the daily intervention of episcopal authority in matters of religious discipline.

The Church made laws on the authority of Jesus Christ, its Head, who, having founded a new people, now guided them as Lawmaker.[2] Church law exists side by side with public law and private law, in fact it is above them; or as they said in those days — above the law of Caesar is a law of Christ which man must not and cannot betray, not even under torture.[3]

Human law, both public and private, and Christ's law could coexist in the Christian conscience up to a certain point, and this indeed longed that the two might coexist in their entirety. But the law of Christ demanded that idolatrous laws and those infringing on liberty be abrogated. Indeed these were abuses of law. But frequently the price of this demand was blood, for it tended to suppress ancient and vital institutions, and to transcend territorial boundaries[4] and traditional customs.

To the pagan mind, Christians were men without a country who lacked a founder, a national lawgiver. Celsus regarded them as nothing more nor less than deserters from the Jewish race, from the national laws of Israel.[5] But the Christians would retort that they had a head, a king, a lawgiver, the founder of a new people, the Church, which he had endowed with legislative power that binds and loosens, judges and re-

2. ὁ καινὸς νομοθέτης, the new lawgiver (Justin, *Dial.*, XVIII, 3). Lucian also calls him thus in *De morte Peregrini*, XIII.

3. The author of the *Liber de laude martyrii* (attributed to Cyprian) says that thus *"suo iure" Christus constituit* (XVII).

4. Ancient lawgivers and wise men could not transmit their laws and teachings beyond their own countries; only today "all of Hellas and the barbarian lands embrace innumerable persons who, having abandoned the laws of their country (τοὺς πατρῴους νόμους) and the would-be gods, now cultivate the Mosaic laws and the teachings in the discourses of Jesus Christ" (Origen, *Peri Archon*, IV, 1).

5. Origen, *C. Cels.*, II, 1.

strains.[6] And insofar as the Christians are soldiers, they must obey the orders of their general, Christ.[7]

Christ's right is absolute, primordial, superior to the rights of family and state, of blood and country, for it can impose upon us even the sacrifice of ourselves, of our children and our relatives, as it did with Abraham ("and for him Christ had not yet been killed") and with the martyrs.[8]

THE CHRISTIAN'S FREEDOM AND THE POSITIVE LAW

Christ's law has been established for man's benefit.[9] By virtue of his law, man, who has been a slave, rediscovers his liberty. Hence the existent body of laws concerns man as the slave of sin, and, reflecting as it does all the defects and limitations of human culpability tends to limit his faculties, to restrict him within more or less narrow boundaries; but the law of Christ, which is the new law, is superior because it breaks all boundaries and unifies all races into one people in one land.[10]

The servile character of pagan law was due principally to idolatry. Did not the ancients make the law derive from the gods? Well, by subjecting the idea of divinity to reprehensible images and rites, they had been the very ones to degrade the law, so intimately bound up with their religion.[11] The Christian religion, being free from the demons — the active "energies" of polytheism — is thus free from falsehood and from the deficiencies of a legislation conceived in an atmosphere saturated with untruth. That is, even from the juridical point of view, Christianity raises the dignity of man, formerly prostrate before mythology.

---

6. *Ib.*, V, 33.

7. Cyprian, *Ep.*, X, 1.

8. Pseudo-Cyprian, *De laude martyrii*, XVIII.

9. Origen speaks of legislation salutary and out of love for man (*C. Cels.*, III, 8).

10. *Maior est igitur legislatio quae in libertatem, quam quae data est in servitutem; et ideo non in unam gentem, sed in totum mundum diffusa est* (Irenaeus, *Adv. Haer.*, IV, 9, 2).

11. "Law was born of the concept not of justice but of religion.... It was one of the aspects of religion." (Fustel de Coulanges, *La cité antique*, ed. 13, Paris, 1890, p. 226).

The instruments of idolatry had been the pagan priest, the very philosophers and still more those poets who, like Orpheus, had corrupted men's souls with song, destroying "that beautiful freedom of mankind under the heavens" in order to make them slaves of myths and diabolical enchantments.[12]

The Church is the depositary of the law of Christ and she enforces it for him in its absolute entirety, using to this end, the *episcopi*[13] as her principal organ, and next the *presbyteri*. The *Didache* is a kind of prelude to the codification of Christ's law.

Consequently, the Church was giving its members not only a new social conscience, but also a new concept of the state; it limited political authority simply by placing its own law, as the law of God, above and even against the law of the state when the latter was irreligious or immoral. When, for example, Tertullian asked that the anti-Christian *institutum* be abrogated, it was an enormously bold request in the light of the civic morality of the ancients for whom the laws, once promulgated, were sacred, fixed, proceeding from divinity. A law might easily fall into disuse; it was not easily abrogated. The *Digest* of Justinian was a collection of laws that were centuries old. Tertullian dared to propose a revolutionary moral standard, namely, that the justice of a law was determined by the conscience of the citizens for whom it had been made. In that atmosphere of ever-growing imperial absolutism, the ruler, who was a god, considered himself the source of the laws; he determined their justice, for he was the source of the moral standard. On the other hand, Christianity made the ruler also, as a man, subject to an extrinsic moral law, the natural and supernatural law, that is, the law preached by the Church. As a result — and this was a revolutionary result — a Christian must not obey a law which offends his conscience. In fact, he

---

12. Clement of Alexandria, *Protr.*, I., 3, 1.
13. *Der Bischof war jedoch nicht nur dux, dominus, iudex und rex, sondern in erster Linie pastor, magister und sacerdos* (Harnack, *Verfassung und Recht der alten Kirche*, p. 95).

does not obey the law when it commands him to swear by the emperor, to call him Lord, to abjure Christ. The heretic goes even further and refuses to obey at all when it calls him to military service or even when it confers on him a wreath for valor. Without this conflict there would have been no martyrs. St. Paul bade the Christians to be subject to the authorities "but not in order to avoid martyrdom, but to inspire you to live virtuously even with respect to them [the authorities], who are co-operating with justice, and are ministers of divine judgment."[14]

This means that divine judgment stands above the temporal authorities. Therefore, there is no such thing as the divinity of the law since there is no such thing as the divinity of the state. To test the equity of its legislation, the state must accept the criticism and collaboration of the citizens for whom the law stands. In other words, the law has two authors, he who commands and he who obeys, and it is not infallible.

Since the state did not accord its citizens this right of controlling the law, its Christian citizens automatically accorded it themselves whenever the law against the Christians was involved. And with every resource at their disposal except, naturally, violence or the repudiation of their faith, they took pains to elude the law by fleeing, bribing their jailors — a matter which Socrates would have condemned as being prejudicial to the public authority[15] — and carrying off the bodies of the mar-

---

14. Tertullian, *Scorpiace*, XIV. "Then after quoting St. Paul (Rom. 13:4-7), he adds: *Condixerat scilicet Petrus, regem quidem honorandum; ut tamen tunc rex honoretur, cum suis rebus insistit, cum a divinis honoribus longe est; quia et pater et mater diligentur, cum Deo non comparabuntur. Caeterum super Deum diligi nec animam licebit.* In the *Apol.*, IV, 13, he says: *Nulla lex sibi soli conscientiam iustitiae suae debet, sed eis, a quibus obsequium exspectat. Ceterum suspecta lex est, quae probari se non vult, inproba autem, si non probata dominetur.* He is repeating a thought already expressed in the *Ad. Nat.*, I, 6: *Nulla sibi lex debet conscientiam iustitiae suae, sed eis a quibus captat obsequium. Ceterum suspecta lex est si probari se non vult.*

15. Plato, *Criton*, XI. Socrates imagines that the Laws and the City appear before him to admonish him as he attempts to escape from prison: "Tell me, Socrates, . . . with this act which you are about to do, do you not plan, perhaps, to ruin, as far as you are able, us the Laws, and the whole City? Do you think a City can endure . . . in which the pronouncements of the courts are thwarted by private citizens?" Socrates goes on to show that all the laws must be respected, the whole body of law. The Christians, on the other hand, dis-

tyrs. This was because the law was contrary to justice; when the laws were just, on the other hand, Christian obedience went so far as to demand the inner consent of the conscience.

On this point, there was no possible surrender on the part of the Christians. The example of the Apostles, steadfastly rebellious to the decisions of the Sanhedrin, was testimony of this.

Thus, with regard to the evangelical invitation to abandon father, mother and brothers for the Gospel and Christ in order to be eternally blessed, Clement of Alexandria, speaking of martyrdom, writes that "mother" was allegorically, the fatherland, the land that has nourished us; "father," on the other hand, means the laws of the state. "But these the just man, of great soul, must disregard readily when it is a question of becoming the friend of God and winning a place at the right side of the sanctuary: thus have the Apostles done."[16]

The exemplary citizen in ancient times sought by scrupulous obedience to be called the "friend of Caesar." The exemplary citizen of the new era insists that the laws should not create a conflict between his actions and his conscience, for his conscience is the important thing, and therefore he must judge the laws according to religious and moral principles. Through these he criticizes laws and when necessary rejects them, as, for example, the laws permitting prostitution,[17] which, after all, are contrary to the austerity of the old Greek legislators, like Solon, and the Roman lawmakers as well (with allusions of this sort, the Christians satisfied their patriotic conscience).

This does not mean that the Christian minimizes the value of the laws, which are expressions of authority and must be obeyed even when they are punitive. For the lawmaker is like the surgeon, who, even when he cuts and burns and admin-

---

criminate between one law and another and reject those which are unjust. For them it was permissible, as it was not for Socrates, to flee into other cities.

16. *Strom.*, IV, 15 (*P. G.*, VIII, 1229).
17. Clem. Alex., *Paed.*, III, 3 (*P. G.*, VIII, 585).

isters bitter potions, does so for the health of the sick man and not because he hates him. But precisely because his function is repressive and formative, the lawmaker, like Moses, must look to the Logos (Reason) for his standard and inspiration; he must be what the philosophers call the wise man.[18]

In opposition to the Platonic (*Gorgias, Crito*) and Stoic theories that the individual is absolutely subject to the laws of the state, and contrary to the tendency supported in ancient times by Protagoras to consider the positive law the source of right, Origen went back to a summary discussion of the origin and end of the state and established the preëminence of natural law over positive law. He thus made a real contribution to the movement, then gathering momentum, to make the legal code conform always more and more to the natural law.

Celsus had objected on the basis of the political ethics of ancient times, repeating that justice consisted in obedience to the nation's institutions, whatever they were. Therefore — replies Origen — the Scythians and Indians who eat their friends and relatives in obedience to the local customs do not commit injustice! He answers with the Christian and Stoic criterion which distinguishes between natural law and positive law. "In the beginning, there are two laws: one, that of nature, fixed by God, the other, that written for the states; when the written law does not conflict with that of God, it is well for the citizens not to desert from it to follow after foreign laws; but when the law of nature, that is, of God, ordains things contrary to the written law, see if reason does not demand that we bid a glad farewell to the written laws and the intentions of the lawmakers, and obey the only lawmaker, God, and regulate our conduct by his ordinances, even at the price of danger and infinite tribulations and death and dishonor. Some ordinances pleasing to God are not in accord with other ordinances acceptable to the cities, and it is impossible to please God and the authors of these laws at the same time; in such cases, it

---

18. *Strom.,* I, 25 and 26 (*P. G.,* VIII, 916).

would be absurd to scorn the works which make us pleasing
to the Author of the universe, to embrace those, with which,
though we become displeasing to God, we remain loyal to
unjust laws and their authors. Now if it is logical in every
case to prefer the natural law, insofar as it is the law of God,
to the law written and conceived by men in the spirit of opposition to the divine law, then how much more reasonable is it
to do this in the case of laws which regard God himself?"[19]

With the help of Stoic thought, Origen is giving philosophical form to this distinction, the nature of which was already
firm and clear in the Christian conscience in the second century
along with all the dangers it involved by setting the faithful
in deliberate opposition to the state, dangers which they necessarily accepted. Justin himself, for all his natural serenity and
attempt at conciliation, is nevertheless a rebel, for this attempt
is inevitably based on the effort to persuade others, the authorities and the enemies of Christianity, to withdraw from their
positions, in short, to yield, because Christianity cannot withdraw in the slightest degree from the stand it has taken. The
others must make concessions; Christianity has nothing to con-
cede nor can it sacrifice any of its morality or dogma to the
state. Now whoever does not submit to the laws is a rebel;
whoever wants to change the established order for a new one
is a dangerous innovator, a revolutionary. After all, Justin himself is often aware of this and shows it in those outbursts which
flash now and then like lightning across the uniform tran-
quillity of his words. Whenever his line of reasoning, notwithstanding his logic, and his feelings, notwithstanding his purity
of intention, clash with the pagan concept and the judiciary

---

19. *C. Celsum*, V, 37. Since human laws derive their power from God, they
complete the divine laws. The commandment in the Acts of the Apostles,
(15:28-29) prohibits only the eating of things sacrificed to idols and things
strangled. . . . But it does not thereby give sanction to murder, adultery, theft,
sins against nature and *caetera crimine quae divinis et humanis legibus puni-
untur.* No, because these crimes are punished by human laws, the Holy Spirit
has considered it "superfluous" to forbid them with divine law (Origen, *Ep. ad
Rom.*, IX, 28; *P. G.*, XIV, 1228).

system, he explodes: "Oh, finally, you may kill us; but who cares aught for death? It is worse for you if you do not listen to us and kill us." This is an unusual challenge, and an insolent one from his adversary's point of view. When he mentions the prohibition, under pain of death, to read the books of the prophets and to aid in the diffusion of the new faith, he speaks clearly: "You may indeed suppress us: but we read and teach just the same. And if this declaration sounds hostile to your ears, you can do no more than kill us!"

"You can do no more than kill us!... Bleak consolation for a Roman autocrat, who was, besides, a philosopher."[20]

In truth, Justin's attitude is not exaggerated when we compare it with that of others who confessed the faith. Melito, who tries not to reproach the just Marcus Aurelius for his anti-Christian laws, does, however, say at one point that they would not be used even against a barbarous enemy.

In conclusion, whenever Roman law conflicted with Christian law, the Christians rejected it and denied altogether that it was law. Otherwise, there was no difficulty; in fact, those who knew Roman law rather professed admiration for it. This is implicit in Tertullian's words and is indeed explicit in the youthful and therefore academic and redundant prose of one of Origen's disciples, Gregory of Pontus, who is to become bishop and be surnamed Thaumaturgus. In his panegyric for his teacher, Gregory, who was studying the Latin language and Roman law, calls the laws which govern the empire "admirable" for they are "wise, well-considered, various, admirable, and, in short, most Hellenic; composed and written in a language — that of the Romans — which is a stupendous and magnificent language befitting the glory of the Empire."[21] And this was at the frontier, the edge of the territory to which Roman sentiment might penetrate.

---

20. I. Giordani, S. *Giustino Martire, Le Apologie*, Florence, 1929, introd. p. 73.
21. *Paneg.*, I.

MARTYRDOM THE PRICE OF RELIGIOUS LIBERTY

Melito's attitude is the most submissive in the second century. The others brought face to face with the authorities designated to enforce the laws assume an attitude always of strength, often of defiance. We have seen how even Octavius became enthusiastic at the sight of the martyr insulting his judge.

The martyr brought to trial is a wrestler facing his challenger, a soldier facing his enemy, a free man facing a tyrant. If he does not surrender, he is the victor and deserves a wreath in the army of Christ.[22] These are not merely figures of speech. From Clement, in fact, from St. Paul to Origen, they are a burning conviction nourished by direct and daily experience. It was only in the peace of later days that they withered into an abuse of rhetoric. We must plunge them back into the spirit from which they burst to appreciate the white-hot vigor of their forcefulness. Brought before their judges, the Christians, divested of all cowardice, consider themselves champions of their own social order, human and divine; they inspirit one another to hold firm, and when one falls in the struggle they bend every effort to bring him back into the arena to renew the combat. The *Acts* of the martyrs of Lyons express this fact in language of defiance and victory, irrepressible and fervid for all that it is austere and staid.

Not only was it possible for the positive laws to be in part erroneous or immoral, but, from the point of view of Christian ethics they were all inadequate and in many cases impotent. We have already noted Justin's and Tertullian's arguments regarding the inadequacy of the legal sanction when it is possible for criminals to hide from or flee the authorities. This inadequacy is due to the transitory nature of the state, which is governed by men and therefore subject to error. There is in-

---

22. Resisting the torture of inquisition is a struggle: *caeleste certamen, certamen Dei, certamen spiritale, proelium Christi;* it brings glory with victory (Cyprian, *Ep.*, VIII).

stead a higher law which has no loop-holes, which no act nor thought may evade, the moral law of the Christians.

With such precise reasoning as this the apologists were asserting that the Christian contribution to the orderly functioning of the state was both great and positive. But the state could not accept the logic of this, not because of such concrete results as the good conduct of the citizens who were followers of Christ, but because of the principle on which it was based and the ethical result to which it led, involving again as it did that divorce between religion and politics, morality and government which the ancient state fought against because it halved its power and importance.

Such reasoning meant a diminution of the power of the state. It brought pressure to bear upon it in order to coördinate it with and subject it to a law promulgated by a society extraneous to it, which at best could barely hope to be tolerated and admitted among the other already existing factions.

And we must remember that, in effect, the teaching of the Fathers, which explained the teachings set forth by Jesus and reiterated by St. Paul, punctured in more ways than one the swollen pantheism of the state, for it was outlining a form of government that would have to collaborate with its citizens on the one hand and the Church on the other if it wished to achieve its ends with a certain degree of completeness. The defenders of omnipotent and omnivorous statism could not, then or later, do less than oppose with force such curtailment of its jurisdiction.

Above the uniform, stagnant civic conscience of antiquity, stultified in idolatrous prostration at the feet of the state, rose the voice of the individual conscience, the heart of the new personality. And it stated that most daring requirement of the religious conscience for continuing to live in the political order, namely, spiritual autonomy. So daring is it, that though it is repeated for centuries it has rarely or almost never been completely realized even under the most liberal governments. The voice of the calm apologist of Rome is vibrant with enthusiasm and determination when he recalls the solitary figure of the martyr standing before the despicable instruments of death, fearless in the defense of his freedom of conscience.

"What a wonderful spectacle it is for the Lord when the Christian faces pain, when he prepares to fight against threats, punishments, torture; when he laughs, mocking, at the crash of death and the horror of the executioner, when he asserts his own individual liberty against kings and princes, and surrenders only to God, to whom he belongs, and like a conqueror rebels against the judge who has pronounced sentence upon him!"[23]

These are tremendous statements to make. Martyrdom — that obstinacy perdurate even in the face of death under torture — becomes "the affirmation of true liberty,"[24] "the foundation of life and of faith, the fortress of salvation, and the bond of freedom and honor" before the omnipotent head of the state.[25] It is a declaration of war and of independence. We have already seen how Lucius joyfully accepted the sentence of death from the prefect Urbicus because it freed him from a regime of unjust laws. In short, it was only the blood of martyrs that could redeem the spiritual conscience from political slavery.

In virtue of this conscience of his, the new man, as a citizen, recognized that he was subject to the state; as a Christian he declared his independence. In the spiritual field both the subject and the sovereign were men, that is, equals; the one to rule over them both was God. In short, the social, moral, and religious autonomy of Christianity, united in the *ecclesia,* split the social, juridical and religious unity of the ancient state, on which every expression of social living was based. It is only natural that this should provoke disturbances, reprisals, con-

---

23. Minucius, *Oct.,* XXXVII, 1.
24. *Ib.,* XXXVIII, 1.
25. *Quid tam magnum atque pulcherrimum, quam inter tot circumstantium gladios libertatis suae Dominum ac salutis auctorem, repetita saepius voce, profiteri? et maxime si ante oculos tuos ponas nihil detestabilius esse dedecore, nihil foedius servitute* ... (Ps.-Cyprian, *De laude martyrii,* VIII).

flicts, that is, a reactionary movement on the part of the old order of things striving to restore its equilibrium.

Tertullian flashes back at one accusation, saying, "It is not the gods who have made the greatness of Rome, but her political expansion has been of service to the gods of Rome." And this was historically true. The worship of Jupiter, and later of Caesar, followed the legions wherever they went. "Rather," continues the African, who in the fury of the counterattack always overshoots his mark, "rather this expansion has been effected by sacrilegious acts such as the destruction of cities and therefore of temples, images, etc., and the massacre of the citizens, and the priests among them, and booty which included also the sacred treasures." In that concise style of his, which makes such good use of vivid antitheses, he writes that the Romans "either grew by doing injury to religion, or injured it by their very growth"[26] — with acts of violence, therefore.

From such a political system, which endures to the detriment of the Christian population, the latter begs for religious peace in freedom of worship. All the apologists, along with Tertullian, are one in insisting upon this point, religious liberty. Their creed is more noble and more pure, and the only true creed among all the others. If the pagans, however, wish to continue to believe in their fables, let them do so. But they must not presume to oblige the Christians to do so. They are not to commit again the error committed against Socrates, who asked only that he be permitted to follow freely his own daemon. Since no crimes against the community can be discovered in the behavior of the Christians then let them enjoy the rights of the community. If anyone of them brought to trial should be proved guilty "then let him be punished, yes, but because he is guilty and not because he is Christian."[27] If the Christians

---

26. The two parts of the sentence balance each other and rhyme. It is an artifice which Apuleius had liked and which will be used and abused by another African, Augustine. *Religionem aut laedendo creverunt —aut crescendo laeserunt* (*Ap.*, XXV, 17). The thought is imitated by Minucius, *Octavius*, XXV, 1-5.

27. Justin, *I Ap.*, VII, 4.

profess doctrines which in part disagree with those of others, let this not be considered a crime. Even among philosophers there are many and serious differences of opinion. "And if some of our doctrines agree with those of your celebrated poets and philosophers and if we affirm others which are nobler and divine, and if we only can give proof of them, why are we so unjustly hated beyond all others?"[28]

But even for the most abstruse dogmas of Christianity, such as the Incarnation, the Resurrection, the Virgin-Birth, parallels (or diabolical imitations) can be found in the Greek myths; then why must the Christians alone be tormented when the Egyptians are permitted to adore the onions in their gardens, and mice, cats and crocodiles? Every province, every city has its own divinity; only the Christians may not have their own religion. Every god may be adored except the true God. Now to take away religious liberty is a crime,[29] the real crime against religion. Thus once again we find the principal accusation reversed: he is an atheist who keeps others from adoring God according to their conscience; therefore the Roman state is atheist.

"Let one man adore God, another Jupiter; let one raise his supplications to heaven, another to the *Ara Fidei;* let one, if you will, count the clouds as he prays, another the beams in his ceiling. . . . No one wishes unwilling adoration, not even a man."[30] If our doctrines "seem to you to conform to reason and truth, esteem them; if they seem frivolous, then scorn them as such; but do not for this condemn innocent men to death as if they were enemies."[31] In short, there is no reason

---

28. *Ib.,* XX, 4. As for other philosophers, Tertullian speaks right out regarding the *licentiam impunitatemque disciplinae* which they [the philosophers] enjoy; they are free to criticize idolatry and mythology and no one forces them to offer sacrifice and light lamps at noonday at the entrance to their houses, etc. (*Apol.,* XLVI).

29. *Libertatem religionis* (Tert., *Ap.,* XXIV, 6). "*Ex-lege,* impious and atheist" is he who wanders from the precepts of God (*Acta Apoll.,* IV).

30. Tert., *Ap.,* XXIV, 5, 7.

31. Justin, *Ap.,* LXVIII, 1. Cf. Tatian, XXI, 2. "When you have examined your stories, accept ours too, since, at the worst, we recount fables even as you."

for the existence of a special law against the Christians; they wish to live under the law that governs everyone else. All the apologists strive to establish this point.

Again in 212-213, when the rigorism of his Montanist belief led him to sharpen rather than blunt the point of conflict, Tertullian once more struck his former note, as in the *Apologeticus,* when he undertook the defense of religious liberty against the sanguinary Scapula: "Every man has, as a natural right, the freedom to adore whom he believes best. . . . It is not the office of religion to force religion on one, for he must embrace it of his free will and not because he is forced."[32]

If the state had accepted this principle of natural right, reasons Tertullian, there would no longer have been any motive for opposing the Christians, who are enemies of no one and least of all of the Emperor or the Roman Empire.

Even the gentle Octavius, when he defines freedom of conscience and the revolution Christianity has wrought on this point, becomes intransigent, fiery, almost rude. By refusing to participate in any way in the sacrifices to the idols he asserts true liberty;[33] "for the free man (and according to the law of the Word, all are free, even women and slaves) even if a tyrant threatens him with death, even though he be cast into prison, or exposed to danger of death or even if he be made to run the risk of losing everything, will never be torn away from the adoration of God no matter what be the means employed against him."[34]

The request of the apologists is based on three points: a refutation of the charges made against the Christians, a demonstration of the rationality and legitimacy of their own creed, and freedom of conscience. Theirs is the first request for freedom of conscience made to a state to which it was unknown,

---

32. *Ad Scapulam,* 2.
33. Minucius, *Oct.,* XXXVII, 1: *Cum libertatem suam adversus reges et principes erigit, soli Deo, cuius est, cedit; ib.,* XXXVIII, 1: *Quod vero sacrificiorum reliquias et pocula delibata contemnimus, non confessio timoris est, sed verae libertatis assertio."*
34. Clem. Alex., *Strom.,* IV, 67, 2.

and it is a reasoned and sorrowful request. The toleration at which they aim and which they will obtain only with the edict of Milan is not pagan agnosticism or indifference toward the various gods and cults; it presupposes that Christianity is the true religion and that the others are false. We find, however, even in the intransigent Tertullian, the clear assertion that adherence to a specific faith is a free act of the will, that violence is opposed to religion, which is a relationship of love toward God and men.

THE LIMITS OF CIVIC OBEDIENCE

As for the religious significance of the charge of atheism, Christian apologetics, being the expression both of the Church's teachings and its practice, cannot yield a tittle; in fact, its intransigence stiffens to the point of seeming hostility, for the Christians not only refuse to worship the idols of Rome and therefore the god-Caesar along with them, but they consider the national gods mere empty names, incarnations of demons, thieves of divinity. Since these gods are not gods, the real atheists are the pagans. Thus the principal charge against the Christians is also reversed. Naturally, this did not make for any possible understanding between Christian and pagan forces and that explains the three centuries of persecution. The struggle against the national idols tended to destroy the foundations of the ancient state, and the state defended itself, mustering all its subordinate gods, for they also were threatened with destruction.

What did it matter that Aristides, Justin, Athenagoras, Tertullian, Clement of Alexandria, Origen and Melito bent every effort to prove the austere morality, the patriotism and the innocence of the Christians when all the suspicion and charges regarding these points were the consequence of the Christian refusal to swear by the divinity of Caesar, to offer incense or to recognize the Roman gods? In fact, it would be sufficient for the Christian to offer one grain of incense or say that he no longer believed in Christ and the whole fabric of accusations would crumble. "The only charge that you can make against us is that we do not adore your gods."[35]

By way of refutation the apologists bring forth all the arguments against idolatry, which actually were not very original with them. On this point they agree with the most enlightened pagans. But if Jupiter and Mars and Venus were phantasms, Caesar and Rome were realities, and they demanded worship as a sign, a proof of patriotism.

When Tatian declares that he is prepared to pay taxes, to serve and obey the emperor but not to pay him the tribute of worship because "a man is to be honored as a man, and only God is to be feared," and because the public authorities are not to be considered more important than God;[36] when the martyrs, even the women among them, declare openly to the judge, "We give Caesar the honor due to Caesar, but we fear God alone";[37] and when Tertullian keeps repeating that the Christians fear God and not the proconsul;[38] then all of them, since they deny the divinity of the state and say they have no fear of its quasi-omnipotence, since they withhold a tribute essential to its honor and therefore essential to its spiritual power, are true rebels in the eyes of the authorities.

None of the Fathers of this period cast any doubt upon the fact that the Christians, as subjects, owe the state obedience, but they explain it and make it clear that it goes only so far as the moral conscience permits. The conscience is the measure and the limit of civic obedience.

"We have been taught to render to the authorities and powers established by God the honor which is due them, provided, however, that this honor work us no injury," says Polycarp to the proconsul.[39] He means, of course, injury to the soul.

---

35. Justin, *I Ap.*, XXIV, 2.
36. IV, 1 and XXVII, 2.
37. Thus speaks the martyr Donata (*Act. Mart. Scill.*).
38. *Ap.*, XLV, 7.
39. *Mart. Pol.*, X, 2.

When the judges promise the martyrs the much sought after title of "friends of Caesar," they know it is a tempting plum even to the Christians, especially if they come of a wealthy family, like Alexander, the fifth son of Felicitas. But that imperial honor is offered as the complement to Christian dishonor; and the faithful, as usual, reply that they prefer to be the "servants of Christ" or, actually "the royal friends of God"[40] rather than of Caesar at that price. The responsibility lies with those who created the conflict between Christ and Caesar.

In the field of politics, the Apostolic and post-Apostolic Fathers follow in the footsteps of the Evangelists and Apostles. With regard to politics — says Clement of Alexandria — we follow the precept of Jesus: "Give to Caesar what is Caesar's and to God what is God's."[41]

As for Caesar's rights, they declare always that his power, like every power, is derived from God. Caesar is Caesar because God wills him so; therefore God is before and above Caesar. It is God who makes the Caesars, and not vice versa as in polytheism. In the beginning, Romans and Greeks, and not they alone, admitted that power came from God. But since polytheism had had no Revelation and lacked an authorized instrument of the will of God, it had easily happened that the government confiscated divinity.

For Origen even the authority "which persecutes and fights against the faith and assails religion" comes originally from God; but in its development, its use, it has become wicked and goes against its source, God. It is like the senses of sight and hearing of which, though they also have been given us by God, we may make impious use. That is, precisely because it does come from God, all power must be exercised according to the law of God: "Whoever exercises the authority received from

---

40. Clement of Alexandria exhorts the "gnostic" to be the "royal friend" of God (*Strom.*, IV, 7; *P. G.*, VIII, 1264).
41. *Paed.*, III, 12.

God in accordance with his own wickedness and not the divine laws" shall render a just account of it to God.[42]

Whoever resists the authority resists the ordinance of God, St. Paul had said (Rom. 13:2). "But here he is not alluding certainly to those powers which persecute the faith," to which we must rather apply the commandment to obey God rather than men. St. Paul is speaking "of the ordinary powers which are feared not by those who do good but by those who do evil."[43]

Theophilus, the bishop of Antioch, though he does typify the obedient, irreproachable citizen, does not push civic loyalty beyond the limits set by conscience: "I shall honor the emperor," he declares to Autolycus who upheld the totalitarian claims of the pagan state; "I shall not, however, adore him, but I shall pray for him. I give adoration only to the one true God, by whom I know the sovereign has been made. You will ask: Why then do you not adore the emperor? Because it is his nature to be honored with legitimate obedience and not to be adored; he is not a god, but a man whom God has ordained to administer justice, not to receive adoration. The administration of the state has in a certain sense been entrusted to him by God; and just as he does not permit any of his subordinates to bear the name of emperor, which is proper to himself, and may not lawfully be applied to any other, just so no one may be adored except God. Honor, therefore, the sovereign with devotion, obeying him and praying for him; and, so doing, you

---

42. *In ep. ad Rom.*, IX, 26. Origen says that in speaking of the sinful judges, Scripture does not say that they "governed the people" but that they "seemed to govern" (Dan. 13:5-6) and he comments thus: *Qui enim bene praesunt populo, regunt populum; qui autem tantum nomen habent judicum et iniuste praesunt populo, regere videntur populum, magis quam regant (Strom.,* X, fragment; *P. G.,* XL, 101-102).

43. *Ib.,* IX, 27 (*P. G.,* XIV, 1226-7). Origen inclines, however, to avoid Caesar's sphere and restrict himself to the things of the spirit. He does not say so, but he shows that he does not willingly come in contact with the political world, all the more because it is pagan and it is the world, and he confines himself to the mysteries. Religion suffices him and fills him completely. In a Christian world he thinks everything will be religion.

will fulfill the will of God, whose law says: My son, honor the Lord and the king: and do not disobey either one; for they will swiftly punish their enemies (Prov. 24:21-22)."[44]

This is a clear assertion of good citizenship and it becomes a lesson in Christian politics, in which the new concept of the origin of authority is balanced by the actual behavior of the good citizen of the faith. The state, like Autolycus, does not accept it. Obedience, prayers, taxes are all very well, but there must be adoration also above all else, and that means the unconditional surrender of the conscience to the state.

Thus there was no basis for mutual understanding. The argument went wandering around in a vicious circle. The circle could be broken and Christian insistence did break it with the sword of Constantine, the statesman who understood the new times, the new conscience. But how much martyrs' blood had flowed before this came to pass!

This drama of struggle between the civic and the religious conscience had also been felt to a certain degree by some of the pagan philosophers, for they too were guilty of living according to reason and seceding from the tyranny of the common prejudices. Socrates was the most famous of these, and he too was imprisoned, writes Justin, as being "sacrilegious, a conspirator . . . ; a victim of the same charges which are brought against us"; and in fact they said of him "that he was introducing new divinities and that he did not recognize the gods honored by the city."[45] Even the rabid anti-Hellenists like Tatian make an exception in favor of Socrates. The Christians of Palestine immediately saw a new Socrates[46] in the sophist Peregrinus Proteus, who was imprisoned for the faith. Socrates' example fit the Christian case like a glove; it was evidence of the same kind of political blindness, which condemned the free experience of the rational and reasoning spirit as a political

44. Theophilus, *Ad Aut.*, I, 11.
45. Plato, *Apol.*, 24b, in Justin, *II Ap.*, X, 4-5.
46. Lucian, *Peregr.*, XII.

crime. And it fit the more exactly because here was the prince of philosophers held up as an example to princes who were philosophers. But they were Stoic philosophers, that is to say, they were pagans, and so far as they were concerned, the gods, from a religious point of view, could be anybody's invention, but from the political point of view they were symbols of the state and had to be respected.

CHAPTER VI

THE CITY OF GOD

THE NEW PEOPLE

THE conduct and the teachings of the Christians proceeded from the new-born consciousness that they belonged also, and especially, to a City of God. Beside and above the *civitas Caesaris* the Holy Spirit raises up the *Civitas Dei,* which is the Church. She is at once a temple, a house, a governed society; she is a people and an army of divine institution; she is the kingdom of God; she is a queen.[1] Her dignity derives from her origin, her membership and her government, which make her a perennial emanation from God.

The Christians are her citizens, who have become so in baptism through the fruits of the Redemption. Incorporated in the Church, they acquire the consciousness of a new sociality which so binds them that they are welded into one organism at the head of which is Christ; it is, therefore, a suprahuman sociality. From it they derive their new rights, divine strength, the goal of all their living, the certainty of immortal life; and this fact inspires in them a tender, filial gratitude toward this Mother — as they call her — who is stern but gentle, who gives them nourishment and protection, namely, her teachings and her sacraments.

Even a scholar like Clement loses his dry academic manner when he speaks of her: "Oh, mystical wonder!" he exclaims.

---

1. ... *aedificat Ecclesiam, templum scilicet et domum et "civitatem Dei"* (Tertullian, *Adv. Marc.,* III, 23). Clement of Alexandria speaks of τῆς ἡμετέρας πολιτείας, "our republic" (*Paed.,* II, 5). Origen also speaks of the *City of God,* πόλις τοῦ Θεοῦ, superior to the cities of men (*C. Cels.,* III, 30). Cyprian says *commissum nobis divinitus populum et exercitum in castris caelestibus constitutum* (*De exhort. mart.,* II). For Justin (*Dial.,* LXIII) and for Abercius (*Epitaph,* ll. 13-18) the Church is a queen and Christianity a kingdom, with its own people.

"One is the father of all; one is the Word of all, and one is the Holy Spirit, everywhere the same. One also is the Virgin Mother, and thus it delights me to call the Church. . . . She too is virgin and mother, inviolate as a virgin, loving as a mother."[2]

The faithful who compose the Church form a "people," a social body, in which the living and the dead are united in their one common life in Christ.[3] Celsus did not consider the Christians a people and therefore condemned them as a civic minority, in fact, a real civic absurdity. But the new social conscience, which the Christians derive from their new customs, from their organization and life in the Church, and from the teachings and the origin of their faith as well as from the reactions of the world about them, is integrated by an always clearer feeling that they do form a new people, the third race whose "king" and "chief leader" is Christ.[4] He is the new law-giver, judge, guide, king, founder of his people. His is a new people and a new kind of kingdom. Even his standard — the cross — is different from any other, for wearing "no diadem on his head, nor sceptre in his hand, nor any other mark of distinction in his dress; but alone, the new king of the new times, he, Jesus Christ, has raised on his shoulders the standard of the power and the dignity of the new glory, that is, the cross."[5] Christian dogmas such as the Incarnation, the immortality of the soul, the resurrection, free will and monotheism formed a bloc apart in the imperial social structure.[6] The most concilia-

---

2. *Paed.*, I, 6 (*P. G.*, VIII, 300).

3. Cf. the delightful inscription found in Rome which addresses a dead infant thus: *Quam te letum excepit mater ecclesia de hoc mundo "revertentem." Comprematur pectorum gemitus. Struatur fletus oculorum* (cf. Leclercq, *Afrique chrét.*, vol. I, p. 75).

4. I pay the taxes, obey all the just laws, and pray for the emperor: *ceterum liber sum illi: dominus enim meus unus est Deus omnipotens, aeternus, idem qui et ipsius* (Tertullian, *Ap.*, XXXIV, 1). Justin (*Dial.*, CXXXVIII, 2) says: "Christ, the firstborn of all creation, has become the head of another race" (cf. *ib.*, XXIV, 2).

5. Tertullian, *Adv. Marc.*, III, 19 (*P. L.*, II, 348).

6. This tenet repelled and astounded the learned pagans: τὴν θαυμαστὴν σοφίαν τῶν Χριστιανῶν (Lucian, *Peregr.*, XI). The explanation regarding the assistance given to Peregrinus, in chains, defines the new teaching, social and legislative, of the Christians: "for those unfortunates have taken it into their

tory of the Christian teachers affirmed that as the Athenians obeyed the laws of Solon, the Greeks those of Phoroneus, and the Spartans those of Lycurgus, so the Christians followed the laws of the Old and the New Testaments, their own particular laws, just as heaven[7] was their particular fatherland. And his disciple, Origen, contemplating that vast intermixing of creeds and customs which Christianity had provoked, foresaw the establishment of a *civitas christiana* which would furnish the only and logical solution to the conflict. By recognizing Jesus Christ, he says, the Christians compose the "kingdom of God" and in it "they separate themselves and stand aloof from all strangers to the City of God (πολιτείας τοῦ Θεοῦ) who are alien to his covenants — in order to govern themselves according to the rule of the heavens, coming toward the living God and the City of God, the heavenly Jerusalem. . . ."[8] This means that the Church constitutes a new *civitas*, a system of government, a regime, the City of God. It is a greater fatherland, and to the extremists it may appear the only one, or it may seem a country opposed to our earthly one.

In fact, in the second and third centuries, that period of persecution and not always systematic theorizing, we have anything but a clear and consistent notion of what the relations between the two orders were. The majority, in actual practice, achieved a harmony between the two sets of duties and loyalties. But not rarely some one found in them a dualism productive of inevitable conflicts that could be resolved only if the Church absorbed the state. In short, there was the danger — and it was not always surmounted — that the body of citizens would be actually disunited and arbitrarily redistributed into

heads that they will all be immortal and will live in eternity: and therefore they scorn death and of their own will and in great number surrender themselves to death; besides, their first lawgiver (ὁ νομοθέτης ὁ πρῶτος) convinced them that they are all brothers, if having once passed over to Christianity, they deny the Greek gods and adore that crucified sophist of theirs and live according to his laws" (ib., XIII). Christ gave laws: ἔθετο νόμους, καθ' οὓς οἱ βιοῦντες μακάριοι ἔσονται (Origen, *C. Cels.*, IV, 32).

7. Clem. of Alex., *Protr.*, X (*P. G.*, VIII, 225).

8. *C. Cels.*, VIII, 5.

two classes, the Christians and the non-Christians, the Christians loyal to the Church, the non-Christians loyal to the state. This was above all an error in perspective, which would only have perpetuated the persecutions, and since it was shared also by non-Christians or those imperfectly christianized, it frequently led to conflicts even after Constantine.

An example of this is to be found in the matter of holding public office.

"Celsus," recalls Origen, "exhorts us to assume public office in the nation when it is necessary for the protection of the laws and religion. But we know that in each city there exists another kind (σύστημα) of nation, created by the Word of God, and we exhort those who are capable of government by virtue of their eloquence and upright morals to govern the churches. We do not accept those who are ambitious for authority, but we thrust it upon those who, because of their great modesty, do not care to assume rashly the general concern for the Church of God." They are the magistrates of that which is our nation according to God, namely, the Church.[9]

This was all very well, but the fact that the Christians made this distinction seemed to pagans like Celsus a sign that they formed a secret and mysterious association (κοινωνίας σύνθημα).[10] Today he would have called them gangsters.

The "philosopher" Aristides gave them a separate place in his three-part (or four-part) division of the human race: Hellenes, Jews, and Christians (or according to the Syriac version: Barbarians, Hellenes, Jews and Christians);[11] and he asserted that "this is truly a new people,"[12] a people, that is

---

9. *C. Cels.*, VIII, 75.
10. *Ib.*, 17. Cf. Minucius, *Oct.*, XXV.
11. *Ap.*, II. "Hellenes" ordinarily is taken to mean pagans.
12. *Ib.*, XVI, Syriac version, ed. Harris. Cyprian presents Christ as the teacher of the new people *vivificans credentium populum et vivificatis consulens in aeternum* (*De op. et eleem.*, VII). Cf. Tertullian (*Scorpiace*, X): *Illic constitues et synagogas Iudacorum, fontes persecutionum, apud quas Apostoli flagella perpessi sunt, et populos nationum cum suo quidem circo, ubi facile conclamant: — Usque quo genus tertium?* — Except that the Christians are not a *gens* like the Jews and the Egyptians, but their members, scattered among all the races, form one people (Origen, *Hom. I in Ps.*, XXXVI, 1).

to say, organized under their own autonomous government.[13]

This people is composed of individuals who have come
from all the other races and who, after the death of the Just,
and as a consequence of his death, have blossomed into another people, "a holy people" and therefore not to be despised
almost as if they were "a barbarous tribe, or a band of Carians
or Phrygians"; they are "a nation that is united in faith, pious,
just."[14] With these words Justin answers the charges of the
Jewish rabbis as well as those of the conservative pagans, to
whom the Christians seem not only an abominable sect with
its own different and peculiar thought and customs but a real
latebrosa et lucifuga natio, with which strong language Caecilius brands it.[15]

It is a new people, yes; but not another race. The Christians
want to appear a new body of people but not another race.
Their characteristic is universality, not ethnical particularism.
They rise above all races precisely to compose a greater people.[16] In this they are not at all different from Roman imperialism nor from Stoic cosmopolitanism, which, with Zeno, tends
toward universal brotherhood,[17] except that the Stoic looks to
one state, the Christian to one Church.

The tomb of Abercius reminds us that he has been in Rome,
the sovereign city clothed in gold, and that there he has seen
"a people that wears a shining seal," that is, the Christian people, who stand out as different in the cosmopolitan population of the capital.

---

13. Clem. of Alex., *Paed.* II, 5 (*P. G.,* VIII, 445) speaks of a "state"
(πολιτείας), which has the authority to outlaw from its ranks certain types
of professions.

14. Justin, *Dial.,* CIX, *passim.* Cf. Tertullian, *Ap.,* XLII, 1.

15. Minucius, *Oct.,* VIII, 4: "a nation which hides and flees the light."
This accusation will be made up to the time of Namatianus.

16. "The Christians are not a race (*gens*) but one people deriving from all
the races . . . : they might be called thus, the race of all the races" (Origen,
In ep. ad Rom., VIII, 6; *P. G.,* XIV, 1173).

17. Cf. J. Bidez, *La cité du monde et la cité du soleil chez les stoïciens,*
Paris, 1932. When they were asked to what city they belonged, Socrates and
Diogenes also used to answer, "the universe."

Ignatius had perceived two economies in the supernatural order, one of them represented by the "old regime," the other, "the new, represented no longer by the Sabbath but by Sunday."[18]

St. Paul's idea of the new man and St. Peter's idea of the new people influence the Christian conscience. The Christians knew it was their duty to cleanse themselves of the old prejudices and customs, to renew themselves, to be born again in order to be worthy of the new word; to be a new race (καινὸν γένος), characterized by a new way of life.[19]

But this desire for rebirth could have its effects on the social order also if not on the political one, and at all events could well seem a program of innovation and therefore invite the thunderbolts of the conservative Empire. Not all the Christian writers explained very well that this people apart were "a part chosen" for God and not a particular party or faction within the state.[20] And at all events, the fact that the Christians did live to themselves within the great body of citizens, that they differentiated themselves by their mode of life, their language and even by mysterious signs of recognition and greeting[21] alarmed the custodians and theorists of the established order, who regarded them as a menace. And they were potentially a menace, as Tertullian himself declared.

But this was inevitable after the Christians began to stay away from the public places (amphitheatres, hippodromes, temples) where the social and political life of the time had its fullest expression. And by way of reciprocity, the faithful of Lyons and Vienna were forbidden to go near the public buildings, the fora, the baths, or to be seen in any place on the eve of the great market days or the persecutions. They were untouchables; or, more precisely, they were like those radicals

---

18. *Ad Eph.*, XIX, 3; *Ad Magn.*, IX, 1.
19. *Ad Diogn.*, I. Also Clement of Alexandria (*Paed.*, I, 6; *P. G.*, VIII, 289): "reborn a new and holy people."
20. Clem. Rom., XXIX. Cf. *2 Clem.*, II.
21. Cf. Minucius, *Oct.*, IX, 2.

who are always being watched and who, on the eve of national holidays, are taken out of circulation.

On the other hand, even if this separation, this aloofness were avoided in daily intercourse, it was inevitable in the spiritual order. Even the gentle Justin speaks of *your* Rome and *your* senate, and the other apologists speak of *your* laws, *your* poets and the like.[22] It is a world which, tossed between sympathies and antipathies, detaches itself from the Jewish-Graeco-Roman bloc even while it takes care not to break all ties with it. In fact it succeeds in accomplishing the miracle of being a world in itself without rejecting a past which is not its own. In a certain sense we might say, with today's philosophers, that it surpasses it by resolving it in itself. "It is different from the others though it does not separate itself from them," as Trypho said to Justin.[23] Even the uncompromising apologists like Tatian and Hermias, Minucius and Theophilus, who reject the whole system of pagan thought in its entirety, do, without admitting it, use its best elements, which will be incorporated into Christian philosophy with almost unanimous consent.

The truth and nothing else — said Tertullian, who did not like the popular interpretation of this establishment of a new people — is what divides the two worlds. But in reality the truths which the ancients had divined were also part of the religion and ethics of his contemporaries.[24]

Justin, by way of vindication in his controversy with Judaism, says, "After the death of the Just we have blossomed into a new people," hated by the Jews, "and by all other men who are notwithstanding our brothers in nature," and protected

---

22. Cf. Tertullian, *Ap.*, XVIII, 4: *De vestris fuimus; Ad Nat.*, I, 7: *proverbiis vestris.* The pagan apologists paid them back in the same coin: "Can it be that the Romans do not command even without *your* God, that they do not rule and enjoy the fruits of the whole world, and that they are not lords even over *your* people?" (Minucius, *Oct.*, XII, 5).

23. *Dial.*, X, 2.

24. *Satis enim est nobis sola veritate a vestra positione discerni. Tertium genus dicimur, cynopennae aliqui, vel sciapodes, vel aliqui de subterranea antipodes (Ad Nat.*, I, 7). And so he treats with fine irony the deformation the adversaries of Christianity have wrought on this *tertium genus* in their estimation of it.

by Christ, "the head of another race," against a formidable coalition of adversaries.[25]

Through Christ, the scattered, amorphous "races" subject to idolatry and therefore to vice, had received the proud heritage of Israel and become a people, a chosen people; "the true spiritual race of Israel, the race of Juda, of Isaac and of Abraham, which, without circumcision, has received from God the testimony of its faith"; we, the Gentiles, are the people "blessed and called the father of numerous peoples." The idea of being a people — a holy people — which is an organic term of relationship to God, derives from Judaism, where it had ripened after the exile; it now becomes more deeply rooted and extends beyond physical connotations. With its "popular" sociality it affects both religious and civic life. In his relations with this "people," God has made a "new covenant";[26] he has made of scattered and unknown peoples, of "a plurality of men," a unity, "people and church."[27]

This distinction plays into the hands of Christianity's enemies, who pile the most slanderous charges on Christian isolation.

Well, retorts Tertullian, if that is the case, do you not see that you also form a "third race" with us, for the crimes you charge to us are committed privately and repeatedly by you? By attributing them to us you make us your equals; but, since we have not committed them, we are different from you.[28]

THE CHRISTIAN COMMUNITY AND THE RIGHT TO ORGANIZE

Apostolic and post-Apostolic Fathers keep repeating and emphasizing that Christian society, the Church, is a new people.

---

25. *Dial.*, CXIX, 3; CXXXIV, 5; CXXXVIII, 2.
26. Justin, *Dial.*, XI, 5. Cf. *ib.*, XVI, CXXXI etc.
27. *Ib.*, XLII, 3. The democratic character is brought out in the typical double epithet δῆμος καὶ ἐκκλησία. Justin also says that the Christians are "united [with Christ] in one soul, one synagogue and one Church . . . , which is established by his name and shares his name; in fact we all are called Christians" (*Dial.*, LXIII, 5).
28. Tertullian, *Ap.*, IV. Cf. *Scorpiace*, X.

They insist on its solidarity and describe it as an army in which each man stands at his post in the ranks, an exemplary soldier. There are subalterns, officers, leaders; all form a pyramid at the peak of which is Christ, the judge of all, the sovereign, the emperor, the King of kings, to whom, "everything is subject in heaven and on earth." The Christians fight under his banner and whoever wanders away from it is a deserter. Baptism is "a shield; faith, a helmet; love, a lance; patience, armor; good works, your stored-up earnings, that when the time of your service is over you may receive your proper recompense."[29] These were figures of speech that could appeal to the imagination of the simple faithful and inculcate in them the feeling of obedience, but they were also such as to irritate the sensibilities of pagan imperialism the more the latter kept strengthening its disciplinary organization through its hierarchical bureaucracy and unifying its religious organization about the emperor, who was, as it were, at the peak of all cults. On the one side was the emperor who made himself a god; on the other was a God who made himself emperor.

This new society was developing outside the pale of the law and consolidating itself into a hierarchical system, while the heart of its organization and the center of its greatest prestige was actually Rome, the capital of the sole kingdom of the god-Caesar. Besides, in describing its structure it used military terms and concepts at the very time when the Roman Empire, becoming more and more totalitarian, was becoming also more and more suspicious of every kind of organization.

St. Paul had called it a "body." Tertullian calls it *corpus,* and *corpus* was the legal term to denote a society which was recognized by the law as a moral person.

The Church owns property as a moral person, unrecognized by the law but existing *de facto* and firmly fixed in the conscience of its members. It makes no illicit traffic of the gifts of Christ: "as it receives gratis, so does it give gratis."[30] This

29. Ignatius, *Pol.,* VI, 2. Cf. St. Clement of Rome, *Ep.,* passim.
30. Irenaeus, *Adv. haer.,* II, 32, 4, in Eusebius, *H. E.,* V, 7, 5.

means, however, that it "receives" money and other gifts. In this period it was above all a matter of the monthly contributions, which were voluntary (*nemo compellitur,* notes Tertullian) and were intended to be used to feed and bury the poor, and to help orphans, the aged, servants, the shipwrecked, prisoners, or those exiled for the faith.[31] They served also to defray the expenses of religious services and to support the clergy. This was not equally true everywhere, however, for if we find the clergy supported by the community in Rome, there is an expression in Tertullian which makes us doubt that this was so in Carthage.[32] The deacons have charge of the funds of the community.[33]

Almost as if it were one of the associations which were recognized by law as moral persons, the Church, at least at the end of the second century, possessed movable and immovable goods, for example, the place of worship, cemeteries, and the community funds (*arca communis*). In the beginning the cemeteries probably belonged to richer members of the community who had put their *areae* at the disposal of their fellow-members for burial ground. But at the end of the second cen-

---

31. Tertullian, *Apol,* XXXIX, 5-6. Callixtus, the future pope, when he returned from the mines in Sardinia, was retired on a pension to Anzio as a confessor by Pope Victor. Caius (in Eusebius, *H. E.,* V, 28) narrates that the sect of Theodotus persuaded the convert Matalis to become its bishop with a salary of one hundred and fifty *denarii* a month. Natalis accepted, but later, tormented by remorse, he resigned.

32. The church of Rome supported forty-six priests, seven deacons, seven subdeacons, forty-two acolytes, fifty-two exorcists, readers and porters, and more than fifteen hundred widows and poor people: "so great a throng, and so necessary in the Church; a vast number rich in the providence of God" (Cornelius, *Ep.,* IX, 3).

33. Pope Cornelius, in a letter to Cyprian of Carthage, accuses the deacon Nicostratus of having, among his other crimes, committed this *quod est illi ad perpetuam poenam reservatum: Ecclesiae deposita non modica abstulisse (Ep.,* V). See also *Ep.* VII: Nicostratus *"diaconio sanctae administrationis amisso, ecclesiasticis pecuniis sacrilega fraude subtractis, et viduarum et pupillorum depositis denegatis...."*

Some manuscripts of the *Liber Pontificalis* have this information inserted in them: *Stephanus missus est in carcerem cum novem presbyteris....Ibidem in carcere ad arcum Stellae fecit synodum et omnia vasa ecclesiae archidiacono suo Xysto in potestatem dedit vel arcam pecuniae; et post dies sex exiens sub custodia ipse caput truncatus est.* The Bollandists have rejected this piece of information; De Rossi considers it highly probable.

tury, Zephyrinus, who succeeded Victor in 198 or 199, summoned from Anzio the future pope Callixtus, an active and clever freedman, a business man and ex-banker, and entrusted to him among other things the management of the community cemetery, the famous cemetery of St. Callixtus on the Appian Way.[34]

A *lex Julia* of the time of Augustus had restricted the foundation of *collegia* (societies), permitting them to be formed in Rome and Italy only after the deliberation and consent of the senate, and in the provinces only upon imperial authorization. Industrial societies (i. e., societies of merchants, artisans, shipbuilders) could, especially in Asia Minor, obtain authorization when they were directly serving the state, even though the Flavian and Antonine emperors had more or less relinquished traditional state monopoly in the Orient.

There were numerous religious associations formed by Oriental sects, for example those of Isis and Serapis from Egypt, Adonis and Astarte from Syria, Mithra from Persia, Cybele and Sabatius from Phrygia. They were, therefore, infiltrations from the outskirts of the Empire and they appealed mainly to the lower classes, to artisans, freedmen, clients, slaves, women, soldiers, etc. Because of this the churches might have seemed to be similar societies, whereas in fact Christian universality found those pagan organizations to be so many citadels of resistance.

Many societies were of the mutual benefit variety. Of this type were the *collegia tenuiorum,* that is, societies of poor people the purpose of which was to insure burial for their members. They were supported by monthly contributions (*stips menstrua*) and they obtained authorization more easily, it being

---

34. If Pope Zephyrinus made Callixtus manager of the Church cemetery, and if Alexander Severus in a lawsuit between the Christian community and a society of wine-merchants, decided in favor of the former, (Lampridius, *Alex. Sev.,* XLIX) and if in 271 Aurelian, in another lawsuit between two bishops, assigned the church building to the one who was in communication with the bishops of Rome and Italy (Eusebius, *H. E.,* VII, 30, 18-19), then we may suppose that the Church possessed immovable goods as well.

sufficient for them to make a formal request to the prefect of the city, that is, the chief of police, and present their list of members. These societies owned, as corporations, the burial ground and their meeting-place. They met generally once a month and gave banquets now and then which had also a religious character since these associations always bore the standard of some god. The members were called *fratres, sodales, socii*. Now Justin, and, more clearly, Tertullian describe for us Christian communities which meet periodically. Their members contribute to the common treasury (*arca communis*) to help the poor and bury their fellow-members, etc., and these contributions, like those of the *collegia tenuiorum,* were called, according to the African, *stips menstrua* because they were collected monthly. Because of this and other similarities, Giovanni Battista De Rossi thinks that the Christian communities might have continued to exist contrary to the anti-Christian law, by organizing as funerary societies, *collegia tenuiorum.* But the activity of a Christian community was richer than that of a simple association of slaves and workers, and its members came from all classes. Therefore it had a character all its own likely to excite the suspicions of the police, who could easily see in these Christian organizations so many *collegia illicita,* which were prohibited by law and against which Trajan particularly took severe measures. We know that in 111 he refused to give Pliny, who had dissolved the societies (of hetaerae) in Pontus and Bithynia, permission to keep a guild of firemen, as he thought necessary, in Nicodemia. The state tolerated only those associations which excited absolutely no suspicion and in no way disturbed the peace — this was the measure of Roman tolerance, and it became suppression as soon as any disorders broke out. It tolerated therefore the *collegia tenuiorum* under certain conditions and it tolerated and protected the guilds of shipbuilders, merchants, etc., who directly served the state. In the Orient it also permitted societies of shopkeepers and artisans employed in special industries which had probably been carried on at one time with professional secrecy by the families of priests.

Septimius Severus (193-211) was probably not the first to extend to the provinces the authorization for funerary organizations; he did so on condition, however, that they met no oftener than once a month and that they did not "cover" illegal organizations.[35]

Such being the case, the Christian communities would have been able to carry on only under great difficulties even as *collegia tenuiorum*. Thus Duchesne thinks they constituted rather those *collegia illicita* which the state tolerated in times of peace provided they did not cause disturbances or meddle in politics.[36] Such associations were not permitted to own property as corporations, but in actual fact a common ownership of property on the part of all the members was recognized.

We have few documents to help us understand clearly just how this situation developed, especially in the second century when the churches began to own property. Evidently the Christians, who were really outside the pale of the law, took advantage of its every concession and tolerance. They probably also formed *collegia tenuiorum* and met — this much is certain — in private homes, which were often offered them by their wealthier members. And they must have also accepted burial-grounds near the family tombs of some of these richer persons. In short, their society lived on the edge of the law between tolerance and clandestinity, and they intended to obey Caesar's law when it was possible but not beyond what was obligatory to obey the law of God. In any case they were careful not to attract the attention of the authorities with disturbances of any

---

35. *Permittitur tenuioribus stipem menstruam conferre, dum tamen semel in mense coëat, ne sub praetextu huiusmodi illicitum collegium coëat* (cf. the article *Collegia* by J. P. Waltzing in the *Dictionnaire d'archéologie chrétienne*). For example, under the pretext of honoring Bacchus numerous secret crime societies had been formed. Severe penalties and even the death sentence awaited the guilty.

36. Tertullian, *Apol.*, XXXVIII ff. He laments the fact that Christianity has been placed among the *factiones illicitas*, when it is in no way like them, that is, it never provokes public disorders.

kind. And if they did not disturb the peace, then the authorities were not likely to take action against them.

On the other hand, just as they had become the target of popular hatred, the Christians, since they were so well organized, were struck down by the emperors and officials who were most loyal to the severity of Roman law. But to rise again they made good use of the pauses between persecutions and the very fact that the latter were intermittent and rarely broke out throughout the whole Empire at once.

CHURCH UNITY AND DISCIPLINE

To the conscience of the new writers the principal society is the Church, not the state. The soul's polestar is the Church. When the state approaches it, it is only to persecute it. If the state remains indifferent, then it seems a distant thing because of the earthly aims it pursues and the pagan spirit in which it lives. Salvation always seems to be Christ, not Caesar. The Christian prays for Caesar, but he dies for Christ. And love for Christ is expressed in the Church.

Since in the Church, the Christians form a *corpus,* more real and more solid than any of the societies held together merely by personal interests or human sentiments, they consequently have an obligation to God himself not to violate in any way the integrity, unity and harmony of its structure, and therefore to act one toward the other in a spirit of mutual helpfulness and accord, working together toward that integrity and unity. This spirit finds expression in their daily moral and social acts. The ideal which Clement of Rome outlines in accordance with St. Paul's teaching is organic from the Christian and the Roman point of view.

"Let us then serve as soldiers, O brothers, with all intensity, under his irreproachable orders. Let us think of the soldiers serving under our leaders, with what discipline, submission and subordination they carry out their commands. Not all are proconsuls, nor tribunes, nor centurions, nor captains of fifty, and so on, but each one in his own rank carries out the commands of the emperor and of his superiors. The great cannot do without the lowly, nor the lowly without the great; there is a certain commingling of all things, and in that lies their advantage.

"Let us consider our body: the head is nothing without the feet nor are the feet anything without the head; even the very smallest members are necessary and useful to the whole body; in fact, all contribute to the health of the whole body, all being subordinate to it.

"Look therefore to the health of the entire body which we form in Jesus Christ and let each one be subject to his neighbor, according to the rank in which he was placed by grace. Let the strong protect the weak and the weak respect the strong; let the rich help the poor and the poor thank God for having granted him assistance in his poverty; let the wise man show his wisdom not in words but in good works; let the humble not give the testimony of himself but let others give testimony for him; let the chaste not boast in his flesh, recognizing that it is another who gives him continence. Let us reckon, therefore, O brothers, of what material we were created, who and what manner of men we entered the world, from what pit and what darkness he has brought us into his universe."[37]

To make any attempt against such unity, in which, according to St. Paul, each Christian lives for all and all for each one, to violate its hierarchical organization or the harmony of the souls composing it is to violate the body of Christ: "Why is there strife, anger, dissension, schism and war among you? Is not then the God we have one God, and is not Christ one, and is not the Spirit of grace infused in us one, and is not our vocation in Christ one? Why then do we tear and rend the members of Christ and rise against our own body and rush into such madness that we forget we are members one of the other?"[38]

---

37. Clement of Rome, XXXVII-XXXVIII.
38. *Ib.*, XLVI.

Discord — today we should say individualism — which serves earthly ambitions has brought social rupture. It has made men place their selfish interests above the common good while it is the duty of all, great and lowly, to "pursue what is to the common advantage and not their own particular advantage." But in order not to fail in that duty it is necessary to preserve oneself in the spirit of humility and to treat others in the spirit of love, in which all difficulties are dissolved and all personal interests are harmonized.[39] If we have that spirit, rather than harm another we prefer to depart from a place and submit to punitive measures inflicted by the community, provided that "the flock of Christ may live in peace with its duly authorized priests."[40]

Among these writers it is naturally the bishops who insist most upon the duties of discipline, the fruit of which is unity. In the bishops, unity, in a certain sense, is incarnate, because their authority unifies men's souls in one doctrine and one common feeling just as their succession guarantees men's heritage from the Apostles.

St. Ignatius of Antioch is a passionate and eloquent exponent of the solidarity which should exist between the faithful and their bishop, in whom the authority of the Apostles lives again and through whom they are united to Christ. There is no church without a bishop; one cannot be in accord with the Gospel if he is not in accord with his bishop.

Polycarp, the bishop of Smyrna, shows that he felt the same way about it.[41]

Irenaeus writes against the heretics who split this essential unity of the Church, while Cyprian bends all his energies with great courage and in the very midst of persecutions to defend this same mode of feeling and believing against the busy growth

---

39. Clement of Rome, XLVIII, XLIX.
40. *Ib.*, LIV; cf. LV.
41. One day when he met the heretic Marcion, the latter asked him: "Do you recognize me?" — "Yes," answered Polycarp, "I recognize the firstborn of Satan."

of dissenters, for "here begin the heretics, and here originate the attempts of the ill-intentioned schismatics: in pleasing themselves and in disdaining with haughty arrogance their superiors."[42]

One of the causes of persecution, according to the Carthaginian bishop, is the discord among the Christians themselves, which he calls the scourge of God. He is sure that once love reigns again and discipline is reëstablished, God will pardon them.[43]

And the martyrs of Lyons, while in prison, wrote to their brothers in Asia and to Eleutherius, bishop of Rome, seeking to make peace, and at the end, having confessed Christ, "conquerors completely, they went to God; having always loved and counseled peace, in peace they went to God, without leaving a patrimony of anxieties to Holy Mother the Church or of dissension and war to their brothers, but joy, peace, concord, and love."[44]

In short, the post-Apostolic Fathers faithfully follow St. Paul's teaching regarding the essential nature of the Church. Tertullian sums it up when he writes: "We are a body in the consciousness of our religion, in the unity of our discipline, and by the bond of our hope."[45]

Discipline is a requirement and a guarantee of unity, concord and orthodoxy. When crowds of lapsed Christians who broke beneath the trial of martyrdom come thronging back to be readmitted to the Church and have recourse to disorderly expedients and undue pressure, Cyprian tries to safeguard the discipline of the Church by making a calm investigation of each one's case, followed by sacramental confession and a suitable penance; he does not want the authority of others, be they even martyrs and confessors, to be set above the authority of the bishop.[46]

---

42. *Ep.*, LXV, 3.
43. *Praecessit disciplina, sequetur et venia* (*Ep.*, VII, 7).
44. Eusebius, *H. E.*, V, 2, 7.
45. *Apol.*, XXXIX.
46. Cf. *Ep.*, XI, XVII, etc.

He feels the paternity and severity of his office; for him "discipline is the guard of hope, and bond of faith, the guide on the road to salvation; it stimulates and nourishes a good spiritual formation, teaches virtue and makes us remain always in Christ, live constantly for God, and come at last to the celestial promises and the divine rewards: to keep it is salutary and to oppose or disregard it is fatal."[47]

THE ORGANIZATION AND LIFE OF THE CHRISTIAN COMMUNITIES

Each individual church is the community of the faithful in a given place, with its hierarchy organized to take care of religious worship, instruction and assistance to those who need it. It is divided into two groups: the ministers and the laymen.[48]

At the head of both is the bishop whose dignity derives through the Apostles from Christ and therefore from God. The Apostolic Fathers constantly insist upon inculcating in the faithful a sense of this most noble dignity of the bishop and consequently of the submission and reverence which they all owe him; and they strive to keep his election and his office free from party conflicts and the ambitions of those without proper dispositions.[49] The bishop is chosen by the very "Father of Jesus Christ, who is the universal bishop"; to obey him, to keep in communion with him, is the same as obeying God. Where the bishop is, there is the Church; without him there can be nothing but conventicles which have no right to exist.[50]

Under the bishop, who stands in God's place, is the body of presbyters who represent the Apostles. And under the presbyters, the deacons, charged to "serve Jesus Christ,"[51] "ministers of the mysteries of Jesus Christ . . . not merely dispensers

---

47. *De hab. virg.*, I.
48. Clement of Rome, XL, XLII.
49. *Ib.*, XLIV, XLV.
50. Ignatius, *Magn.*, III, IV.
51. *Ib.*, VI, 1.

of food and drink, but servants of the Church of God."[52]
Without the deacons, presbyters and bishops, the Church would
not be the Church. From the second century on there is no
more mention of prophets, doctors and apostles as members of
the ecclesiastical hierarchy, as there was when the churches
were first being organized.

And finally, the laymen, gathered about their bishop, who
is the guarantor of harmony and concord, and about the presbyters and deacons, and united by the tie of love, which is not
a fleshly but a spiritual love in Christ, complete that union
which is the image ($\tau \acute{\upsilon} \pi o \varsigma$) of eternal life.[53] The laymen who
stand not within but apart from the sanctuary, "that is, those
who act independently of their bishop, the college of presbyters
and the deacons, have not a pure conscience."[54]

From these short quotations we can understand what an
essential part of the new religious life this organization was
which endowed its members with a sense of order, discipline,
solidarity, harmony and responsibility.

There is frequent intercourse among these churches, a frequent exchange of letters, missionaries and assistance. They
feel they are parts of one sole body. Itinerant missionaries and
Christian merchants bind them together and carry information
about their activities and doctrine. When Ignatius is led to martyrdom, the bishops and faithful of the churches of Asia Minor
gather along his way to greet and comfort him. A lively sense
of solidarity binds them all together. When peace is once more
established in the community of Antioch, which had been upset
by dissensions, the principal churches of Asia send messengers
and letters bearing congratulations and thereby show how the
life of each church was included in the life of all of them. Later
when Polycarp dies for the faith, the church of Smyrna com-
municates the news — as the document says — "to all the Christian communities in the world which constitute the holy, uni-

---

52. *Id., Trall.,* II.
53. *Id., Magn.,* VI, 2.
54. *Id., Trall.,* VII, 2.

versal Church." And when the martyrs of Lyons are sacrificed for Christ, the churches of Lyons and Vienne inform the others of what has occurred.

While in prison the martyrs of Lyons had sent the presbyter Irenaeus to Rome with a letter regarding Montanism, and he had conferred on the matter with the Roman bishop Eleutherius. Differences in ceremonial and in dogma lead them to seek the opinions of other churches in order to reëstablish the orthodox creed in harmony with all. And it is to Rome as to their source that they go principally to seek doctrine and unity.

To Rome, after Peter and Paul, go Hegesippus, Justin, Tatian, Rhodon, Marcion and Apollo, Valentine, Heracleon, Ptolemy, Polycarp, Irenaeus, Origen, Praxeas; for the churches are many numerically, but only one substantially, and they must have a center. Rome was the church where sat the successors of Peter and Paul.

As names change and the field of conversion grows wider, the fact that the bishops are the successors of the Apostles soon appears to be the rule and principal guarantee of orthodoxy in the other churches too. These communities could never have been able otherwise to live on and preserve their hierarchy, authority and autonomy, but would rather have separated in time and developed each in its own restricted circle. At the first sign of conflict they would have nullified one another, drawn apart, ignored one another. Instead of the Church there would have been an aggregate of clubs. A unitary organization was in the very nature of things. We have already seen that it was in the intention of the Founder.

The rationalist critics say that this unitary — catholic — organization came later, when the first signs appeared that the faith was weakening, and that therefore it was determined by the necessity of bolstering the faith by organization. Instead we find the proof of the unity of all the churches in the authority of one bishop, the bishop of Rome, not at the end but at the beginning of this increased organizing activity. The Bishop of Rome, between 95 and 98, used his authority to settle a dispute that had broken out in the community of Corinth, passing judgment on the two contending parties with gentle firmness. And he excused himself for having intervened so late because of the persecutions that had afflicted the church of Rome under Domitian until 95 or 96. Ignatius of Antioch, writing to the church in Rome, repeated the special praises of St. Paul and recognized its "preëminence in love," and this, in Christian terminology, has also been interpreted as meaning the universal Church itself.[55]

On the other hand, the church of Rome had the tradition to "do good to all the brethren, in various manners, to send help to the many churches in all the various cities, in one place giving financial aid to the needy, in another helping the brothers in the mines with funds which — acknowledges Dionysus, Bishop of Corinth, writing to Rome in 170 — you have been accustomed to send them from the beginning; thus preserving, as it befits Rome, a hereditary tradition of the Romans, which your blessed bishop Soter has not only kept but also developed."[56] Irenaeus, bishop of Lyons, recognizes the necessity for each church to be in accord with (*convenire*) that of Rome. Cyprian informs the Roman clergy of his refuge and justifies himself to them. Rome asks Origen for an explanation of the oddities in his exegesis and summons the powerful primate of Egypt back to orthodoxy.[57] For the heresies which break out, usually in the Orient, a settlement and solution is usually sought in the Occident, in Rome. Montanists and Gnostics seek to corner the consent of that church which continued the authority

---

55. It is Funk's interpretation. "From the observation that προκαθημένη can mean only a place or a community, and from Ignatius' frequent use of the word ἀγάπη (love) as a synonym for ἐκκλησία — he says in fact: 'the love of the Ephesians,' 'the love of our brothers in Troad' to denote the respective communities — he concludes that the word ἀγάπη in this case, so placed, means the Church in the catholic sense, the universal Church, the concept of which, like the word he uses to describe it, is clear in the mind of Ignatius. This Church does not preside over Rome, but over all Christian love, over all the Church, from a place in the region of the Romans: the circumlocution brings out the difference" (I. Giordani, *S. Clemente Rom.*, p. 31).

56. Eusebius, *H. E.*, IV, 23.

57. Cf. Duchesne, *op. cit.*, I, p. 538.

and dignity of St. Peter and St. Paul.[58] Even differences in rite were settled there, so much so that when Polycarp and Anicetus failed to come to any agreement, the latter's successor in the Roman see, Victor, excommunicated in 190 the churches of Asia that refused to accept the Roman custom of a movable Easter.

Excommunication is an act of coercion based on the authority of the Church. In the gatherings of the faithful "exhortations, punishments and religious censures are meted out. Judgments are passed also, with great deliberation as befits persons who are sure they are in the sight of God; and it is a most serious anticipation of future judgment if one has sinned to such a degree as to be excommunicated from public prayer, from the gatherings and from every religious relationship."[59]

Outside the Church there is no salvation: "One cannot live outside the Church, because the house of God is one, and there can be no salvation for anyone except in the Church."[60]

---

58. Cf. Tertullian, *De praescript. haer.*, XXXVI. The primacy of Peter and his death in Rome are solemnly proclaimed in the "Clementines," *Ep. Clem. ad Jac.*, 1; *P. L.*, II, 33-35. The most important documents are collected in the ninth fascicle of the *"Florilegium patristicum,"* entitled *Textus antenicaeni ad primatum romanum spectantes*, ed. G. Rauschen, 1914, and H. Vogels, 1937.

59. Tertullian, *Apol.*, XXXIX; cf. Origen, *In Iesu Nave, Hom.*, VII, 7.

60. Cyprian, *Ep.*, LXII, 4. "Outside this house — the Church — no one is saved" (Origen, *ib.*, hom. III, 5).

CHAPTER VII

THE NEW CIVIC CONSCIENCE

Christian Imperialists

WE USE the terms "imperialism" and "imperialists" with great caution. By them we mean strictly the feeling not only of loyalty but also of acceptance and devotion toward the Antonine house and the Roman Empire, as the existing regime; or, as Athenagoras wrote to Marcus Aurelius and Commodus, "the feeling of obedience and zeal for your House and the Empire." We exclude any connotation of military and political expansion since there is no trace of any in the writings of the Fathers.

Tertullian was in the main current of Christian teaching when, from the fact of the divine origin of authority, reaffirmed by the Apostolic Fathers, he deduced the daring corollary that since God had invested the emperor with his power, he was to be considered as belonging more to the Christians than to the pagans. Thus the new society also drew into its own orbit the political authority divested of its idolatrous superstructures, just as it had annexed to itself the Jewish prophets, extricated from rabbinism, and the Greek philosophers, cleansed of the crust of paganism. This was a logical process of assimilation indispensable to a universal society in which Christ was to be all and was to absorb all individuals and groups even to their least thoughts.

But this attitude can hardly, or only superficially be considered imperialistic, especially in the modern sense of the term. For just as it was Christianity which baptized Platonism and not the latter which platonized Christianity, so it was Christ who re-claimed the civil authority and not the civil authority

143

that subjected Christ. In other words, Tertullian, along with Clement, Polycarp, Athenagoras and Theophilus, wanted the emperor to come down from the pedestal where he received idolatrous worship, and become a Christian; the Christians were not to prostrate themselves before his altar. This ideal was to receive a tremendous development and come to maturity in the Middle Ages. Now it flashed like a sudden intuition across the Christian conscience. Tertullian himself did not foresee that it could be realized; in fact, in an attack of ascetic pessimism he stated that it was humanly impossible to realize it: "The Caesars would have believed in Christ if the Caesars had not been necessary to the world or if the Christians could have been Caesars."[1]

This was a pessimistic view of humanity and of the world, here considered irremediably antithetic to Christ. And it was a view based on the past, but not confirmed by the future, not even by the immediate future; for about 206 in Edessa presided a Christian king, Abgar the Great, the protector of Bardesanes, who made Christianity the state religion at the same time that he remodeled his kingdom after the pattern of Roman civilization. This offered a typical example of how the two orders might well live together, while pagan apologists were daily pointing out how opposed they were to each other. It is true, however, that Abgar's experiment did not last very long.

In any case, having once denied that there was any antithesis between Christians and Romans and having by a process of strict logical deduction reduced the whole question of antithesis to one between Christians and pagans, Tertullian and the Church itself went no further than that. In fact, Tertullian's own temperament carried him to extremes again and he stated that nothing interested him and his fellow Christians less than public affairs. This was true in part, that is, so far as direct and daily participation in politics was concerned, but it was not true

---

1. *Ap.*, XXI, 24.

when it came to renouncing any influence over the ethics of the state and its conduct toward its subjects in general and the Christians in particular. Clement of Alexandria, who always seeks a balance in all things and whose point of view is more practical, asserts that political activity is also licit "for it is not at all forbidden to busy oneself with an unworldly mind with worldly things according to the will of God."[2] Tertullian, however, was for the moment more concerned with the question of being able to live within the Empire than with anything else.

The Christian attempt to win citizenship for the faithful brought out various aspects of the feelings they nourished toward the Empire as such. The Church professed that authority comes from God but it did not therefore declare that the government of Rome was entirely at peace with God's law. There was complete freedom of judgment regarding the government's actions; and such judgments were indeed free, varying, of course, from one period to another and according to diverse temperaments.

They may be summed up under three principal headings. First there were those who were Roman in feeling, who loved the Empire and wished to introduce Christianity into it as a positive factor even of civil and political well-being; who accepted the existing dynasty with zealous loyalty but distinguished between it and the trappings of idolatry which surrounded it. The second attitude, which seems the most widespread at least in the second century and which probably corresponds to the actual practice of the Church rulers, is represented by those who quite realistically face the fact that the Empire is there, that it is strong and cannot be overthrown. These try rather to win from it a legal or *de facto* recognition for the Church and the enjoyment of ordinary rights and of the bene-

2. Τὰ ἐν κόσμῳ κοσμίως, he says with a play on words. His principle is: ἐξὸν δὲ ἀκροᾶσθαι μὲν σοφίας Θεϊκῆς ἀλλὰ καὶ πολιτεύσασθαι ἐξόν ("it is permitted to listen to divine wisdom, but also to take part in public life" — *Paed.*, III, 11; *P. G.*, VIII, 656).

fits of good administration and internal peace without mixing in politics; in fact, they prefer to avoid public office although they do express the desire that the Empire recognize the rights of Providence over the state and renounce its own deification. But in the end they take refuge in the conviction that the world will endure only a brief time, that its end is near and that then all present difficulties and injustices will be resolved by eternal justice. Lastly, the third attitude is that of the intransigents for whom the distinction between the new order and the old means complete division and antithesis; hence they identify the throne of Caesar with the throne of Satan, Rome with Babylon, so that they hate her and oppose her, as much as possible, as the incarnation of evil.

This is, of course, only an approximate division at best because very often in the same author we do not find one attitude entirely distinct from another; rather they are fused under the pressure of events and various emotions. In the light of the documents we possess, however, the thesis that the Christians formed a nucleus of imperialists who were conscious and deliberate adversaries of the quiritarianism entrenched in the senate[3] is absolutely untenable. It is enough to consider that the most ardent professions of Christian loyalty to the state were made under the Antonines and for their senatorial regime, which tried to rescue the Christians from the violence of the populace and protected them from the hatred of the Jews. On the other hand, the most hated emperors were Nero and Domitian, who were as anti-quiritarian as anyone could be.

Related to this and equally untenable is the thesis that there was a Catholic imperialism, which in this century supposedly took the form of a secularization of Christianity expressed in the Church's effort to model itself after the Empire, to copy its organization and its centralization in Rome.[4] The Roman

---

3. This is the thesis of U. Benigni, *Storia sociale della Chiesa*, vol. I, p. 173 ff.

4. The thesis of Harnack, *Dogmengeschichte*, I, refuted by Batiffol, *Eglise naissante*, 274-6. In this regard see R. Murri, *L'idea universale di Roma*, chap. II, Milan, 1937.

church exerted no pressure whatever to subject the other communities, some of which had been organized before she had. As we have already mentioned, her superior function as guide appears historically to have been a spontaneous and accepted development of principles proper to Christianity.

In the first current of thought listed above we can more or less include Clement of Rome, Melito of Sardis, Abercius, Athenagoras, Apollonius, Theophilus and perhaps Dionysius of Corinth. It is evident, though decreasingly so, as long as the Antonines govern, and it appears again under Constantine, a sign that it sprang up as a consequence of the very nature of the regime of various emperors.

In the second tendency we may include Quadratus, Justin, Tertullian as a Catholic, Clement of Alexandria, and Origen in part.

The passage from the first current of feeling to the second is a gradual one as is also that from the second to the third, that of the rigorists who carry their intransigence over from the political to the intellectual field and oppose not only the imperial rule but also pagan culture. In this third tendency we may place Tatian, Hermias, even Minucius, Hippolytus, the authors of the eighth book of the *Sibylline Oracles,* the *Apocalypse of Baruch,* and the *Fourth Book of Esdras,* the traditional lists of the *Didache,* Papias, Irenaeus, the writer of the *Epistle to Diognetus,*[5] the author of the *Second Epistle of Clement,* the Montanists and Tertullian as a heretic.

Under the influence of these three currents of thought, which sometimes fuse and sometimes supplant one another, the new society was being fashioned with a physiognomy all its own, differentiated from pagan society but not cut off from

---

5. "The anonymous author or authors of the *Didache* confidently await the coming of the Lord; Papias, in Asia Minor, dreams of a true earthly paradise; Irenaeus, an emigrant from Asia, recalls the dreams of the Millenarists and of Papias, but as a protest against the existing Roman rule. Under and with this lively expectation of a happy era to come, spread the vision of a fire, a universal upheaval which would put an end to the Empire opposed to God. . ." (P. Ubaldi, *Taziano,* Turin, 1921, p. XI).

it; for it accepted both the most sound moral and philosophical contributions of paganism and also its social and political structure, pruned of idolatrous worship and the injustices most opposed to the precept of charity.

The bishop of Rome, Clement, who was a freedman or the son of freedmen in the service of a family related to the emperor, felt that as a citizen he was quite purely and simply a Roman and that the duties of citizenship were refined by Christian charity.

Others, who perhaps were functionaries or close to the authorities, or who were influenced by their own political tendencies, more easily cultivated in exceptionally loyal Asia, constantly believed in spite of everything in the possibility of a reconciliation between Church and Empire and a peaceful coexistence of the two. They were the extreme conciliationists, who loved both the Church and the Empire and wished them to live together in harmony. From the uneducated and anonymous author who doctored the *Gospel of Peter* (he lived about 120) and with great ingenuousness acquitted the Romans and Pilate[6] of every responsibility in the execution of Jesus, throwing all the blame on the Jews and on Herod whom he transforms into a judge, to the author of the still older[7] *Gospel of the Twelve Apostles,* who makes the Roman Empire a creation of God entrusted to Augustus, attributes to Tiberius the intention to make Jesus a king and has Pilate weeping over the shroud of Christ killed against his will,[8] on down

---

6. Some critics have thought they saw a similar purpose in the apocryphal *Acta Pilati, Anaphora Pilati* and *Ep. Pilati;* but the information is too vague to deduce that there was any specific apologetical intent in them. Even Tertullian, *Ap.,* XXI, 23, makes Pilate have Christian sympathies. For the date, and the problems resulting from the discovery of the *Gospel of Peter,* see L. Vaganay, *L'év. de Pierre,* Paris, 1930.

7. According to Origen this is earlier than the Gospel of St. Luke, who in the introduction to his Gospel is supposed to have had this and the *Gospel of the Egyptians* in mind. See Revillout, *L'év. des douze apôtres,* in *Patrologia Orientalis,* II, 123 ff.

8. *Patrologia Orientalis,* II, pp. 146, 152, 172. This apocryphon says that the emperor's representative in Palestine, a certain Carius (Caius?) sends the Apostle John to Tiberius, and when Tiberius learns what Jesus is doing he orders

to Melito, Theophilus, and Abercius — three Asiatic bishops, notice — they do not realize that there is any substantial incompatibility between Christianity and Roman sentiment.

Melito, the bishop of Sardis, carries his submission to the authorities almost to the point of not complaining against the recent anti-Christian measures (perhaps edicts) passed in Asia. He complains only that "shameless spies greedy for the belongings of others, who rob and plunder with impunity night and day" the houses of the Christians take advantage of these measures. If the emperor is truly responsible for them, the bishop asks, then let the forms of orderly procedure be respected, let them be carried out according to the law "since a just sovereign could never establish anything illegal. And we willingly accept the reward of such a death."

Here Melito certainly exaggerates the matter of loyalty and skids into adulation, so anxious is he to capture the imperial good will.

"Only this do we beg of you," he continues, "that you yourself first scrutinize those who have conducted these investigations, and judge fairly whether we merit death and punishment or salvation and peace. But if this mandate and this unheard of edict, such as would be unbecoming even against your barbarous enemies, does not proceed from you, then with all the more reason we beg you not to leave us the prey of this public thievery."

He follows this request with another which is more ingenuous or more daring, namely, that Christianity be accepted as the natural ally of the Empire since God has brought them into being together to accomplish a good purpose. Christianity's appearance in the Roman states, he explains, was an auspicious omen for the nascent Empire: "from then on, in fact, Roman power grew greater and more splendid; you have been the heir of this power under good omens and you shall

---

that he be made a king. The one who opposes Pilate on this point and says to him: "You are a Galilean, Philistine, Egyptian Pontus" is Herod, who from then on becomes Pilate's enemy (4 fragm.).

continue to be so, and your son as well, if you will protect the philosophy[9] that developed and took its rise with the Empire inaugurated by Augustus and was respected also by your ancestors with all the other religions.

"The most important proof that our teaching has progressed to mutual advantage with the Empire so felicitously risen, is that the Empire has suffered no calamity since the reign of Augustus, but on the contrary has flourished in a splendid and magnificent manner, such as every one could desire. Nero and Domitian alone among all, because of the instigation of malicious persons, sought to incriminate our teaching."

Tertullian uses this artifice too. From a distance the persecutions seemed to be localized in the reigns of those two emperors if only because their persecutions were systematic and particularly savage and were carried on with no guarantee of legality even in procedure. Their name was detested also by the philosopher-emperors who had come up from the senate; for of the membership and prerogatives of the senate those two despots had made a shambles.

This was a curiously ingenuous dialectic device, but it can be justified when we consider the faulty information of the period; it is noteworthy too as an attempt to erase any incompatibility between the two orders, even historically.

"From those two the calumnies against us have been spread about even down to our own day, because the reports of the informers are accepted without conscience."

"Your pious forefathers," however, exerted themselves to correct the errors of that legislation with numerous measures, among which are the rescripts of Hadrian to Minucius Fundanus, and of Antoninus to the cities of Greece like Larissa, Thessalonia and Athens, where disorders were deliberately provoked in order to condemn the Christians for them. The good Melito concludes that Marcus Aurelius, since he is still

---

9. Christianity is presented as a philosophy according to the ideas of the period, and in order to make it more acceptable to the philosopher-emperors.

more humane and more of a philosopher than his ancestors, will continue their benevolent policies.[10]

Melito is not the only one to consider it a providential co-incidence that Empire and Church were born at the same time. It showed a naïve faith in their compatibility and the possibility of their collaboration in a harmonious development of both, a Utopia in view of the actual state of things; but this was the view accepted by the political conscience of the Middle Ages.

Origen, who was more realistic but no less farsighted, noted that the birth of Christ had coincided with the institution of the Empire, which was an aggregate of peoples that favored the evangelization of all races; but he foresaw the victory of the barbarians and their conversion and so he conceived a grandiose spiritual unification of all races in Christian unity,[11] a unification in Christ, not in Caesar.

In the petition sent to Marcus Aurelius and Commodus, his partner in government, Athenagoras is not at all sparing with praises either. Rather he exaggerates them in the attempt to demonstrate his own complete loyalty. Besides he is cordially devoted to the sovereigns and, with his great confidence in their sense of justice, he expects them to resolve that misunderstanding which is the anti-Christian law.

They are "great among princes"; they have assured the peace of the whole universe and of all classes (why then should the Christians not benefit from it?), with "gentleness, mild-

---

10. Melito, in Eusebius, *H. E.*, IV, 26, 5-12.

11. *C. Cels.*, VIII, 68, 72. Origen considers it a sign of Christ's power and divinity that he manifested himself at the moment of the creation of the Roman Empire. "In those days justice sprang up, and abundance of peace" (cf. Ps. 71:7). God wished all peoples to be well-disposed to Christ's teaching and so he provided that they be gathered together under the one Roman emperor, for a division among peoples would have interfered with the Apostles' work in fulfilling Jesus' command, *Go and preach to all nations.* Augustus unified all peoples in one Empire and during his reign, Jesus was born. "A number of different governments would have impeded the dissemination of Jesus' doctrine throughout the whole world ... because people everywhere would be compelled to take up arms and fight each for his own country" (*C. Cels.*, II, 30).

These are seeds of the ideas that will bear fruit in the Middle Ages, when the Empire will seem a divine institution like the Church.

ness, love of peace in all things, and humanity" giving to "private citizens equal justice under law and to cities due honor." They are "most great, most humane, most learned emperors, versed in philosophy, endowed with all learning"; so that "as they surpass all other men in intelligence and kingly power, so do they surpass them also in the full possession of all learning, for in every branch of knowledge they may boast as no other man may, not even he who has specialized in only one" and this includes a knowledge of the Sacred Scriptures of the Jews.[12] Athenagoras pays homage also to their unsurpassed devotion to the divinity.[13]

Praises like these are scattered throughout his exposition. Like the writing of Melito, it tries to touch the most sensitive cords in the heart of a man, sovereign and father like Marcus Aurelius, who, out of affection for his son, ruinously changed the system of succession to the throne. "Now you who are, with all men and in everything, by nature and education, good, moderate, benevolent and worthy of the Empire, nod your royal head [in assent] to me who have refuted the accusation and demonstrated that we are religious, meek and continent in spirit. Who, indeed, deserves to obtain what he asks more than we who pray for your authority in order that you may transmit the sovereignty, from father to son, as is most just, and that your authority may increase and develop with the submission of all men? For this is also to our advantage, permitting us to lead a quiet and tranquil life[14] and gladly accomplish what is ordained."[15]

We cannot accuse Athenagoras of insincerity although we must admit that hyperbole has its part in this as in other documents of the sort. But when we view it as a whole, his prudence in speaking of Christianity without ever naming Christ

---

12. Athen., *Suppl.*, I, II, VI, XXIII, XXIV.
13. *Ib.*, VIII.
14. I Tim. 2:2.
15. Athen., *Suppl.*, XXXVII.

or the Christians or casting the least aspersion on the idols[16] makes it clear that effectively his aim was to reach the sovereigns' hearts with a sincere exposition of Christian life and teaching. These would prove the upright civic loyalty, not merely innocuous but even serviceable, of the Christians, "people who do no harm to anyone and who are most devout and most observing of justice toward the divinity and your Empire."[17] It is evident that it hurts him to see excluded from the Empire's peace and indisputable benefits such a compact nucleus of excellent citizens, "cast out, robbed, persecuted" without reason.[18] He wants to remain within the Empire on an equal footing with his peers; in fact, he wants to vie with its best citizens in respect for authority and obedience to its laws.

Justin also appreciates the benefits of the peace in the Empire, of controlled administration and orderly legal procedure. He recognizes the fact that without the Antonines the hatred of the Jews would have continued to stir up persecutions of the Church.[19] Neither does he attribute the persecutions to the emperors; he makes the devils, who goad on the sycophants, responsible for them, nor does he consider the latter "obstinate" in all cases.[20]

This is his conviction and he declares it also to the Jews: "You hesitate to recognize Christ ... in order not to be persecuted by the authorities, which, incited by the evil spirit of error, the serpent, will not cease to kill and persecute whoever confesses the name of Christ." And so he foresees that, due to the ethical conflict between the forces of evil and Christianity, the latter will constantly have to meet vexations of one

---

16. Athen., *Suppl.*, XVIII. Not mentioning the name Christian was a common expedient in speaking with adversaries animated by prejudices. Minucius does the same thing.

17. *Ib.*, I.

18. *Ib.*, I.

19. "You [Jews] no longer have the power to coerce us, thanks to the present rulers: but whenever you had it, you used it" (*Dial.*, XVI, 4; cf. *ib.*, XCV, 4).

20. *Ib.*, XVIII.

sort or another until Christ returns again and destroys them all and rewards each man according to his works.[21]

Athenagoras still more explicitly throws the blame on the fanatical and irresponsible populace and especially on the villainous informers.[22] But it will become clearly impossible, or at least extremely difficult, to hold this view after Septimius Severus and his various successors issue edicts reviving and intensifying persecution. Then it will no longer be possible to doubt the anti-Christian intentions of the pagan Empire.

THE CATHOLIC HIERARCHY AND THE EMPIRE

The Church took a middle course. In the face of a hostile law that had endured for almost three centuries, she undertook no total political opposition to the state as such nor did she reject the state. She offered moral opposition to that law only and to the political idolatry from which it emanated; and indeed this was enough to justify the reaction of the idolatrous state. In the field the Church considered her special province, she could not permit the intrusion of the state without destroying herself; hence with tenacious resistance she strove to make the state withdraw. Her opposition was confined therefore to that particular field.

Some of her uncompromising members perhaps desired a complete opposition on the part of the Church, or better, they transferred their intransigence from the field of theology to that of politics. But the Church, though she had condemned the idolatrous worship of Caesar (the state-god), did wish to go on living; and without compromise she realistically sought to distinguish between the emperors, especially the Antonines, and the principle of idolatry. She recognized their authority, prayed for them, and as an ecclesiastical hierarchy she refrained from any direct political activity which was not within her competence. Rather than exile herself from imperial society, she

---

21. *Dial.*, XXXIX, 6.
22. Athen. *Suppl.*, I.

desired to enter into it, to dispel its suspicions and win ordinary rights for her members. In short, she desired to convert it, not subvert it, and she requested and finally obtained first tolerance, and then liberty. She did so not through compromise, but by making the force and reason of her arguments prevail against the unreasonableness of the persecutions; the apologias and writings of the period prove this. It should be noted that it was volunteer defenders who engaged in controversy rather than the responsible heads of the Church. As rulers the latter chose to be prudent. Probably with their authoritative intervention or their own private dealings with the authorities, they obtained not a few of those general or local respites of tolerance which cross and re-cross the blood-red cycle of persecution. Ignatius of Antioch knew that the Roman community with its influence could save him from martyrdom and he asked them not to use it. At heart the majority of Roman functionaries realized that the Christians were the most innocuous of citizens and that their entire guilt could be reduced to a religious obsession. Therefore, when they could, they winked one eye or both and did not refuse to listen to the arguments of the bishops and presbyters who must have come to try their powers of persuasion on them. The authorities saw to it that the public peace was not disturbed. If the mob did not disturb them or the central government did not insist, then most of the time they did not go stirring up hornets' nests of their own accord. In short, with regard to dogma the Church was unshakable and uncompromising; with regard to the government she was flexible and adaptable.

In the second and third centuries, the Church, in accord with Gospel teaching, was loyal to the state in the political field but opposed to it in the field of religion. It was the pagan state which invaded religion and made a political problem of something that was not political at all. The official Christian requests that the anti-Christian law be abrogated never went beyond what the law allowed. The Church was anything but insensible to the benefits of Roman peace and the administration which, in the second century, was the best the ancient world had seen. Besides, her very opposition on religious grounds remained always purely passive (harmful to the state only indirectly) for she took care to render good for evil. Certainly the fact that the Christians kept insisting on their loyalty to the Empire and the prayers they were obliged to offer for the emperor must have done much to temper the severity of the law and the hostility of the government and render the persecutions less rabid than might have been expected from unyielding Roman authority. Tertullian cites the names of more humane judges who even had recourse to legal expedients to save the faithful from death.[23]

"And there is," he adds, "an even more compelling motive which obliges us to pray for the emperors, for the stability of the Empire and the power of Rome: we know that immense catastrophe hangs over the whole world and that the end of time, which will bring horrible calamities, is retarded by the existence of the Roman Empire. We do not wish to experience this catastrophe and therefore in praying that it be delayed we are lending our suffrages to the continuance of Roman power."[24]

"When the imperial power is shaken and with it all the members of the Empire, we also, however foreign we are to the tumults, shall be somehow overwhelmed in the general collapse."[25]

Tertullian was shrewdly interpreting the thought of the official Church with regard to this subject in this particular period. The dispenser of kingdoms is God to whom belong the earth and all men. It is God who confers power on rulers and therefore on emperors also, who are set above all men and beneath God alone. But "let them take into account within what limits the

---

23. *Ad Scap.*, IV. As an example of a humane and extremely moderate judge we might recall that Perennis who had to condemn Apollonius (*Acta Apol.*).
24. *Apol.*, XXXII; cf. also XXX.
25. *Ib.*, XXXI.

power of their sovereignty prevails, that is, let them understand God: and since they have no power against him, let them recognize that the power they have is from him."[26] The emperor is great because he is inferior to God.

Now the men most acceptable to God are the Christians. Therefore, since they pray to him for the emperor also, they are more likely than any others, in fact, they are the only ones likely to obtain grace from heaven for the head of the state.[27] The Scriptures teach this attitude of prayer and submission toward the ruler. He who rules has been set in power by God; therefore, there is to be seen a "judgment of God" in the emperors. "We know that God's will is realized in them, so that we too will the security of what God has willed. . . . But it is useless for me to dwell on the loyalty and devotion of the Christians toward the emperor: let this suffice, that we honor him as the person especially chosen by our Lord, so that I could with all reason say: Caesar is more ours than yours, having been established by our God."[28]

ANTI-IMPERIALISM AND ESCHATOLOGICAL · SOCIAL THOUGHT

There was another current of thought, less widely diffused and existing almost entirely on the outskirts of the Empire (Syria, Assyria, Africa) which differed from the view of the conciliationists either because it did not think any accord possible with Rome or because actually it did not want any. Naturally we cannot draw a definite line between the two. Tertullian's civic loyalty borders on opposition, and Tatian's opposition makes concessions to civic loyalty. The arguments of St. Paul and St. John, or we might say the political arguments based on the principles of St. Paul, found various applications, moderate or extreme, with varying temperaments, places and times.

---

26. *Ib.*, **XXX**.
27. *Ib.*, **XXX**.
28. *Ib.*, **XXXII-XXXIII**. Tertullian's model is I Tim. 2:2 and Rom. 13:1-2, which is also the inspiration of Origen in *C. Cels.*, **VIII**, 65.

Certainly it was easy for the Christians to proceed from religious to political universality and to set this against Roman imperialism. In the same way it was easy to exaggerate the competence of the Church and conceive it to be an order not only distinct from the state but its rival. The most austere ascetics identified the corruption of the time with the moral life of the Empire; and their flight to God, with its feverish expectation of the end of the world and a chiliastic palingenesis, was for some of them a spiritual flight from the Empire, an escape from the laws of the state, an interior revolt. The state rejected them and they departed from it, some by becoming absorbed in God and some by building apocalyptic vengeances in their excited fancies. In respect of these latter, the persecuted Christian and the Jew deprived of his fatherland were in perfect accord. Origen took refuge in metaphysics and allegorical symbolism. When he compared the two orders, he saw on the one side well-ordered churches illuminating the world through which they move, their "senates" worthy, their leaders virtuous; and on the other, superstitious and disorderly assemblies, corrupt senates and magistrates without dignity: in other words, the City of God, with all its fine organization, set above and against the city of men.[29] Probably the hatred of the populace and the iron-fisted hostility of Roman law had something to do with the exodus of the fanatics of Phrygia who went seeking a new, free and peaceful country in the plain of Pepuza. In time, as anarchy and definite hostility toward the Empire grew more widespread, this minority became the majority, without, of course, the fringe of exaggerations like those mentioned above. Irenaeus and Hippolytus were in line with Tatian, and so was Origen, at least in part; for as the Empire gradually became more and more totalitarian and tried more and more energetically to rid itself of Christianity in which it saw a centrifugal force of opposition, the Christians came to take less and less interest in the state, to draw

---

29. C. Cels., III, 29-30.

aside, to feel foreign to it and, in certain localities at least, actually hostile. The world treated them as intruders, and they were inclined, at least during the persecutions, to consider themselves such, to feel themselves exiles made for another world. For Clement of Alexandria, the earthly country disappeared into the heavenly country;[30] for Tertullian[31] and Tatian, there was, besides the Empire, the world of which they considered themselves citizens. Marcus Aurelius also used to say that as a man he belonged to the world; and this Stoic cosmopolitanism sometimes went hand in hand with Christian universalism and coincided with the sentiments of the middle classes in general, which were composed of people from the country and of freedmen, strangers to ordinary imperial patriotism. If they had been able to speak freely, the exponents of this current of thought would perhaps have inveighed against Rome with fiery energy; but because of the activity of the police and the system of paid informers, they were obliged either to hide their feelings in restrained phrases, which certainly meant more to their contemporaries who were aware of all this than they mean to us, or to give vent to their emotions in sibylline invectives.

The Church, when it secured first peace and then protection from the state, ignored the semiclandestine documents of political opposition which had been circulated in the centuries of oppression; and thus many of them were lost. Some — and this is significant — have been preserved only in Syriac or Ethiopic or Armenian.

In the little that does remain, however, we can glimpse a deep resentment against Rome. She pacified, governed, unified; but there were numerous layers of subjugated peoples in burdensome civil and economic inferiority, and there were nationalistic individuals in the provinces who were not exactly resigned to the submersion of their respective countries in the

---

30. "We have no country on the earth, and so we can despise earthly riches" (*Paed.*, III, 8).
31. *Apol.*, XXXVIII.

general uniformity of the Empire, which frequently extended its sphere with the iron claws of plunder and extortion. To rebel was impossible; and yet desperate groups here and there tried it.

Their religion gave the Christians the strength to support a yoke that was often particularly heavy because of the persecutions, and it inspired them to seek an accord with the state in order to live in peace with it. But in not a few groups, Christianity, forging as it did a new collective conscience, only strengthened their aversion for the whole imperial structure; and once they convinced themselves that the Empire was the realization of the rule of evil, they went so far as to hate it, and then they did not pray for it, but rather prayed for the vengeance of God upon it.

We can be certain that the majority of Christians did pray for the emperor, though perhaps with breaking hearts; but there was a minority that invoked fire and brimstone upon the savage Babylon with her seven hills as cruel as the seven heads of the hydra. This latter feeling was expressed, or hidden, in various forms, from anti-Hellenic polemics to the tenacious refusal to answer the judges, from the Christian desertion of public affairs to the propaganda of the apocryphal apocalypses.

Tatian entered the great polemic tournament as the impetuous enemy of Greek culture, a kind of champion of the barbarian world. He had learned Greek rhetoric, but he had remained at heart an Assyrian with a residue of nationalistic hatred for all that was Roman tucked away inside of him. He thought that in Christianity he had found the dynamic force of at least a spiritual rebellion which would exact revenge of a superior order for the humiliations inflicted by the arrogant tyrants. He was contemplating a spiritual revenge, yes, but with a feeling of violent disgust for the corrupt and infamous world with which political Rome was identified. He did not say so explicitly; prudence warned him to veil his opinions. But along with the millenarists and the Judaizing writers of apocrypha he contemplated with joy the palingenesis which would accomplish that vengeance. Thus his scorn for the "scientific imperialism of the Greeks" was associated and fused with a scorn for their "social-moral imperialism."[32]

Other attacks against the existing state of affairs were launched from extra-cultural sources, that is, by asceticism and messianism. Ever since the destruction of Jerusalem in 70 A. D., the shattered soul of the Jewish people sought to re-galvanize the faith of its scattered sons by placing in circulation pseudo-canonical books of the Bible, in which the calamities they had suffered were explained as a temporary punishment visited upon them by God for their sins, as a people and as individuals; and these books announced at the same time the palingenesis to be brought about by the reconstruction of Jerusalem as a messianic kingdom of glory and peace for the just, and of shame and destruction for the pagans.

These writings, in which Judaism was purifying and strengthening itself, circulated also among the Christians, who often introduced into them allusions and explanations with Christian meaning and drew from them the strength to endure the spectacle of the triumph of an idolatrous power over Christ's people, who were being robbed, banished, massacred, and treated generally like a pack of mangy dogs.

Thus at the same time perhaps that St. John, on the island where he had been exiled, was writing his *Apocalypse,* a Jewish writer was publishing an apocalypse of his own, fortifying it with the name of a famous Biblical personage: *The Fourth Book of Esdras.* Christian hands later touched up the first two and last two chapters. These aimed to prepare the people for the Last Judgment, which, according to calculations then widely accepted, was to bring to an end the Roman Empire and the messianic age.

In his second vision, Esdras weeps because the Law and the benevolence of God are no longer reserved to one race, and

32. Ubaldi, *op. cit.,* p. 61, n. 6.

the latter had been scattered among the pagans; but in the fifth vision he describes the appearance of a proud two-headed eagle that rises to rule the whole earth and all its inhabitants without encountering any resistance whatever. However, its twelve wings fall off one by one, and its two heads droop until a lion comes and with a human voice cries aloud the list of frauds the eagle has continuously perpetrated, the truth it has trampled under foot, the meekness and humility it has oppressed, the falsehood it has exalted, the wealth it has squandered, and the peaceful cities it has laid waste. But the Most High, the Strong, will now wound it to the death and thus free the earth. The eagle represents the fourth kingdom of Daniel and symbolizes the Roman Empire. The lion is Christ who will inaugurate a regime completely opposed to the Roman, that is, a rule of peace and joy that will last until the day of Judgment.[33]

Toward the end of Trajan's reign, an apocryphal *Apocalypse of Baruch* (in the Greek text of which some Christian inserted his own convictions) again set forth the agonized question as to why God had trodden on the just and glorified the idolaters. The question was answered by the assurance that there was to be an eschatological revolution in which the just would have their revenge in glory and the wicked would meet the most overwhelming punishment through the destruction of the last empire, Rome, wrought by the Messias. The *Paralipomena of Baruch,* composed about twelve years later, prophesy the reconstruction of Jerusalem. Groups of Christians appropriated this document too, if they were not actually the ones to publish it around 130 A. D.

Bitter feelings of hatred for the Empire were injected by some Judaizing Christian into the *Sibylline Oracles,* in which the national Jewish religion had for centuries been gathering teachings to convert the pagans along with cries of vengeance

---

33. For the text see *Die Esra Apokalypse* (IV. Esra). hrsg. von B. Violet, 2 vols., Leipzig, 1910-24, (*Die griech. Christl. Schriftsteller*). The various readings that have come down to us are arranged in six columns.

invoked upon their heads. The eighth book is typical; it is a kind of cento, a Jewish, pagan and Christian patchwork put together at the time of Marcus Aurelius. This book says that after the empires of the Egyptians, Medes, Persians and Macedonians, the last is the Roman Empire, the most illustrious and the most iniquitous, with cruel tyrants and fearsome laws, and it will come to an end in a final catastrophic conflagration.[34] With her wretched gods Rome will fall from her lofty height nor will she ever rise again, and wolves and foxes will prowl among her smoking ruins and the shattered remnants of her standards and eagles. The hated *Urbs* will be destroyed with all of Italy. Oh, when will that day come when the ruins of the pagan Empire will be greeted with the cry of liberation of the people who are everywhere oppressed and the Messias will establish on the earth an eternal reign, and call to life again the dead? The Christian writer salutes Sion, freed from the yoke of unjust laws.[35]

Another writer addresses Rome as the source of all the evil in the world and the object of the hatred of all the peoples she has subjected: "Unstable, perverse, destined to evil calamities, great beginning and end of sufferings for men, since through you nature perishes, and then is saved, oh fount and origin of grief. . . . Who among mortals has ever loved thee? Who does not quiver with wrath within himself? . . . All things have been ruined by thee, all evil is gathered in thee. . . ."[36]

THE CHILIASTIC PALINGENESIS

As for this vision of an eschatological kingdom of God established after the destruction of the universe (which the

34. The statue of Daniel, pointed out to Nebuchadnezzar, was a "symbol of the world." The head of gold represented the Babylonians, then in power; the silver represented the Persians who succeeded them and ruled for two hundred and forty-five years; then the Greeks of Alexander of Macedon, who reigned three hundred years (bronze); finally the Romans (iron) "men strong as iron"; these will be followed by the *digiti pedum, testa et ferrum . . . democratiae futurae* (terra cotta and iron) (Hippolytus, *In Dan.*, v. 30; *P. G.*, X, 672-3).
35. *Sibyll.*, VIII, 37 ff.; 126 ff.
36. *Ib.*, V, 227 ff.

Stoics also taught would take place in a cataclysm of fire at the conclusion of great cosmic cycles), it was not difficult even for the most gentle Christians to set it against the spectacle of the earthly kingdom of Caesar, the persecutor of saints, seated on a throne supported by immeasurable corruption. And the meekest martyrs were easily led to view death, the passage to eternal life, as a liberation from a political regime which condemned the Church and legalized the brothel. As imperial hostility grew more bitter, the spirit of the *Apocalypse* became more diffused; and since the Empire was persecuting Christ, the Christians began to couple Caesar with the Anti-Christ. Thus in some sections they came to identify Caesar with Christ's adversary, that is, to carry to extremes the antithesis between the Christian Church and the pagan state. We must remember that the Church did not follow these extremists; while she held her slain in her arms, she hoped always to come to some understanding with the state.

In the Jewish apocalyptic writings, the enemy of God had been successively identified with Antiochus Epiphanes, Pompey, Herod the Great and Caligula. Christian apocalyptics, which were influenced by the Jewish writings and drew on the same sources (Daniel, especially, besides St. John) identified the Anti-Christ with Nero principally, who was expected to return (*Nero redivivus*) at the head of the Parthians. It was believed that his name contained the 666 of the *Apocalypse*. Irenaeus proposed three other names: Teitan, Euanthos and Lateinos. Hippolytus preferred the last, for he identified with the Romans the tyranny of the Anti-Christ, which leveled all men in idolatry.[37]

This belief after all was completely orthodox: some future form of government is always better than the present regime. But in their passionate yearning for justice, the early Christians cherished the hope of a better regime to be established in this world, a reign of justice for all, of universal peace, with bread

---

37. *De Christo et Antichristo*, 48-50.

in abundance too; for this expectation was a reaction not only against present political corruption but also against social and economic injustices. There was too much hunger to be satisfied, and it was not only the hunger for justice. And in eschatology early Christianity wrote some of its plans for political and social reform, the first pages of its radical sociology. This began with the fully orthodox like Justin and persisted in unbroken continuity down to heretics like Montanus.

Justin's ideas concerning Christ's second coming were developed from the visions of Daniel and were excited by his trembling expectation and desire to see the present distress of tortured Christianity finally ended. He counted over the time and foretasted the joy of that kingdom which would encounter no opposition from one sea to the other and would be governed by justice for the liberation and exaltation of the good. The Christian chanted the messianic Psalms (or those that appeared such to him) to God, king of the earth ... king over all the nations, seated on his hòly throne (cf. Ps. 46:8-9).

Like his first advent, in shame and suffering, Christ's second coming, in power and glory, will be made manifest in Jerusalem, where the prophecy of Micheas (4:1-7) will be fulfilled: Christ will judge among numerous peoples, he will rebuke strong nations even to the most distant lands, and the weapons of war will be transformed into the tools of labor, the arts will flourish in peace and all the oppressed will be reinstated in their rights.[38]

In addition Justin did not envision this empire of peace, faith, hope and love among men as the antithesis of the Roman Empire. At least he did not give that impression. He saw it rather as the glorification of Christ in contrast to his denial by the Jews. He not only transferred many messianic aspirations to Christ's second coming, he also made it the beginning of a social-political regime on earth that was to last a thousand

---

38. Justin, *Dial.*, XXXII and ff.; XXXVIII-XL; LXXXVI; CIX.

years under the sceptre of Christ with its capital in Jerusalem, "rebuilt, and made larger and more beautiful."[39]

The *Apocalypse of Esdras* foresaw a kingdom that was to last four hundred years.[40] From a literal interpretation of St. John's *Apocalypse,* Justin derived the idea of the millennial kingdom which would be composed of all the just among the Jews with the prophets and patriarchs at their head, and all the just among the Christians led by the Apostles and martyrs, all made co-sharers in the kingdom.

He is a broad-minded and tolerant man; he knows that not all the Christians "even of pure and pious doctrine" believe in the millennium, but he and "the Christians who are complete-ly orthodox," do believe in it firmly, basing their faith on the prophecies of Ezechiel and Isaias and "John, one of the Apos-tles, the author of the *Apocalypse.*" There will be a new heaven and a new earth and the memory of former things will vanish, for only joy shall live and no longer will any lamentations be heard; there will be no more infants born before their time, no more old people who will die before their hour is come. The youth will be a hundred years old. Nor will one man build a house and another inhabit it, nor one plant a field and an-other harvest it. Each man will enjoy all the good things of earth. And the wolf and the lamb will feed together.[41] The millennium will end with the Last Judgment.

This millennium is the last in a series of seven that repeat the cycle of the creation of the world, which, including God's day of rest, lasted seven days, each one thousand years long. Jesus Christ became Incarnate on the sixth day, that is, in the sixth millennium,[42] at the end of which he will return to estab-

---

39. *Ib.,* LXXX, 5.
40. *IV Esdras,* VII, 28, Latin text.
41. Cf. Is., 65:17-25.
42. For these reckonings cf. Barnabas, XV, 4-5; Irenaeus, V, 28, 3; Hippo-lytus, *In Dan.,* IV, 23-24; and Justin, *Dial.,* LI, 2, LXXXI and CXXXIX, 4, where they are accepted and it is taken for granted that the reader knows them. In 2 Pet. 3:8, we find: "One day with the Lord is as a thousand years, and a thousand years as one day."

lish the millennium of the just reign of rest and joy which corresponds to God's rest after the work of creation.

In the *Epistle of Barnabas* we already have chiliastic calculations and beliefs. The ingenuous Papias had also acquired from the "presbyters" the belief in a millennial kingdom of material enjoyments for the just, in which the animals would live in peace and the earth would bring forth luxuriant harvests: the vineyards would each have ten thousand vines, each vine ten thousand branches, each branch ten thousand tendrils, each tendril ten thousand clusters, each cluster ten thousand grapes. Dreams like these of social well-being thrive on the faith of devout souls. Even though Asia's production of grapes was now fairly good, wine must still have been expensive in the market and beyond the means of the poor man. And in the most simple souls there was also a thirst for good wine, in order to forget, in a little exhilaration, their endless succession of sufferings.

The belief in the millennium goes back to Asia Minor particularly, where it developed in all probability through an inaccurate interpretation of the *Apocalypse* and under the influence of the Jewish world with which the Christians there came in contact. Besides Papias, who had been the disciple of the "presbyter" John[43] it had been accepted also by various heretics. Among the latter was Cerinthus[44] whose interpretation seems even more grossly materialistic, his millennium being a succession of orgies. These more earthy aspirations perhaps flowed through popular channels into the current of Moslem eschatology, and in them various groups of both Jews and Christians found the most concrete expression of their consuming desire to fill their hunger at last, to enjoy themselves

---

43. Eusebius, *H. E.*, III, 39, 1.
44. *Ib.*, III, 28, 2; VII, 25, 2-3. Dionysius of Alexandria says that Cerinthus believed in a completely earthly kingdom of Christ, in which men would indulge unrestrainedly in the pleasures of eating and drinking and carnal joys of every sort (*ex l. II de promiss.*, 3, *P. G.*, X, 1241-44). Cf. Gaius (in Eus., *H. E.*, III, 28, 2), who says that Cerinthus was expecting a reign filled with passions and pleasures to last through a "thousand years of nuptial feasts."

finally, after having watched for decades from a distance the banquets of the few nabobs[45] while their own stomachs were half empty.

In Lyons, the millennium was accepted by Irenaeus, who had been a disciple of Polycarp and belonged among the traditionalists. On the other side of the Mediterranean, it was accepted because of the same traditionalism by Nepos in Arsinoë and Tertullian in Carthage. The latter was already inclined toward the messianic sublimation of the Montanists. In the third century the belief began to lose ground amid bitter controversies even though among its exponents were Hippolytus, Methodius of Olympus, Commodianus, etc.[46]

The Montanists reheated the chiliastic expectation among their own frenzies and went so far as to persuade a great crowd of men and women to sell and abandon homes, relatives and goods in order to go and await the descent of the heavenly Jerusalem on the plain between Pepuza and Thymion in Phrygia, a land fertile in pseudo-mystic exaltations. Since the chiliastic capital did not descend they transformed those two towns into a Jerusalem of their own and put their strict regime into practice under the disciplinary guidance of prophets and prophetesses, finally winding up in anarchic communism.

The chiliastic aspirations were not necessarily associated with hatred for Rome, just as not all the Christians looked forward to an eschatological revolution in the world's economy as being also the end of and a vengeance upon the existing social-political order. But the learned pagans who inquired into these beliefs saw in them the threat of ruin.[47] In all cases, they indicate a social aspiration for a better political and civil order, an ideal that went far beyond the actual accomplish-

---

45. *Nam et confitemur in terra nobis regnum repromissum; sed ante caelum, sed alio statu; utpote post resurrectionem in mille annos, in civitate divini operis, Ierusalem caelo delata . . .* (Tertullian, *Adv. Marc.*, III, 24).

46. Chiliasm had almost disappeared in the fifth century, persisting only in some stray heretical sects.

47. Cf. Minucius, *Oct.*, X: *Quid? quod toti orbi, et ipsi mundo cum sideribus suis minantur incendium, ruinam moliuntur?*

ments of the Empire. The great and more practical Origen will establish this kingdom of God on the earth and within the existing economy; it will be a reality when all the world is Christian and the new "city," complete and sufficient in all things, will be the Church. He is another precursor of the author of the *De Civitate Dei*.

THE FATHERLAND AND THE WORLD

It was inevitable that the Christians should be differentiated from pagan society, and this had advantages and disadvantages as far as their relations with the authorities were concerned. The advantages were to fall due in the far distant and uncertain future; they had occasion to experience the disadvantages every day.[48] Besides, according to the notions of the time, any justification for treating the Christians as a people apart served also to vindicate for them the right to have, like other peoples, their own Divinity and their own particular worship.

In the *Epistle to Diognetus* and the *Shepherd* of Hermas, one the expression of a refined intellect, the other of an ingenuous soul, we find diffused beneath the mystic impulse a deep-rooted disdain for the world, a great indifference toward what goes on in it. We can feel that many Christians are truly "strangers" to the world, not only from the religious but also from the social point of view, because they have substituted for it a loftier society, the perfect and true society. And in this these two authors resemble the compilers of the *Didache* and the *Epistle of Barnabas*.

"Even if the vineyard does not bear fruit," asserted Cyprian by way of argument, "and if we have no oil, and the grasses are parched with the drought, what does it matter to the Christians, the servants of God, whom paradise invites and all the graces and the bounty of the kingdom of heaven await? They

---

48. "Without miracles the disciples [of Jesus] would not have been able to persuade those to whom they were transmitting a *new* word and new doctrines to accept them even at the risk of death, leaving Τὰ πάτρια" (Origen, *C. Cels.*, I, 46).

are always joyful in the Lord . . . and they endure with strength the misfortunes and adversities of the world."[49]

The Christians abstained from all forms and expressions of idolatry in proportion to their faith. In large cities, if they did not form a strong nucleus, they could do this without attracting too much attention. So far as the rest of their daily life was concerned, outwardly they did not seem different from the rest of the body of citizens. The difference was within, in the spirit; and the author of the *Epistle to Diognetus* is keen enough to perceive this. He points out what a reserve of moral leaven, and indirectly what social and political leaven — revolutionary from the point of view of the old order — was contained within the deposit of the new ethics placed in circulation by these Christians, who otherwise ate and dressed like other men. He objects strongly to the attempt of the mass of people and the intellectual minorities to segregate them from civil intercourse, and he insists that they have a specific function in society which, though it could be tolerated in the theory of some Cynic or Stoic, evidently becomes dangerous when numerous and compact groups of citizens attempt to carry it out. "The Christians do not distinguish themselves from other men because of their dwellings, nor their language nor their customs. They do not inhabit particular cities, they do not use a different language, they do not lead an eccentric life. Their teaching has not been patterned by fancy or by the notions of busybodies, nor do they propose a human system of opinion, as certain others do."

That is, the Christians do not wish to be confused with any philosophic sects or political factions. As citizens, they are like all the others and they do not wish to be shut up in distinct groups and thus lose contact with the rest of the world. Their way of understanding life is indeed different. In fact, "though

---

49. Cyprian, *Ad Demetr.*, XX. This is a reply given in argument and is therefore a little exaggerated and not quite true to the thought, which is: the Christian is serene because he does not make his life depend on the vine but on possessions which do not perish.

they inhabit Greek or barbarian cities according to the lot that
has befallen each one, and though they follow the local customs
in dress, in eating and in other civil practices, they display a
mode of life that arouses wonder and is indisputably singular.
That is, they inhabit their own cities, but like pilgrims. They
take part in all that happens like other citizens, but everyone
treats them like foreigners. Every foreign land is as their
native country, and any native country is for them as a foreign land."[50]

They had, therefore, a different concept of their civil and
social obligations, which derived from their new concept of
religion and was actualized in a way of life rich in unusual
expressions.

The Stoic used to say that as a man he was a citizen of the
world. The Christian said this too but he immediately explained
the relative and transitory nature of this citizenship, which was
that of a "foreigner." People spoke of "the pilgrim church in
Rome ... the church that passes, a foreigner, through Smyrna,
etc." While Clement of Alexandria taught that conversion to
Christianity was a kind of desertion,[51] Tertullian, a centurion's
son, went so far as to say that he recognized "the world as the
one sole state of all men."[52] The pagan Celsus had said that
the unification of Asiatics, Europeans and Africans under
the same laws "even to the ends of the earth" was a beautiful
ideal but a utopian one. Origen answered that it was a sure
and reasonable thing to expect that one day the Logos (Reason,
the Word) would transform all souls in its own perfection and
unify them under its own law.[53] He expressed thus the Christian aspiration that Christian universality would be realized in
a kingdom that also was universal, but for that very reason

50. *Diogn.*, V. Cf. 1 Pet. 2:11 ff.; the address of *I Clem.*; Tertullian *Ap.*, I;
and *Recognitiones*, IX, 7; [*Christianus*] *sit tanquam peregrinus et advena atque
alterius civitatis civis*.

51. Μετανοήσωμεν οὖν, καὶ μεταστῶμεν ἐξ ἀμαθίας εἰς ἐπιστήμην. . . .
Καλὸς ὁ κίνδυνος αὐτομολεῖν πρὸς Θεόν (*Protr.*, X, 93, 1-2).

52. *Ap.*, XXXVIII, 3. Cf., Minucius, *Oct.*, XVII, 2: *hanc communem
omnium mundi civitatem*.

53. *C. Cels.*, VIII, 72.

spiritualized. This general feeling helped the Christians to endure banishment and not to fear exile, which was the cruelest punishment of all for the citizen of ancient times. Cicero, Ovid, Seneca, banished from Rome, did nothing but complain despite all their fine philosophy. The Christians took advantage of exile to spread the Gospel, that is, the City of God, and later to begin monastic life as an organic revolt against the established order that had driven them out.[54]

Christian universalism and Stoic cosmopolitanism were loosening, though unwittingly, the bonds of nationalism which obliged the Roman to view the foreigner as an enemy or at least as a stranger. Even the barbarian, even the enemy entered into the new brotherhood and this sounded like scanty patriotism or outright treason to the pagan apologists. Their exclusivism was combated in the vigorous controversy which Aristo of Pella and Justin, especially, waged with the last defenders of Jewish racial and religious exclusivism within the orbit of imperial society, and which pushed the last Jewish-Christian communities to the edge of heresy. The Church freed herself of the latter with a definitive excommunication at the end of the second century.

We must also note that patriotism as such was not strongly felt in that leveling atmosphere of imperialism, which had substituted for it the religious, idolatrous devotion to the head of the state. This substitution had weakened patriotic feeling at Rome, its very center, where it had been replaced by centralized bureaucracy, and it had obliterated patriotism in the provinces. In so far as it had led to idolatrous concepts and expressions, it had alienated the Christians, to the most loyal of whom belongs the merit of bringing patriotic sentiment back within human, and therefore acceptable, limits.

The Empire itself was fundamentally to blame for this loss of patriotism since its whole political make-up favored a class

---

54. Thrasea was wont to say: "I had rather die today by violence than be sent tomorrow into exile" (Epictetus, *Diss.*, I, 1, 26).

of privileged citizens in the cities, set above the anonymous classes of exploited peasants and the proletariat. There was not even any feeling of race, for the conquests and Roman legislation as well as commercial intercourse had mixed or equalized the various races gathered in the Empire. Nor could the national religion serve any longer to bolster patriotic feeling since the Christians had abandoned the worship of the gods, which, as a whole, was one of the most characteristic national* institutions, and syncretism was divesting the deities of their ethnical character.

In this period, municipal governments were still active and exerted a strong influence, but their power also was growing weaker as imperial officials gradually replaced elected office-holders. Besides, this municipal sentiment had also centered about religious traditions and local idols, so that when the Christians abandoned and ultimately destroyed these latter, they destroyed also the last hopes of independence and liberty that still persisted, especially along the outskirts of the Empire.

On the other hand, the concept of the fatherland had to undergo a profound transformation in Christian thought because the *polis,* the state, no longer constituted the final end of the individual and society. This was the kingdom of God, in relation to which the state became merely a means to an end. What had seemed in the past an absolute value now became a contingent thing. And naturally the state, which robbed and killed the Christians, rejecting them as its enemies, was not likely to inspire patriotic feelings in them.[55]

Perhaps when the deacon Sanctus at Lyons, his body mutilated by the most refined forms of torture, refused persistently to tell from what country he came, answering only in Latin, "I am a Christian," his attitude was a reaction to the state's rejection of the Christians, and certainly he was expressing the

---

*Translator's note: *patrie* (Τὰ πάτρια: the fatherland).

55. During persecution, *Relinquenda erat patria et patrimonii facienda iactura. Cui enim nascenti atque morienti non relinquenda quandoque patria et patrimonii sui facienda iactura est? Christus non relinquatur, salutis ac sedis aeternae iactura timeatur* (Cyprian, *De lapsis,* X).

Christian consciousness that they belonged to a different order, well-constituted and completely sufficient. His answer implied a complete spiritual and social universality because "he asserted that that title for him was his name, country, race and all things," although they burned the most sensitive parts of his body with red-hot tongs.[56]

This is a denial of the fatherland! — said the people of the provinces.

The Roman conquests were a religious enterprise! — objected the theorists who defended the deified state.

A fine religion, and fine justice indeed! — retorted Octavius ironically. — Rome was founded and grew on crimes and terror; granting them immunity and sanctuary, she received in the beginning "desperate criminals, violent men, beginning with Romulus himself, her head and lawgiver, who, in order to be superior to his worthy people even in crime, committed fratricide. These are the first auspices of the religious city!" The second set are tarred with the same brush: the rape of maidens and other men's wives and war with their parents, their fathers-in-law! And then, look at Rome's territorial expansion achieved by driving the owners from their land — the sacred land! — destroying cities with their temples and altars, taking captive her enemies. Wars and blood: this is the heritage bequeathed by Romulus to his successors. "Thus all that the Romans hold, adore, possess is the booty of violence,"[57] and of irreligion.[58]

An invective like this from the gentle Octavius is important not only because it upsets the belief in the divine origin of Rome, which is therefore eternal as Horace and all the Romans sang of her, but also because, coming from a Roman subject,

---

56. *Act. Mart. Lugd.*; cf. Eusebius, *H. E.*, V, 1, 20-21.
57. Minucius, *Oct.*, XXV, 1-5.
58. Tertullian, *Ad nat.*, II, 17: *Tot sacrilegia Romanorum, quot trophea; tot de deis quot de gentibus triumphi. Manent et simulacra captiva.* The same idea recurs in *Apol.*, XXV: "It is not possible to believe that the Romans have become powerful through their religious merits, for as we have indicated, they either developed their religion by violating it or violated it in developing it."

it sounds like a condemnation of the moral origin of the government to which he is subject. This is not a Roman speaking; it is a judge who condemns (and this is important) as a Christian, who, because he is a Christian, brings the history of society to trial before his own individual conscience and feels outside and opposed to a regime built in contempt of the ethical law.

Is the state right then in considering the Christians public enemies? To judge this accurately we must remember first that not all the Christians share Octavius' opinion: there are others who believe the Roman Empire to be a providential institution; secondly, that these statements are high-lighted in the heat of argument; thirdly, that his is the opinion of an African, who naturally would not be fully sensitive to the greatness of Rome. Minucius is less skillful than Tertullian and falls right into the trap of his adversary, who is trying to picture the Christians as anti-Roman. Tertullian, as we have already pointed out, reduces the antithesis to its true terms: the Christians are anti-pagan.

In any case, Octavius does not state that since the origin of Roman power is unjust there must therefore be a rebellion against its laws or that the existing regime should be overthrown. As a good Christian he probably prayed for the emperor and paid his taxes; and even though he calls the worship given "princes and kings" "false adulation," he holds it is licit (*fas est*) to honor them "as great and chosen men, honor being more truly rendered to an illustrious man, and love an offering more pleasing to a very good man."[59] As we see he is an orderly citizen, and he is introduced to us as a respectable one. Therefore he is not an enemy of the state.

On the other hand, once we have weighed whatever polemical sentiment and resentment there is in Octavius' words, we find that his judgment on the origins of Roman power — and on all regimes in general that have been fashioned by armed violence — is the inevitable Christian one. It will be

59. *Oct.*, XXIX, 5.

further developed by St. Cyprian and still more by St. Augustine. When the moral standard is applied to the political world, then its infractions of justice are condemned.

Thus Octavius' (or better Minucius') attitude presents an aspect of the process of breaking down the old order, in so far as it was associated with idolatry and immorality or at least amorality, with the intention either of building a new order or of directing the existing one toward acceptance of the ethical law, which is superior to the state and the individual; in short of christianizing it.

It is certain that in this way Christianity breaks up the solidarity with the nation's past of the Empire's Christian subjects. On this point it collides with nationalism, the primary factor in which is the indiscriminate cult of the glories of the past. The new citizen weighs and sifts these glories; he reëvaluates them and when necessary rejects them.

The reaction of extremists like Tatian is quite understandable. They rejected the Roman "law," justifying their attitude by pointing out the conflicting variations in legal norms and customs from one country to another. According to them, there should have been one norm only, ruling one people in harmony. Athenagoras, on the other hand, used that variety in laws and customs as an apologetical argument to ask citizenship and tolerance also for the law and customs of the Christians. But Tatian hammered like a battering-ram against his adversary's position without noticing the contradictions in his own arguments or paying too much attention to their practical consequences. He sought no understanding with the other side; he was setting forth the reasons for the conflict. His universalist concept of political society, however, was accompanied by other elements of disintegration in the already enfeebled patriotism of the time, particularly of the middle classes, made up of country bourgeois and city freedmen, and also of the working classes, to whom this new universal and equalitarian order offered those rights which the imperial system of privileges and favoritism refused them.

Thus Tatian was fashioning a kind of nationalism in reverse; we might call it spiritual Irredentism. His attempt to divest the pagans of any creative originality in their arts, institutions and literature, to picture them as magpies strutting in other birds' feathers,[60] and to establish the source of learning among the barbarians, certainly sprang more from the resentment of his race than from the deposit of charity in his belief, even if we make due allowance for the stress and strain of debate. This confusion of two different and fundamentally antithetic ideas clouded Tatian's faith and ultimately dragged him out of the Church. From then on a large part of the Christian heresies sprouted in that same composite soil of nationalistic religion or religious nationalism.

Thus mysticism and asceticism, under the stimulus of the Roman persecutions, were strengthened by this belief that the world was a "foreign dwelling," the antagonist of the eternal dwelling, so that the soul's chief concern is to leave it "without fear" knowing that to be attached to worldly goods is the same as "deserting the path of justice."[61] We cannot serve two masters: "the present world and the future world are two enemies: one teaches adultery, corruption, avarice and fraud; the other renounces these things. We cannot be friends of both.... But we believe that it is better to hate our present possessions."[62]

The basic practical aim of the Church was to christianize the world; that is, not to flee it so much as subdue it, forcing it to use rightly even the goods of this earth. When, however, it seemed impossible to thus master the world, the Christian, by deserting it, fled the danger of being dominated in his turn.

"The brave Germanicus [although a youth] ... eager to leave as soon as possible the society of unjust and evil men [the pagans] attracted the wild beast, provoking it to attack him."[63] This was certainly a rigid application of the ascetic

---

60. *Orat.*, XXVI, 1.
61. *2 Clem.*, V.
62. *Ib.*, VI.
63. *Mart. Pol.*, III, 1.

ideal of opposition to the world in its concrete expression as the social and civil organization which was persecuting him.

And another martyr, out of hatred for the world, had already arrived at a principle of amazing force: "nothing that we see is lasting. . . . " Christianity, when it becomes a mark of hatred for the world, is "not a work of passivity but of greatness."[64]

The anti-Christian world was ugly and low; Christianity hurled in its face the challenge of its own greatness of soul.

WAR AND MILITARY SERVICE

"All the world," groaned St. Cyprian, "is wet with fraternal blood; and murder, when it is committed by private citizens, is a crime; if it is committed by the state it is called valor: this means that it is not the stamp of innocence but the vastness of the slaughter which bestows impunity on crimes."[65] Thus all kingdoms, including that of the Romans, were born of crime and violence, and their development has been similar to their origin.[66]

The Roman state was a military one built by weapons and developed by wars; and the emperor was the head of the army, while the Empire was founded "on a theology of imperial victory."[67] Certainly, therefore, it could not accept the judgment which condemned war as crime on a large scale. Nor could many other pagan societies accept it.[68]

But the Carthaginian bishop, and with him the majority of those who incidentally touch upon the subject, were looking

---

64. Ignatius, *Rom.*, III, 3.
65. *Ep.*, I, 6; *P. L.*, IV, 205.
66. Cyprian, *Quod idola dii non sint*, V.
67. J. Gagé, "La théologie de la victoire impériale," *Revue historique*, CLXXI, 1933, 1-43.
68. The ancient Germans believed that whoever died in combat was received into Valhalla no matter what the morality of his life had been; this is bellicosity carried to a paroxysm of brutality and ferocity (cf. F. Wagner, *Les poèmes mythologiques de l'Edda*, p. 5). We find a similar belief among the ancient Japanese and Mohammedans, etc. Christianity transfigures this: whoever dies in that battle of faith which is martyrdom is received among the saints, that death being a kind of new baptism which purifies him of every guilt.

to the Christian ideal, which is an ideal of peace. War is violation of charity; it severs brotherhood and annuls sacramental and ecclesiastical kinship. Wars are made for lust of power or greed for wealth, "while peace and charity, simple and quiet sisters, have no need of weapons."

Since the Church's ideal is peace, the Roman Empire, a military organization with an ideal of victory, could not view it with a favorable eye. Celsus was interpreting the sentiment of the ruling classes when he called the Christian a kind of deserter who took up arms to defend the emperor quite unwillingly. On this point there really was a cleavage between the two orders.

Origen does not refute Celsus' charge; he justifies it. Military service, he argues, is murder, and for this reason the Christians will have none of it. They are moved by a religious feeling similar to that which exempts the priests of the idols from bearing arms in order that they may not offer sacrifices "with bloody hands, fouled with slaughter." The Christians have much greater reason to be exempted for they are "priests and worshipers of God, who, keeping their hands pure, fight with prayers before God, thus waging war for those who campaign for a just cause and those who govern according to justice, and their aim is to overthrow all the opposition set in the way of those who act with justice."[69]

Origen, therefore, accepts real loyalty to the state but not military service. The Christian's military service takes the form of prayer. He does not offer it unconditionally, however, but only when the conflict is in conformity with justice and the authorities in no way offend justice; in short, only in the case of a just war. He accepts a just war, but not military service! That distinction can be made as long as the Christians are a minority in the state; but what happens when the state is completely Christian?

---

69. *C. Cels.*, VIII, 73.

Origen, by a process of logical and abstract deduction, reasons that in a Christian universe (which he did not consider impossible or too difficult of attainment) there should be no more wars. Conflicts are inspired by devils who make men violate treaties and disturb the peace. But wherever the Christians are active the devils are overthrown and therefore the causes of war disappear.

If the Romans had the Christian faith, "they would conquer their enemies with prayer; they would not fight in battle at all, since that divine Power would defend them which once promised to preserve five cities unharmed for fifty just men."[70] In short, God would fight for the Romans if they became just, Christians. Celsus had said it was impossible for the Romans to adopt Christianity since the God of the Christians was not a warrior god and had permitted Jews and Christians to be miserably overcome.[71]

This is another way, then, in which the Christians serve society, i.e ., with "just prayers" and austere morals. These are spiritual weapons and with them they fight for the emperor more than his other subjects do. They do not fight *under* him "even though he might wish to force them to" (for Origen war is murder and therefore to be rejected at all costs) but they fight *for* him with prayer. Only in this sense may the Christians also take up arms "for the fatherland."[72] If Celsus had read that reply he would have been horrified. Origen answered his appeal that the Christians take up arms for their sovereign with abstractions that bordered on the utopian. He was looking at the problem more as a theorist concerned only about his logic than as a student of society.[73] He failed

70. Cf. Gen. 18:26.

71. *C. Cels.*, VIII, 69-70.

72. *Ib.*, VIII, 73, 74. F. Cavallera has attempted to justify Origen's opinions, "La doctrine d'Origène sur les rapports du christianisme et de la société civile," *Bulletin de litt. eccl.*, 1937, 30-39.

73. — Whence do we come? — We come from every side called by Jesus, at whose command we convert the weapons and instincts of war into the tools and attitudes of peace (as Isaias and Micheas prophesied): "We no longer take up arms against nations, nor do we any longer learn to wage war, for we have been

to make the proper distinctions, and in the heat of argument he forgot that even in a completely christianized world the influence of original sin would still be active, and one of its manifestations is war.

Tertullian's attitude toward military service, due to his own personal rigorism, eventually contradicts his own previous statements and the actual practice of the Church. The Church did not disturb the soldier's conscience with discussions concerning the legitimacy of his profession. She was satisfied if he exercised it in a Christian spirit, that is, without hatred, abstaining from idolatrous acts[74] and divesting himself of that greed for plunder which for centuries converted every passage of troops through a country into disaster for the population. She asked the soldiers attached to the administrative offices or local garrisons also to conduct themselves with uprightness and moderation.

In 211, when Scapula begins his violent persecution, Tertullian considers it a proof of his belief that there can never be any conciliation between Christian society and the pagan system. It seems that soldiers were gathered in the plain of Lambesis to receive the *donativum* distributed on the occasion of the accession of Caracalla and Geta to the throne. The soldiers presented themselves "wearing on their heads a laurel wreath or crown. But one of them, a soldier of God more than of men, and more consistent than the other brethren, who had presumed to be able to serve two masters (Caesar and Christ), bare-headed with the useless wreath in his hand, shone in solitary splendor, revealing himself a Christian by that very act."

Before his officers he confesses who he is and asserts his

---

made through Jesus the sons of peace: for he is our leader instead of the generals of our nation" (Origen, *C. Cels.*, V, 33). We can see that there was danger here of falling from pagan monism, which identified religion with politics, into a Christian monism that would absorb politics in religion.

74. This was not easy. The soldiers had their own particular deities (Hercules, Mars, Victory, etc.) and worshipped their standards also, in each of which there was a "genius" and which were kept in shrines. The Roman eagle was adored as the image of the emperor.

duty not to adorn himself like the others; and before the pre-
fects, he casts off (or they strip from him) the "heavy, cumbersome" armor of the soldier, including "the sword which is not
necessary for the defense of the Lord"; and "now, purple-clad
with the hope of shedding his blood, shod with the preparation
of the Gospel, girt with the much sharper word of God, armed
from head to foot with the precept of the Apostle, and crowned,
more purposefully, with the shining diadem of martyrdom, he
awaits in prison the largesse of Christ."[75]

This episode — which after all concerns only one Christian
among all the other "brothers" — is an expression of Tertullian's radicalism. He makes service to Christ incompatible
with service to Caesar and places the soldiers in a dilemma:
they must be either soldiers or Christians. Instead of rejecting
as the other apologists do the antithesis formulated by their
adversaries, Tertullian makes it his own and defines it with a
radicalism which, though it was originally inspired by the
idolatry implicit in the military wreath and military service in
general, had in it the seeds of dissolution for any civil society,
the seeds of real political revolution.

To defend his thesis that the wreath is idolatrous, Tertullian
knows that he cannot use the Scriptures, which contain no prohibition to adorn the head with flowers. He says that he is
basing his argument on tradition, which, in the practice of the
faith, has the force of a norm and a law. With his usual skill,
he fortifies himself with brilliant sophisms: flowers on the head
are against nature because they were made to be smelled and
therefore to be placed, ungarlanded, beneath and not above
the nose; the natural law gives testimony of and takes the place
of the divine law. But then he leaves aside this play of sophistry
and takes up the thesis that lies nearest his heart: can the
Christians be soldiers? The answer is no, because they cannot
place a human oath before a divine oath; they cannot have
any other master after Christ; they cannot renounce their father

---

75. *De corona*, I.

and mother, to whom they owe the greatest honor after God, and they cannot renounce their neighbor to whom they owe love; they cannot use the sword, which bears Christ's condemnation, whereby he who wounds with the sword perishes by the sword; they are obliged not to engage in combat, being sons of peace, bound not even to quarrel; they may not make others suffer chains and imprisonment and torture, for they are forbidden to take revenge even for personal injuries; they may not guard the temples which they renounced in baptism and protect by night the demons which they put to flight by day with exorcisms; they may not, in short, commit a series of acts which are contrary to religion and morality. A soldier who becomes a Christian must either leave the service or face martyrdom. For Jesus, "both the soldier is a faithful pagan, and the pagan a faithful soldier." The military profession is irreconcilable with the duties of the faith. The Christian belongs to the supernal city, the heavenly Jerusalem, and not to the earthly city (that is, Rome). If the latter laughs, he weeps. In conclusion, he is no longer merely a pilgrim in a foreign land; he is an enemy in the country of others.

It is not surprising that Tertullian had left the Church when he wrote like this. For heresy in those days consisted in isolating one or two Christian elements and carrying them to extremes. Usually, it lost sight of charity, which marks the limit for the various precepts of the faith.

The Church followed neither Origen nor Tertullian on this point. From the time of Pope Soter she has rather boasted of the loyalty and merits of Christian soldiers and she celebrated the miracle wrought in the thirst-ridden army of Marcus Aurelius by the prayers of the Christian soldiers in the *legio fulminans,* whose plea for rain God granted.[76]

---

76. The miracle is pictured on the Antonine Column in Rome, where it is attributed to the gods. Perhaps an echo of this is to be seen in Cyprian: The Christians have their possessions in God.... *Et tamen pro arcendis hostibus et imbribus impetrandis et vel auferendis vel temperandis adversis, rogamus semper et preces fundimus, et pro pace ac salute vestra propitiantes ac placantes Deum diebus ac noctibus iugiter ac instanter oramus (Ad Demetr.,* XX).

CHAPTER VIII

RATIONAL EDUCATION

PRINCIPLES AND OBJECTIVES OF CHRISTIAN PEDAGOGY

THE aim of classical education was to form an ideal man, or better, citizen, according to a rational program of virtue (ἀρετή, *virtus*). Virtue was taken to mean the sum of one's natural and moral endowments, the balanced combination of which resulted in virile beauty and goodness (καλοκἀγαθία). In fact, the term implied a harmonious composite of physical beauty, nobility of birth, health, wealth, control over the passions, fortitude and above all moderation in all things. Thus these attributes were the object of an educational effort exercised only on free and wealthy citizens and denied to the humble laborers, to those conquered in the struggle for existence, to the slaves and barbarians[1] who, conversely, were the κακοί (the wicked).

In this humanistic type, beauty and wisdom or goodness were convertible terms, and goodness was the equivalent of usefulness, success, well-being; in short, *eudaemonia.* Aristotle considered that the requisites for happiness were friends, wealth, political influence, noble birth, handsome sons, personal beauty, fame, etc.[2] Seneca added an elegant house, a beautiful wife, lands and money for trade. Martial would have also liked a fortune acquired not by labor or effort but through some inheritance, a profitable estate, a fire always burning on

---

1. Cf. A. J. Festugière, *L'idéal religieux des Grecs et l'Évangile,* Introduction: *L'idéal grec.* Cf. also Clement of Alexandria, *Strom.,* II, 21 (*P. G.,* VIII, 1073). According to the Aristotelians, "neither the man who is poor, or without fame, nor the sickly man nor one who is a slave is happy." This is quite different from the evangelical beatitudes!

2. *Eth. Nic.,* I, 8, 1099.

184

the hearth, rare social calls, a healthy body, prudent sincerity, friendship, serenity, etc.[3]

This well-being, as we see, was the ideal aspiration of an ethical system which derived its law from man and took nature as its model. Therefore, in actual practice its brightness was pierced with the sharp and terrible shadows of ego-worship, social injustice and corruption, which perverted this eudaemonia and made it hedonism, while an implacable fate shed the poison of mystery and death over man's every day. Besides, this fusion of physical and moral health, of religious, civil and military virtues, of leisure and political activity was, along with the whole body of philosophy, the educational endowment of a privileged minority; it was virtue that found expression only among persons of equal rank. Whenever slaves or poor people were concerned, *virtus* no longer had any *raison-d'être*, or it was expressed in different degree; for they were not the "good and beautiful" but the mob not permitted the leisure of the wise man, the wicked, *les gens qu'on ne reçoit pas.*[4]

Christianity is theology and, unlike the pagan religions, it is also ethics. It teaches God to man and it teaches man the way to pattern himself after his Creator. Christ, the Logos, is a teacher: he teaches the kingdom of heaven and the way of life we must follow to reach it. He is the pedagogue *par excellence;* and the Christian writers who shape the new society seek in the Gospel the rules for practical living, omitting not a single act in the Christian's day, either when he is alone with his own conscience or when his actions relate to his neighbor. Christian pedagogy is born as instruction in the way to live a good life, to make our daily acts reflect God. And it also produces teachers: Justin, Aristides, Panthenus, Clement, Bardesanes, Origen; in a sense, every episcopal see becomes a school.

The Christian attitude toward pagan education, which, in the period that concerns us here, boasted teachers like Quintilian and

---

3. *Epigrams,* X, 47.
4. Festugière, *op. cit.,* p. 33.

Plutarch, varied, of course, according to temperaments, times and places. A stern and ascetic moralist like Tertullian or one with a Jewish background like Pseudo-Barnabas does not trouble himself to educate according to the Graeco-Roman program, or rather, according to its naturalistic principle. From the ethical point of view, he attaches no importance whatever to physical beauty, political power or economic wealth. But this is a cenobitic ideal, which it was easy for the *simpliciores* to accept, for they were already excluded by tradition from the benefits of the Greek system of education. When, however, in another African center, where he unwittingly acts as a corrective for Tertullian's rigorism, Clement of Alexandria finds that he must lecture on pedagogy to an audience composed of philosophers, rhetoricians, elegant youths, sumptuous ladies and middle-class people imbued with Hellenic maxims, he feels that just as he cannot ignore the values of Greek education in philosophy neither can he do so in the matter of pedagogy, which is its practical application. And just as the rich pagans took lessons from philosophers, whom they considered their spiritual directors, so the wealthy Christians, or those inclined to Christianity, took lessons from Christian philosophers; and neither the one nor the others felt it necessary to abandon the traditional ideal. In the Church everybody was a philosopher, rich and poor, old men and children, as we have seen, because the Gospel was the true philosophy and by its virtue the Christians possessed the key to all of truth. But in the Alexandrian *Didaskaleion* we see the recurrence of an intellectual *élite,* the return of the Greek παιδεία, reserved for a minority. The difference is that this *paideia* is christianized; that is, it becomes, practically speaking, a mixture of philosophic maxims and Biblical apothegms directed to the education of the Christian.

Clement has in mind to form a man living after the image of God according to reason; that is, to train him to regulate every act of his mind, his emotions and his body according to the teaching of the Logos, Reason, which is personified in Christ. This is rationality derived from Greek philosophy but directed toward another end, thanks to the fact that Reason was identified with the Founder of Christianity, who was represented as the divine Pedagogue. This concept inspires the famous treatise called precisely *Paedagogus,* which is the first systematic treatise on Christian pedagogy.

THE COMPLETENESS OF THE *"Paideia"*

This Christian education is concerned with the whole personality, molding the individual's inner life and his social and religious relations according to a standard of perfect equilibrium, of measure, which affects his physical life also; for the pupil in this system is sound and vigorous in mind and body. Far from permitting any kind of excess, this pedagogy seeks moderation in all things[5] and so is "forceful but not forced."[6] It fashions the ideal type of man by alternating gentleness and severity, praise and blame, by repressing his evil passions and developing his good tendencies, by mixing love and fear in intelligent doses.

In actual practice, this is a handbook of good behavior which starts with the spirit and regulates the daily acts of life, casting them in the unity and universality of the religious ethics of Christianity. It must have helped minds imbued with classical education to approach Christianity, presented to them as a system of rational morality, and at the same time, with its detailed maxims and its instructions for every eventuality of the day, it injected Christian virtue into the social organism

---

5. Ἡ συμμετρία, ἣν πανταχοῦ βοηθὸν ἐπικαλούμεθα τῷ βίῳ (moderation, which we call the universal mainstay of daily life), *Paed.,* III, 9 (*P. G.,* VIII, 620).

6. *Paed.,* I, 12 (*P. G.,* VIII, 369): Οὐ γὰρ ὑπέρτονος ἡ τοιάδε ἀγωγὴ τοῦ Λόγου, ἀλλ' εὔτονος. Another definition which echoes those of the Greek philosophers is *ib.,* III, 12 (664):
Ἡ δὲ ἀρίστη ἀγωγὴ εὐταξία ἐστί, παντελὴς οὖσα εὐσχημοσύνη, καὶ δύναμις τεταγμένη βεβαία, τῶν ἑξῆς ἀλλήλοις κειμένων ἐν ἔργῳ καλῶς ἀποδοτική, κατ' ἀρετὴν ἀνυπέρβλητος.

with the help and protection of the rational and natural ethics of the ancients.

If the *paideia* of old produced harmony between private and public life, the new education realizes a greater harmony which includes a man's individual conscience, his civil life and his life in the Church. Its objective is to create a person who, in all these three phases of living, acts in conformity with a single ethical aim. He may not change his morality by changing his place of abode, like the cuttle-fish, which is said to match any rock to which it clings. In all his daily relations the Christian must be as he is in Church: pious, chaste and charitable. After singing praises to God he cannot sing obscene songs or indulge in frivolous chatter with the pagan sentiment, "Eat and drink today, for tomorrow we die!" Whoever holds this thought is already dead to God.[7]

In short, it might be said that the Church is always everywhere. In fact, the "didaskaleion" *par excellence* is the Church; the pedagogy *par excellence* is religion in so far as it is "knowledge of God's worship, instruction for learning the truth, right education which leads to heaven."[8] "It is right ordering of truth to the contemplation of God and the pattern of holy conduct in the eternal dwelling-place."[9] Our last end, therefore, lies beyond the orbit of earthly existence in the eternal supernatural.

The gymnasiarch is the Logos who forms us "in simplicity, modesty, and, in a general sense, in love of liberty, humanity and beauty, so that we are like to God by means of our virtue. — Labor and do not be discouraged, for you shall become what you dare not hope to be. For there is one mode of training philosophers, one for training rhetoricians, another for athletes; so is there still another which is the training of Christ and results in a generous disposition, suitable to the noble act of choice. It regulates all our actions: our gait, our reclining, the

---

7. *Paed.*, III, 11 (*P. G.*, VIII, 657-60).
8. *Ib.*, I, 7 (*P. G.*, VIII, 313).
9. *Ib.*, I, 7.

food we take, our sleep, our going to bed, our regimen and the rest of our daily life. This education by the Logos is not over-strained, but sweet and harmonious."[10]

Clement seems to have been successful enough in his attempt to reconcile the Greek with the Christian ideal. He has looked at life approvingly; he has christianized pedagogy and made it the preparation for a new social life in charity and spiritual equality; he has purified beauty, seeking to spiritualize it, and he has not rejected but rather cultivated, in virtue, the very health and beauty of the body. He dreamed of a serene fusion of the old and the new centered about the Logos, Christ, a synthesis of matter and spirit, of the rights of the individual and the rights of the community. With smiling gratitude he took what was good and beautiful from all about him.

Then, in the *Stromata,* he sketched the perfect type among the mass of average Christians, the *gnostic,* in order to set against the false gnostics of his day the Christian who realizes in himself the perfect equilibrium of all virtues; and principal among these are apathy, of a slightly Stoic flavor, understood to be a serene detachment from the interests and affections of the world, and secondly charity, essentially Christian, which keeps apathy from freezing into egoism and makes it instead an instrument of action.

Free Will and Virtue

The essential difference between Christian and Stoic virtue lies in the freedom of the will and its attendant personal responsibility, which principle the Christian apologists energetically defend in the face of deterministic pagan philosophy. Even an intellect tainted with heresy, like Bardesanes, joins in this defense.

The Stoic also makes a heroic effort to achieve an inner liberty of his own; but his effort is based on extreme pride which makes him withdraw from the multitude and shut him-

---

10. *Ib.,* I, 12.

self up in the ivory tower of an impassiveness that remains undisturbed even in the face of death. This is the opposite of becoming all things to all men. For charity, whose most forceful interpreter is the ex-Pharisee of Tarsus, is centrifugal; *ataraxia,* the expression of Stoic wisdom, is egocentric. The former is a four-way lodge thrown open to all outside who suffer; the latter is a house whose doors and windows are bolted against the grief and pain of brothers.

The two have a different basis: charity is born of humility, which obliges us to purify ourselves so that we may feel we are nothing but creatures in the hands of God. *Ataraxia* is born of pride, which rejects God's help and stands on its own strength alone.

On this point Christianity offered radical opposition to Stoicism, and to all extra-Christian thought. It might be said that this is one of the marks of distinction, in fact, the most characteristic difference from the moral point of view between the Christian system and all others. It is associated with the concept of sin and redemption, from which man derives his feeling of humility and his dignity. He is responsible because he is free; and Christianity is a system which guards and strengthens that freedom, the requisite of an eternal destiny.[11] Christian authors defend this point in constant and vigorous polemics, addressed not only to the pagans but also to the heretics. Heresies, especially in this field, seem pagan contaminations of Christianity.

That set of heresies which flourished in the second and third centuries particularly and are known by the term Gnosticism had accepted the slavery of absolute fatalism, of Heimarmene, with overwhelming moral consequences that in some cases resulted in monstrousness. Man was no longer responsible for his salvation, which was made subject instead to the

---

11. *Est ergo omnis creatura rationabilis laudis et culpae capax; laudis, si, secundum rationem quam in se habet, ad meliora proficiat; culpae, si rationem recti tenoremque declinet: propter quod recte etiam poenis et suppliciis subiacet. Quod etiam de ipso diabolo et his qui cum ipso sunt et dicuntur eius angeli, sentiendum est* (Origen, *Peri Archon,* I, 5, 2).

tyranny of the stars.[12] With regard to salvation men were divided into three classes: 1) the *hylici* who are not saved; 2) the *psychici* who may in some cases be saved; and 3) the *pneumatici*, who are saved no matter what they do, "a privileged people, a chosen seed, the Church elect, the sons of Kings. . . ."[13]

Almost all the Christian writers defended the freedom of the will against pagans and heretics. They understood that this was the key to the basic problem existing between the new religion and all the rest.[14]

Virtue makes us like God, but only because it is the fruit of an effort that is as courageous as it is free.

"The nobility of truth, judged in the beautiful nature of the soul, marks the slave, not by the fact of being bought or sold, but by the fact his spirit is not free. It is fitting for us not to seem but to be free, being educated by God and adopted by God. Therefore, at rest and in motion, in our gait and in our dress, in short in all the acts of life we must conduct ourselves in the greatest freedom possible."[15]

The pedagogy of the Logos is a process of regeneration, of becoming perfect; it transfers man from the corruptible to the incorruptible, but it does so through a free act of his own will, which is determined to tear him free from the slavery of tradition, customs and prejudices.[16] "Acts which are not free are not to be judged. Whether they be done through ignorance or necessity, they involve no condemnation. . . ."[17]

Man is not born virtuous by nature nor does he become so by merely growing up. He becomes virtuous only if he wills

---

12. From Exodus, 4:21, they deduced *non esse in potestate nostra ut salvemur* (Origen, *Peri Archon*, III, 1, 8); this was later adopted by Protestantism.

13. Cf. H. C. Puèch, "Où en est le problème du gnosticisme?" *Revue de l'univ. de Bruxelles*, 1934, 298 ff.

14. Origen, who repeatedly rises in defense of the freedom of the will, adds that there is also "a blameworthy freedom and a praiseworthy slavery," for we may be free from or slaves to justice, wisdom, mercy, etc. (*Ep. ad Rom.*, VI, 5). He is toying with words.

15. Clem. of Alex., *Paed.*, III, 11 (*P. G.*, VIII, 632-3).

16. *Ib.*, I, 7.

17. *Id.*, *Strom.*, II, 14.

to, and virtue is a good which no one may take from him unless he consents. Sin is not to be attributed to the devil; temptation is the devil's but the sin must be attributed to the one who commits it. As a consequence praise or blame follow good or wicked actions.

Freedom of the will does not exclude the action of grace; in fact, "God helps the virtuous man, honoring him with the most attentive care ... breathing into him who has resolved to lead a good life, the strength to attain salvation.... As the doctor cures those who coöperate with him in regaining their health, so God gives eternal salvation to whoever coöperates with him in order to possess knowledge and good works."[18]

Liberty is a requisite of rationality: "every rational soul is endowed with a will that is free and the power of choice."[19] Reason serves to discern liberty and to choose between good and evil. Education can accomplish a great deal on this point; it can transform the most lecherous and savage beings into models of continence and meekness.[20]

In defending free will, which makes God no longer responsible for the evil in the world, the orthodox Christians are united. This was the point on which the heretics deviated from orthodoxy just as it was the point of ethical difference between paganism and Christianity. It can be said that Christianity, by introducing the principle of moral responsibility with its consequences in eternity, elevated man's dignity and made him judge between two extremes, and at the same time it educated him to generous sentiments, tempered his spirit for the struggle and revealed to him the secret of resistance.

CHARACTER

The point of departure even for pre-Christian morality was the virtues of "courage, prudence, judgment, justice, forti-

---

18. *Strom.*, VII, 7 (*P. G.*, VIII, 468).
19. Origen, *Peri Archon*, I, *Praef.*, 5.
20. *Ib.*, III, i, 3-5.

tude, patience, continence, and above all piety."[21] These virtues follow and condition one another. Although their possession depends upon our own will, yet there are circumstances which hinder their exercise. The most serious of these are sickness and poverty. Not all men, caught between illness and virtue, are able to dominate the former and at the same time not neglect the latter, "and if one does not resist it is as if he fled."

Sickness is to be conquered by strengthening the spirit so that it rules the body in all cases. "Do not, therefore, fear the illnesses that threaten you, nor the company of old age which the years bring you; even sickness will cease if we do the will of God with all our hearts. Knowing this, dispose your soul to be strong against sickness; be as courageous as the strenuous fighter in the stadium, to overcome your trials with indomitable fortitude. Do not allow yourself to be depressed with sadness, neither through sickness nor any other misfortune which may overtake you. . . . "[22]

"Let the same be said of poverty, because it also distracts the mind from what is necessary, that is, from contemplation and the avoidance of sin; and it obliges him who has not completely consecrated himself to God through charity to earn his sustenance. Good health, on the other hand, and the possession of the necessities of life keep the soul free and independent if it knows how to use earthly goods wisely. . . . We must be busy with material concerns not for themselves, but for the body, the care of which is required by the very care of the soul, to which all things must tend."[23] The true gnostic, who has made his soul the temple of the Spirit, "rises against every fear, every danger, not only of death, but also of poverty, sickness and dishonor."[24]

---

21. *Strom.*, II, 18.
22. *Id., Fragm.* V (44).
23. *Strom.*, IV, 5.
24. *Ib.*, VII, 11 (*P. G.*, IX, 489).

Our worst enemies are our passions "great antagonists, Olympic champions," against which we must fight indomitably if we wish to keep our peace and liberty.[25]

Thus virtue engages in free combat; it molds character, it makes man a "true athlete," in the stadium of the universe.[26]

HYGIENE, BEAUTY, HEALTH

It was a characteristic of Marcionism and various other heretical movements to condemn matter, and therefore the body, as being associated with evil; and they ended by exacting the cessation of physical life, that is, of life on earth. Even Tertullian, already imbued with Montanist asceticism, vehemently condemns so absurd a doctrine, which would ultimately rob the Church also of its members. The body has been truly consecrated by Christianity because it is the instrument of the soul's perfection, and it is destined with the soul to be sanctified first and then to rise, just as, with the soul, it was directly created by God. It is through the flesh that the soul may exercise its directive influence, enjoy the gifts of nature, wealth, "nourishment," and experience the gamut of the sensations.[27]

It remains a basic Christian thought that the health of the body must be cared for and also its beauty, if it has any, as being a gift of God. But this care must be governed by morality; these are not ends but means to our true end, which is the sanctification of the soul. We must take a religious care of the body to make it a collaborator of the Spirit, a temple of the Spirit, destined to rise again. It must be kept chaste; we must not adulterate it in life with the counterfeit of cosmetics and theatrical make-up, and in death, it must not be cremated because the noble work of the Creator may not be destroyed. The body contributes to the most lofty dignity of man, whom God loves with a special love since he created him

---

25. *Ib.*, II, 20 (*P. G.*, VIII, 1065).
26. *Ib.*, VII, 3 (*P. G.*, IX, 424).
27. Tertullian, *De resurr. carnis*, VII. Cf. his *De carne Christi*.

directly with his own hands while all other beings were created at his mere command.[28]

The Alexandrian examines the whole problem with the feelings of a Christian and the mentality of a Greek philosopher; he also argues with the Marcionites, who, out of contempt for the Creator of the body and matter, inveigh against their own flesh and go so far as to give it over to a vain death, offering their bodies in a false and useless martyrdom. "Let them know that a well-regulated body contributes to intellectual beauty. Therefore Plato, in the third book of the *Republic,* so often wrongly quoted in argument against procreation, affirms the obligation to 'take care of the body for the harmony of the soul'; hence whoever preaches the truth must live and live rightly; for it is through life and health that one may arrive at *gnosis.*"[29] This is an explicit affirmation of the value of existence and health, linked philosophically with the values of the life of the soul.

"The free flower of health is beauty." But this is attained by sobriety, which beautifies the mind with good morals and flowers externally in true physical beauty, and also by movement and exercise, which favor the circulation of the blood and the elimination of toxic materials[30] — exercise but not athleticism.

Naturally, for the Christian it is not this beauty that fades which has substantial value, but the beauty of spiritual grace, of virtue, which never ages. This the Church educates, adorning it with intellectual beauty too by means of instruction

---

28. Clem. of Alex., *Paed.,* I, 3.

29. *Id., Strom.,* IV, 4.

30. *Paed.,* III, 11 (*P. G., VIII,* 640): Ἄνθος δὲ τῆς ὑγιείας ἐλευθέριον τὸ κάλλος. Festugière (*op. cit.,* p. 31, n. 12) recalls that Greek ἀγαθία is also καλοκἀγαθία; and that Greek morality therefore includes the care of the body. The author of the Discourse to Demonicus (14) lists the duties toward the body after those toward the gods and parents: "Attend to the exercise of the body, not to those which aim only at acquiring strength, but those which bring health" (ὑγίειαν); and he advises his readers not to exercise to the point of weariness. *Hygiene* is an essentially Greek word and idea and is part and parcel of the classical *paedeia.*

which is offered, as Athenagoras notes, even to humble women. The beauty of the intellect is not at all opposed to physical beauty, which, far from being considered evil, is to be contemplated as the work of "the hand and mind of God," the Supreme Artist; hence "the more beautiful the body is, the more it is worthy of respect," the respect which protects its loveliness from obscene and destructive abuses.[31]

But true beauty patterns itself after God;[32] it is the imitation of the Absolute, a value of the spirit, not of the body. There must be perfect harmony between the interior and the exterior, not a hypocritical falsification; the spirit is the master and the flesh is the slave. Christ humiliated his Flesh; yet, through it he redeemed the flesh of all of us for the resurrection.[33]

Good Greek that he is, Clement appreciates the value of gymnastic exercises, which, he says, are good for young people's health and excite the desire for glory, thereby benefiting at the same time the health of the body and the joyousness of the spirit. Hence they are factors in that harmonious, natural and salutary development of body and soul which is the central aim of his pedagogy. He is a good psychologist too. He affirms that "the gymnasium is enough for boys, even though the baths be available"; but sports must be graduated according to age, sex and circumstances. Wrestling and racing are not suitable for a woman, and her natural exercises are feminine tasks; suitable exercises for a man are wrestling, playing ball, especially in the sunshine, walks in the country, excursions into the city, reading aloud, besides occupations copied, and not ignobly in truth, from agricultural labor, such as hoeing, going to draw water, splitting wood, fishing, etc.[34]

Sports, however, must never be indulged in to the detriment of health (as, for example, when one becomes exhausted, for

31. *Suppl.*, XXXIV.
32. With regard to beauty cf. also what is said of womanhood in chapter IX of this volume.
33. Clem. of Alex., *Paed.*, III, 1 (*P. G.*, VIII, 555 ff.).
34. *Ib.*, III, 10.

weariness from the point of view of health is equivalent to idleness and opposed to leisure) nor of other more important and noble activities. Neither must their object be vainglory, but health; and therefore they must be engaged in with moderation and (as in wrestling) with all fairness and without cunning or tricks.[35]

The baths in those days were great centers for recreation and the display of luxury. But the Alexandrian does not condemn them for this reason. Being a good Greek he appreciates the usefulness of the bath and the fact that for his countrymen, and especially for his audience, it is a necessity. He knows that people frequent baths for four reasons: for cleanliness, to cool and refresh the body, for health, and for lust. Only the last motive is to be condemned. Women should bathe for cleanliness and health; men only for hygienic reasons, for baths taken merely for refreshment are superfluous and weakening to their strength. In all cases, there should be moderation.[36]

Because it excites sexual emotions, mixed bathing is to be condemned[37] and still more to be condemned are those baths where the women denude themselves in public and have the slaves massage them. The men should mortify them, fleeing their sight and blushing for them. All the water in the pools cannot wash away so much lewdness.[38]

Side by side with this moderate care of the body through bathing and exercise, we have ascetic instruction in the mortification of the body, by fasting and other austerities. The Alexandrian also recommends moderation in food, but he is still concerned with health, which is endangered by over-indulgence in eating. Another tendency, which is sometimes fused

---

35. Cf. p. 62 of the present volume.
36. *Paed.*, III, 9 (*P. G.*, VIII, 617). Polycarp knew that the Apostle St. John took baths and that one day at Ephesus he rushed from the building when he learned that Cerinthus, the "enemy of truth," had entered it, fearing that the whole edifice would collapse on his head (Irenaeus, *Adv. haer.*, III, 3, 4).
37. Cyprian forbade virgins to go to the mixed baths (*De hab. virg.*, XIX).
38. Clem. of Alex., *Paed.*, III, 5.

with and sometimes distinct from the first, varying with different temperaments, is captained by Tertullian,[39] who counsels
rigorous corporal discipline for sinners as a means of expiation.
The basic teaching of the Church on this point declares care
of the health reasonable and physical penances heroic. But the
Alexandrian teacher has in his head the Greek idea of the
golden mean, the *aurea mediocritas*.

From the ethical point of view, food has a most conspicu-
ous importance. Man does not live to eat: he is not his belly.
The purpose of food is not to develop voluptuousness but to
contribute to two vital factors in his life, health and strength;
this means "just" strength, naturally, for that of the professional athlete is extravagant, hence he makes the meal a particular necessity.

Like Seneca and the physician Antiphanes, who maintained
that the majority of diseases were caused by complicated dishes,
Clement exalts frugality and condemns the excessive use of
condiments. He shows that dainties and tidbits are not nourishment and he, too, states that "the single cause of illness is the
variety of foods."[40]

Thus Christianity on the one hand rejected the excesses and
extravagances of a culinary art that was associated with appalling economic injustice, and on the other hand it reëstablished the legitimacy of all natural foods in contrast to the
various Jewish prohibitions. All foods are good; abuses and
excesses are morally bad, and adulterations are harmful to
health.[41] Thus it was not a question of food but of moderation.

Origen says that many Christians follow the maxim of the
Pythagorean Sextus: "whether or not one eats flesh-meat is

---

39. *De poenitentia.*
40. Clem. of Alex., *Paed.*, II, 1 (*P. G.*, VIII, 380).
41. Like St. Paul and the Pythagoreans, Clement thinks it is well not to eat
meat or drink wine; however, he who does so does not sin. The important
thing is to do these things with moderation. He recommends onions, olives,
greens, milk, cheese, fruit, and when necessary, roast or boiled meat (*Paed.*,
II, 1). In short, he is a vegetarian, or a "nature food" exponent, for he thought
vegetables were better raw.

immaterial, but to abstain from it is more rational." However, whether one eats meat or not, the important thing is to use it with reason, for nourishment and not for gluttony; because even in eating we glorify God.[42] This is a far cry from the exaggerations of some heretics and rigorists who attached capital importance to the selection of certain foods and abstention from others.

DRESS, COSMETICS AND LUXURIES

Various non-Christian ascetics used to dress simply in nothing but white linen. Among them were the "therapeutae," and, in the third century especially, the Neo-Pythagoreans.

Dress must serve to cover the body and not to adorn it. It is a means and not an end. Rich dress is an image of false beauty, a kind of slavery to public opinion, a repudiation of true beauty and elegance. In fact, since the purpose of clothing is to protect the body from cold and heat and to cover the private parts, there is no reason why men's clothing should differ from women's, just as the food which they take to nourish themselves does not differ, its purpose being the same in one and in the other. If there is any concession to be made, then women may be permitted the use of softer materials, but not elaborate costumes made of silk, or dyed, or embroidered with gold. Dye is an adulteration of nature and serves to encourage the corruption of morals, while it adds nothing to the protective properties of the cloth and is a blameworthy thing because it excites concupiscence through the sight. On the other hand, white and simple garments are those suitable for innocent and simple souls.[43]

For moral reasons, dresses must not be too short (they should come at least below the knee) and women would do well to cover all parts of the body, even the neck, and not wear purple dresses, which excite lust. The precious and rare

42. *C. Cels.*, VIII, 30, 31.
43. Clem. of Alex., *Paed.*, II, 10.

materials used by capricious women and effeminate men are an offense against modesty. The teacher of the *Didaskaleion* does not even consider the interests involved in the silk and dyeing industries and the manufacture of purple dye; he sees only the ethical side of the question, and so far as this is concerned it seems to him that elegant clothing is bought at the price of human dignity. Like the Stoics, he asks his audience to consider that the person is more precious than his garments; as the "statue is more precious than the temple, the soul more precious than the body, and the body more precious than its dress." Instead individuals pay ten thousand talents for clothes, who, if they were to be sold, would not bring a thousand Attic drachmas, a sign that they consider themselves to be of less value than their apparel.[44] Opposition to excessive expenditure for objects of luxury was of benefit, directly or indirectly, to society at large.

Sobriety, therefore, is the ideal also in matters of wardrobe, and so is simplicity, but this does not mean lack of elegance, because "one's apparel should be suited to one's age, person, figure, temperament, and occupation," the Alexandrian concludes. Then, as always, he adds (he sometimes merely tacks on) a religious meditation, recalling that the Apostle invites us to put on our Lord, Jesus Christ; and, almost fearful that he has gone too far in his condemnation of luxuries, he softens his remarks by saying: "Wearing gold objects or softer garments is not to be absolutely forbidden: the important thing is to restrain the irrational impulses of the mind so that they may not through excessive laxity drag us into weak and wanton conduct."[45]

Particular attention is given footwear, which was the outlet for all the whims of feminine and even masculine fashion. Shoes are useful, perhaps even necessary; but they must be simple, while "certain haughty women" become extremely

---

44. *Paed.*, II, 10.
45. *Ib.*, III, 11 (*P. G.*, VIII, 629).

fastidious about this article of clothing and are not even ashamed to wear shoes embroidered with gold or gems, or ornaments etched with obscene figures: Attic and Sicyonian half-boots, and Persian and Tyrrhenian buskins . . . that have been brought at great price from the centers of fashion. The Alexandrian Father condemns all this commerce, carried on to the detriment of the chaste and simple beauty of the soul. He thinks footwear should also be simply a protection, especially for women, who ought always to wear shoes in order not to expose their bare feet. But men "may easily do without them unless they are in military service: for there is some similarity between being shod and being bound."[46] It is healthier to go barefoot, or to wear, at the most, simple sport shoes (the *konipodes* of the Athenians).[47]

Men and women seek other means of sensual allure in perfumes, cosmetics, and in their attire. Pearls, purple trimmings and bracelets hide what God has made manifest and superimpose an invention of the devil on the true human form that has been received from God. It is contrary to the way in which God has created us to pierce the ears in order to hang *pretiosa grana* from them. For the same reason, the adulteration of the eyes, cheeks and hair with dyes and cosmetics is of diabolical instigation: it is an art invented by the apostate angels when they lost heavenly grace. And it results in the alteration of the truth of our divine creation.[48]

Those cities did well, Clement says, which forbade by law the buying and selling of perfumes, cosmetics and cloth-dyes;

---

46. G. Bardy, *Clément d'Alexandrie*, p. 155, compares this opinion with Musonius, in Stobeus, *Flor.*, I, 84. In this book Bardy has collected and arranged various moral teachings of Clement.

47. *Paed.*, II, 11.

48. Cyprian, *De hab. virg.*, XIV. He advises all women — not only the virgins (XV) — not to adulterate the *opus Dei*, the truth of the human body made to the image of God. Beauty aids make it the image of Satan; the latter pretends to improve, correct — almost as if it were imperfect — the handiwork of the Creator. It is a *praevaricatio veritatis* to adulterate the body with *flavo colore, vel nigro pulvere, vel rubore*. Cf. Tertullian, *De cultu fem.* V: *quod nascitur opus Dei est. Ergo quod fingitur diaboli negotium est.* Cyprian uses almost the same words.

for a city which professes to worship the truth cannot permit adulterations in the persons of its citizens. Women who paint their faces deserve reproach, but even more so do the men who become effeminate in the use of cosmetics; the latter should have the odor of virtue, the former should breathe forth Christ, the Anointed, the true royal ointment. They should breathe the odor of heavenly unction, not that of the things with which they mar their bodies.

On the other hand, perfumes are not completely to be condemned, for that would be the same as condemning the sense of smell, which has been given us to use. Women may use them moderately, that is, in such a way as not to make men's heads reel. Perfumes in large amounts are used to good advantage in anointing corpses, not living persons. And the men of the stadium may be permitted the use of hygienic oils. For the author means to censure what is vain and harmful, not what is useful. Thus those perfumes may be used moderately which do not excite the passions or invite to impurity but which do aid health, are good for headaches or clear the brain when the strength is enfeebled, and which ward off catarrh, colds, bad humors, etc. It is also helpful to massage the feet and other odorous members with perfumed oils. But utility is one thing and voluptuousness another, for the latter is the invention of courtesans and a love philter. Hygiene is one thing, effeminacy is quite another. It is all a matter of abuses, which, above all, are unhealthy.[49]

Women spend a great deal of care and time in arranging their headdress, and so do the men, who dye their hair to look younger and only grow white before their time, for whiteness is due to the excessive drying out of the hair.[50] It is even worse when men have their hair arranged in the coiffure of harlots and then put on soft, thin, shining garments and chew mastic (the ancient version of chewing gum). And they support a

49. *Paed.*, II, 8 (*P. G.*, VIII, 472 ff.).
50. *Ib.*, II, 8 (*P. G.*, VIII, 476-7).

whole series of beauty shops where they go to be smoothed with the pumice stone, to have the hair removed from their bodies, to be massaged and shaved, etc. This is the degeneration of hermaphrodites who deceive themselves into thinking they can delay death and who are ashamed of old age, in which natural dignity is inherent, so much so that God had himself called the "Ancient of days" (Dan. 7:9). The man who adulterates his body cannot have a pure soul. It is the spirit which is to be rejuvenated, not the hair.

A woman should be womanly; her face should wear no make-up and her hair, when necessary, may be softened with oils and fastened with a brooch or pin at the neck, but it must not be dyed nor twisted into complicated braids held in place with costly combs and pins. Much less should she adorn her head with false hair (how can the priest bless her when his hands rest on dead hair?). And men must not get themselves up like women by shaving themselves and rubbing pomade on their hair and curling it. With the beard on his face and the hair on his chest, Nature has given him an appearance of leonine strength; a natural and rational pedagogy teaches that it is impious to do violence to virility. The beard may be shortened but not shaved off; the latter is ridiculous and not at all fitting for the members of "our society" who should appreciate the gravity which the beard contributes to their appearance.[51]

Clement confines himself to precepts based on nature; but I believe he is aiming his remarks against the sexual degeneration (sodomy, emasculation) associated with effeminate headdresses. The emasculated priests of certain goddesses dressed like women altogether.

Another unnatural adulteration is the glamor achieved with gems. They have the same attraction that bright objects have for imbeciles or fire has for babies. "Giddy women wear gems

---

51. *Ib.*, III, 3.

in bracelets and necklaces: amethysts, ceraunites, jasper, topaz, Milesian emeralds, pearls. . . . "[51a]

Precious stones are used most commonly in rings. A woman wears a ring, not for ornament but as a token of fidelity. It is especially ridiculous for men to adorn their fingers with rings as the women do. It is enough for them to wear one on the little finger, which they use for a seal. But this must not be cut with the image of idols, swords or bows, but rather with religious emblems and emblems of peace like the dove, fish, ship, lyre or anchor, or the figure of a fisherman, which serves to recall the Apostles, or that of children rescued from the waves. These symbols are appropriate for persons who seek truth and peace. And since they are also sober and temperate people they will not have seals cut with a goblet and much less with the figures of nude lovers or mistresses.[52]

In short, Clement, who is well-acquainted with the frivolous, restless, luxurious and sensual society of the great Mediterranean city in which he lives, wants to recall its men and women to a greater appreciation of their own persons and wean them from the spell of artifice. The drastic sketches of frivolous women and libertines which he includes in his catechetical instructions bring out more clearly sections of society obscured by the false refraction of luxury and vice. He has before him as he writes many of those dandies and hetaeras whom the comedy-writers he had studied caricatured so mercilessly, branding their frivolity and turpitude for what it was.

Those women who rouge their cheeks, weigh themselves down with gold ornaments, curl and tint their hair, shade their eyelids, wear exaggerated high heels in order to look taller, and squeeze themselves in or pad themselves out to look thinner or more shapely, and who are all the day long busy and anxious about their toilette are like Egyptian temples; these are graceful and precious without but once you enter

---

51a. *Ib.,* II, 12.
52. *Paed.,* III, 11.

and approach the priest, who, after the proper hymn, solemnly draws aside the draperies for you, what is revealed to you in the niche, stretched upon the purple, but a crocodile, a dead cat, or a serpent. ... If you scrape off a little of the crust of pomade or remove those sumptuous veils, what you see is not beauty but filthiness. Beneath the woman decked like a goddess with perfumes, gems and dazzling colors, crouches the beast, the serpent, on a cushion of lust.[53]

BANQUETS, MUSIC, CONVERSATION

The Alexandrian, living among wealthy people, has had occasion to observe Sybaritic banquets, and his apt analysis of them is full of information regarding the customs of his times. The wealthy were madly anxious to import goods from over the sea, to have wines from the best cellars and cooks who could prepare the most refined delicacies; they reduced their own persons to a devouring "jaw" and nourished their spirit with the smoke of the kitchens, sinking every good thought in the gutter of a shameful life, stuffing their intellects and ruining their health. ... The table — the highest aspiration of so many clients, parasites, procurers, and wandering or poverty-stricken gladiators — became a center of low-mindedness, adulation and violence. Hence the Christians were counseled to hold their banquets by themselves, not because the foods served had the power of infecting them with evil, but rather that they might not contaminate their conscience or cultivate the friendship of the devils.[54]

The Christians did hold banquets by themselves, the agapes, which gave the rich the opportunity to exercise charity and fraternity toward the poor. But they were not to degenerate into the usual social affair and thus lose their original character, from which their name derived. They were not prepared for the

---

53. *Ib.*, III, 2.
54. *Paed.*, II, 1. With regard to these nabob banquets, the dinner of Trimalchio described by Petronius is highly informative. And cf. Carcopino, *La vie quot. à Rome.*

enjoyment of the palate, nor did they *per se* fulfil God's promise as some Christians ingenuously believed. They were "heavenly nourishment, a rational feast," the true love St. Paul speaks of (1 Cor. 13:7-8; Luke 14:15). Not that the meal in itself was love; but it was an indication of love, "a sign of generous and social benevolence."[55] In this interpretation there is a little of that anxiety, characteristic of the Alexandrian school, to allegorize and spiritualize everything, though without failing to appreciate the social (κοινωνία) and economic value of the custom.

Banquets offered the most dangerous occasions for disorder of various kinds. The history of the Empire is linked not a little with the chronicle of convivial orgies. For the Christians, a pagan banquet might also furnish occasions for idolatrous acts; therefore, St. Paul had counseled prudence and tact in the matter of receiving invitations.

Clement of Alexandria is developing St. Paul's thought. He does not even condemn the partaking of elaborate dishes when Christians are invited to banquets, and he tells them to answer the invitations with courtesy and to make the very food and drink bear witness to the benevolence between host and guest and strengthen mutual friendship. When such sentiment of affection prevails, the guests at table will be careful not to provoke arguments and quarrels, preferring to keep silent rather than contradict one another. In every case, the Christian will be nourished also by a feeling of gratitude toward God, a feeling that will keep him from taking unreasonable care for or delight in his food. He will take his place at table with the modesty and gravity which should never leave him, thereby giving good example. He will not therefore abandon himself to voracious eating and acts of gluttony, to excessive drinking and consequently to unseemly laughter. The figure of the man who is stuffed with food and wine is the most ridiculous and

---

55. *Paed.*, II, 1. (*P. G.*, VIII, 388): δεῖγμα δὲ εὐνοίας κοινωνικῆς καὶ εὐμεταδότου.

unsightly that one can imagine. He makes a skin-sack of his belly almost as if he had been created just to eat, like the irrational animals. Food and drink are means, not ends; if they are used sparingly they contribute to one's health and strength. We must be masters, not slaves of food. At table also, we are in the presence of God.

Music and singing during banquets titillate the senses or excite them to lust. Therefore there is no place at a Christian banquet for instruments whose music is warlike, amatory or riotous, for they are unsuited to the pedagogy of the Logos. Not that musical instruments are to be condemned in themselves. If a Christian wishes to study the lyre, the cithara or singing let him do so by all means. David did, and the Scriptures are full of references and invitations to praise God with singing and music. It is a question of changing the use and the character of the music, of creating a new, sacred music. As we praise God before the meal, so in drinking we may praise him by singing a psalm. The important thing is that the melodies be not effeminate or suggestive, but grave and chaste; and in all cases, chromatic harmonies (a kind of refined and enervating music) are forbidden for they belong to the music of harlots.[56]

"We must learn music to sweeten and refine our manners. ... But let vain music be forbidden."[57]

The same rule of moderation applies to conversation, which is the expression of the inner mind. The Christian must abstain absolutely from foul talk, "which is speaking of indecent things." The names of certain parts of the body and certain sexual acts are not obscene in themselves, but they become so when they indicate illicit and immoral actions like adultery and pederasty. The Christian should also rebuke such language in others with a severe look, and, if it is opportune, with words of reproach. He should never, through adulation or weakness,

56. *Paed.*, II, 4 and 7.
57. *Strom.*, VI, 11.

smile at a salacious jest; rather should he blush. Whoever indulges in such things is a mediocre man and a pagan. The true
Christian is an aristocrat in his speech, knowing, like Menander
that "evil conversations corrupt good morals." For this reason,
special care should be taken not to let children hear such talk.
This condemnation includes obscene recitations on the stage.

The Christian, in fleeing foul talk, should also refrain from
talking too much, which does nothing but heap one nonsense
on another and is boring.[58] Likewise, this most precious gift of
speech is not to be wasted in ridiculous chatter; the ridiculous
is ugly to see and to do, and it indicates bad morals. Grace
in speaking, the smile, refined humor are an ornament to the
person; but unrestrained clowning at the expense of man's
morals injures his dignity.

Laughter is a natural gift but it must not be abused, just
as the horse does not whinny all the time. Unrestrained laughter
in women reflects unchaste tendencies, in men vanity.[59] When
dinner is over, the Christian blesses God and goes to bed. And
his rest also is evaluated from the moral point of view. First
of all, in order to sleep men do not need soft and luxurious
couches with embroidered coverlets and frames, which, among
other things, are harmful to the digestion. Beds with silver
legs and ivory inlay are not permissible for "holy men" for they
are "a lazy contrivance for rest." "Their use is not prohibited
those who own them; but it is forbidden to take thought for
these things." This is another of the teacher's typical good-
natured concessions to the Alexandrian gentlemen, which would
probably have scandalized the austere Tertullian. Besides, he
does tactfully suggest that they use simple beds which restore
the original function of sleep, and that is rest, not idleness; its
purpose is to restore our energies that we may return refreshed
to our occupations, affairs and studies (and women to their

58. *Paed.*, II, 6.
59. *Ib.*, II, 5.

spinning). We must always remember the relation of our life to God, whose praises we should do well to repeat even in our sleep.

Since sleep is like death and unprofitable, and since it robs us of half our life,[60] it would be well to sleep in more moderate measure and awaken early.[61]

---

60. Cf. Plutarch, *Moral.*, p. 958 D.
61. *Paed.*, II, 9.

CHAPTER IX

SOCIAL RELATIONS

THE CHASTE LIFE OF THE CHRISTIANS

CLEMENT'S pedagogy aimed to form the "rational" man, the first step in the formation of the "gnostic," who is the perfect Christian. But meanwhile the Church, with less intellectualistic worries and without bothering about distinctions or degrees or types, was working for the reform of society's morals.

Like the majority of pagans who became Christian, most of the apologists were converted to the Gospel by the spectacle of the austere morality of the Christians and their serene courage in the face of martyrdom.

The Apostolic Fathers, while molding the community into a harmonious organization, were seeking to form a strict moral sense or conscience in its members, to fashion a Christian personality in each one of them. Before Lucian had ever dramatized the theme, which after all was already well-known in classical literature,[1] the *Didache,* and later Pseudo-Barnabas, set the Christian, the new Hercules, at the crossroad of good and evil and invited him to choose his way: one — the road of life — was the path marked out by the Ten Commandments and the Christian precepts of continence, chastity, charity and self-denial; the other, the road "of death, evil above all others and full of malediction: murders, adultery, concupiscence, fornication, theft, idolatry, magic, poisonings, rapine, false witness, hypocrisies, insincerity, deceit, pride, malice, arrogance, avarice, foul talk, envy, insolence, pomp, ostentation; persecutors of

---

1. In the period which concerns us here, we find comparison of the two ways also in Irenaeus, Εἰς ἐπίδειξιν 1. Cf. Harnack, *Die Apostellehre und die jüdischen beiden Wege,* Leipzig, 1886.

the good, haters of truth, friends of falsehood, ignorant of the reward of justice, far from the good and from just judgment, vigilant, not for the good but for evil; people far indeed from meekness and patience, that love vanity and seek rewards, that have no mercy on the poor, never take thought for those who suffer, and do not know their own Creator, that kill their children and with abortions destroy the creatures of God; that turn away from the needy and oppress the unfortunate; advocates of the rich, unjust judges of the poor, inured to every form of guilt. — Flee, my sons, from such vile persons!"[2]

In developing and popularizing the ethical-religious concept, already perceived by that pre-Christian theologian, Plato, Christian catechesis establishes the exercise of virtue as the indispensable requirement for enjoying the sight of God, for perceiving him with the eyes of the soul, because guilt obscures spiritual vision. Whoever wishes to contemplate God must be, specifically, "neither adulterer, nor fornicator, nor thief, nor robber, nor purloiner, nor insolent, nor slanderer, nor be wrathful, nor envious, nor arrogant, nor proud, nor a cutthroat, nor covetous, nor disobedient to his parents, nor must he traffic in his children."[3]

Here we have lists of the most serious and common vices of the time[4] balanced with lists of the most rare and austere virtues. The senatorial martyr, Apollonius, presents just such a catalogue of virtues to the proconsul Perennis: "[Jesus] taught us to put aside our wrath, to bridle our greed, to master pleasure, to cut sadness from us, to hold all our possessions in common,[5] to increase friendship, to lay aside all ostentation,

---

2. *Didache*, V.

3. Theophilus, I, 2. Cf. Justin, *Dial.*, IV, 3.

4. Juvenal, *Sat.*, I, speaks of eunuchs who married, wealthy libertines, slaves covered with rings, informers, men who became old ladies' lovers in order to wheedle an inheritance from them, tutors who debauched their wards. "What is disgrace so long as your money is safe?" (v. 48) ; "to their crimes they owe their gardens, their villas, their tables, their old silver and the goats embossed on their goblets" (vv. 75-76). Fiancées are corrupt and boys are already adulterers. The descendants of the Trojans besiege the door of the rich man for a wretched portion of food.

5. κοινωνικοὺς γίνεσθαι.

not to seek revenge on one who injures us, to despise the death to which we are sentenced, since we are victims of injustice — an injustice suffered and not committed — to obey the divine law, to honor the emperor, to adore the Immortal God only, to believe in the immortality of the soul and the judgment after death.... "[6] This is the morality preached by the Pedagogue Christ, who teaches "frugality, simplicity (the rejection of pomp and show), the love of liberty and of our neighbor."[7]

The popular writer, Hermas, attempted to outline the genealogy of the virtues, from faith in God to love of neighbor: "From faith is born Continence, from Continence Simplicity, from Simplicity Innocence, from Innocence Chastity, from Chastity Knowledge, from Knowledge Discipline and Charity."[8]

In controversy with the defenders of idolatry, Christian teachers insisted that God is not to be honored with the sacrifice of two-footed and four-footed animals, but with virtue and works of charity. "The man who cherishes innocence sends prayers to God; he who cherishes justice pours libations to God; whoever refrains from cheating propitiates God; he who snatches a man from danger sacrifices the most acceptable victim of all. These are our sacrifices, these are our ceremonies: and thus, among us, he is most religious who is most just."[9]

The popular charge of incest wounded the Christians in their most noble and moral feelings and works. The Church's writers answered it by insisting that their brother Christians vigorously and truly belied the charge with their irreproachable conduct; and they painted for their adversaries, sometimes in colors warm with emotion, the picture of the chaste life led by Christian individuals and communities — the latter an inexhaustible atelier of good, which was bestowed on everyone even in return for evil.

---

6. *Acta Apoll.*, XXXVII.
7. Clem. of Alex., *Paed.*, I, 12 (*P. G.*, VIII, 369).
8. Hermas, *Pastor*, Vis. III, 8, 7.
9. Minucius, XXXII, 3.

Sometimes the apologists themselves were amazed by the complete change in morals wrought by every sincere conversion. In truth, this marked one of the most salient and striking points of contrast between Christianity and the world which surrounded it. The behavior of these converts first marked them as different and then became a daily reproach to the many dissolute members of pagan society, which often exploded its hatred against them in revenge.

"Once you ran to the temple; now run to the Church. First you shed, but now free others' blood; once you dissipated others' wealth, now give your own possessions to others; once your eyes sought women or other things to covet with your glances, now let them seek the poor, the weak and the wretched to console them.... Let the tongue which once spoke indecencies now bless God and proclaim the truth."[10]

Do we delude ourselves? "The source of our illusion is beautiful if it converts us from intemperate to temperate, from unjust to just, from imprudent to prudent, or inclined to prudence; and if it makes us manly and strong who were timid, cowardly and weak.[11]

When a man was converted he was truly severed from a whole way of life.[12] The reaction began sometimes in the family; the conversion of one member, changing the tenor of life within it, created conflict and furnished fuel for quarrels to the point where a husband turned informer against his wife who had become chaste,[13] a father disinherited the son who had become obedient and a master sent to the galleys the slave

---

10. Origen, *In Ep. ad Rom.*, VI, 4.
11. *Id.*, *C. Cels.*, II, 79.
12. The author of the *Oratio ad Graecos* is a pagan who has been converted or, as he says, separated ἐκ τῶν ὑμετέρων ἐθῶν. Whoever was converted to Mithra did not give up his ancestral customs. He who is converted to Christ repudiates and changes ἔθη, including the poets and philosophers (Clement of Alexandria's view is not a little different). These ἔθη, this civilization from which he divorces himself is identified with Homer, Hesiod, mythology, sumptuous rendezvous, with music, flowers, perfumes. To these things, which are its ethical expression, he opposes "an incomparable philosophy" (*ib.*, V).
13. Justin, II *Ap.*, I, 2; II, 1.

that had become trustworthy.[14] They preferred the complicity of the old vice to the new virtue; they even preferred to suffer loss or damage to their own interests rather than keep in the house the object of their hatred.[15]

People said, "That Gaius Seius is a good fellow; what a shame that he's a Christian." Or "I am amazed that so fine a person as Lucius Titius could turn Christian all of a sudden." They never asked themselves if perchance Gaius was so good and Lucius so wise because they were Christians, or if they were Christians because they were so wise and good.[16]

Now a Christian's relations with others are regulated by a divine and natural moral law which controls even his thoughts and which may not be evaded because its sanction is pronounced by God in eternity. It purifies all relationships, controlled by scrupulous honesty and animated by a charity which looks beyond the body to the soul.

"And therefore according to their age, some are as sons and daughters to us, others like brothers and sisters; and the oldest we venerate like our fathers and mothers. But when we call them brothers and sisters and give them other names of kinship, we take the greatest care that their persons be not outraged or violated, because our doctrine teaches: If any one shall give a second kiss because it gives him pleasure . . . ;[17] therefore we must be cautious in kissing or rather in the act of respect, since it would shut us out from eternal life if it were the least sullied in thought."[18]

Athenagoras is alluding to the embrace which the Christians exchanged, irrespective of sex, as a sign of charity and brotherhood. When faith or continence were deficient unchaste

---

14. Cf. Tertullian, *Ap.*, III, 4.
15. *Ib.*, "One's interests are not worth as much as his hatred of the Christians."
16. *Ib.*, III, 1.
17. This is a *logion* (cf. Resch, *Agraphon* 137 [A9]; *T. U.*, n. F., XV, 3-4 Hft., p. 177 ff.) which is unfinished in the manuscript, but it is easy to complete it: "commits a sin" or something similar.
18. Athenagoras, *Suppl.*, XXXII.

thoughts might intrude upon the liturgical act, and Clement of Alexandria had to complain that some could do nothing but "make the churches resound with the smack of their kisses without possessing within themselves any benevolence toward the brother or the sister they had kissed."[19]

This embrace, by malicious implication, had given rise to the charge of incest, that is, of intercourse between members of the same family, brothers and sisters, sons and mothers. These were Christian names; but in the erotic language of the Romans, brother and sister meant nothing more nor less than lover.

The truth was that the idea of universal brotherhood was indeed difficult for the ancients to understand precisely because the majority of them had no concept of universal sonship in God, no idea of being children of one God. Lucian spoke of it as a curious paradox: "Their first lawgiver has put into their heads the conviction that they are all brothers . . . and in truth they show an incredible zeal every time something happens which affects their common interests: nothing then seems hard or painful to them."[20] This is so true that Christians can be distinguished from pagans by their love for one another, while the pagans are distinguished by their mutual hatred.[21]

But Christian love is the chaste love of one brother for another. When the pagan Caecilius called it an incestuous love with rape as its object, Octavius retorted briskly that such malicious slander was due to the hatred of men, who, for their part, recognized one another as brothers only in parricide.[22] In fact the Church maintained a rigid discipline over those who violated her moral laws; she required the guilty to make expiation by confession and by performing penances that were sometimes very arduous, and she excommunicated the most serious offenders, such as murderers, adulterers and apostates,

19. *Paed.*, III, xi, 81, 2.
20. *Peregr.*, XIII.
21. Tertullian, *Ap.*, XXXIX.
22. Minucius, *Oct.*, IX, 2 and XXXI, 8.

considering that they had betrayed their baptismal pledge. Even in the third century the latter could not be completely reinstated in the community even after they had repented; and when Pope Callixtus permitted carnal sinners to be reconciled to the Church on their death-bed, he drew down upon his head the caustic criticisms of Tertullian and Hippolytus.

Thus in the second and third centuries, Christianity kept trying to press out of that amalgamation of races, castes and diverse interests a harmonious society in which the warm and generous lifeblood of charity would circulate freely, spreading joy, communicating the well-being of each to all and of all to each, melting away the barriers of inequality and counteracting concupiscence.

VIRGINITY

Christian instruction, writings and prayers taught that purity and modesty should be a general habit of life.[23] To lead a chaste life was the duty of men and women in every class of society. Chastity reached ascetic perfection in virginity, which seemed ever more clearly to be the most noble state in the moral life; and in grateful admiration the faithful clothed it with an ever brighter ideal beauty, seeing in it a radical revolt against the eroticism in which the society about them was decaying.[24] Some even went to fanatical excess and emasculated themselves, misunderstanding the words of the Gospel: "For there are eunuchs who were born so from their mother's womb; and there are eunuchs who were made so by men;

---

23. The *Epistle of Barnabas* interprets Moses' command not to eat pork as a command not to associate with men who live like pigs, that is, who wallow in pleasure and forget the Lord except in moments of need (10). Tertullian's treatise, *De Pudicitia*, begins with this summary: *Pudicitia flos morum, honor corporum: decor sexuum, integritas sanguinis, fides generis, fundamentum sanctitatis, praejudicium omnis bonae mentis; quamquam rara, nec facile perfecta, vixque perpetua, tamen aliquatenus in saeculo morabitur, si natura praestruxerit, si disciplina persuaserit, censura compresserit. Si quidem omne animi bonum aut nascitur, aut eruditur, aut cogitatur.*

24. Clement of Alexandria paints a vivid picture of the frenzied lust of the period, *Paed.*, III, 4 and elsewhere.

and there are eunuchs who have made themselves so for the kingdom of heaven's sake. Let him accept it who can" (Matt. 19:12).

In Alexandria, a cultured and wanton city, a commercial center and marketplace for *cinaedi,* procurers and hetaeras, a Christian asked the governor Felix for permission to emasculate himself, and when he did not receive it he kept himself chaste.[25] Later the famous Origen castrated himself "for the kingdom of heaven's sake" and was greatly admired for it by his contemporaries. But then he recognized his error, the essence of which had been given Christian definition by his teacher: "The true eunuch is not he who cannot but he who will not yield to lust."[26] A eunuch, Melito, is listed among the most glorious saints of the Asiatic churches in a letter sent to Pope Victor by Polycrates in the name of the bishops of Asia.[27]

The Church never sanctioned those excesses with which the ascetico-erotic customs and instincts of the Asiatic religions were attempting to force her door. What she preached was continence, that is, the mortification of the will, not emasculation or hatred of the flesh; for "we are not children of concupiscence, but of the will."[28] In the second century it was already easy to find Christian "men and women who had grown old without marrying because of the hope of uniting themselves more closely to God. And if remaining virgins and celibates brings us closer to him, even the very thought of impure desires separates us from him."[29] Virginity and celibacy seemed a kind of youth whose flower did not fade even in advanced old age.[30] Men and women consecrated themselves to it, but of their own free will.

---

25. Justin, *I Ap.,* XXIX, 2-3.
26. Clem. of Alex., *Paed.,* III, 4. Cf. Tertullian, *De resurrect. carnis,* 61: *"Quot spadones voluntarii! Quot virgines Christo maritatae! Quot steriles utriusque naturae!"*
27. Eusebius, *H. E.,* V, 28, 5.
28. Clem. of Alex., *Strom.,* III, 7 (*P. G.,* VIII, 1161).
29. Athenagoras, *Suppl.,* XXXIII.
30. *Quidam multo securiores totam vim huius erroris virgine continentia depellunt, senes pueri* (Tertullian, *Ap.,* IX, 19).

The apologists extolled this blossoming of virginity in Christian society, contrasting it with the lasciviousness which raged in pagan society, even within the temples and among the few virgins sacred to Vesta.[31] They went so far as to say, not without exaggeration, that there had been more Vestals condemned to death for unchastity than had escaped it, and the latter had done so through good luck and not through virtue.[32] In fact, Christian asceticism on this point was of great originality and power. Classical paganism was almost totally unacquainted with virginity, and the Oriental religions for the most part substituted castration for it when they did not celebrate — and it was an almost universal celebration — the feasts of their divinities with the "sacred" prostitution of "girls and women." Christianity exalted the Virgin Mary, who was offered to the Temple at the age of three as a "virgin of the Lord";[33] but in Babylonia, Asia Minor, Syria and even in Greece to prostitute oneself was considered an homage to the divinity — to an Astarte, Aphrodite, Mylitta or Baalath — and the custom spread throughout the Empire with the diffusion of the Oriental cults.[34]

The Christians attributed so great a value to chastity that the most hateful punishment some pagan judges could think of to inflict on Christian maidens was to condemn them to the brothel, to give them to a panderer instead of a lion.[35]

---

31. Those converted to Christ's teaching abstain from obscenity, impurity and all sexual indecency, living like "perfect priests" in the service of chastity, and some remain virgins. Such mortification does not require potions, sedatives or hemlock as one Athenian hierophant thought necessary for his chastity (Origen, *C. Cels.*, VII, 48).

32. That is what we read in the *Octavius* of Minucius, XXV, 10.

33. *Protevang. Iac.*, VIII and IX, 1.

34. Cf. C. Vellay, *Le culte et les fêtes d'Adonis-Thamouz*, Paris, 1904, p. 169 ff. (*Annales du Musée Guimet, Bibl. d'Etudes*, t. XVI).

35. *Nam et proxime ad lenonem damnando christianam potius quam ad leonem, confessi estis labem pudicitiae apud nos atrociorem omni poena et omni morte reputari* (Tertullian, *Ap.*, L, 12). This happened in the case of the virgin Serapia, who was given to two libertines. Palladius in the *Historia Lausiaca* quotes from Hippolytus the incident of a virgin of Corinth who was sent to a brothel because she refused to satisfy the desires of an influential man. For a

Whoever did not have the intention or the necessary fortitude to remain a virgin, the Church invited to marry with a pure spirit. For her, chastity is beautiful and so is matrimony; the mother is holy and the virgin is holy: vice attaches itself to the spirit.[36] But we know that not a few Christian couples, after being married, decided at a given moment to consecrate themselves to chastity and live together as brother and sister; in fact, this is what Hermas says of himself.[37] For they considered that virginity substituted a mystic union with God for marriage with a human creature.[38]

The Fathers begin to vie with one another in exalting the state of virginity, in which they see one of the most precious acts of homage to God and one of the most effective examples for society. Tertullian extols the virgins as brides of Christ, holy, sacred and vowed to him; and he considers that all the Apostles except St. Peter were virgins.[39] Origen sees in the

---

few days she found an excuse to protect herself from various clients until a young man, Magistrianus, had himself introduced to her room and persuaded her to put on his clothes. She was able to leave without being recognized. When the young man was discovered he was condemned to a horrible death; and thus he met, says the author, a twofold martyrdom: one for his own soul and one for her chastity. "Christ in his mercy granted him a double honor and two palms" (St. Hippolytus, *De virgine corinth.*, *P. G.*, X, 871-874).

36. Clem. of Alex., *Strom.*, III, 18. Cf. *Paed.*, II, 10 (*P. G.*, VIII, 509): "It is absolutely necessary either to marry or to be completely pure from matrimony."

37. *Pastor*, Vis., II, 2, 3.

38. (The virgins) *malunt enim Deo nubere, Deo speciosae, Deo sunt puellae: cum illo vivunt, cum illo sermocinantur, illum diebus et noctibus tractant: orationes suas velut dotes Domino assignant* (Tertullian, *Ad ux.*, I, 4). The virgin who falls *non mariti sed Christi adultera est* (Cyprian, *Ep.*, LXII, 4). The *Epistolae Clementis ad Virgines* celebrate virginity as a sublime office, a royal priesthood, a holy nation; but virginity is only a means not an end, because the kingdom of heaven is won with the efficacy of our works of faith. Its purpose is personal sanctification, with God as the ideal and Christ as model. But it must not be selfish, because our own personal sanctification is always associated with that of our neighbor, according to St. Paul's ideal, through prayer and good works; visiting the orphans, widows, the poor and the sick. The greatest reserve is recommended in relations with Christian women. Thus there is a distinction between the ascetics and the ordinary faithful; and virginity becomes a special state, a vocation, which implies *mortifications* and *poverty,* since heaven is its only goal, and perhaps a private *vow* also. (Cf. Martinez, F., *L'ascétisme chrétien*, Paris, 1914, p. 170 ff.)

39. *De monog.*, VIII.

virgins a wreath of flowers that adorns the virgin Church and he places them next in rank after the martyrs.[40] A half-century after Tertullian had written in Carthage his treatise on the duty of virgins to wear veils, we find painted in the Catacombs of Priscilla at Rome a very beautiful scene showing the giving of the veil to a virgin consecrated to God.

MATRIMONY

Next after the virgins, Origen places the continent. We know that in this period married people sometimes vied with the virgins in practicing chastity.[41]

According to Marcion the true Christian does not marry; and if he is married, he divorces his wife. According to Tertullian, turned Montanist, marriage is a kind of legal adultery to be tolerated only as a necessary evil.[42]

The orthodox Christian writers, who accept neither the dualism of the Marcionites nor the pessimism of the Montanists, proclaim instead the legitimacy and sanctity of matrimony. The philosopher Clement of Alexandria is aware that this doctrine differs from the teaching of not a few Greek philosophers, like Democritus and Epicurus, who reject matrimony because of all the annoyances and bother it entails, and the Stoics, who consider it, like procreation, an indifferent thing; but it is in harmony with the ideas of Menander and Musonius, etc. According to the Alexandrian, "there must certainly be marriage for the nation, for posterity and for the perfection, so far as it depends on us, of the world."[43]

The very infirmity of the human body leads to marriage, a kind of intimate society which completes the physical life also:

---

40. *In epist. ad Rom.,* IX, 1.

41. Christian epigraphy in this period calls married people also *virginii* and *converginii* (cf. Grossi-Gondi, F., *Trattato di epigrafia cristiana latina,* Rome, 1920, p. 100).

42. *De exhort. castit.,* VIII-IX. In the apocryphal *Acts of Paul,* St. Paul is accused of turning women away from marriage almost as if he preached that absolute continence was necessary for salvation.

43. *Strom.,* II, 23 (*P. G.,* VIII, 1089).

the care, for example, which a wife gives a sick or aged husband has no substitute, nor can it be equaled by the care administered by his closest relatives and friends.

The Encratites supported their repudiation of marriage with detached phrases from the Scriptures or with outright apocryphal texts liks the *Gospel of the Egyptians.* Clement refuted them with passages from the very same apocryphon and denied that procreation was a sin or that parenthood was a bitterness and a distraction from holy works. "I have noticed," he writes, "that many of those who have refrained from marrying have not proceeded according to holy wisdom; they have fallen into misanthropy and have let the fires of charity go out."[44] Certainly one can sin in matrimony also; some even become bestial. The fault, however, does not lie in matrimony itself but rather in the intemperance and ethical irrationality of those who so fall. "We must therefore judge matrimony favorably and approve it since the Lord wills that humanity increase and multiply. But he does not will that we abandon ourselves to excesses and lust as if we were beasts."[45]

The Christian will remember that God sees him also in the darkness of the night, in the privacy of his chamber. Darkness does not cover us, for the light is within us. "He debauches matrimony who uses it in the manner of whoredom."[46]

Matrimony is holy in itself; the acts of nature performed

---

44. *Ib.*, III, 9.

45. *Ib.*, III, 7 and *Paed.*, II, 10 (*P. G.*, VIII, 512).

46. *Paed.*, II, 10 (*P. G.*, VIII, 516). The Alexandrian gives a series of intimate rules for moderate regularity in the use of the marital act, justifying his treatment of such a subject by saying that for purposes of instruction it is permissible to name even the secret parts of the body "since God was not ashamed to create them." When the embrace has been completed and the wife has become pregnant then we must not disturb nature with acts which would no longer have a rational purpose but would instead be lasciviousness excited and accompanied by luxuriousness, wines and excessive eating. Abuse is enervating. Matrimony is legitimate but wantonness is not. The former is the expression of the desire to beget children, not the inordinate excretion of the seed. The marital act must be chaste; it must not be performed as with prostitutes, with wanton words and positions. Whoever befouls marriage is dead to God and abandoned, like a corpse, by his Logos and the Holy Spirit. Clement's successor, Dionysius of Alexandria, also preaches on these moral questions.

in matrimony are to be revered. It is false modesty to believe that the marital act is sinful or impure. Excesses of lust bring wantonness; but within its own natural limits, matrimony is blessed by God.[47]

Marriage remained strictly monogamous. Justin, in his controversy with Trypho, exhorted his Jewish listeners to follow God rather than the blind rabbis who still permitted them to have four or five wives.[48] In the new law each husband has only one wife and each wife only one husband. "Each of us has as his wife the woman he has married according to the laws we have established," affirmed Athenagoras,[49] emphasizing the strictness of the monogamous principle and at the same time the ecclesiastical legislation that supplemented the deficiencies in the civil law. And he added, in explanation of the purpose of matrimony, "We use this woman only for the procreation of children.[50] As the farmer who has sowed his field awaits the harvest without sowing any more seeds therein, so for us the measure of our desire is the procreation of children"[51] — "the most bitter enjoyment of children," the pessimistic Tertullian calls it.[52]

Thus marriage exists between one man and one woman.

---

47. Tertullian himself recognizes this in one of those contradictions he falls into in argument, when, to refute a heretic he comes back to orthodox doctrine: *Natura veneranda est, non erubescenda. Cuncubitum libido, non conditio foedavit. Excessus, non status est impudicus. Siquidem benedictus status apud Deum, "Crescite, et in multitudinem proficite"* (Gen. 1:28). *Excessus vero maledictus, adulteria, et stupra, et lupanaria* (*De anima*, XXVII, P. L., II, 695).

48. *Dial.*, CXXXIV, 1.

49. κατὰ τοὺς ὑφ' ἡμῶν τεθειμένους νόμους (*Suppl.*, XXXIII. Benigni, *op. cit.*, I, 271, reads "according to *your* laws").

50. Cf. Justin, *I Ap.*, XXIX, 1, which says that the Christian must either marry in order to raise children or remain chaste. There is no other alternative. And Minucius, *Oct.*, XXXI, 5: *Unius matrimonii vinculo libenter inhaeremus, cupiditate procreandi aut unam scimus aut nullam;* and XXXV, 6: *Vos enim adulteria prohibetis, et facitis; nos uxoribus nostris solummodo viri nascimur.* Tertullian echoes the same thought, *Ap.*, XLVI, 11: *Christianus uxori suae soli masculus nascitur;* and *ib.*, IX, 19.

51. *Suppl.*, XXXIII. This thought, derived from pagan literature, recurs in Clem. of Alex., *Paed.*, II, 10, 102, 1. Cf. also *Strom.*, III, 58, 1-2.

52. To dissuade his wife from every marrying again he writes: *Adiciunt quidem sibi homines causas nuptiarum de sollicitudine posteritatis, et liberorum amarissima voluptate* (*Ad uxorem*, I, 5).

Some Gnostic sects shared their women in common.[53] But the Church, though she encourages wherever possible the common use of property, does not tolerate any such promiscuity: "We share everything except our wives. We dissolve our community of goods on that very point where others begin to practice it (and this is the only case in which they do practice it). They not only usurp the wives of their friends, but they patiently give their own wives over to their friends, after the example, I believe, of their most virtuous ancestors, like the Greek Socrates and the Roman Cato, who shared the wives they had already married with their friends in order to have children even outside their own houses. I do not know whether the wives yielded unwillingly to this or not: and why should they have taken thought for their chastity when their husbands gave it away so easily?"[54]

At the beginning of the century, the bishop Ignatius had declared that whoever dishonors the family with adultery will lose what God has promised, insisting on St. Paul's warning, "Remind my sisters to love the Lord and to remain faithful to their husbands in body and soul. Likewise, in the name of Jesus Christ, tell my brothers to love their wives as the Lord loves his Church."[55] The Church already had adequate laws regulating the sacrament of matrimony, the reception of which was a religious and social act "with the approval of the bishop, in order that the thought of God and not passion might preside at the wedding."[56]

---

53. We read in Eusebius, *H. E.*, IV, 7, 9, that Carpocrates had made this common use of women a condition for reaching the perfection of the mysteries; hence the notorious accusation against all the Christians. Clem. of Alex., *Strom.*, III, 2, refutes the Carpocratians and shows his disappointment that Plato in the *Republica* should have introduced such a practice. Elsewhere (*Strom.*, III, 4) he says there are those who call public prostitution a "mystic communion" (κοινωνίαν μυστικήν), corrupting the meaning of a word that is suitable only to express "a community of money, food and clothes." The other is the community of the brothel and the pigsty.

54. Tertullian, *Ap.*, XXXIX, 11-13.

55. *Ad Pol.*, V, 1. Cf. *Ad Eph.*, XVI, 1.

56. Ignatius, *Ad Pol.*, V, 2. In the second century the Bishop Dionysius of Corinth wrote a letter on this subject to the churches in Pontus but it has been lost (Eusebius, *H. E.*, IV, 23, 6).

Church practice in this matter aimed to establish marriage as a religious act and lift it ever more definitively from the field of natural law to that of divine law, transcending the civil law, which was necessarily inadequate and changeable. The Christian was impressed by all the care and guarantees with which his marriage was surrounded and gradually became aware of the vital importance of a union governed by an unchangeable law like that of the Gospel, in the light of which the usual cases of separation and infidelity and the ordinary concerns regarding them and the length of the marriage no longer had any *raison d'être;* and God became the indissoluble bond between man and wife.

In practice, a just marriage was one that grew out of the social life of the Church; it was the marriage of two of the faithful whose acquaintance and relations with each other had developed under the eyes of their brethren and above all of their superiors and had been accompanied by the prayers and exhortations of the latter; whose union had been pronounced, ratified and blessed by the Church on earth and therefore by God in heaven.[57] The Church was like a mother to them, and their superiors like fathers. In non-Christian society also good marriages are often those arranged by parents and entered into with their consent.

Tertullian cherished a strict ideal of matrimony from the first years of his conversion. As a young man he had written a little essay (now lost) on the trials of married life (*De angustiis nuptiarum*) that was recommended by St. Jerome. The thought of those trials did not keep him from marrying, however, and becoming a convert, although, because of his increasingly pessimistic view of life, they seemed to loom bigger and bigger throughout his other works on marriage. He addressed one of these treatises to his wife, *Ad uxorem,* to teach her what her conduct should be in case she were widowed. In it he re-

---

57. Tertullian, *Ad uxorem,* II, 9.

peated that virginity is a higher state than matrimony with such emphasis that it is clear he was becoming more and more convinced that the latter was a state barely to be tolerated and nothing more. He advised against second marriages and he condemned with a variety of lively arguments any marriages between Christians and pagans. Nevertheless he concluded the treatise (at least what is considered its second book) with an impassioned description of the religious harmony in Christian marriage.

"Who can enable us to express the happiness of those marriages which the Church performs and the offering[58] confirms, which a blessing consecrates, the Angels proclaim and the Father ratifies? Even earthly children marry well and legitimately only with the consent of their parents. Oh how sweet is the yoke of two of the faithful who are one in hope, one in faith and one in the service to God! Both brothers, both servants of God without any estrangement in body or soul. They are truly 'two in one flesh'; and when the flesh is one so is the spirit. Together they pray, together they prostrate themselves, together they fast, instructing, exhorting and supporting each other. Both are in the Church and equal, at God's table, in their trials, in persecutions, and when relief comes; one does not hide from the other, one does not avoid the other, one is not a burden to the other. They are free to visit the sick and to aid the poor. They give alms without danger of torture,[59] they offer sacrifice without scruples, and daily exercise their zeal undisturbed. They make the sign of the cross without stealth, their thanksgivings are free of anxiety, their benedictions need not be silent. Psalms and hymns rise from their lips and they vie with each other in singing the praises of God. Christ, who sees and hears such things, rejoices and sends his peace down

---

58. This is the holy *oblatio,* the sacrifice of the Mass, which accompanies the nuptial ceremony.

59. The torture to which the pagan husband subjected his slaves in order to discover how and to whom his Christian wife had given alms.

upon them. Where two are, there is he in person, and where he is, the evil one is not."[60]

In short, husband and wife compose a miniature church, a society which fulfils its natural obligations like a prayer, in strictest chastity[61] and within the fold of Christian law. The Christian family, through the exercise of these virtues, becomes a bond woven of strong, chaste, serene affections that reaches from the aged grandfather down to the youngest grandchildren and the slaves.

"Where is justice to be inscribed except in a wise soul? Where charity? Where purity? Where meekness? These divine inscriptions must be cut in the soul.... Sons deserve good fathers because they have taken refuge with the Father; fathers deserve good sons because they have recognized the Son; wives deserve good husbands because they are mindful of the Spouse; slaves deserve good masters because they have been redeemed from extreme slavery."[62]

The mad eagerness of men and women to adorn themselves with wreaths like the pagans is a stupid thing. The true crown for a woman is her husband, for a man it is marriage, and for both of them it is the children which "the divine husbandman gathers in the meadows of the flesh." The crown of old men is their children's children, and the glory of children is their father. The glory of all is the Father of the world, in whom all families form one single family; and the crown of the Church is Christ about whom centers the life of every institution and individual.[63]

But in this ideal picture of married life, faults and weaknesses must also be considered, and the moralists begin to sketch various examples across the fabric of Church practice.

---

60. Tertullian, *Ad uxorem*, II, 9 (*P. L.*, I, 1302-4).
61. The married couple are to be so chaste that the Pedagogue exhorts the husband not to kiss his wife in the presence of servants (Clem. of Alex., *Paed.*, III, 12; *P. G.*, VIII, 664). Cato expelled from the Senate a man who had kissed his wife in the presence of his daughter. Plutarch (*Coniug. praec.*, XIII) said that a husband should caress and rebuke his wife in private.
62. Clem. of Alex., *Protept.*, X (*P. G.*, VIII, 224).
63. *Id., Paed.*, II, 8 (*P. G.*, VIII, 480).

" 'I command you,' says the Shepherd to Hermas, 'to preserve your chastity and do not permit to enter your heart the
thought of another's wife or of fornication or any similar corruption. For if you did so you would fall into serious sin. If
you keep your wife always present before your mind, you will
never sin. But if such a desire should arise in your heart you
would sin, and you would likewise fall into guilt if any other
similar wicked thoughts should enter it. For a servant of God,
such a desire is a serious sin; and if one commits such an evil
action, he earns death. Listen therefore: refrain from this concupiscence; for where chastity dwells, there iniquity cannot rise
in the heart of the just man.'

" 'I ask him: — Sir, permit me to ask you a few questions.
. . . If a man have a wife faithful in the Lord, and he finds her
out in some adultery, does the husband sin if he lives with her?'

" 'So long as he is ignorant,' said he, 'he does not sin, but
if the husband knows her sin, and the wife does not repent, but
remains in her fornication, and the husband go on living with
her, he becomes a partaker of her sin, and shares in her
adultery.'

" 'What then,' said I, 'sir, shall the husband do if the wife
remain in her vicious practices?'

" 'Let him put her away,' he said, 'and let the husband
remain by himself.' " Not even adultery dissolves a marriage;
it merely justifies a separation. In fact, the Shepherd continues,
"But 'if he put his wife away and marry another he also commits adultery himself.'

" 'And if the wife, after she has been put away, repents and
wishes to return to her husband, must he not receive her?'

" 'Most certainly!' he answered. 'If the husband did not
receive her he would sin, and he would sin grievously; one who
sins and repents must be received;[64] not, however, frequently,

---

64. The Montanist Tertullian regarded this as outright laxity, and so he
wrote: *Scriptura Pastoris, quae sola moechos amat . . . ; et utique receptior apud
ecclesias epistula Barnabae illo apocrypho Pastore moechorum* (*De pudic.*, X,
10 and 20).

because for the servants of God there is one penance. Because of repentance, therefore, the husband must not marry another. This is the rule of conduct for the husband and for the wife. . . .

" 'Not only,' he said, 'does a man commit adultery when he pollutes his own flesh; but he is also an adulterer who acts as the pagans do. Hence, if a man persist in actions of that kind and does not repent, flee from him and do not live with him. If you do not do this, you become a partaker in his sin. That is why it was commanded you, whether man or woman, to remain by yourselves: for in these things there may be repentance. And I do not offer an opportunity for laxity, that such an action be committed, but that the sinner may sin no more.' "[65]

The Shepherd is a teacher of penance. He regards marital fidelity, even after a husband or wife has been put away, as a means of giving the latter the opportunity to repent and to restore the unity, which has not been broken (for that is impossible) but which has been, in a certain sense, suspended. For Hermas, receiving the adulterous wife who has repented does not mean inviting her to sin again but rather inviting her to change her life.

Divorce is not even mentioned, because that would be absurd among Christians. But at that time among pagans it had "become the fruit of marriage"[66] and was so frequent that there was less adultery.

Second Marriages

The early Church did not look favorably on a second marriage. Some considered it a kind of adultery, "an honorable adultery," as Athenagoras says. He believes that the marriage endures even after the death of one spouse; hence "whoever frees himself of his first wife, even if she is dead, is an adulterer in disguise, who is forcing God's hand, since God in the beginning created one man and one woman only; and he is dis-

---

65. Hermas, *Pastor,* Mand. IV, 1.
66. Tertullian, *Ap.,* VI, 6.

solving the unity of flesh with flesh established for the act of procreation."[67]

Adam and Eve were the models: one man and one woman. Then the Jews went astray; but Jesus reëstablished the original unity of marriage as it had come from the hand of the Creator.[68]

The Church continued to entrust its responsible positions to men and women who had been married only once.

What Athenagoras considered adultery in disguise became a kind of outright bigamy for the Montanist Tertullian who, with great sarcasm, pictures the plight of a husband besieged by two wives, one dead and one living, while he prays for one and the other, standing before the Lord with two wives at once![69]

"When the husband has died by the will of God, then the marriage has also died by the will of God. Why should you rebuild what God has destroyed?"[70] And do not let anyone come saying that he seeks a wife as a partner in the management of his household, to superintend the servants, to keep the chest and the keys, to spin and to free him from the numerous cares of the home. For if he really needs a housewife, let him take "a spiritual wife, choosing, from among the widows, one who is beautiful in the faith, having the dowry of poverty, and distinguished for her years; and thus he will make an excellent marriage. And it pleases God that a man have even more than one such wife."[71]

Ideas like these belong to an asceticism that is excessive and perhaps foolish, but they were quite in harmony with the rigorism of the Montanists who absolutely forbade second marriages as adulterous. Indeed, since they had already created for the faithful the dilemma of choosing between celibacy and divorce, they had destroyed first marriages also.

---

67. Athenagoras, *Suppl.*, XXXIII.
68. Tertullian, *Ad uxorem*, I, 2.
69. *De exhort. cast.*, XI.
70. *Ad uxorem*, I, 7.
71. *De exhort. cast.*, XII.

Clement of Alexandria also deems second marriages an evil, though as usual he takes into consideration human weaknesses and customs; and these make him tolerate such marriages as an evil that is perhaps inevitable.[72]

For the Carthaginian priest, continence is the rule and standard in all sexual relations, and it is practiced in three ways: by virginity, by the voluntary chastity of married couples, and by widowhood after a single marriage.[73] Origen agrees with him, exhorting women "to preserve the grace of virginity. If they cannot and then lose their husbands, let them remain widows." In fact, while their husbands are yet living, let them make a vow that if he should die they will never remarry. Instead, the author moans, "we meet second, third, fourth marriages and even more if we must speak the truth. But we know that such marriages cast us out of the kingdom of God." Whoever remarries (a bigamist!) belongs, if he is good, to an inferior rank of Christians saved in the name of Christ but not crowned by him.[74]

Thus Tertullian had exhorted his wife not to marry again if he should die first. And he did so not through jealousy but through concern for her own interests. For a woman remarries either from concupiscence or ambition. The Christian widow will do well to consecrate herself to God, becoming his spouse, always young and beautiful in him.[75] In many ways she is superior to the virgin, because she earns with her works the merits which the other attains with the help of grace. One knows pleasure and abstains from it with conscious self-control; the other does not desire it because she does not know it. "More glorious is that continence which is aware of its right and understands what it has seen. The virgin may be more blest, but the widow will have the more difficult victory: the former because she has always possessed that good, the latter because

72. *Strom.*, III, 12.
73. *De exhort. cast.*, I and II.
74. *In Luc. hom.*, XVII (*P. G.*, XIII, 1846-7).
75. *Ad uxorem*, I, 4.

she has acquired it."[76] If she should wish actually to remarry then let her not wed a pagan, but in order to avoid a whole series of difficulties and dangers in the fulfillment of her religious duties, let her choose a Christian. Thus Christian society becomes more homogeneous.

The picture of the difficulties which a pagan husband might place in his wife's way in the practice of her religion is so gloomy, that, even allowing for Tertullian's touch of exaggeration, it explains the Church's assiduous care to prevent mixed marriages because of the danger of apostasy or of laxity. For the African that picture is bristling with one set of reasons why the pagan world of Satan can never be reconciled with the Christian world of God. A holy thing can never be joined to a thing that is cursed. A woman cannot serve two masters; she cannot serve the Lord as a Christian, and a pagan as his wife.[77] It is clear that "the faithful who contract marriages with pagans are guilty of fornication and should be driven out of the community of brethren."[78]

Because of this clear and definite condemnation of marriage with the unbaptized, many women found it impossible to find a husband of equal or higher social rank, for the Church abounded in poor people. Tertullian solves the difficulty with strict Christian logic: a woman that marries a brother in religion who is poorer than she, makes a great gain; for, since the kingdom of heaven belongs to the poor, he will enrich her with his merits. By becoming his equal on earth, she may win the same rank as he in heaven.[79] And she will do in holiness what so many matrons do through lust or selfishness, who give themselves to slaves, freedmen and eunuchs.

---

76. *Ib.*, I, 8.

77. In the ecclesiastical language of the period the Christian is the servant (*servus*, literally "slave") of God; the pagan is here called *servus diaboli* (*Ad uxorem*, II, 3-4) ; and the wife is *in Domino conserva* (*ib.*, I, 1).

78. *Ad uxorem*, II, 3.

79. *Christianam fidelem fideli re minori nubere piget, locupletiorem futuram in viro paupere? Nam si pauperum sunt regna caelorum* (Matt. 5:3) *quia divitum non sunt, plus dives in paupere inveniet maiore dote. Sit illa ex aequo in terris, quae in caelo forsitan non erit* (*Ad uxorem,* II, 8).

If instead she marries a pagan for worldly interests, she sacrifices her whole life, subjecting herself to a daily contradiction and struggle between her own religious aspirations and her actual conduct in a society to which she does not belong. If she makes the sign of the cross over her bed or on her own person, she will arouse suspicions of magic. If she blows on an impure object to drive out the spirit of evil in it, or if she arises in the night to pray, she will not be spared the surprised rebuke and suspicion of her husband. At the beginning of the year and of the month, and on the festivals of the sovereigns, whether she wishes to or not, she will have to breathe the perfume of incense burning in honor of demons and see her own door garlanded and illuminated. And then she will have to accompany her husband to meetings of the societies to which he belongs, and to inns; and she will have to listen everywhere to conversation which is either strange to her or blasphemous.[80] Her life will be a hell. On the day of the "station" her husband will want to go to the baths. On fast-days he will want to give a banquet. If there is a service in church, he will keep his wife busy at home in domestic affairs. Much less will he permit her to visit her brothers in the faith, in the poorest hovels here and there throughout the city, or to go out at night for the vigil services, or to go to the Eucharistic banquet which the pagans interpret as a cannibalistic feast, or to drag herself on her hands and knees across the dirty floor of a prison to kiss a martyr's chains. And then will he permit her to give the kiss of peace to any of her brothers, to wash the feet of the saints, to shelter foreign Christians and to give alms?

In the face of so many difficulties, a woman will in the end either oppose her husband, to whom she ought to be obedient, or she will lose her faith, or at least the observance of her faith and the chastity of Christian thought and life, in order to adapt herself to her husband's mode of living; and then she is lost to the Church.

---

80. *Ib.*, II, 4-6.

This differèntiation between pagan and Christian within the bosom of the family necessarily engendered bitter resentment and suspicion.

WOMAN AND HER FUNCTION IN SOCIETY

The controversy over chastity hinged upon the Christian concept of woman and of the nature of the relationship between the two sexes. On this point, Christian austerity was never mitigated; rather it was intensified in its conflict with the unbridled immorality which surrounded it.

Woman achieves very great prestige by virtue of her purity. Perpetua, a lady, and Blandina, a slave, as well as Felicitas, Symphorosa, Mercuria, Dionysia[81] and so many others rise in heroism above their male companions in martyrdom. Women already occupy a most notable place on the rolls of the Martyrs[82] as valiant soldiers of Christ, who renew in themselves the examples of Deborah and Judith. "With our own eyes," says Origen, "we have often seen women and girls suffer the tyrannical torments of martyrdom, in the flower of their youth, when the frailness of a life that was still a novelty added to the weakness of their sex."[83]

Woman, in her virtue and in the immortality of her soul, is holy; to look on her with dishonest pleasure is already an act of adultery:[84] The Church educates her, keenly aware of her influence on the morals of all society.

"Let us direct our women toward the good. Let them show us the lovable habit of chastity; let them prove the resolute sincerity of their meekness; let them, through their silence,[85] make evident the moderation of their tongues; and let them

---

81. ἡ σεμνοπρεπεστάτη πρεσβῦτις Μερκουρία καὶ ἡ πολύπαις μέν, οὐχ ὑπὲρ τὸν κύριον δὲ ἀγαπήσασα ἑαυτῆς τὰ τέκνα, Διονυσία. . . (Dionysius of Alexandria, *Ad Fabium Antioch.*, VI).

82. Cf. Clement of Rome, VI.

83. *In Iudic. hom.*, IX, 1.

84. Athenagoras, *Suppl.*, XXXII.

85. Clem. of Alex., *Paed.*, II, 7, recalls the dictum of Sophocles: "Silence for women is virtue."

practice charity, not according to their preferences, but in equal measure toward all who fear God."[86] From this passage we can see that the Roman church, and naturally the others also, after St. Paul's example, directed women's activity toward works of charity irrespective of their personal likes or dislikes, to which they are most sensitive.

Among the reasons why Tertullian condemns second marriages is the difficulty the Christian woman would encounter in performing these charitable works, such as visiting the sick and the poor, offering hospitality to pilgrims, comforting those in prison, etc.

The new woman is fashioned; she is no longer the agent of lust, but the agent — the most solicitous, tactful and desired — of social service. She no longer carries her charms to brothels, rendezvous of doubtful reputation, or frivolous gatherings; but with thoughtful and smiling face, she carries the gentle light of maternal solicitude into the darkness of a prison or a hovel to shine upon the suffering and abandoned. She renounces herself for others. She does not poison, kill or ruin; she revives, cheers and helps. A new and limitless field of action opens up before her; and innumerable daughters of Eve dedicate themselves to it with heroic ardor. Their character is formed in a strict school, which makes them strong and capable of "virile tasks."[87]

Clement's ideas are echoed by Polycarp: "Educate your women to remain firm in the faith granted them, in love and in chastity; to cherish, in all sincerity, affection for their husbands; to have charity toward all others in equal measure with purity of intention; and to bring up their children in the fear of God."[88]

Principles such as these were being taught in Rome, Smyrna, Carthage and other lascivious cities teeming with wily streetwalkers as well as with the clever, refined, elegant, lo-

---

86. Clem. Rom., XXI, 6.
87. *Id.*, LV.
88. *Epist.*, IV, 2.

quacious and superstitious courtesans devoted to Magna Dea, Isis, Adonis and Dea Bona, and especially devoted to money and their own beauty. Ovid had satirically remarked that the only chaste woman in Rome was the one no one sought after, and that husbands did well to wink both eyes.

Epictetus said that when a girl is fourteen, men already call her a lady, and from then on she believes she has nothing to think of but pleasing them, when she should instead be learning that she is esteemed only for her modesty and decency;[89] but Christianity requires that every woman be chaste, whether she be wife, virgin or widow.

The Church does not entrust women with any of the duties of the ministry although in the second century we still find prophetesses.[90] The Montanists, on the other hand, besides making them prophetesses and rulers, also confer on them the power to administer the sacraments. Before becoming a Montanist, Tertullian does not believe that a woman can administer even the sacrament of baptism.[91] He believes that woman's place is in the home, consecrated to the humble tasks of serving and assisting others. Therefore she should dress modestly, conscious of the law of sacrifice and pain to which she is subject because of Eve's fall, the cause of the ruination of all mankind. She must wear no gold nor gems nor beauty-aids, no cosmetics, no colors, nothing luxurious. These are tricks of the devil to tempt feminine chastity and humility, and the patrimonies of entire families are dissipated because of them.

Tertullian's rigorous asceticism leads him to a misogynist interpretation of woman's function in society, for he contemplates her under the fatal curse pronounced upon Eve, whereby she is destined to bring forth children in labor and

---

89. *Ench.*, XL.
90. Cf. Justin, *Dial.*, LXXXVIII, 1. From the mention in Rom. 16:1-2, of "Phoebe, our sister," Origen argues: *Et hic locus apostolica auctoritate docet etiam feminas in ministerio Ecclesiae, constitui.... Ideo locus hic duo pariter docet, et haberi, ut diximus, feminas ministras in Ecclesia, et tales debere assumi in ministerium quae astiterint multis, et per bona officia usque ad apostolicam laudem meruerint pervenire (In epist. ad Rom., X, 17).*
91. *De bapt.*, XVII.

suffering and to be subject to her husband. She is the instrument of perdition, "the gate of the devil, the first violator of the divine law," and as such, she has caused the downfall of man, who is "the image of God"; and the fruit of this is death, and on it hangs also the death of the Son of God. This is a mistaken notion of Church doctrine. Tertullian goes on to say that a woman should prepare˙her body for martyrdom with severe penances and in scrupulous chastity, but instead Christian women vie with their pagan sisters in making themselves beautiful, setting their ornaments with gems, wearing golden bracelets, painting their cheeks and eyes, and bleaching or dyeing their hair. Yet they have no need for all these artifices, for rough and unadorned, they had already awakened passion in the fallen angels.[92]

The woman who is faithful to Christ should disdain trying to please. It is enough for her to please her husband by cherishing her true beauty, which is the beauty of her mind and way of life. Naturally these restrictions, which aimed to do away with temptations and to correct frivolity and vanity, apply also in large measure to those men who are just as giddy in their attempts to please the women, who are constantly looking at themselves in the mirror, who dye their hair, cover themselves with pomade, and smooth and polish their bodies like wanton girls.

Though a woman's true and characteristic virtues should be humility and chastity, Christian women are not wanting who, in their frantic desire to cut a fine figure, kill humility with their apparel (*cultus*), the sin of ambition, wearing gold and silver ornaments, gems and ornate dress; and who kill chastity with cosmetics, the sin of prostitution, altering the appearance of their hair, skin and members of their body in order to attract attention and to seduce.

The Christian man or woman is simple in his dress and in his thought, and he is clothed with a dignity that is born

---

92. *De cultu feminarum*, I, 1 and 2.

in his conscience. The Christian woman loves her home where she tends to her spinning (and thus the Roman matron lives again). If she must go out, she does not go gadding about to gossip, or to strut her finery, but she goes to visit the sick and to pray in church.[93]

After 208, the Carthaginian priest busied himself about the dress of maidens in particular in the impetuous treatise *De virginibus velandis*. He had also written on this subject in Greek, it seems. He wanted young Christian maids to cover their heads with a veil. This was the custom in many churches in the Orient and Greece, in some churches in the Occident also, and among the married women of Carthage. Some girls in this latter community veiled themselves on the street and then uncovered themselves in church, or else they wore no veil at all. For the sake of a uniform discipline in the Church and above all for moral reasons, the puritanical Montanist wants all virgins to be veiled. They should avoid allowing themselves to be looked at, because to permit this partakes of the sinful concupiscence aroused in men who look at them. A holy man who stares at a virgin is ashamed; and a holy virgin is ashamed when a man stares at her. The maiden who uncovers her head exposes herself to the public and invites rape; she is no longer a virgin. Married women also should cover their hair, but not with little caps only nor with thin and tiny handkerchiefs that leave half the head and the ears uncovered: "let them remember that the whole head is woman." Whether she be mother, sister or daughter, let her cover her

---

93. *De cultu feminarum*. Clement of Alexandria, *Paed.*, III, 3, also rebukes the effeminate men who are busy beautifying themselves like silly women. With regard to sports, he says women should not be exempt from physical exertion; they should not, however, be encouraged to wrestle and race, but to spin and weave, and if necessary, let them help to cook and make bread; and let them help the poor and exercise a charitable hospitality, etc. (*Paed.*, III, 10). Cyprian wants them to dress modestly, for *ornamentorum ac vestium insignia et lenocinia formarum non nisi prostitutis et impudicis feminis congruunt* (*De hab. virg.*, XII). Virgins *sericum et purpuram indutae Christum induere non possunt* (*ib.*, XIII). Cf. the preceding chapter, pp. 199-205.

head for love of her children, her brothers, or her parents. Her liberty is a danger for everybody.

Yet, beneath these rigoristic ideas, there throbs a most lively and exquisite feeling of respect for virginity in particular and for womanhood in general.

WOMAN'S RELATION TO MAN

In Greek thought, man's kingdom was the "city," the world, and woman's kingdom was the gynaeceum; the relations between them were condensed in the command, "Rule over the woman."[94] In Christian thought, man and woman have the same duties toward virtue; from the ethical point of view also they are equal, and this was in contrast with the then prevalent notion that woman was inferior. "One only is the God of both, one the Instructor and one the Church; theirs is the same temperance and modesty, the same food, and the same monogamous marriage; one and the same is their breathing, their sight, their hearing, their knowledge, their hope, their obedience, their love, everything. As life and grace and salvation are common to both, so are their love and education. For in this life only is the female different from the male. . . ."[95]

Thus Christian pedagogy reëstablishes in religion an equality created by nature itself. "Nature is the same in each individual, and each is capable of the same virtue. Woman does not have one human nature and man another. They both possess the same nature and the same virtue. If we said that prudence, justice and similar virtues are masculine, we should have to conclude that only man must be virtuous and that woman should be intemperate and unjust; but this it would be disgraceful even to say. Woman, like man, must cultivate prudence and justice and all the other virtues, whether she be

---

94. Inscription in the gymnasium of Miletopolis: γυναικὸς ἄρχε.
95. Clem. of Alex., *Paed.*, I, 4.

free or a slave, since there is one identical virtue in their one identical nature."[96]

Christianity makes oneness in faith and ethics correspond with this oneness in nature; hence in the natural and in the supernatural order, it purifies woman as well as man, and the slave with the free man, and makes them all, without distinction, "philosophers." Consequently, external or social conditions can in no way limit either the dignity or the spiritual obligations of each individual, not even in the face of martyrdom. "For, if it is beautiful for a man to die for virtue, for liberty and for himself, the same is true for a woman, because this is not a privilege of the masculine sex but a natural right of virtuous beings." And a woman may be virtuous even against the will and in spite of the actions of her husband.[97] This means an autonomy for woman which, in the second century, is still incomprehensible to the pagan mind.[98]

It also constitutes a dignity which vests woman with an interior beauty that needs no artificial aids or adornments. "Beauty and ugliness reside in the soul alone; only the virtuous man is beautiful and good, and only the good is also the beautiful, according to the words of the poet: 'It is virtue alone that shines in the beauty of the body.' And it blossoms in the flesh, it bestows a pleasing aspect on inner temperance, when good morals shine radiant in the face. For the beauty of all beings, even of plants and animals, emanates from their virtue." True beauty is "justice, temperance, fortitude and fear of the Lord"; the form of the Word, the resemblance to God, for beauty is altogether a perfect transformation in God.[99]

---

96. *Strom.*, IV, 8.

97. *Strom.*, IV, 8.

98. Just as the wife must have no friends but her husband's, so she must have (and venerate) no gods but her husband's, and she must shun foreign superstitions: "for secret sacrifices offered by a woman are not pleasing to any god" (Plutarch, *Coniug. praecept.*, XIX).

99. *Paed.*, II, 12; III, 1. Celsus did not understand this and asked, "Was the mother of Jesus, therefore, a beautiful woman and because she was beautiful did God espouse her, who by nature cannot be enamored of a corruptible body? And was it truly proper that a God should be enamored of her if she was

Such a woman is an essential factor in the smooth running and the joy of the household. She has a care for both her virtue and her domestic duties; "for their own toil best confers true beauty on women, exercising their bodies, and clothing them with their own proper adornment; not the adornment produced by others' labor, which is not attractive and is suited to slaves or courtesans, but that which a good woman owes only to the work of her own hands and earns with her own labors." In other words, she makes her own clothes and manages the household for her husband and children. And only thus "are they all joyful, the children because of their mother, the husband because of his wife, the wife because of her family, and all of them because of God. In short, 'A valiant woman is a treasure of virtue';[100] she has 'not eaten her bread idle,' — the 'diligent woman is a crown to her husband' (Prov. 31: 27; 12:4)."

Hers is a complete moral strength which is not shaken by the blandishments of luxury; it governs her manner of speaking, her walk, her dress, and requires her to be sincere and natural. Such a woman does not imitate the gestures and mannerisms of actors, nor the gait of dancers, nor does she droop and languish when she walks. She does not speak in an artificial little voice, nor does she cast languid and covetous glances about her to captivate, nor does she chew gum. These are harlot's tricks, which the Alexandrian priest castigates with the sarcasm of the comedy-writers and the irony of Anacreon. In church (as everywhere, because the Lord is present everywhere) woman must dress modestly without exposing any part of her body, not even her neck; she must be pure in body and in spirit, like Aeneas' wife, who was modest and veiled even during the burning of Troy.[101]

---

neither rich nor of royal birth, and if no one knew her, not even her neighbors?" (Origen, *C. Cels.*, I, XXXIX.)

100. This is a verse of the comic poet Alexander. Cf. for this paragraph, *Paed.*, III, 11.

101. *Paed.*, XIII, 11.

If she is not married, she thinks only of God. If she is married, she divides her life between God and her husband. If she acted any differently she would become the victim of vice. "The modest woman who tends to her husband sincerely adores God; but the woman who cultivates her personal elegance separates herself both from God and from chaste wedlock, and puts her elegance in her husband's place."[102]

By virtue of her dignity woman becomes an instrument in ennobling man, just as with her impurity she can become the means of brutalizing him.

The good Hermas regarded a chaste wife so highly that he said sin can be avoided merely by keeping her image in mind.[103] In her lives again the grace of Susanna, who was not beautiful because of the cosmetics on her skin and the color about her eyes (such as Jezebel used), but rather with the beauty of faith, chastity and sanctity.[104] In her also lives again the conjugal fidelity of Sara and the wives of the patriarchs.[105]

The shameless and greedy woman is, according to whoever compiled the *Gospel of the Twelve Apostles,* the one truly responsible for the betrayal of Christ. In fact, Judas was supposed to have let himself be led astray by a woman, as Adam had been by Eve.

The Apostolic Fathers keep insisting on chastity and humility in chastity, especially for women, who are more exposed to exploitation and fall more frequently. In their polemical writings the apologists compare the Christian woman, chaste, sober and industrious, with the pagan woman, dissolute, grasping

---

102. *Ib.,* II, 10.

103. *Pastor,* Mand. IV, 1 (already quoted).

104. Hippolytus, *In Susannam,* V, 30 (*P. G.,* X, 696). Cf. Cyprian, *De op. et eleem.,* XIV-XV: *Quae matrona in Ecclesia Christi locuples et dives es, inunge oculos tuos, non stibio diaboli, sed collyrio Christi. . . . Quae talis es, nec operari in Ecclesia potes. Egentem enim et pauperem non vident oculi tui superfusi nigroris tenebris et nocte contecti.*

105. *Discant mulieres exemplis patriarcharum, discant, inquam, mulieres sequi viros suos. Neque enim sine causa scriptum est quod Sara stabat post Abraham, sed ut ostenderetur quia vir si praecedit ad Dominum sequi mulier debet* (Origen, *In Gen.,* hom., IV, 4).

and wretched. Naturally, the colors are exaggerated in the heat of argument and the effort to generalize. But there is great truth in Tatian's statement that the Christians honored virgins, widows and chaste mothers, while the pagans celebrated above all concubines and women given to vice. He found an evident rebuke in the number of statues representing hetaeras, which were exposed to the admiration of the public as masterpieces of Greek sculpture. This idolatrous art devoted to amoral women invited imitation of their life by others. The Christians were derided because they wasted time instructing lowly women, girls, boys and old men; but this was a care given the minds and hearts of creatures who were despised by Greek intellectualism.

Greek artists had immortalized poetesses whose verses burned with unbridled sensuality: Lysippus carved a statue of Praxilla, and Silanion of Sappho, "a madly erotic hetaera who sang of her own lust"; and the courtesans Phryne, Glycera and Pasiphaë were all enshrined in statues by the greatest sculptors of Greece. These are fine models of feminine behavior, the apologists observed ironically. But we must also remember that, above the herd of vain and frivolous women, Stoic teaching formed wives and mothers of austere virtue, who were independent and fearless while adulation was the universal practice; and in the families of laborers and peasants there were still good women faithful to a traditional or natural morality.

In any event the strict principles of Christian teaching reëstablished the institution of the family, the axis of which, in so many respects, is woman. The purity of her morals, her control over the bodily appetites, her chastity do not make her any less a person; they do mean that she is freed from the abuse to which she was so often subjected and which made her a tool for pleasure while she was young and for labor when she was old — the frequent object of exploitation. They mean a renewal of the charm of ideal beauty, which outlasts the decay of physical beauty. The only misogynist writings in

Christian literature that spring from this ascetic and moral re-
habilitation of woman either border on heresy or are outright
heretical; they are due to a misunderstanding of moral obligations, characteristic of the crabbed and morbid rigorists and
those who could not rise to a comprehension of the synthesis
of all virtues.

PROCREATION, ABORTION, EXPOSING THE NEWLY-BORN

The natural purpose of matrimony is not the remedy of
concupiscence but the generation of children. Thus it has a
basis that may be called juridically solid in view of the Church's
"laws" governing marriage. The determining factor in marriage is not pleasure nor even the *affectus maritalis* of Roman
law but the children, even aside from the religious bond. This
had been originally the concept of Roman law also.

A principle like this, which made the parents participants
in the work of Creation, penetrated like a burning wedge the
base and depraved mentality of the pagan cities of the second
and third centuries, whose more comfortable citizens had become sterile through selfishness, while the proletariat learned
to ape them. Trajan and Hadrian had had no legitimate children. A family of five children was held up as an example to
the whole Empire. If it had not been for the Christian reaction, there would have been an appalling decrease in the
population.

The birth of a child, among Christians, is the first fulfillment of conjugal union: "If a child is born to one of them,
they praise God; and if the infant dies they praise God the
more as for one who has passed through the world without
sin."[106] For begetting children is not an end in itself; it is a
means of creating candidates for eternal beatitude.

This teaching is quite different from what the freedman
Encolpius and his companions learn in the *Satyricon*. When
they are shipwrecked on the shores of Croton, a peasant tells

---

106. Aristides, *Ap.,* XV (Syriac version, ed. Harris).

them that, to make a fortune in that city, they must know how to cheat and lie; and they must also not have children, for whoever does have any can be sure of never being invited to dinner or to parties. Only those who have no children are esteemed and welcomed. Paganism in all ages, like the citizens of Croton, has considered children a burden; Christianity has deemed them a dutiful contribution of members to the Church and to society, and an offering of souls to God.

Clement of Alexandria teaches that "marriage is the first legal union of man and woman for the procreation of legitimate children."[107] Just as he condemns Carpocrates' heresy that women should be shared in common, so also does he condemn the heresy of the Marcionites, who, because they believed nature to be evil and did not wish to populate a world made by a creator who was just but not good, refrained from marrying and begetting children, though they did not abstain from food and air, which are also the work of the same creator. They practised continence toward God; they were false ascetics who condemned as nefarious the very union by which they themselves had been brought into being. But the seed of saints is holy, and from it come the Church's children. The Marcionites said that marriage is fornication; hence the Lord did not marry. But they forgot that Christ has a bride, the Church, and that he was not an ordinary man who needed a helpmate. "Hence not even chastity is a good unless it is kept for the love of God."[108]

Against Marcion and Valentinus, who were Gnostics, and against Cassianus, who was a Docetist, Clement defended procreation as a good, opposing to their false and sterile asceticism the example of the Lord who came into the world by birth, and that of the Virgin who conceived him. He buried under a mass of Scriptural quotations their unnatural and antisocial

---

107. *Strom.*, II, 23 (*P. G.*, VIII, 1085).
108. *Strom.*, III, 6 (*P. G.*, VIII, 1153) and *ib.*, III, 3.

doctrines of hatred of the flesh — that flesh which the Lord himself assumed and that body which he himself healed for so many sick.[109] The Alexandrian priest's orthodox views naturally collided with the Carthaginian priest's catastrophic — and by now heretical — ideas, based as these were on the assumption that the world was soon to end. Tertullian believed that if there were no more births it would hasten the ruination of a Satanic world and of a state whose laws, tribunals, commerce and temples all bore the stigma of idolatry, while any children that might be born would only furnish the mob in the amphitheatre with the opportunity to yell: "The Christians to the lions!" And he commented: "That is the acclaim they want to hear who desire to have children."[110]

The Alexandrian is consistent, however, and even criticizes his beloved Plato, some of whose opinions seem to disparage the creative act as opposed to the virtue of speculation; and he criticizes as well those poets who have opposed procreation by celebrating the lack of children as the finest state in which to enjoy life. In compensation, he finds, there have been other poets who have deplored a childless marriage as "incomplete" and have declared that marriage happy which is crowned with many children as with a wreath of flowers. Procreation continues the work of creation.[111] He who is afraid to have children goes against nature.

Naturally, the purpose of marriage, precisely because it is procreation, must not be adulterated or supplanted by lust, which is contrary to nature and reason. "In order that all of life may be lived according to reason, it is necessary to train ourselves early to rule the passions." But, and this is an answer for the Malthusians of the period, "criminal means must not be used to prevent the propagation of the human race according to the plans of Divine Providence. And yet we see women

109. Cf. *Strom.*, III, 17 (*P. G.*, VIII, 1205).
110. *De exhort. castit.*, XII.
111. *Strom.*, III, 9.

who use poisonous drugs to kill the fruit of their womb and who, in destroying it, divest themselves of every feeling of humanity."[112]

Minucius sums up thus the pagan crimes against children: "I see you expose new-born infants to wild beasts and birds, or rid yourselves of them by giving them a wretched death by strangling; and there are women who kill the seed of the future creature with medicinal potions, and commit, as it were, infanticide before they have given birth."[113] His voice quivers with scorn that is in marked contrast with his delightful and delicate pictures of prattling children and little boys playing at throwing shells into the sea on the beach at Ostia on a charming October day.

The preceding volumes of this series[114] have mentioned how the people of ancient times used abortion and exposed infants on a large scale to rid themselves of the burden of support and education. Christianity immediately defines abortion as a crime; it is murder. The Christians were accused of murder for cannibalism, and they demonstrated the absurdity of the charge by showing that their moral law forbade so much as the sight "of a man's execution, even if he has been justly condemned . . . , and the gladiatorial combats and the combats with beasts . . . for they maintain that to assist at the killing of a man is almost the same as killing him. . . . " How can they be murderers when they consider that whoever "brings about an abortion with medicaments commits a murder, and that he will have to render an account to God for that abortion? In fact, a man cannot believe the fetus is a living being and that as such it is under the protection of God and at the same time kill it when it has been born."[115]

112. *Paed.*, II, 10.
113. *Octavius*, XXX, 2.
114. *The Social Message of Jesus*, ch. VII; the *Social Message of the Apostles*, ch. VIII.
115. Athenagoras, *Suppl.*, XXXV.

The pagan accusation was due to a mistaken and malicious interpretation of the Eucharistic banquet at which they thought an innocent was consumed. Tertullian retorted that real infanticide was committed in the past by the national god Saturn, who devoured his children, and in the present by the anti-Christian accusers and judges, who became assassins through abortion, which is murder in advance. They not only commit homicide but actual murder of their own children by preventing them from being born; but for the Christians, since all murder is forbidden, "it is not permitted to destroy the fetus while it is still in the womb and the [maternal] blood flows through it to form a man. To prevent birth is to be beforehand with murder; and it makes no difference whether one kills a life already born, or suppresses it at birth. He is already a man who is about to be one; and every fruit already lives in its seed."[116]

Another criminal expedient to rid oneself of children was to kill newly-born infants by "drowning them in water, exposing them to the cold, to hunger or to the dogs."[117] Babies were exposed more frequently by the noble and the rich than by the poor; there were wanton matrons who spent fortunes on peacocks, parrots and other birds from India, as well as nightingales, monkeys, and monstrous clowns, and then, in order not to have any bother at all, exposed their own babies.[118] And these became the property of whoever took them in. They were called *alumni* and differed from slaves only in the fact that their parents could redeem them if they wished to, though this was rare. Justin describes the lot of these poor innocents: "Far from doing evil or committing sacrilege, we hold that it is a crime to expose new-born infants; in the first place, because we see that almost all of them are dragged into prostitution, and not only the girls, but also the boys. As it is told

116. *Ap.*, IX, 6.
117. *Ib.*, IX, 7.
118. Clem. of Alex., *Paed.*, III, 4.

of the ancients that they bred herds of oxen, goats, sheep and horses, now people raise adolescents for the sole purpose of abusing them obscenely. . . . In the second place, we do not expose infants for fear that one of them, not being taken up, might die, and then we should become murderers. Therefore, in principle, we must either marry for the sole purpose of raising children or, not marrying, must remain completely chaste."[119]

Tertullian also condemns giving one's children to wealthier persons for adoption because of the danger that they may become "material for incest."[120] In this crime, the pagans imitated their gods — another apologetical argument. "Saturn did not expose his children; he ate them outright. And rightly did parents in certain parts of Africa sacrifice their babies to him."[121]

It could happen that those unfortunate parents, after a few years, might commit incest with their own sons and daughters without recognizing them. The apologist Minucius describes this not imaginary danger when he refutes the charge of incestuous practices among Christians, which his fellow-countryman Fronto had accepted without troubling to verify it. Such practices are common among pagans, if anything: "In Persia, the law permits intercourse with one's mother; in Egypt and Athens it is lawful to wed a sister; your stories and tragedies make a show of incests, which you take pleasure in reading and listening to; and you likewise adore gods who have had incestuous unions with a mother, a daughter, a sister. With cause, therefore, is incest often discovered among you, and constantly practiced; even without knowing it you may fall miserably into illicit acts. For since you practice free love and scatter your progeny here and there and frequently expose to the mercy of others even the children born to you in your

---

119. *I Ap.*, XXVII, 1; XXIX, 1.
120. *Ad Nat.*, I, 16.
121. Minucius, *Oct.*, XXX, 1.

house, then necessarily ... it is possible for you to fall upon your own creatures and have intercourse with your own children. Thus even without conscious guilt you weave tragedies of incest."[122]

---

122. *Octavius*, XXXI, 3-4. In ancient Egypt, exposing infants was forbidden. The Greeks introduced it there. The *Gnomon of the Idiologos*, a papyrus probably of the second half of the second century A. D., contains in Nos. 41 and 107, a fiscal provision which says: "If an Egyptian takes an infant from the dunghill and adopts him as his son, he shall be punished at his death by the confiscation of one-fourth of his fortune." Here we see the racial hostility characteristic of the Greeks and Romans, who preferred that their children die in the streets rather than be adopted by an Egyptian, one who belonged to an inferior race; this reveals also the odiousness of the revenue system. (Cf. F. Maroi, "Intorno all'adozione degli esposti nell'Egitto romano," in *Raccolta di scritti in onore di G. Lumbroso,* Milan, 1925, p. 377 ff.)

"While by order of her ἀστυνόμοι Athens recruited public slaves to clear the streets of the tiny bodies of exposed infants, Christianity, from its very beginnings, was recruiting neophytes, who ... searched on the infamous κοπρῶνες for the tender little shoots of human lives. ... " The apologists speak of this cautiously in order not to give strength to the charge that the Christians gathered up these children in order "to kill them during the ceremony of initiation of the neophytes." The accusation is in itself a proof that they did rescue them.

St. Paul often speaks of adoption (Rom. 8:15-17, 23; 9:3, 4; Gal. 4:6; Eph. 1:5). The concept of "υἱοθεσία in St. Paul comes to be intimately associated with the concept of *Ecclesia";* "it is a mystical grafting which joins us as members to Christ. ... Now it is exactly this type of mystical adoption ... which furnishes the model for the *adfiliatio* of orphans and exposed babies in the first centuries of Christianity." Thus unwittingly Christianity "corrodes and disintegrates the framework of Roman legal institutions" (F. Maroi, *op. cit.,* pp. 400 and ff.).

Maroi cites various instances of the exposure of infants, which were due to Greek influence, as they are recorded in the papyri. A certain Hilarion writes to his wife Alis: "If you give birth to a male-child, keep him; if it is a girl-child, expose her" (1 B. C., *P. Oxy.,* IV, 744). He narrates also that "from among the infants exposed on the public κοπρῶνες there must certainly have been recruited in large number the most wretched elements of Alexandrian society, those who formed that crowd of *cinaedi,* expert performers of obscene dances, not to mention *istriones scurraeque mimarii et praestigiatores* (the very etymology of their name κοπρία or *copreae* is significant) who gave Alexandria that primacy which was all her own" (*ib.,* p. 388).

When the Romans came they did not change these conditions; the exposing of infants was for them part and parcel of the *patria potestas.* Children exposed on the dunghills were destined usually *vel ad servitutem vel ad lupanar* (Lactantius, *Inst. div.,* VI, 20); and the term "exposed" is usually the equivalent of slave. Hence the various names common to slaves: *Stercorius, Stercoria,* κοπρία (and *Proiectus, Proiecta,* etc.). In the papyrus document cited above there is "the odious restriction regarding juridical capacity" before religious law (No. 92). Christianity, on the other hand, took priests from the lowliest classes.

The Fathers use strong language to castigate that murderous egoism of parents which was destroying the family; but it was not until the time of Diocletian that selling one's children was forbidden by law. Children must be neither killed nor exposed but educated by their parents, who are conscious of their responsibility before God. This command is written first among the popular Christian precepts: "Do not neglect your son or your daughter; but teach them from childhood the fear of God."[123] The father must not slight the care of his family for the business of this world.[124] He must know how and when to pardon and to punish, and he must not be indulgent toward faults because of excessive love. That provokes the wrath of the Lord and also brings ruin on the house. The father must courageously strengthen the virtue of the members of his household with constant instruction. "As the blacksmith, by beating on the shapeless metal with a hammer, forms it into the object he wishes, thus daily instruction in integrity conquers any wickedness." Therefore let the father not weary in admonishing his children.[125] And as for the youths, they have the duty to be obedient, docile and chaste.[126]

Another criminal abuse of children at that time was pederasty. In the second century, despite the Scantinian law, it received its official apotheosis in the person of the Apollo-like Antinoüs, who was loved by the Emperor Hadrian. The latter raised statues in his honor, dedicated a city to him and decreed that he be worshiped as a god.[127] The practice of this unnatural vice must have grown widespread and intense, as all the apo-

---

123. *Didache*, IV, 9.
124. Hermas, *Pastor*, Vis. I, 3, 1.
125. *Ib.*, Vis. I, 3.
126. Polycarp, V, 3.
127. Cf. F. Gregorovius, *L'imperatore Adriano; un quadro del mondo greco-romano ai suoi tempi* (It. tr., Rome, 1910), ch. XXI, *passim*. Mention is made of this in Hegesippus (Eusebius, *H. E.*, IV, 8, 2); and in Theophilus, *Ad Aut.*, III, 8. "All, through fear, were forced to venerate as a god this Antinoüs, who had just died, although they knew who he was and whence he had come" (Justin, *I Ap.*; XXIX, 3).

logists with one voice brand it with their most violent condemnation: "The pederasty forbidden by barbarians, the Romans surround with privileges."[128] The youth, like the virgin,
has the closest resemblance to the purity of God; pederasty is
the most shameful abuse of his body and his soul. Justin reports
that boys were raised and trained expressly for this "with a
whole mob of women, hermaphrodites, and infamous persons
teeming with their perversions in the midst of the people."
They were a source of gain for private individuals and of taxes
for the state.

"Some, besides having impious, immoral and unrestrained
relations with these people, abuse, if they have the opportunity,
even a son, a kinsman, or a brother. There are even those who
prostitute their children and their wife.... "[129]

Bardesanes in his review of the customs of various peoples
brings out the public practice of pederasty among the Germans,
among whom "handsome youths act as wives to men, who
even marry them."[130]

Christianity made its own Juvenal's admonition that the
greatest reverence is due to youth. Clement of Alexandria
taught that Christians are to regard all youths as their children,
with paternal eyes.[131]

"Woe to you, O Rome," thundered the anonymous Sibyl
amid the discontented populace; "punishment will overtake
you, because you have yearned for poisons, practiced adultery
and nefarious intercourse with young boys, O city, cesspool
of vices, iniquitous, evil.... Woe to you, O impure city of
the Latin land."[132]

---

128. Tatian, *Orat.*, XXVIII, 2.
129. Justin, *I Ap.*, XXVII, 1-3. Tatian also denounces (XXVIII, 2) "the
herds of boys, like droves of horses at pasture"; and Clement of Alexandria
(*Paed.*, III, 4) stigmatizes the wealthy "trainers" of "herds of beautiful boys,
like sheep, whose beauty is milked from them." For these and other un-
mentionable practices, see Minucius, *Oct.*, XXVIII.
130. *Liber legum regionum*, XXXV (*P. Syr.*, II, 393).
131. *Paed.*, II, 10 (*P. G.*, VIII, 504).
132. *Sibyll.*, V, 164-167.

And just as Pseudo-Barnabas had compared the one who corrupts young boys to the hyena, so all Christian writers with equal force condemned the no less widespread practice of sodomy. Thus the Christian work of curing the moral disease of society was carried on along a single front and invaded every secret hiding-place of vice. It was like a rushing stream of fresh pure water, sweeping through a vast Augean stable to make it clean.

CHAPTER X

WEALTH: ITS VALUE AND USE

THE PHILOSOPHICAL CONCEPT OF WEALTH

THE ascetics made every effort to center all life's interests upon the things of the spirit; and those who believed the end of the world to be imminent were indifferent to the things of earth, absorbed as they were in securing for themselves the eternity of glory. But as Christianity became more widely diffused and the faith in a proximate second coming of Christ grew dimmer, the persecutions, the obligations imposed by evangelical love and the very renunciation of wealth produced any number of economic and social problems — problems of assistance, labor, distribution and administration. Hence the Church was obliged to pay increasingly active and close attention to the things of this world also. We do not maintain with some that the bishops (and the deacons) were simply administrators of temporal things as their name might suggest,[1] but certainly their office included these too. If the Church wanted to build up brotherhood, equality, peace, labor, the very kingdom of God on earth, then she had to labor to establish even the human factors of success. A church cannot be built out of a mob that has been systematically brutalized by hunger and the lash. It is necessary first to nourish them — perhaps as a kind of prerequisite — to restore their hope and their moral and physical energies in order that they may be disposed to think of the problems of the spirit.[2] Even today

---

1. Perhaps this may be said of the chief administrator (*epitropos*) of the Montanists who had the grave responsibility of provisioning the crowd of refugees at Pepuza and of managing the funds that derived from the sale of their goods.
2. This is the thought we glean from the later writings of Clement of Alexandria, although in the beginning he also had stated absolutely that "there

253

missionary activity is social, educational and remedial as well
as religious. If, while it preached the life of paradise, Christianity had not regularly and effectively aided men to procure
the means of earthly life also, especially through that long,
vast, unceasing labor of redistribution of wealth known as
charity, it would never have accomplished the revolution it did.

When the industrial revolution in England had revived
and worsened the wholesale slavery of men, women and children, and when the conditions of the poor were at their very
worst, Lord Shaftesbury found it necessary to declare that his
efforts to reëmancipate these unfortunates with laws protect-
ing their interests were opposed by the "Saints," that is, the
theorists of an individualistic and purely "mystical" religion,
who, safe in their sacristies and temples, refused to lower their
glance to the miseries of this world. But the majority of the
saints of the first centuries lived intensely that solidary social
life in which they made their own the joys and the sorrows of
their least brother; and they realized the Gospel precept in
that active solidarity which reflects the life of the Godhead,
the meaning and the essence of charity. The sharing of property was one phase of the intense community life of the Church
carried out in the knowledge that that only was good which
was done in the spirit of unity.[3]

We have no proof that the other religious and philosophic
currents of the time took any active or systematic interest in
economic problems; and one of the human factors responsible
for the more rapid success of Christianity in comparison with
the other religions supported by the state or spread by the army,
was precisely this interest which the Church brought to the
solution of the human problems of property, money and labor,
a solution conditioned by the precepts of charity and justice

---

is no impediment for him who strives to know God: not the lack of children,
not poverty, not the lack of glory, nor of independence" (*Protr.*, X, *P. G.*,
VIII, 221).

3. Cf. Ignatius, *Magn.*, VII, 1.

and definitively dependent upon the very problem of eternal salvation.

It is first necessary to give wealth its proper value. *Per se,* it has no ethical value whatever. It does have a religious one; for, while pious but superficial ascetics regarded it as unquestionably the creation of the devil, the more intelligent and discerning writers viewed it, in itself, as a creation of God. Nature with all its various elements and products, earth, water, animals, vegetation, metals, etc., has been fashioned by the divine Artisan. Goods, therefore, are truly in themselves what their name implies: *good.*[4] Secondly, if they have been created by God, they are for the use of all created beings, and originally they belong to everybody.[5] Therefore, they should at least be available for use in common.

---

4. Theophilus, *Ad Aut.*, Liber II, *passim*. According to Origen (*In ep. ad Rom.*, IV, 9; *P. G.*, XIV, 995) there are *good* things, *indifferent* things (which are neither good nor bad: for example, wealth, beauty, strength) and *bad* things.

The indifferent things become good if they are christianised: if strength is used in the service of God and wealth in the service of the poor; then the indifferent things also are such that we may glory in them, that is, they become *good*. Vice versa they become *bad* if they are destined to a bad use: for example, strength used to oppress the weak and wealth used to trample on the poor.

5. "God made all things for everybody. Therefore, all things are common property and let the rich not claim more for themselves than the others.... God gave us the power to use his wealth, but only insofar as it is necessary, and he wishes us to use it in common. It is therefore unjust for one to feast and revel while many live in poverty" (Clem. of Alex., *Paed.*, II, 12).

God has created all things and given them an unchangeable order; "and he has placed them all in man's service, while he has willed that man alone be free" (Novatian, *De Trinitate*, I). What God has made is a work of goodness and is a good thing: and the goodness of created things is testimony of the goodness of God the Creator; for God cannot be the maker of anything evil (*ib.*, IV). Therefore we must reject the Jewish discrimination between pure and impure foods; God made all things, including food, *valde bona*, according to Gen. 1:31 (*Id.*, *De cibis iudaicis*, II). — *Quodcumque Dei est, in nostra usurpatione commune est, nec quisquam a beneficiis suis et muneribus arcetur, quominus omne humanum genus bonitate ac largitate divina aequaliter perfruatur. Sic aequaliter dies illuminat, sol radiat, imber rigat, ventus aspirat; et dormientibus somnus unus est, et stellarum splendor ac lunae communis est. Quo aequalitatis exemplo qui possessor in terris redditus ac fructus suos cum fraternitate partitur, dum largitionibus gratuitis communis ac iustus est, Dei Patris imitator est* (Cyprian, *De op. et eleem.*, XXV). Cyprian tears the soul away from the greedy pagan world; he frees it from the material influence of wealth, which is poisonous, and places the fruits of wealth in common use, according to the plan of the Creator.

Practically speaking this language was revolutionary, but it was not new to Greek philosophy or to other ancient thought. Stoicism still taught, though only in theory, the essential goodness of the natural state, in which life would be easy and there would be sufficient wealth and peace and justice for all. Seneca is a precursor of Rousseau in maintaining that the difficulties of existence are the products of civilization, which has divided men through avarice and lust and, by means of their differences and hatreds, has created property and consequently poverty. Apart from the doctrine of the uncorrupted goodness of nature, these ideas had a certain affinity with the Christian teaching regarding the origin and use of created goods.

Among the Christians themselves there was, at least apparently, great confusion of thought between goods in themselves and the practical use made of them, and this confusion was at the bottom of the radical condemnation of wealth we find in some writers.[6]

Judging wealth in the abstract and apart from the fact that it was created by God, Clement of Alexandria finds that it is intrinsically neither good nor bad, that it involves no ethical judgment.

Juvenal stigmatizes the "most holy majesty of money."[7] It is a usurped majesty that violates human dignity; for in themselves riches, whose expression is money, are void of any value whatever. Their value derives from their use. Gems, for example, pearls, gold and silver owe their worth to their rarity. When it comes to actual usefulness they are inferior to the less valuable iron. "Among certain barbarous peoples, prison chains are beaten of gold because this metal abounds among them: and whatever may be had in abundance loses in value."[8] These observations, while not original, bring back to first principles

---

6. For example, Origen himself in speaking of the origin and history of words laments the fact that the words *bonus* and *bene* have been applied also to "blind wealth" and material things (*C. Cels.*, I, 24).

7. I, vv. 112-3.

8. Tertullian, *De cultu fem.*, I, 7. Cf. Clem. of Alex., *Paed.*, II, 12.

that disesteem for wealth of which asceticism makes such vigorous application in questions of the use of wealth.

But from this lowered estimate of the thing itself, the next step was usually a reëvaluation of its use, which must be made to harmonize with the Christian precepts of brotherly love, humility and the preëminence of the spirit over matter. First the Christians built their platform; then they worked to erect on it an economic life that would be less unjust than the existing one, which, especially since Hadrian's time, had been resolving itself into a cleavage between the minority of privileged *honestiores* and a majority of exploited or neglected *humiliores.* In Italy, the old and the new aristocracy invested in lands, to live on the modest profits they yielded. But through lack of well-planned and intensive farming and because of the gradual dwindling of the market, the countryside also became impoverished and the fields lay idle across ever-widening estates. Pliny the Elder had already deplored this situation.[9] The Antonines tried to remedy it but without result. First trade and then industry were more profitable, and in these the new men who had come up from slavery or the country grew rich. But the center of wealth was moving from Italy to Gaul, Spain, Africa and Asia. The declining birthrate and emigration began to depopulate the cities and turn the countryside into a solitude, while a growing and top-heavy bureaucracy circumscribed private initiative and then stifled it with taxes.

---

9. Cyprian mentions these estate-owners (*ad Donatum,* 12); they are insatiable and drive the poor from their boundaries in order to widen their fields, *infinita ac sine terminis rura latius porrigentes.* But they are slaves of their own wealth; they do not possess it, they are possessed by it. (Cf. Seneca, *De vita beata,* XXII: *Divitiae meae sunt, tu divitiarum es,* and his *Ep., CXIX.* After all it is a fairly common theme among the writers of the Empire.)

In addition Cyprian condemns the greed of the authorities who make the cost of living higher, dry up the sources of wealth, and cut off all aid from the poor and all care from the sick. The magistrates attend only to *impia lucra,* greedy for the spoils of the dead (*Ad Demetr.,* X). They all plunder; *avaritia palam saevit, et, ipsa audacia sua tuta, in fori luce abruptae cupiditatis arma prostituit. Inde falsarii, venefici inde, inde in media civitate sicarii tam ad peccandum praecipites quam impune peccantes. . . . Impunitatem consequuntur mali* (*Ad Demetr.,* XI). It cannot be said the good bishop lacked courage.

The Church certainly could not remedy injustices like these with political measures, both because of her very nature and because she could not in any way directly influence a state which had outlawed her. She did, however, remedy them in part by putting into circulation the resources that came to her through charity. First of all, she made the rich contribute of their wealth and she instilled resignation in the poor.

"Your spirit must not be disturbed at the sight of the unjust who enjoy wealth and the servants of God who live in poverty."[10] "The possession of the ends of the earth avails nothing; the kingdoms of this world avail nothing. It avails us more to die for the name of Christ than to rule the ends of the earth."[11]

If principles like these had remained isolated, they would have contributed nothing to the relief of economic distress, which, particularly after the second half of the second century, became truly serious. But their enunciation by ascetics was accompanied by the activity of men who were in closer contact with the people; and on the other hand, they served to fix in men's minds that new moral evaluation of money which alone could give rise to a more just distribution of wealth. Nor could closer examination of the economic problem be expected in those days from any of the pagan writers either.

As wealth (*fastidium opulentiae*, Tertullian calls it) lost its prestige, so did those who possessed it. The mistaken judgment of the world gave them a preëminence based on mere external show and unjustified by any spiritual motive.

"Take their adornment from the matrons, and take the slaves away from their masters, and you notice that in no way do these people differ from the slaves they have bought at great price: not in their gait, not in their countenance, not in their speech. But in all things they resemble their inferiors; and if they do differ in anything it is in the fact that they are

---

10. *II Clem.*, XX.
11. Ignatius, *Rom.*, VI, 1.

weaker than the latter and because of the manner of their up-
bringing they are more susceptible to disease."[12]

The Christian could not adapt himself to the moral domi-
nance of extrinsic values. His standard was always the spirit
and so he scorned wealth insofar as it meant social privilege,
and even free citizenship insofar as this was a mark of extrinsic superiority.[13] His asceticism was socially revolutionary.

THE ETHICAL VALUE AND SOCIAL FUNCTION OF WEALTH

In defining the Christian attitude toward the goods of this
earth, the Apostolic Fathers stay within the limits of the teachings of Jesus and the Apostles. But we can already note an
emphasis on the ascetical side, and it grows stronger in the
second and third centuries under the pressure of government
persecutions and the economic crisis.

"Let not the wise man glory in his wisdom, and let not the
strong man glory in his strength, and let not the rich man glory
in his riches," says St. Clement of Rome, quoting Jeremias.[14]
"Christ belongs to the lowly and not to him who exalts himself above his flock." He came in humility and poverty as the
spirit of prophecy had foretold: "For the wickedness of my
people has he come to death. And I will give the ungodly for
his burial, and the rich for his death." And in the prayer, God
is called the bestower of poverty and riches.[15]

It is a fact that between wealth and poverty, Christ chose
poverty.[16]

---

12. Clem. of Alex., *Paed.*, III, 6.
13. Athenagoras, *Suppl.*, I.
14. Clem. Rom., XIII, Jeremias, 9:23.
15. *Id.*, XVI, XLIX. The quotations are from Isaias, 53: 8-9; and I Kgs.,
2:7.
16. *Matrem de qua nasceretur elegit pauperem, et patriam pauperem, de qua
dicitur: Et tu, Bethlehem, minima es in millibus Iuda* (Origen, *In Lev. Hom.*,
VIII, 4). Origen justifies Jesus' poverty by comparing it with that of Socrates
and other Greek philosophers: Democritus, Crates, Diogenes etc. (*C. Cels.*, II,
41). Jesus' words, "It is easier for a camel ... etc." (Matt. 19:24) Celsus
regards as a plagiarism from Plato, who said, "It is impossible for a man who
is good to an eminent degree to be rich in an eminent degree" (Origen, *C. Cels.*,
VI, 16; cf. Plato, *De leg.*, V, 743).

Despite the fact that they are not always clear, these writers condemn the use made of wealth and not wealth itself, at least not explicitly. In fact, what they hammer at most is greed.

Polycarp repeats with St. Paul: "The desire of money is the root of all evils" (1 Tim. 6:10); and he is paraphrasing St. Paul when he writes: "He who permits himself to be conquered by covetousness will be contaminated with idolatry and judged a heathen."[17] For happiness does not reside in wealth.[18]

The widespread belief in Fate helped to establish wealth as a privilege, for since riches were considered an unavoidable gift of destiny, it was useless for the poor man to react in any way. This a bestial Fate, Tatian argues, and in fact it resides in the Zodiac, which is the circuit of animals. "And the wrathful and the patient, and the chaste and the dissolute, the poor and the rich are made to depend on such legislators of procreation."[19] Instead the Christian rebels against this quiescence and lack of responsibility; he rebels according to the Christian program of revolution, overthrowing in the realm of the spirit the foundations of the existing social and economic system. "How can I admit that procreation depends on *heimarmene* when I see its ministers of such a breed? I do not wish to rule, I do not long to be rich, I refuse a military career, I detest fornication, I am not interested in maritime commerce for love of money, I do not frequent the palestra to win wreaths, I have renounced the mad pursuit of glory, I scorn death, and I rise above every sickness, I do not enslave my spirit to sadness. If I am a slave, I endure slavery; if I am free, I do not parade my

---

17. IV, 1; XI, 2. "We cannot be friends of God and at the same time friends of the body and the pleasures of the body. The friend of pleasure will love riches, the friend of riches will be necessarily unjust.... Even though his sacrifices are hecatombs and though he adorn the temples with thousands of votive offerings, he is impious, atheist and sacrilegious in thought. Every voluptuous man must be avoided as impure and atheist" (Porphyry, *Ad Marcellam*, 14). Then, like a typical Greek, he says we must not speak with those whose ideas we do not approve of; we must not teach God to the unworthy.
18. *Diogn.*, X.
19. Tatian, *Oratio*, IX, 1.

noble birth. I see that there is one and the same sun for every-body, the same death for everyone, midst pleasures and midst poverty. The rich man sows, and the poor has a share in the same sowing; the richest die, and beggars move within the same limits of human life. The rich have the greatest needs, and they grow poor through vainglory, while the poor man, with his moderation, keeping within the limits set by his means, fulfils his obligations more easily.... Die to the world re-nouncing its madness."[20]

These are the extremists of the ascetical revolution, which is, however, negative and destructive rather than constructive. It does not make the reparation expected by those who thirst after justice.

In Hermas we have the ascetic who comes from the business world (the modest business world of the little rural bour-geoisie), and he therefore values money with the eye of a man of action. It might be said that two currents of thought meet in him: the one is strictly ascetic and resolves the problems of wealth by renouncing it altogether and embracing poverty; and the other is more practical, insisting on the divine origin of earthly possessions and on the fact that their use may be good or evil. This latter attitude asserts rather that good use must be made of wealth and moves the problem toward a compro-mise solution with due consideration for the exigencies both of piety and of everyday life. It christianizes property, labor, finance, money and even capitalism, insofar as we may use the term in speaking of those times.

According to Hermas, then, wealth also has been given us to use as a means to earn merit. The Christian must keep only what he needs and give the rest away in order to win riches in heaven where his true country lies. For he is on this earth as a foreigner, and therefore it is not fitting that he should trouble so much to build "edifices and homes that are com-

---

20. Tatian, *Orat.*, XI, 1-2.

pletely useless," to buy estates and surround himself with luxury. Whoever did this would show that he considers his dwelling, the earthly city, to be not temporary but permanent. Earthly possessions are "foreign" to the Christian, "subject as they are to the jurisdiction of others." The two cities, the two rulers are incompatible: either the Christian serves the "foreign" city and obeys its laws, or he lives for "his own" city, obeying other laws. Since he is merely passing through this earthly city, a pilgrim, the Christian does not provide himself with anything beyond the mere necessities, and so it will not be painful for him to leave it when its king sends him away for disobeying its laws.[21]

The same idea occurs in another writing of the same period: "The Lord says, 'No servant can serve two masters' (Lk. 16: 13; Matt. 6:24). If we tried to serve God and Mammon both, it would be to our loss. What does it profit to gain the whole world, but then to lose one's soul? The present world and the future world are two enemies: the one preaches adultery, corruption, greed and fraud, the other renounces them. . . . We believe it is better to hate our present riches because they are trifling, short-lived and corruptible, and to love those others which are good and incorruptible."[22]

"In the moment of tribulation," that is, persecution, rich Christians apostatize through love of their wealth in order to avoid its being confiscated. But in order to become useful stones in the Christian edifice, they must detach themselves completely from riches. There is Hermas' personal experience: when he was rich he was useless; now that he has lost his riches he is "useful to life."[23] Hermas' anxiety regarding the difficulty riches create in the hour of trial echoes through the other Fathers, especially the bishops. Cyprian observes that during

21. *Pastor*, Sim. I.
22. *II Clem.*, VI.
23. Hermas, *Pastor*, Vis. III, 6.

persecution riches have been a chain on faith and virtue.[24] In recompense, however, the rich man who endures martyrdom has more merit than the poor man, for besides his life he sacrifices his fortune, and God repays him a hundredfold.[25]

Contrary to Hermas' ideas, Clement of Alexandria asserted that in time of persecution possessions may constitute an obstacle only if the mind is passively attached to them; and he objected that it was not a question of external persecutions and peace, but of internal persecutions and peace, for even far from the instruments of the executioner, one may be tormented by the passion to acquire more wealth, and this tears and cuts the heart with much more terrible goads and stings.[26]

In any case, this ascetic ideal of complete detachment from the things of the world is influenced by Christianity's position in civil society; for the Christian lives constantly in danger and is threatened every moment with the possibility of being expelled from that society, of being sent back to his own kingdom, heaven, via persecution. Asceticism is a heroic solution for extraordinary times, but what of ordinary times?

Hermas examines the question with his usual good sense. According to a popular notion, shared also by the Jews, riches are the property of God. Man is merely their administrator and he must administer them according to the will of their owner, that is, he must invest them in good works in order to

---

24. During the persecution of Decius, the Christians of Africa apostatized in great number merely at the threat that their goods would be confiscated. Persecution, according to Cyprian, is a punishment because we do not obey the commandments: *Patrimonio et lucro studentes ... saeculo verbis solis et non factis renuntiantes* (*Ep.*, VII, 1). And elsewhere: *Dissimulanda veritas non est. ... Decepit multos patrimonii sui amor caecus, nec ad recedendum parati aut expediti esse potuerunt quos facultates suae velut compedes ligaverunt.* Riches have made victims for the serpent that devours the earth. If the rich sold their goods and gave them to the poor in accordance with Matthew, 19:21, they would not perish; if they had their treasure in heaven, their hearts would be there and not here (Cyprian, *De lapsis*, XI). *Sequi autem Christum quomodo possunt qui patrimonii vinculo detinentur? Aut quomodo caelum petunt, et ad sublimia et alta conscendunt qui terrenis cupiditatibus degravantur? Possidere se credunt qui potius possidentur, census sui servi, nec ad pecuniam suam domini, sed magis pecuniae mancipati* (*ib.*, XII).

25. Origen, *Exhort. ad mart.*, XV-XVI.
26. *Quis dives salvetur?*, 25.

reap the profit in that which is his true country. These investments are not lost at death; in fact, they are found again in
the new life and they give a happiness that has nothing to do
with the joys of voluptuous living poisoned as they are by the
worries and disappointments that cluster about one's houses,
lands and luxury here below. "Use your money as your state
in life requires, to procure this happiness. Do not defraud in
any way nor covet the property of others."[27]

Thus while riches as they are commonly used form an obstacle in the path of perfection, they become, as the Christian
uses them — in the service of the needy — a means of perfection; and the rich man and the poor become partners in a
society whose capital is securely invested. For with respect
to our eternal end, the rich and the poor are as the vine and
the elm; one needs the other in order to bear fruit. The great,
new social, moral and religious function of wealth is this, that
when it is used in accordance with the Gospel precept, it permits the rich to rise and lean on the poor, as the vine grows
leaning on the elm-tree; but if it drags along the ground it
bears dry and scanty fruit. This simile has flashed clearly and
spontaneously across the mind of the farmer-ascetic. And as
he develops it, it seems to him that the elm gives more than
the vine, for it gives the vine its moisture in times of drought
and helps it to bear fruit in full abundance. "The rich possesses much, but being a prisoner of his wealth, he is only poor
in the sight of God: and his prayer is weak, without the strength
to rise to the Lord. . . . The poor man is instead rich in prayer
and generous in recognizing the glory of God, before whom
his requests have great importance. . . . "And so the enlightened rich man helps the poor man to live in this life by supplying his wants; and the poor man helps the rich to live in eternity by supplying what he lacks. Each gives what he has; their
collaboration is made up of various elements which are fused

---

27. Hermas, *Sim.*, I, 11.

in the one result that benefits both partners. Naturally this is possible when they are both Christians, that is, when for both of them their joint and supreme end in life is eternal happiness. Thus religion influences economics and its influence is fundamentally revolutionary. Hermas, the ex-slave and ex-peasant and the brother of the Pope, had found for the poverty-ridden economic system of the Empire the most obvious and most eloquent formula, the formula of that solidarity and coöperation among all classes[28] which is the concrete expression of their equal responsibility, and of their unity in the Church.

In short, wealth has a function of its own: it is to serve the good of all men. If it serves only the selfish use of a few, it betrays its function.[29] The miser who removes a part of the world's wealth from circulation to keep it sterile and inactive in his coffers and chambers sins against its function. He does not possess it; he is possessed by it. He is not a master, but a slave, the slave of matter.[30] To avoid such a danger, such a social and theological sin, the perfect Christian, just as he frees

---

28. *Sim.*, II. For other exhortations to the rich urging them to assist all the needy, see *Vis.*, III, ix.

29. "Wealth is not to be employed for our empty enjoyment, but *to be put in common use*" (εἰς μετάδοσιν κοινωνικήν), Clem. of Alex., *Paed.*, II, 1.

30. Wealthy misers do not give of their substance either to their clients or to the poor (*cum indigentibus nulla partitio*). *Possident ad hoc tantum ne possidere alteri liceat. Et, o nominum quanta diversitas! Bona appellant ex quibus nullus ullis nisi ad res malas usus est* (Cyprian, *ad Donatum*, 12). "Whoever lays aside his earnings places them in a sack that is full of holes." This is a saying of the prophet Aggeus (1, 6) quoted by Clement of Alexandria (*Paed.*, II, 3). To the wealthy miser Cyprian says: *Pecuniae tuae captivus et servus es, catenis cupiditatis et vinculis alligatus es, et quem iam solverat Christus, denuo vinctus es. Servas pecuniam, quae te servata non servat. Patrimonium cumulas, quod te pondere suo onerat.... Quid divitiis tuis solus incubas? Quid in poenam tuam patrimonii tui pondus exaggeras, ut quo locupletior saeculo fueris, pauperior Deo fias? Redditus tuos divide cum Deo tuo, fructus tuos partire cum Christo, fac tibi possessionum terrestrium Christum participem, ut et ille te sibi faciat regnorum coelestium cohaeredem* (Cyprian, *De op. et eleem.*, XIII). "The best wealth is to have few desires" (Clem. of Alex., *Paed.*, II, 3). *Usibus sanctorum honeste et decenter, non quasi stipem indigentibus praebere, sed censum nostrum cum ipsis quodammodo habere communem, et meminisse sanctorum sive in collectis solemnibus, sive pro eo ut ex recordatione eorum proficiamus, aptum et conveniens videtur* (Origen, *In ep. ad Rom.*, IX, 12, *P. G.*, XIV, 1220).

himself from his senses to protect his chastity, detaches himself from wealth in order to protect charity, which is the essence of his life in Christ.[31]

THE WEALTHY AND PARADISE

In Alexandria, however, that varied, rich and busy market, in the *Didaskaleion,* attended by cultured and generally wealthy people, and in that Egypt where the praise most sought after by the priests and "prophets" was to be called "happy, rich and illustrious,"[32] the learned and gentle Clement examines with a more realistic eye the whole problem of the relationship between wealth and the salvation of the soul, and he corrects, perhaps too much, the views of the extreme ascetics. Certain extremists regarded the renunciation of wealth as an act of self-liberation meritorious in itself, almost as if that alone were sufficient to widen the road to heaven, which is so narrow for the rich. If this were taken literally, it was to be feared that it would cause a useless waste of wealth and general impoverishment and thus introduce into the life of the spirit a much more goading anxiety over one's daily food or one's house, dress and future, that it would bring conflicts and worries in its wake which would take their toll of piety itself.

Because it defended the position of the rich in the Church and the use of money in relation to salvation, Clement of Alexandria's *Quis dives salvetur?* (Τίς ὁ σωζόμενος πλούσιος) enjoyed great popularity. Actually it is a homily on the episode

---

31. In the Our Father the Christian asks only for one day's bread and does not worry about the future. Christ *docet non tantum contemnendas, sed et periculosas esse divitias, illic esse radicem malorum blandientium, caecitatem mentis humanae occulta deceptione fallentium* (Cyprian, *De orat. dom.,* XX). In the *Testam. in Galilea,* LVII (*P. O.,* IX, 228), we find among the counsels which the risen Jesus gives the Apostles: "Preach and teach what is true and just, without making exceptions and without fearing anyone, particularly the rich who are opposed to those who follow my commandments. . . . But I speak also for him who is not rich. If the rich man gives and at the same time prides himself on being superior to him who possesses nothing, then he will be called benefactor by his fellow men in vain."

32. Cf. F. Cumont, *L'Égypte des astrologues,* Brussels, 1937, p. 120.

of the rich young man in the Gospel who goes to ask Jesus what he must do to win eternal life.

" 'If thou wilt enter into life, keep the commandments,' " the Divine Master answers him. The young man has kept them all. Then Jesus adds tenderly: " 'One thing is still lacking to thee' " — " 'If thou wilt be perfect, go, sell what thou hast, and give to the poor, and thou shalt have treasure in heaven; and come, follow me.' But when the young man heard the saying, he went away sad, for he had great possessions."[33]

Up to this time the exegetes had interpreted Jesus' command literally. They saw in it an exhortation to the heroic renunciation of wealth in order to attain perfection, to be the closest followers of Christ. Consequently all Christians, if they wished to be heroically Christian, would have had to rid themselves of their fortunes and follow Christ.

Clement sees an enormous peril in such a procedure: economic anarchy. And for the peace of heart of the rich Christians who could not make up their minds to be poor, he re-examines Jesus' precept and gives it a different interpretation from the popular one, from that given it by the superficial and uncultured, as he rather harshly calls them. He is aided by the characteristic tendency of Alexandrian exegesis to interpret the Scriptures allegorically and spiritually, and he shows a certain disdain for the crass literal interpretation.

His treatise effectively strikes at ascetic exaggeration, but it evades the explicit precept of Jesus and the work of redistribution which was being accomplished to a certain extent by that very sale and sharing of goods in the community. It is the first skillful apologia of the ethics and legitimacy of wealth.

There had been a general evolution in the author's own thought on the subject. In the beginning, in accord with those who took the Scriptures literally, he also had confined himself to stating that nobility does not reside in heaps of gold but

---

33. Matt. 19:16-22; Mk. 10:17-22; Lk. 18:18-22.

in the temperate use made of it and its distribution according to the biblical saying: "He hath distributed, he hath given to the poor: his justice remaineth, for ever and ever" (Ps. 111:9). He had also censured "the wealth that makes men beasts,"[34] and like those who applied Jesus' words to the letter and believed that wealth was to be distributed, he had perceived the significance of the evangelical revolution: "Not he who possesses and guards his wealth is rich but he who distributes it; its redistribution, not its possession, makes a person happy; a good that is shared becomes a fruit of the soul, and this is wealth of the soul."[35] Blessed, therefore, is he who sells his goods and gives to the poor. "Wealth is like a serpent; if you do not know how to pick it up safely by the tip of the tail and hold it away from you so that it cannot hurt you, it will wind itself about your hand and bite you. In like manner, wealth may encircle one in its folds and bite him, depending on whether he who takes hold of it is an expert in managing it or not."[36]

In conclusion he had said that the true rich are the Christians because they are endowed with virtue. But in the *Paedagogus* he had already begun to place the emphasis on the function of wealth, which he believed should be social. Contrary to the capitalistic custom of the period to amass wealth in the form of precious objects, garments and stores of provisions and household goods (a custom that was one of the causes and also the result of economic stagnation), he asserted that wealth kept in an inactive investment is against reason because thus it is of no use or benefit. It may at the most be of some use to the individual and a few of his parasites; but if it were redivided among those who have nothing, then it would avail the rich man for paradise. The wealth contained in such objects represents a superfluity, a waste; it is withdrawn from general consumption. For the frugal man and woman a

---

34. *Paed.*, III, 7.
35. *Ib.*, III, 6.
36. *Ib.*, III, 6.

little is sufficient. Works of charity are like a well: the more water that is drawn, the more it fills up again. And the charitable man is never in need. In short, earthly goods find their justification in their use for society, not in the luxury they buy for one individual. And the money used for leisure, unrestrained pleasures, gems, gold, silver, vases, etc., is uselessly spent.[37]

In the homily we are here considering, which is later than the *Stromata,* Clement no longer teaches that one's possessions are to be sold and distributed among the poor; he teaches that they are to be kept and used to benefit the poor also. To forestall any eventual charge that he has gone over to the rich, he begins by stating definitely that anyone who praises the wealthy for their wealth is guilty of more than adulation and throwing away his independence. He is also impious because he diverts to man the honor due to God. He is also treacherous because riches in themselves corrupt the morals of him who possesses them; hence to praise a man for his riches is equivalent to plunging him into pride on their account.[38]

If there are reasons why salvation is more difficult for the rich than for the poor, still the rich are not to be discouraged. The warning about the camel and the needle's eye should serve to inspire them to works of salvation. The "rich young man" should still sell his goods and give them to the poor to be "perfect." This means that simply keeping the Commandments had not made him perfect. Besides Jesus says, "If thou *wilt* be perfect," that is, he respects the freedom of his will, for man is free and "God does not force him: violence is the enemy of God."[39] One thing is lacking to the young man still: he must be more of a Mary in the future, while in the past he has been more of a Martha.

37. *Ib.,* III, 7.
38. *Quis dives salvetur?,* 1.
39. *Ib.,* X. Cf. also XXI: "Only one violence is good: to force God and wring from him eternal life."

The new exegesis makes its appearance; it is the first deviation from the traditional. Clement says that the young man went away sad when he heard Jesus command him, "Sell what thou hast"; but that was because he did not understand. For Jesus did not mean he should literally throw away his money, but that "he should detach his soul from the thoughts of wealth, from greed for it, from the morbid passion for it, from the cares and thorns of living which choke the seed of life. For neither great nor worthy to be desired is the state of one so lacking in possessions that he does not have wherewith to live; for if it were, then that whole swarm of proletarians, derelicts and beggars who live from hand to mouth, all those wretched cast out upon the streets, though they live in ignorance of God and of his justice, would be the most blessed and the most religious and the only candidates for eternal life simply because they are penniless and find it hard to live, lacking the most modest means. To say nothing of the fact that it is nothing new to renounce one's wealth and bestow it on the poor and needy, for that was done by many persons before the coming of our Savior, by some that they might dedicate themselves to the study of literature and dead philosophy, and by others to win empty fame through vanity, like Anaxagoras, Democritus, Crates."[40]

Nevertheless the Lord's command is original, but in a different, more divine and perfect way; and its originality consists not in divesting the body of riches but the soul of vice, in stripping it of all that is extraneous to it. The ancients stripped themselves externally of wealth, but internally they cherished passions and vices, and in fact they drew new pride from the renunciation they had made. Jesus could not have meant anything like this for his precept aimed not at pride but at eternal life. One may give away his substance and keep the desire for it and regret: "it is impossible that a man reduce himself to the point where he lacks the necessities of life and not feel

---

40. *Quis dives*, XI.

regret for the loss of his possessions, or that the thought and effort to recover them wherever and however possible should not distract him from the duties of seeking his own perfection." And therefore?

"Therefore, we must not cast away riches which can benefit our neighbor. Possessions were made to be possessed;[41] goods are called goods because they do good, and they have been provided by God for the good of men: they are at hand and serve as the material, the instruments for a good use in the hand of him who knows how to use them. If you use them with skill you reap a benefit from them."

On the other hand, he who does not know how to use them thus wisely, reaps only loss; but even in that case, the fault lies not with the instrument, the wealth itself, but in the inexpert individual who uses it.

Clement is a copious writer and he develops this idea at very great length, viewing it from every possible angle. He repeats and repeats that wealth, because it is an instrument, must serve and not command its owner. By its very nature it is not *per se* either good or evil; and therefore it is not to be discredited. This is an evident jibe at the preachers who heaped all the evils of corruption on wealth and represented it as incompatible with perfection! With his insistence on this concept (which is substantially that of the majority of the Fathers, but is set forth in much bolder relief in this treatise) Clement of Alexandria is arguing, without naming them, against those who thoughtlessly go about teaching people to abandon their property, money and goods. "Let no one therefore cast away his substance, but rather let him cast away the passion that keeps him from a better use of it. Become good and upright, and then you will be able to use these goods honestly also." And his conclusion is: "The command to detach oneself from

---

41. The author is punning on the Greek words: χρήματα, riches, and χρήσιμα, useful things, and also χρῆσις, use, which have the same etymology, deriving from χράομαι.

all one's goods and sell them is to be understood as referring to the passions of the mind."[42]

It is not the Alexandrian teacher's intention, however, to defend the ownership of property at the expense of the poor or to arrest the distribution of goods accomplished in the community by voluntary contributions. On the contrary, he would like to regulate that process, now irregular and fitful, and make it a continuous and normal activity, an increasing flow of adequate and proportionate contributions of revenue on the part of those who possess and retain capital, property.

"How much more useful would it be, on the other hand, if a man, possessing sufficient, should not feel any loss from his possessions, but should come to the aid of him who requires it! . . . Indeed what could men share in common[43] if no one owned anything?" This is George Bernard Shaw's argument,[44] and it is more specious than not. First of all there would be new acquisitions from subsequent converts, and secondly, if, in the Christian community, all the members placed their goods at the disposal of all, there would gradually develop a regular system of managing such revenues, not only for charitable purposes as the givers intended, but also for organizing a permanent community life. That happened to some extent in the first Christian communities, and it happens today in the various religious orders, in which the voluntary poverty of the individual members does not keep the community from having a normal economic existence.

We can make a similar objection to the Alexandrian's other question: "If all despoiled themselves of their possessions who would give the alms commanded by Christ? Who would give food to the hungry, drink to the thirsty, clothes to the naked,

---

42. *Quis dives*, XIV.

43. *Ib.*, XIII. Here also Clement of Alexandria uses the — shall we say — technical expression for this act: κοινωνία (sharing in common). In the *Paed.*, III, 6, he had already written: "The sharing of wealth is to be accomplished according to reason: it must be shared in the spirit of charity and not of meanness or of insolence. . . ."

44. Preface to *Androcles and the Lion;* cf. the first volume of this series, *The Social Message of Jesus*, pp. 16-17, 269.

and shelter to the pilgrim if all were hungry, thirsty, naked and homeless?" Truly it was not a question of reducing everyone to beggary, but of filling the needs of some from the over-abundance of others, that is, of giving food, drink and clothing to everyone in a society which granted these things — at least permanently — to only a part of its members.

Jesus, continues the Alexandrian, rightly did not condemn property; in fact, he accepted the hospitality of Zaccheus and Matthew, two "rich men and publicans." And he did not command them to abandon their possessions but to use them justly, that is, to set aside a part of them (sharing them in common) for works of mercy. For if the latter cannot be performed without money, and if, on the other hand, the Christian were commanded to rid himself of his possessions, then he would find himself facing a hopeless contradiction: "The Lord would only be commanding us to give and not to give, to nourish and not to nourish, to shelter and to shut outside, to share our goods in common and not to share them in common. This is an evident absurdity."[45] Therefore, we must renounce not wealth, but our passions. It is possible to renounce the first and keep the second; but it is better to renounce the second and keep the first. What is necessary is to use wealth "well, with wisdom, moderation and prudence, and in the spirit of religion."

Therefore the invitation, "Come, follow me," means, divest your soul of the wealth of vice; make it poor in guilt; become poor in spirit, that is, do not be a slave of your substance, whether it be much or little, and when necessary know how to cast it from you. He who knows that riches are from God, knows that he has them and the use of them more for his brothers than for himself.[46] "He who carries riches in his soul, and has gold or a piece of land in his heart instead of the Holy Spirit, who is entirely devoted to increasing his patrimony

45. *Quis dives*, XIII.
46. *Ib.*, XVI.

without end, wishing constantly to garner more and more everywhere, and who is prostrate on the earth and bound by the fetters of the world; how can he aspire to the kingdom of heaven, reduced as he is to a being who has a field or metal where his heart should be?" Since a man's mind is where his treasure is, wealth in this case is pernicious and diverts his attention from God to matter.[47] The ethical evaluation of wealth is to be made in the heart of man. There, wealth and poverty are born and live, according to whether a man deposits virtue or guilt in his heart. When it is virtue, the rich man knows of himself what his duties are and he can free himself of the superfluous possessions which obstruct his path to heaven; and even then he makes a bargain, because he exchanges material values for the spiritual values with which the poor repay him. Money thus becomes a means to salvation. If the rich young man in the Gospel had understood this, he would not have found any contradiction between wealth and virtue, and he would not have turned away.[48] Christ does not forbid you to own property. If greed dominates you, then "give away, throw away, hate, renounce, flee." But if you know how to dominate your riches and make yourself "poor in accordance with the commandments, free, unconquered and immune to the diseases and sins of wealth,"[49] then you may possess it with a tranquil conscience. The Lord cannot intend a man to be damned merely because he is rich: for then why would he have made riches spring from the earth? And why would he have let the man be born rich?[50]

This is the main theme in Clement's little treatise on wealth as related to salvation. It was a counterpoise to exaggerated

---

47. *Ib.*, XVII. In the *Paed.*, II, 3 (*P. G.*, VIII, 437) he had said: "Wealth badly managed is a stronghold of wickedness ... ; the greed for money is the stronghold of wickedness."

48. *Ib.*, XX.

49. *Quis dives*, XXVI.

50. *Ib.*, XXVI, Cf. *Strom.*, III, 6 (*P. G.*, VIII, 1160): The Lord "has taught us to share our goods for love; he has not forbidden us to grow rich justly (καλῶς), but to grow rich unjustly and insatiably."

asceticism, and at the same time it more efficaciously impelled Christians to examine the use made of temporal goods in addition to the now familiar matter of redividing and sharing them.

It is the oldest organic expression of a current of thought which was able to keep the rich from being frightened away on the very threshold of the Church, from being discouraged and even turned away by a prejudicial condemnation which had given them the alternative of either ridding themselves of their possessions or being damned. This must have been a real danger if Clement tries so hard to dissipate it. But, we repeat, he is not the advocate of the rich against the poor. He wants rather to bring them closer together, not by the road reserved only for those courageous enough to become poor and descend to the level of the many, but by the easier and pleasanter road where they may unite in spirit through the "mystery" of charity, in which God himself resides.[51] He created a place in the spirit where they could meet as brothers and equals by eluding the accident (the temporary vesture) of wealth or poverty. Love shatters the selfish exclusivism of wealth, and it endures and grows even in heaven where faith and hope are ended in fulfillment.

Clement envisions a model rich man, beneficent, generous and humble, who knocks down all the barriers which his wealth has raised between him and others; a father among the poor, a capitalist who does not exploit the laborer as an enemy but helps him as a friend. Though his point of departure is different, Clement, like the Apostolic Fathers, cherishes the ideal of a Christian social function for wealth. He does not destroy the rich man's superiority; he modifies it. He offers his ambition the friendship, that is, the intimate familiarity of the poor and their coöperation in the work of winning salvation.

---

51. *Ib.,* XXXVII. He thus also realizes the ethical law, so dear to him, of "measure," of *aurea mediocritas,* which tends toward equality; it is the aspiration of the Christian philosopher, who regards it as the condition most favorable to divine gnosis.

The rich man is to use his means, his social preëminence and his prestige to exercise a primacy in charity; he is to be one of the leaders in the army of the socially inferior.

"Do not be dazzled by appearances, you who have tasted the truth and have been made worthy of the great Redemption; but contrary to what other men do, gather about you an unarmed host (not destined for war nor to shed blood, free from all wrath and stain of sin) of devout old men and pious orphans, of widows armed with meekness and men decorated with love. Secure these with your wealth, and make them your bodyguard, to defend you in body and in soul; for their general is God, and through them even a sinking ship will float, guided only by the prayers of saints; and a tormenting illness will be cured by the touch of their hands; and an attack of thieves will be repulsed, crippled by pious prayers; and the violence of devils is destroyed, hurled back by the stern precepts implicit in their works.[52] All these soldiers and guards stand firm and strong at their posts. Not one is inactive, not one is useless. One can pray God for you, another comfort you in your last illness; one can weep and sigh with compassion for you to the Lord of the universe, or teach you things useful for your salvation; another can admonish you frankly, another advise you with benevolence; and all can love you truly, without deception, without fear, without dissimulation, without adulation and without guile. O sweet servitude of friends! . . . O sincere faith of persons who fear only God! . . . "[53] How many treasures of sanctity there are in those poor bodies!

The exhortation is affectionate and eloquent, and it is also shrewd. Clement keeps insisting on total solidarity, with respect to spiritual and temporal goods, among men who are sons of the same Father. The realization of this solidarity leads toward that relative equality to which the Alexandrian also aspires when, quoting Proverbs (30:8) in the hymn that con-

---

52. *Quis dives*, XXXIV.
53. *Ib.*, XXXV.

cludes the *Paedagogus,* he asks the Lord: "Give me neither poverty nor wealth."[54] The Greek golden mean is christianized. Yet this work does betray the first anxiety over the resistance the wealthy offer the communist, equalitarian program of the more determined ascetics. The Church as a whole harmonized the various currents of thought, treasuring the evangelical liberty that is the heritage of each individual; that is, on the one hand she continued to preach the counsel, "Sell what thou hast and give to the poor," and to grow rich spiritually and temporally through the voluntary renunciation her most generous members made of their possessions;[55] and on the other hand she let the majority of her members possess their goods in peace, asking only that they use them as Christians, governed by the obligations imposed on them by solidarity with their brethren. She christianized wealth too and inspired its use with charity and the solidarity of those who shared in the Redemption, and she thereby reëstablished the original purpose of all earthly goods, created by God for all his children without distinction. She bent money, movable and immovable goods, to social service. And she was the first to exemplify this primary purpose of wealth by her works of charity, by requiring, on the one hand, that her ministers, virgins and widows renounce also their wealth,[56] and by never modifying, on the other, her strict condemnation of love of gold and all

---

54. *Paed.,* III, 12.

55. In one papyrus there is mention made of an *arura* of land which a Christian named Demetrianus has decided to give "according to the *ancient custom* to the community," i. e., the Church. The Church probably used it for a burial-place or other lands which it needed. (*P. Oxy.,* XII, n. 1492. Cf. Ghedini, G., *Lettere cristiane dai papire greci del III° e IV° secolo,* p. 123. The *arura* is an Egyptian measure equivalent to 2756 square meters. Cf. Tertullian, *Ap.,* XXXIX, 5.)

56. Cyprian reminds the wealthy virgin consecrated to God that she has also renounced her wealth, her ornament and luxury, for which she has substituted true spiritual wealth. If, however, she wants to use her wealth, she must do it according to the Gospel. *Utere, sed ad res salutares et bonas artes; utere ad illa quae Deus praecepit, quae Dominus ostendit. Divitem te sentiant pauperes, locupletem te sentiant indigentes; patrimonio tuo Deum foenera; Christum ciba* (*De hab. virg.,* XI).

intemperate forms of enrichment.[57] He who is poor in spirit has already traveled half the road to Eternity.

As a result of such principles the economic life of the Church took the form of an undefined communization of private properties and their redistribution to the needy,[58] while she advanced as much as possible toward that ideal equality which would be the reflection of spiritual equality in economic life.

Then, since the use made of wealth has an ethical value with consequences in eternity, the duties of the rich are paralleled by corresponding obligations on the part of the poor. If the rich must be poor in spirit, so must the poor. Hence not only do the rich who badly use their temporal wealth go to hell, but so do the poor who "ignobly endure their poverty."[59] It might be said that the Gospel requires the poor to be rich in spirit.

In short, material wealth is stripped of the value ordinarily attributed to it and is reduced to a status of relativity which is fraught with responsibility. In the usual Christian reversal of things, the true rich man is the virtuous man, united to God, whom no change of fortune can affect.[60]

---

57. In the *"Gospel of the Twelve Apostles,"* so called by Revillout, Judas betrays Our Lord to get money for his wife. Every day he stole from the common purse for this woman, "robbing the poor in his ministry." And in order to have more money she persuaded him to betray the Master (fragm. 5; *P. O.,* II, p. 156). *Iniustitiae enim auctorem et dominatorem totius saeculi "nummum" scimus omnes* (Tertullian, *Adv. Marc.,* IV, 33). Origen identifies Mammon with evil in general (*C. Cels.,* VIII, 56). *De avaritia triumphus est pecuniam spernere* (Cyprian, *De zelo et livore,* XVI).

58. κοινωνία and μετάδοσις. Cf. Clem. of Alex., *Paed.,* III, 6. To explain what the Savior meant when he said to the rich young man, "If thou wilt be perfect, etc." (Matt. 19:16 ff.), Origen quotes the Acts of the Apostles, 2:44-47 and 4:32-37 regarding the communization of property by selling it and giving the proceeds to the Church (*in Matt.,* XV, 15). Queen Tryphena sends Thecla a supply of garments and gold which she leaves with Paul "for the ministry (εἰς διακονίαν) of the poor" (*Acts of Paul,* XLI).

59. Cf. Origen, *De orat.,* XXIX (*P. G.,* XI, 533).

60. *Quem ille* [*Deus*] *divitem fecerit, nemo pauperem faciet* (Cyprian, *ad Donatum,* 15). The law promises wealth to the just. Celsus interprets this literally; he "follows the letter which kills" and refers to "blinding wealth"; instead Origen interprets it as wealth which enriches the light of the mind, according to I Tim. 6:17-18. In that sense poverty is dangerous (*C. Cels.,* 7:21). For the God of the Gospel is not opposed to the God of the law (*ib.,* 7:20).

CHAPTER XI

LABOR

CHRISTIAN LABOR

THE classic sources of ancient oligarchic wealth were war and usury. The Fathers of this period, though they do not treat of such wealth except incidentally, condemn it explicitly enough and remove it from the sphere of Christian activity at least insofar as it spells violence and greed. In actual practice, Christians were not forbidden to be soldiers and bankers; for generally speaking the Fathers were usually setting forth precepts for complete, heroic virtue and this did not prevent a number of the faithful (the majority of them in fact), who tried to reconcile with virtue whatever profession or state their conversion to Christ overtook them in, from living honorably, like good children of the Church, at the halfway mark.

In his apologetical writings Tertullian himself agrees that the daily activities of the Christians are the same as those of the pagans. They have the same way of life, the same education and furnishings, just as they have the same daily needs; for, he says, we are not a caste of "Brahmins or Hindu Gymnosophists (fakirs) living in the forests and exiles from life. But we remember that we must be grateful to the Lord, our God and Creator. We do not reject any fruit of his works; we merely use them temperately in order not to use them sinfully or immoderately. Thus we do not fail to frequent the forum, the market-place, the baths, the shops, the workshops, the inns, and your fairs, and to have all other relations in which our life with you in this world finds expression. With you we sail the sea, enter military service, work the land and trade in its fruits, just as we publicly sell for your use the products of our trades and labors."[1]

Tertullian analyzes these occupations — which are everybody's occupations — in order to answer the charge that the Christians were inactive and unproductive.[2] Farming, shopkeeping, commerce, the occupations of free men, were the ordinary source of the Christians' income. Labor was not forbidden them but idleness. "There is no one lazy in the house of the wise man."[3]

But since the pagan and the Christian world had two different and basically opposed concepts of labor, there was a conflict on this point too. Christianity does not accept the slavery system as a labor system. It considers labor a debt of expiation owed by every man born on earth whether he be rich or poor. It was ennobled by the example of Christ and the Apostles who earned their bread in the sweat of their brow. Celsus perceives this contrast too[4] and expresses his disdain for a society founded by "a carpenter's son," whose mother was a working woman, whose first disciples were laborers and whose believers, in Celsus' time, belonged for the most part to the proletariat.

The Fathers of the Church reject all social prejudices concerning labor and laborers, although they regard this subject not from the economic point of view (or at least do so only incidentally) but from the point of view of ethics and hygiene.

In the first Fathers we find no mention of capitalistic activity. The few capitalists of Italy and those of the provinces, evidently the majority, kept far away from a religion that set

---

1. Tertullian, *Ap.*, XLII, 1-3.
2. "They charge us with still another insulting accusation: they say that we are unproductive (*infructuosi*) in business," useless to society (Tertullian, *Ap.*, XLII, 1).
3. Origen, *In Gen. Hom.*, IV, 1 (Gen. 18:1 ff.).
4. To face the trials of life seems ignominious to Celsus: "labor seems to him the worst of all evils (πόνον μὲν τὸ μέγιστον τῶν κακῶν) and pleasure a perfect good: this is a theory held by not one of the philosophers, who believed in Providence, fortitude, patience and magnanimity": and the sufferings of Christ do not diminish but increase the faith of the strong (*C. Cels.*, II, 42).

them against the state and thereby exposed their possessions to confiscation, for which too many emperors were more than prone to find an excuse; and they shied away from a moral code that established a kind of incompatibility between the business of increasing one's wealth and the salvation of one's soul. In the writings of the apologists, especially of Tertullian and Clement of Alexandria, it is a voluptuous and immoral wealth that is vividly pictured.

But the Church is principally concerned with small labor and the swarms of working-men with scanty resources, whose pennies are being drained away by wars, bureaucracy and economic disorganization. Labor is accepted as an obligation and practiced as a virtue. It is a means to earn eternal rest — in a certain sense an eternal income — in the bosom of God. The economist evaluates labor from the point of view of its immediate yield; the Christian considers its ultimate yield, and thus brings it back to theology, to its own teleology. Therefore, before solving its problems in the field of sociology, he solves them in the field of charity. The man who does not work not only does not deserve to eat; he shows that he is refractory toward virtue. Toil is expiation and a distraction from idleness. Socially speaking, it permits him to earn his food in the sweat of his brow, as the Lord commands, and to share all or part of his earnings in common with his brothers to support those who cannot work. Origen, explaining the action of Providence in history, says that labor is born of the will of God, who wished to offer human diligence the material on which to exercise itself that it might not remain idle and ignorant. And to that end he made man needy. Need serves to stimulate man's inventiveness that he may find means to live, clothe himself, etc. Abundance, for those who have no concern for the divine mysteries or philosophy, would have given rise to negligence.

"The lack of provisions required for life created farming, viticulture and gardening, as well as carpentry and the metal industries to produce tools necessary for these occupations concerned with food. And the need for shelter produced not only wool-combing, spinning and weaving, but also the building industry, which then developed into architecture by virtue of man's intelligence. Then the demand for useful things led men to seek out products of other regions through navigation and maritime trade and thus to bring them where they were lacking." The animals have no needs because they have no reason and could not think up the ways and the arts to procure the necessities for themselves. What nature gives them (food, fur, feathers, scales) is enough for them.[5] Labor is dignity: "the good worker freely takes his bread, the price of his labors; while the lazy and indolent laborer does not dare look his employer in the face." Thus speaks the church of Rome through Clement, who is pronouncing a truth which the Christians accepted as axiomatic[6] but which did not have a pleasing ring to the Quirites, who had been brought up in beggary to the state and of whom an emperor could speak in terms of a starving herd: "Nothing is more joyful than the Roman populace when it is filled."[7] For hunger was the most shameful degradation to which the dignity of the greatest people in ancient history was subjected.

When a pilgrim knocks at the doors of the Church, he is to be given assistance for two or three days at the most; then he is to be given work. And if he does not know a trade, then it is up to the faithful to find a way to keep him from living in idleness. An idle Christian is a contradiction to his own moral

5. Origen, *C. Cels.*, IV, 76.

6. Clem. Rom., XXXIV, 1. The concept is found in a *logion* quoted by Macar., *De orat.*, X (cf. Resch, *Agrapha*, CLXXXIV (L 45) p. 205): "Even God detests the idle; and the idle man cannot even be one of the faithful.... Idleness is the teacher of much guilt."

7. The emperor Aurelian; see Vopiscus, *Aurel.*, XLVII. In Rome alone in the second century, grain was distributed free to 175,000 persons, heads of families, to feed about six or seven hundred thousand people, that is, half of Rome. In the other half of the population there were 400,000 slaves and 10,000 soldiers. Thus out of a population of 1,200,000 people only about 150,000 lived on their own income. Cf. Carcopino, J., *La vie quotidienne à Rome*, Paris, 1938.

code; he does not follow Christ, he barters him.[8] These admonitions were necessary, for some wily loafer would insinuate himself among the faithful and try to get a free living on the pretext of charity. A typical example of this is that Peregrinus Proteus whose amazing adventures were recounted by Lucian.

In God's providence labor is a means to furnish man with what he needs. Therefore, the fruits of labor belong to all the human brothers and from this fact derives the duty to give alms. Thanks to this concept, labor is no longer degrading or servile in any way; it is a means to attain perfection, to realize the kingdom of God on earth, of God who is the true "nourisher, father, teacher, counselor, physician, mind, light, honor, glory, strength and life, who takes away all anxieties for clothing and for food."[9]

Labor serves to procure us the necessities of life, but not wealth for itself alone, nor wealth for luxury and vice. Its superfluous fruits belong to the poor. He who works to get rich is working for other than Christian aims.[10] Man must labor calmly, therefore, in the love of liberty and his neighbor; that does not mean inertia but "moderation," in accordance with the principal criterion in Graeco-Christian teaching. Hence one man's interests cannot harm another's and temporal motives cannot obtain over spiritual ones.

From this follows a sane balance: "Labor, but not to the point of exhaustion." This represents an advance condemnation of the exploitation of labor and completely condemns slave labor as conceived by Cato and used by so many urban and rural property-holders.[11] A society based on labor alone is

---

8. The *Didache*, which sets forth these practical norms, calls it with a play on words Χριστέμπορος, a strong neologism which establishes a real antithesis between Christian and parasite. Hippolytus repeats it. The first pseudo-Clementine *Ad virgines* denounces idleness as the most dangerous enemy of a chaste life and says that the "idle man, as he is without labor, is also without use" (11).

9. *Diogn.*, IX.

10. Clem of Alex., *Paed.*, I, 12, writes that the breathless pursuit of wealth is war, "and war requires great equipment, and enjoyment requires great expense; but peace and charity, quiet and simple sisters, have no need of weapons."

11. *Ib.*, (*P. G.*, VIII, 369).

therefore materialistic, anti-Christian, like a society based on wealth alone. Both are means, not ends; they are material means toward a spiritual end. The fact that labor also is relative, while it emancipates us from the driving care for tomorrow and the mad ambition to rise above one's state in life, at the same time makes us free, autonomous, sufficient unto ourselves, as the Word desires us to be.[12]

Hermas, whose life has been spent within the orbit of a modest, rural and homely economy, contemplates a labor sufficient to help oneself and others, but no more than that. To his ascetic spirit, a feverish toil, great business activity seem dangerous: "he who does many things also commits many sins, for, occupied with his own affairs, he does not serve his Lord. ... If one attends to a single occupation only, he can also serve God, because his mind will not be corrupted...."[13] Business is like a crop of thistles that chokes the heart; and wealth constricts it with fear, "the fear that others may ask you for something. Such people shall with difficulty enter into the kingdom of God."[14] This is certainly not the road along which legitimized usury will evolve into capitalism!

Hermas cherishes an ascetic ideal, seeing in voluntary poverty a condition of virtue. Consequently, he advises against avarice, luxuriousness, the use of too many foods and the great and stupid luxuries which tend to enervate a man.[15]

From allusions in other writers also, we get the impression that the Christian community of that time lived, or aspired to live, like a monastic community, with, for the most part, a common management of goods sparingly used. Christian effort was directed toward lessening those economic injustices which were so acute in imperial society and remedying the most serious needs of the sick, widowed, orphaned, aged and abandoned. At least such a community was the ideal; as far as actual prac-

---

12. *Ib.*
13. *Sim.*, IV, 5-7.
14. *Ib.*, IX, 20, 2.
15. *Mand.*, XII, 2, 1.

tice was concerned, the repeated and insistent exhortations of the Fathers show us what stiff resistance they found in the individual selfishness of many members. And sometimes even the bishops and deacons seem to have been greedy for money, and hence to have acquired property for themselves, because there was so much insistence on the care with which they were to be chosen.[16]

There were Gnostic sects whose greed for money scandalized even the pagans. In Egypt, "those who adore Serapis are Christians, and they worship Serapis, some who parade as bishops of Christ; there is not a single chief of a Jewish synagogue there, nor a Samaritan, nor a Christian priest who is not also an astrologer, or soothsayer, or magician. Even the famous patriarch when he comes to Egypt is constrained by the one set to adore Serapis and by the others to adore Christ . . .; but the one god of them all is money. It is the divinity adored alike by Christians, Jews, people of every sort. . . . "[17]

Hence while the *Didache* states that the priests should live from their ministry as workmen from their labor, and that, in fact, they deserve from the faithful the first fruits which it would otherwise be well to give to the poor, it nevertheless warns the faithful against prophets who are parasites and apostles who, on leaving, take with them more than a loaf of bread. It calls those who ask for money pseudo-prophets unless they ask it for the needy.[18]

THE CHRISTIAN LABORER

Labor procures a man his food and it gives him dignity. But it too must be governed by the moral law, and therefore a man must labor honestly, without cheating, dissimulation or

---

16. Cf. *Didache*, XV.
17. This is from a letter (there are those who attribute it to Hadrian!), the authenticity of which is not certain, addressed to the consul Servianus; it is quoted by Flavius Vopiscus, *Saturninus*, 8 (*Script. hist. aug.*, ed. Hohl, II, 39). Christians who adored Serapis could not have been anything but Gnostics.
18. *Didache*, I and XI.

lying. The products of his labor must be good, and he must sell them for what they are really worth. He who builds or he who sells must be honest and sincere in all he does, for his thoughts and his actions are scrutinized by God, who rules over the workshop, the field and the market. On these also is based the eternal judgment on each laborer, whether he will be saved or damned. Thus there is a clear and direct relationship between producer and consumer, whether or not there is a middle-man, and it must be a completely honest one. Morality reforms the market-place.

In other words, the Christian, even as a laborer, remains a Christian, that is, subject to a religious and moral law, and this should therefore govern his labor. First of all, every kind of labor, every profession is in itself good provided only it is not opposed to spiritual good. This establishes a distinction between licit trades and professions and those which are not licit. Illicit activities were those which endangered or violated the moral law and those which led to acts of idolatry. And the Church commanded: "Flee evil arts."[19]

Hence most of the occupations of the time were licit; attempt was made only to christianize them by freeing them of dishonesty and the hateful fever for gain. Christians could not, however, serve as priests, caretakers or sacristans in the temples of idols, nor sell or prepare the victims for sacrifices, nor carve statues of the gods. They could not speculate, trade or work in any activity or place destined for idolatrous worship. They could not be "procurers, panderers, bath-attendants,[20] hired assassins, nor merchants of poisons, nor magicians, fortune-tellers, soothsayers or astrologers."[21] And this prohibition did help to clean out the gutters of society, filled with this particular brand of criminal and fraudulent parasitism.

---

19. Ignatius, *Ad Pol.*, V, 1. Lightfoot and Moricca interpret this: "Flee the tricks of the wicked."

20. They also acted as procurers, drumming up business in the baths, which were famous for the pleasure-seekers that frequented them.

21. Tertullian, *Ap.*, XLIII, 1.

Christians could not be actors either because of the moral anathema which hung over the theatres. Much less could they be gladiators or employed in any of the services connected with those legal massacres which were the spectacles in the amphitheatre. Tatian also condemns the street-player, who contorts his body, rolls his eyes, twists his joints, masks his face and plays the trumpet with his nose, all these things being impious falsehood for they deform the human figure as designed by God. For the same reason he despises actors and declares he feels no admiration for the choruses of singers, for the public speakers, declaimers, philosophers and poets because the things they say are empty and immoral. This was a serious condemnation in a period when public-speaking was one of the most popular and ostentatious pursuits of public officials and private citizens.

With Sappho, "that wicked prostitute, erotic to the point of madness, who sang of her own lust," the Assyrian apologist contrasts the chaste women of the Christians, among whom are "the virgins, who, as they tend to their spinning, recite the divine praises more nobly" than the Lesbian poetess could sing. He has no use for athletes who build up their bodies until it becomes an art for them to "carry the weight of their carcass about" and whose activity spells provocation and violence; and he despises still more the gladiators "who for their debaucheries must sell themselves to be killed."[22]

Commerce and trade were not looked on very favorably because of the lying and cheating that characterized bargaining and other negotiations involved.[23]

---

22. *Adv. graecos*, XXXIII and XXIII.
23. *Negotiatio servo Dei apta est? Caeterum, si cupiditas abscedat, quae est causa acquirendi, cessante causa acquirendi, non erit necessitas negotiandi* (Tertullian, *De idol.*, XI).

"Let him who sells or him who buys never give two prices for the thing to be bought or sold: if he give one price only, trying to keep it a just price, even if he does not succeed, by the very fact that he seeks the truth, he drives a bargain (πλουτεῖ) for the integrity of his thought." Let no one therefore swear oaths during the transactions; and let the middle-men in the market and

As we go up the professional scale we find that teaching is not in good odor either because in the educational system of the period instruction was based principally on idolatrous poetry and prose that was false or immoral. Later Julian takes the Christians maliciously at their word and forbids them to teach on the pretense that they use text-books which are condemned on religious and moral grounds.[24] Some writers banned also the profession of sculptor.[25]

It goes without saying that all dishonest trades were forbidden along with the idolatrous professions or those akin to them. For example, during an invasion of Goths in Pontus, there were Christians who, under cover of the general confusion, went fishing in the troubled waters and "drew profit from the blood and ruin of persons who had been wounded, killed or imprisoned." At the request of an unknown bishop, St. Gregory Thaumaturgus braved all the problems of ownership created by the invasion and stated it was not licit to enrich oneself with the goods of people who had been overwhelmed by the disaster and that whatever booty had been taken by Christians in the wake of the invader was to be restored to its owners. He also condemned those who kept anything they had

---

the shopkeepers philosophize in a Christian manner with the words of Exodus, 20:7 ('Thou shalt not take the name of the Lord thy God in vain'). Whoever transacts business dishonestly through greed for profit is driven from his Father's house by God, who does not wish it to become the home of dishonest transactions (Clem. of Alex., *Paed.*, III, 11).

24. Tertullian considered the profession of school-teacher and of the other *professores litterarum* semi-idolatrous because they were related and close to *multimodae idolatriae*, it being necessary to teach the genealogy of the gods and the revolutions of the seven planets named after pagan divinities. To the objection: How then can we be educated when the door to every means of earning a living is a literary career? — he answers that it is one thing to teach (which he forbids) and another to learn (which he permits with caution). Since this and other prohibitions created a great deal of unemployment among the Christians, Tertullian steps over the difficulty by saying that the soul is more important than one's daily bread; it is better to die of hunger than of sin (*De idol.*, X-XII).

25. Clem. of Alex., *Protr.*, IV, based on Exodus, 20:4: "Thou shalt not make to thyself any graven thing, nor the likeness of any thing...." But this application of the commandment was made on paper rather than in practice. Christianity rejected idolatrous and immoral sculpture, but with Christian spirit she cultivated this along with the other fine arts.

taken from the invader and especially those who kept as prisoners persons who had fled from the barbarians.[26]

In conclusion, the Christian was to exercise his trade or profession in scrupulous honesty, "philanthropically," in order to earn what he needed for himself and also the means to help his neighbor, making of his toil, like his prayer, an instrument for the attainment of perfection. For even in his daily work he must remember that he has been created for heaven. Thus the arts and trades are also fixed directly in the one matrix, the Absolute.[27]

"Tend to your farming if you are a farmer; but know God while you labor in the fields. Sail if navigation is your profession, but invoke always the celestial pilot. Was it in a military career that the knowledge of God first came to you? Well then, obey the Commander who orders you to do just things."[28]

THE SOCIAL CLASSES IN THE CHURCH

In the second century even better than in the first, Christian society mirrors proportionately the composition of the society in which it takes its rise, though with an immeasurable preponderance of members from the poorer classes. This last was due both to the nature of Christian teaching and to the relation between Church and state which was such that the rich, attached as they were to their possessions, knew that they might lose them from one minute to the next because of their faith.

Among its numbers the Christian community did count high court officials who, through prudence, stayed more or less in the background but who gave the Church considerable material assistance. We have already mentioned Hyacinth and Carpophorus; we may add the name of the rich freedman Hermetes who died for the faith. And there were members from the wealthy middle classes: the names of the matrons Per-

---

26. *Ep. canon.* This is an interesting document of episcopal action in legal, social and economic matters.
27. Clem. of Alex., *Paed.*, III, 6.
28. *Id., Protr.,* X (*P. G.,* VIII, 216).

petua and Felicitas and of the wealthy and prominent Vettius Epagatus have come down to us in the story of their heroic martyrdom.

And in fact, Christian martyrology reflects better than any other document the various social classes composing the Church. Among the martyrs of the period we find a government official, Hermetes, who, at his conversion, is supposed to have freed twelve hundred slaves; a certain Quirinus, a tribune; the family of the martyr, St. Symphorosa, employed in local administrative positions; philosophers, men of letters and lawyers, like the apologists. St. Irenaeus had come from Smyrna to Lyons when this growing western market was attracting the men of the Orient, who were most active in seizing every opportunity to start commerce and industries throughout the Empire and who gradually supplanted the Latins. In his church there was the martyr Attalus, a Roman citizen "very well-known," who was therefore beheaded instead of being thrown to the beasts. We have already mentioned Apollonius, who was of consular rank.

If many slaves turned informers against their Christian masters, many others imitated their resistance to torture. The Church honors the names of Blandina, Hesperus, Zoë and her two children; and Pamphilius, Mary, etc. Euelpistus, one of Justin's companions in martyrdom, was a slave of the emperor.

Since the Church must forbid its members to exercise certain idolatrous and immoral professions, like acting, we may reasonably suppose that her members were distributed through most of the professional categories. The future Pope Callixtus was a slave who managed a public bank for and with the funds of his Christian master Carpophorus, a sign that the banking profession was tolerated. And we shall see how it will even be honored by not a few of the Fathers. Theodotus was also a banker, a heretic and disciple of another Theodotus, a rich tanner who had come from Byzantium to Rome at the time of Pope Victor in order to preach a doctrine that denied the divinity of Christ.

Just as the Christians found Christian merchants in the market-place from whom they preferred to make their purchases, so in the *tabernae argentariae* they found Christian moneychangers who loaned money and received deposits. The bank of Callixtus may be considered the first known Catholic bank managed by a Christian and having Christian capital and deposits of Christian persons, among whom were poor widows. Unhappily it went bankrupt.

In this period also the Church showed no hostility or diffidence toward the military profession. We have just mentioned the tribune Quirinus (and with him are Getulius and Amantius, the husband and brother-in-law of St. Symphorosa)[29] and the Christians who belonged, according to a contemporary tradition, to the *legio fulminans* whose prayers obtained the saving shower of rain for the thirsty Roman army in the war against the Quadi.

The fact that so many different social elements were gathered into a society which felt itself to be one body and one soul, the fact that its members considered one another brothers and that their associations included sharing the same death for the faith, meant that the Church inevitably became also a kind of social melting-pot, in which all the various barriers disappeared.[30] The rise from one of the *humiliores* to the

---

29. *Passio S. Symph.*, I.

30. As we have said, brotherhood tended toward relative economic equality also, as the perfect ideal of charity. A Judaizing document — the *Clementine Recognitions* — reflects a certain anxiety that this tendency may fail to recognize the "necessity" of "inequality" in the matter of social attributes and also of social classes; for it is this inequality which permits the exercise of charity. *Numquid omnes . . . oportebat esse in hoc mundo reges, aut principes, aut dominos, aut paedagogos, aut legisperitos, aut geometras, aut aurifices, aut pictores, aut fabros, aut grammaticos, aut divites, aut agricolas, aut olitores, aut piscatores, aut pauperes? Hoc certum est quia omnes esse non poterant. Omnia tamen haec officia et multo plura praesens vita hominum requirit, et sine his transigi non potest; est ergo necessaria in hoc mundo inaequalitas* (Recognitiones, IX, 5). *Sed hanc inaequalitatem quae mortalium vitam necessario subsequuta est, divina Providentia in occasionem iustitiae, misericordiae, humanitatisque convertit, ut dum haec inter homines aguntur, sit unicuique causa iuste agendi cum eo, cui merces operis exolvenda est, et faciendi misericordiam cum eo, qui, debilitate fortassis aut penuria intercedente, debitum solvere non potest . . . (ib., VII).*

honestiores had become constantly more difficult since, after Hadrian's death, no more cities had been built where the peasantry might go and ascend the social scale. Outside the Church the various classes and their attendant distinctions were crystallizing into a mold. But within the Church, the exchange between one class and another was kept alive by the spirit of the Gospel. The conservatives, the advocates of the old regime, deplored the proletarian character of Christianity.[31]

The pagan apologist Celsus said that Jesus, while he paraded as a king and raved about a kingdom "went wandering about like a beggar, frightened, suppliant, laden with miseries," until he joined to him a "band of ten or eleven ill-famed and violent men, publicans and sailors who did a shady business, and then he went wandering about with them here and there, trying to find enough to eat midst privations and ignominy."[32]

"Our Jesus," answered Origen for the Christians, "who is despised because he was born in a little village that was not even Hellenic or of any other celebrated nationality, and who is defamed because he was the son of a poor and hardworking mother and because, driven by hunger, he left his country and went to earn his living in Egypt; this Jesus, who was not just an ordinary Seriphos[33] born on some tiny and most contemptible island, but altogether the very lowliest of the type of Seriphos, succeeded in shaking the whole inhabited world, not only more

---

31. Celsus could not be convinced that in an aristocratic order of values like religion and philosophy anyone could accept as a teacher a Palestinian Jesus, "born in a Jewish village of a poor working-woman who was a native of the place." He then alleges that she was accused by her husband, a carpenter, of adultery and rejected by him; "and so driven forth and obliged to wander about in shameful fashion, she gave birth to Jesus in secret; and the latter, because of his poverty, was forced to emigrate to Egypt and hire out by the day" (Origen, *C. Cels.*, I, 28).

Celsus thought he could defame Christianity merely by demonstrating its origin in poor Judea rather than in illustrious Greece, in an environment of poor working-men instead of aristocratic or wealthy philosophers (besides accepting all the calumnies circulated against Mary by the rabbis in order to strike at her virginity, of which the Christians were most proud).

32. *Ib.*, I, 61 and 62.

33. An ignorant person not a Greek who had come to Plato to offer objections to Themistocles' glory.

than Themistocles of Athens but also more than Plato, Pythagoras or any other philosopher, king or general of this world."[34]

The criteria of esteem presented a real antithesis; in the new conscience low birth was transformed into a cause for pride.

The Jews also found a proletarian birth unsavory, like the crucifixion, an execution reserved for the outcasts of society. The Christians granted all that.

"When Jesus came to the Jordan, and men believed he was the son of the carpenter Joseph,[35] he seemed without beauty as the Scriptures had prophesied; and they believed him a carpenter, and in fact as long as he lived among men he worked at the tasks of this trade: plows and yokes. . . . "[36]

It was only the Church that went systematically in search of the poor, with no ulterior motive, to nourish them and educate them, to remake their souls and bodies. It is no wonder that they ran to her in throngs. It is a hard thing to be poor, and it was especially so in antiquity when we consider that at the trial of Apuleius one of the charges against him was his poverty — he had only three slaves. He had replied by reciting one of those rhetorical praises of poverty common in the writings of the philosophers, especially the Stoics, saying, like Clement of Alexandria, that wealth and poverty are in the heart, and true wealth lies in being content: "He will possess more than all men who desires the least: he who desires the least will have all that he shall wish."[37] His countryman Minucius translated the same ideas into Christian terms:

"If, as it is said, the majority of us are poor, this is our glory and not our infamy; for as the mind is enervated by luxury so is it strengthened by frugality. And yet, who can be poor who has no needs; who does not desire what others have; who is rich in the judgment of God? Poorer is the man who,

34. Origen, *C. Cels.*, I, 29.

35. τέκτονος; it is the word used also by Celsus, by the *Gospel of Thomas*, etc.; it comes from Matt. 13:55.

36. Justin, *Dial.*, LXXXVIII, 8. The same detail is in the *Gospel of Thomas*, XIII, 1-2.

37. *Ap.*, XX, 2.

though having much, desires more. . . . No one can be so poor as he comes into the world. The birds live without patrimony of any kind, and the beasts daily find their food. . . . Happier is he who knows how to lift his soul above his poverty rather than sigh under the burden of wealth. And yet if we thought wealth useful to us we should ask God for it; and certainly he, who is the owner of all things, could grant us some part; but we prefer to disdain wealth rather than touch it; rather than wealth we desire innocence and we prefer to ask for patience; we prefer to be good rather than prodigal."[38]

Besides, the charge the pagans (Celsus, Caecilius) made that the Christians gathered in the dregs of society was perhaps due more to the assistance, education and unaccustomed dignity the Church bestowed on the poor, the women and the children than to its actual composition. Indeed, what disturbed the pagan Caecilius was the fact that "persons with no education, uninitiated in literature, ignorant of even the meaner arts" were engaging in debate concerning the supreme Power of the universe and its attributes. "This deplorable, illicit and hopeless faction is composed of the crudest elements and of credulous women of the people."[39]

It cannot be denied that the new community was marked by its prevalently proletarian character. Some of its rich members, who were heroically Christian, became poor voluntarily. But from the tempered character of those humble members, from the glory won in martyrdom by slaves and artisans, from the moral dignity conferred by the Gospel, sprang the more vigorous forces in Christianity's attack on the sumptuous and idolatrous world. This new attitude and consciousness of strength in the social outcasts seemed rash and intolerable to the upholders of class privilege, to that part of the bourgeoisie which then abhorred as dangerous the spiritual rise of the masses, stratified beneath the feet of the privileged. That is

38. Minucius, *Oct.*, XXXVI, 3-7.
39. *Ib.*, V, 4; VIII, 3.

why they clamored that they be ruthlessly repressed. Caecilius' lips curl with hatred when he speaks of these Christians without property who not only take the liberty of making philosophy and theology, but babble and chatter on the street corners, plotting and organizing with obscene rites and oaths; and they carry their insolence to the point of scorning the temples, publicly insulting the gods and sneering at sacred things, "commiserating, miserable as they are, the dignity of the priests, and despising the purple, they who go half-naked. . . . Oh but such an execrable coalition should be torn up by the roots!"[40] A similar scorn must have marked the features of the aristocrats that denounced the insolence of the Parisian laborers who, on the eve of the Revolution, were reading papers and pamphlets and discussing civil reforms instead of working.

The Church deliberately uplifts the lower classes, the majority, whom she calls the elect, although made of people who all the year are cold and hungry, in need of everything, burdened with pain and grief of every sort.[41] The intense community life of the Christians, from their prayers to God to their fulfillment of the precepts of charity, was fashioning a new social conscience, as the natural effusion of their religious life. The Church knew very well that the reëducation of her members inevitably spread the conflict from the religious-political field to the social one since the new conscience of the outcasts could not help reacting with a constant and determined influence on their environment. And she also knew very well that those satisfied with the present order "were intolerant, disgusted and indignant, and lamented because the illiterate, the poor, the ignorant, were discussing celestial things." But she replied that "all men, without distinction of age, sex, or dignity, have been created with the gift of reason and sense, having received the power of knowledge not from their social condition but from nature. . . . Thus the rich, enmeshed in their

---

40. Minucius, *Oct.*, VIII, 4-5; IX, 1.
41. *Ecce, pars vestrum et maior — melior, ut dicitis — egetis, algetis, opere, fame laboratis* (Minucius, *Oct.*, XII, 2).

riches, have become accustomed to speculate more on their money than on heaven; while our poor have found wisdom and transmit it to others. Hence it appears that intelligence is not granted by money, nor is it acquired with study, but it is created with the very formation of the mind."[42]

Such vindication of the lowly and the justification of their presence in the Church were certainly not intended to establish a preëminence for the poor and illiterate over the rich and learned, but to destroy the differences built by the claims of wealth and education, differences that always resolved themselves into class distinction and conflict. Christianity realizes within its fold the peaceful, concordant living together of all classes (their collaboration with respect to labor) seeking order and harmony in every field on the basis of the original equality of souls and the actual brotherhood of the baptized. But such harmony can be achieved only among souls who recognize their own true equality and at the same time the ephemeral and relative nature of distinctions based on caste and class, on wealth and culture.

"Are you a king? You fear as much as you are feared, and however you may be surrounded by a numerous escort, yet in the face of danger you find yourself alone. Are you rich? It is ill to trust oneself to fortune, and the brief journey of life is not equipped but burdened by a great cargo of provisions. You glory in the fasces and the purple? It is a vain human error and a useless worship of dignity to go resplendent in purple and be sordid in thought. Are you noble and do you parade your ancestors? Yet we all have been born to the same destiny, and we do not distinguish ourselves one from the other except by virtue."[43] This is the summary of the Christian evaluation of social prestige and position, which are unstable

---

42. Minucius, *Oct.*, XVI, 5. There was the prevalent conviction that the Apostles had been poor. In the *Recognitiones*, VII, 6, Peter says: *Nos enim a puero, id est, ego et frater germanus meus Andreas, non solum orphani, sed et valde pauperes crevimus et necessitate operarii esse consuevimus* ... (P. G., I, 1358).

43. Minucius, *Oct.*, XXXVII, 9-10.

and transitory; the very fact that they are relative with respect to the eternal values renders them insignificant and sometimes cumbersome, as is the case with wealth. In their stead Christianity introduces the distinctions, the aristocracy, of spiritual merit. These ideas were not exactly original but they became powerful and active by virtue of the Christian teaching on which they were based. Hence, just as they clashed with the claims of pride crystallized in the social register and the assessor's books, so they comforted and ennobled the lowly who thus found a way opened to all of them by which they might rise according to their free and individual merits.[44]

---

44. In the first three centuries Christian epigraphy bears no trace of social distinctions; in the epitaphs we do not find the designation, *servi* or *liberti,* common in pagan epigraphy, nor *ingenui* or *clarissimi,* and not even titles designating military or civil honors or offices, etc., although there were among the Christians high officials and patricians of the highest society like the Flavii, the Caecilii, the Postumi (cf. Grossi-Gondi, *Epigr. crist.,* pp. 100 and ff.).

CHAPTER XII

SOLIDARITY

SOCIAL WELFARE

SINCE each Christian is incorporated in the Church, an organism whose lifeblood is love, he has the duty to be brother to every man in every relationship in life. Christian life, from the social point of view, is service to our brothers.

"A common spirit, deriving from our common Master and Father," must unite each man to his neighbor in a common destiny; for "in one and in the other is the Church, and the Church is Christ."[1]

Since the poor are identified with Christ, the Christian externalizes his faith in good works for the poor; he adores and prays God "every day through almsgiving and works of mercy for men."[2]

Charity is a supernatural virtue. It determines the communion of saints, which establishes a solidarity between the living and the dead, the militant and the triumphant. Thus the Christians begin to include in their epitaphs invocations for help to the deceased,[3] especially to the martyrs.

Solidarity, therefore, finds its first source in the sacraments and its first expression in prayer. In the Lord's Prayer, Jesus Christ, "before anything else, as preceptor of peace and teacher of unity, does not wish us to pray individually and privately in order that we may not pray for ourselves alone. We do not,

---

1. Tertullian, *De poenit.*, 10.
2. *Acta S. Apoll.*, XLIV.
3. One crude and ingenuous one says: *Pete pro parentes tuos* (sic). Cf. J. P. Kirsch, *Die Lehre von der Gemeinschaft der Heiligen in christl. Altert.*, Mainz, 1900, 54 ff.

in fact, say, 'My Father, who art in heaven,' nor 'Give me today my daily bread' . . . ; but we have a public and communal prayer, and when we pray, we pray not for one person, but for the whole people, because we the whole people form unity. God, teacher of peace and concord, who taught us unity wanted each man to pray for all even as he himself bore us all in one."[4]

Almsgiving is among the great means for obtaining remission of sin. It is next in rank after Baptism and martyrdom.[5] It is therefore associated with the direct means of attaining supernatural life. It is nourished by the Eternal, and numberless and infinite are its applications and resources.[6]

By the law of charity, the Christian owes part of his income, as a concrete expression of love, to God and to his neighbor. He gives to God first by giving to the Church.

This was the custom in the religions of antiquity also. The famous Rosetta Stone, which is nothing but a decree in honor of Ptolemy Epiphanes issued by the council of Egyptian priests at Memphis on the occasion of his coronation, celebrates the praises of the king "because he has consecrated to the temples revenues in money and foodstuffs" and remitted the taxes, and because he has restated the obligation of the people to give "annual offerings of foodstuffs and money, and the part due the gods from the fruits of their vineyards, gardens and other lands."[7] In recompense every temple was to erect a statue and a shrine to the god Epiphanes.[8]

A similar custom of setting aside a part of one's income for the expenses of worship prevailed also among the Baby-

---

4. Cyprian, *De orat. domin.*, VIII.
5. Origen, *In Lev.*, hom. II, 4.
6. With regard to Rom., 12:10, Origen says that this is "the first commandment after the first," while in practice men consider it the last *et minus necessarium:* thus we love what we ought to hate and we hate what we ought to love. *Fratres ergo iubemur diligere, non iudicare* (*In ep. ad Rom.*, IX, 6; *P. G.*, XIV, 1219). "There are four elements specially necessary in our relations with God: Faith, Truth, Love and Hope" (Porphyry, *Ad Marc.*, XXIV).
7. Cf. C. & T. Müller, *Fragmenta historicorum graecorum*, I, Paris, 1885, appendix: *Inscription grecque de Rosette*, ed. Letronne, ll. 14-16.
8. *Ib.*, ll. 41-42.

Ionians, Persians and Phoenicians, and still exists today among various primitive tribes. It prevailed also among the Hebrews, from whom it passed over to the Christians, taking in time the form of the tithe, but not everywhere nor with obligation involved.

The offerings to the Church were collected — at least in some communities — usually every month as was the custom also for the *collegia tenuiorum*. There was no fixed quota, but each gave according to his conscience and in proportion to his income. With the funds at its disposal the community gave its ministers a certain recompense, paid for the meeting-place, took care of the cemeteries, and above all remedied the most serious social inequalities by assisting the needy, not a few of whom were completely dependent on it for support: widows, orphans, the aged, the unemployed poor, invalids, prisoners in the jails or those condemned to the mines or to exile for the faith. Help was sent even to those farthest away — an expression of the motherhood and universality of the Church. In order to help the prisoners, the Christians tried to buy the coöperation of the guards, and with gold they also tried to buy back the bodies of the martyrs, though, as at Lyons, they did not always succeed.

Because of Christian universality then, assistance was given to all who could be reached, but it was given first of all to companions in faith and in a spirit of brotherhood that was to be practiced rather than flaunted.[9]

The administration of the funds necessary for this great philanthropic activity — the funds of the poor for whom they were destined and from whom, in part, they were derived[10] — was entrusted to the scrupulous unselfishness of the bishops and deacons. There is record of a few who mismanaged them.

---

9. Tertullian, *Ap.*, XXXIX, 5 ff. In *Adv. Marc.*, IV, 16 (*P.L.*, II, 397) he writes: *Etsi maior est bonitas quae operatur in extraneos, sed non prior ea quae ante debetur in proximos.*

10. The Christians "are poor and bestow wealth on many; they seem to lack everything and instead they abound in all things" (*Diogn.*, V, 13; cf. 2 Cor., 6:10).

This duty was not imposed on or accessory to their office but an organic part of it, for from the beginning it had been the duty of the rulers of the Church to work "with all diligence for the temporal as well as the spiritual . . . in the interest of all." This was a distinguishing mark of good bishops[11] and it was the practical application of the fundamental precept of universal charity.[12]

In fact, one departs from the new spirit when he sins against charity. This is the mystery and the strength in which everything is simplified and christianized. All disagreements are settled in love; all miseries are resolved in love. It is the social virtue by which the ego is destroyed or else is strengthened in the complete offering of self to one's brothers. St. Clement of Rome repeats St. Paul's praises of charity and Ignatius recognized in the church of Rome a primacy of love; and as love is the substance of Christianity, this primacy is without question a primacy in the Church. The serene and broad-minded Clement not only recognizes but commemorates, for example, the heroic pagans who have sacrificed their lives and their personal interests for the good of society, to save their fatherland. Love of country is nothing but love for the brothers who are nearest us. Judith and Esther, through their love of country and the virtue in their hearts, called upon God for help and he saved their people, for whom they faced danger.

This heroism lives again in Christian men and women "many of whom went voluntarily to prison to free others and many of whom sold themselves into slavery to feed others with the price they received."[13] It is a hidden and anonymous heroism and therefore greater than that of Codrus, Lycurgus, Ca-

---

11. "The bishops always protected with their constant ministry the *poor* and the *widows*" (Hermas, *Sim.*, IX, 27, 2).

12. Hermas, *Mand.*, VIII, 10.

13. Clem. Rom., LV. A first list of the "corporal works of mercy" is to be found in the "Clementines" (*Ep. Clem.* ad Iac., X): "Above all feed the hungry; give drink to the thirsty; clothe the naked; assist as much as you are able those in prison; receive pilgrims into your homes with all readiness."

millus, Decius Mur and Cicero, to whom the bishop is probably alluding.

In the great liturgical prayer (of the church in Rome)
which he has passed on to us, immediately after the praises
to God's attributes, we find this Christian charity expressed
in an earnest appeal for all those who suffer:

> "We pray thee, O Lord,
>   to be our help and our support:
> save the afflicted among us,
>   pity the humble,
>   lift the fallen;
> show thyself to the needy,
>   heal the infirm,
>   lead back the sinners of thy people;
> fill the hungry,
>   free our prisoners,
>   raise up the weak,
>   comfort the faint-hearted."[14]

Thus love, which shines on all the sufferings of all human
brothers, is the strongest social bond in the Church. It distinguishes the Christians from the pagans, and the latter are
able to recognize the former precisely by this love they bear
one another, which becomes a real mutual interchange of feelings and works among them, and a pledge of resurrection in
eternity. He who loves, imitates God, who will reward us
"if we abstain from all injustice, greed, avarice, calumny and
false testimony: not rendering evil for evil, outrage for outrage (1 Pet., 3:9), blow for blow, and curse for curse."[15]
There can be no revenge, therefore; only pardon. Love re-
deems; love saves. And "the sign of true and unchanging love
is not to desire our own salvation only, but to desire also that
all our brothers,"[16] by virtue of the principle of universal

14. *Ib.,* LIX.
15. Polycarp, II, 2.
16. *Mart. Polyc.,* I, 2.

solidarity which embraces body and soul. In fact, Polycarp, before being led to the stake, feels the need of praying for all "the great and the small, the illustrious and the obscure, and for all the universal Church throughout the world."[17]

In this way, the nascent Church, truly the living Christ, cared for men's souls and bodies for the sake of eternity. And she made social assistance a means to reach heaven, a constant imitation of God, who never ceases to help his children on earth. She performed her task both as a society and through her individual members. Though the commandments of the Church had not yet been written as we know them today, their content may be found substantially in almost all the writers of the second century.

The ethical patrimony of the Old Testament had been incorporated into the ethical patrimony of Christianity with the conviction, strengthened by the gradual alienation of the Jews, that the ancient holy books lawfully belonged to the new Covenant, that they were a prelude to the new harmonious synthesis. St. Clement of Rome makes his the admonitions of Isaias: Render to the orphan his rights and justice to the widow! And he invites his readers to cure internal disagreements with the loftier nobility of social service. Justin also takes Isaias' most vigorous social pronouncements[18] and makes them his own, and so does Cyprian.[19] According to Hermas, when the Christian has acquired the formative virtues he "must help the widows, care for the orphans and the impoverished, redeem the servants of God from their distress, be hospitable . . . become the poorest among men, reverence his elders, prac-

---

17. *Ib.,* VIII, 1.
18. *Dial., passim.*
19. Cyprian, who is tireless in promoting a true Christian life and in shaping the ecclesiastical community according to the evangelical ideal, wrote a little book entitled *De opere et eleemosynis,* in which he repeats the best of Hebrew thought on the obligation and the value, which is also religious, of almsgiving as a form of prayer, redemption and propitiation "which delivereth from death and . . . purgeth away sins" (Tob. 12:9). Almsgiving and works of charity are the complement to prayer.

tice justice, preserve brotherhood, support insults ... not oppress debtors or the needy."[20]

It is dangerous, as we have seen, for the Christian to acquire property in this world, where his dwelling is only temporary and barely tolerated. It is better, says the Shepherd, "to use your money to relieve the oppressed, each according to his means, and to care for the widows and orphans with constant attention." For the pagan the fever of gain took the form of great investments in farmland and found expression in a passion for building; for the Christian, "let the fields and buildings be represented by widows and orphans. Spend on them the wealth and opulence that you have received from God."[21]

It is the Lord's commandment: "Man is my image, and he is therefore endowed with right reason. Set for him a pure table, without blood, heaping it with good things; if he is hungry, give him bread; if he is thirsty, give him to drink; if he is naked, clothe him; of the fruits of your labor give a generous part; refresh the oppressed, relieve the weary: offer this living victim to him who lives. . . . "[22]

Because the Christians loved one another as brothers and called one another by that name, so that it could be said they loved "even before they knew one another,"[23] then this love, translated into works of charity, created a real and effective solidarity between the rich and the poor, the latter being numerous out of all proportion.

This lifeblood of charity, which heals and rebuilds, flows throughout the whole Christian body down to the smallest capillaries. Because of it, the Christians "do not neglect the *widow* and they free the *orphan* from those who do him violence; and he who has gives to the needy, without complaining; and when they see a *stranger,* they take him to their houses and rejoice over him as a brother; ... and when one of their

20. Hermas, *Mand.,* VIII, 10.
21. *Id., Sim.,* I, 8.
22. *Sibyll.,* VIII, 402-409.
23. Minucius, *Oct.,* IX, 2.

poor dies, if they know it, they procure a *burial* for him according to their means; and if they hear that one of them is *imprisoned* or oppressed for the name of Christ, they all provide for his needs, and if they can, they free him."[24]

Virtue is manifested in works of charity. The most austere virginity is sterile if it does not produce works of charity toward the needy.[25]

At the beginning of the second century the proletariat had in very great measure already lost its purchasing power, thus causing and at the same time feeling the effects of the prevailing commercial and industrial decay. The periodic interventions of the state were merely panaceas of fleeting efficacy. In the general inability of the age to do anything about the social question, the varied social services which the Church carried on as its organic function undoubtedly relieved the sufferings of many. The pagans also performed works of charity, but these were isolated instances and restricted to individual persons, and they had not the efficacy of the Church's organization and universality.

Antoninus Pius established government aid for poor children and Trajan carried it still further but for demographic reasons.[26] Christianity admitted no mundane interests or limi-

---

24. Aristides, *Ap.,* XV (Syriac version).

25. "It is good and profitable to care for the orphans and widows, especially those who are poor and laden with children. . . . It is good and just to care for our neighbor for the love of God. . . . Let us love the poor as servants of God and let us anticipate their needs with our care. . . . It is noble in the sight of God and men to remember the poor, to love our brothers and strangers . . ." (Pseudo-Clem., *Ep. I, Ad Virg.,* XII).

26. Pliny, *Paneg.,* 26-28; Dio, LXVIII, 5. Cf. E. Caetani-Lovatelli, *Varia,* Rome, 1905, 257 ff.: "Le istituzioni di beneficenza presso i Romani."

"We know that Pliny, before he died, had bequeathed an annual income of thirty thousand sesterces *in alimenta ingenuorum ingenuarumque,* that is, for the support of a certain number of free citizens and their children. The same Pliny left large sums for the construction of baths and the foundation of a library in his native Como. He bequeathed in addition a sum for the support of his own freedmen, leaving it in trust in the state treasury and providing that they enjoy the interest during their lifetime and that after their deaths, this interest be used annually to present a banquet for the Roman plebs (*ad epulum plebis urbanae*). We find other examples of this curious generosity, which bequeathed or set aside in some other way a sum of money to furnish public

tations. Its beneficence had to reach out to all whoever they might be, irrespective of size or age, appearance or dress — even to the deformed — for in each man lives the Father and the Son, and our external appearance is nothing but a garment we put on "in order that we may be able to enter this common school,"[27] which is the world.

Wealth that is not spent to do good is lost. He who helps the poor makes a loan to God.[28]

SOCIAL ASSISTANCE IN PRACTICE

Assistance is owed by everyone to everyone. First, of course, the rich owe it to the poor. The rich must feel no repugnance toward the poor or the deformed or the weak, in whose bodies lives Our Lord. And in fact, the rich who embraced Christianity did in numerous instances follow the law of charity to its ultimate consequences and become poor to help their brothers, giving the community houses, lands and cemeteries.[29]

---

banquets for the plebs of Rome or the *municipia*. Caninius, to whom the letter of Pliny quoted above was addressed, was asking his friend Pliny how to invest money he wished to leave for a similar purpose.

"These gifts, examples of which are offered us by eminent persons of ancient pagan society, were certainly signs of noble unselfishness. But their defect was this, that they were confined to very limited groups of persons, or else the use to which they were destined was voluptuous more than anything else (like the public banquets) or purely ornamental (like the library and the baths), and in general these gifts were prompted not so much by a noble impulse of altruism as by a kind of posthumous ambition and vainglory" (S. Colombo, "Le origini della beneficenza cristiana" in *Rivista dei giovani*, Turin, 1931, pp. 375-6).

27. Clem. of Alex., *Quis dives salvetur?*, XXXIII.

28. *Pudeat divites sterilitatis atque infelicitatis suae.... Qui miseretur pauperis Deo foenerat* (Cyprian, *De op. et eleem.*, XV). We must spend our money for the poor; if not, *tentatio est patrimonium grande, nisi ad usus bonos census operetur, ut patrimonio suo unusquisque locupletior magis redimere debeat quam augere delicta* (Cyprian, *De hab. virg.*, XI). Wealth is a temptation to idolatry; the Christian risks confiscation and death; if he loves his patrimony, he denies Christ.

29. As early as 66 the daughter of the Stoic Barea Soranus, a man of senatorial rank, was accused of having sold her trousseau (*cultus dotalis*) and a necklace (*monile*) *quo pecuniam faciendis magicis sacris contraheret* (Tacitus, *Ann.*, XVI, 30-31). H. Jeanne (*art. cit.*, p. 355) thinks it is a case where a rich patrician renounces her possessions to contribute to the community treasury.

But the poor are also bound to help the other poor; and this many poor Christians did, fasting, if necessary, to save a loaf of bread for those needier than they.[30]

Not even parents burdened with numerous children are exempt from the obligations imposed by Christian solidarity, which are the performance of "good and just works"; for they must consider the poor, in whom Christ resides, before their own children, after the example of the widow who gave Elias the hearth-cake she had made for herself and her own son.[31] Parents with large families have more obligations toward the Lord, responsible as they are for the souls of more persons: as Job offered numerous sacrifices for his numerous children, so Christian parents must offer God more alms to redeem more souls from their sins.[32]

And even the father who is infirm should trust his patrimony to God rather than to his heirs, making God the tutor and guardian of his orphans that he may protect them against the harm that may come to them from the world. A patrimony entrusted to God cannot be ruined either by confiscation by the state, or by the burdens of taxation, or by calumnies charged in the courts. On the other hand, he who takes more thought for his patrimony on earth than for his patrimony in heaven entrusts his children to the devil rather than to Christ, and thus commits one crime. Then he teaches them to love their inheritance more than Christ, and thus commits a second crime. This is the teaching of a bishop of the third century,[33] who makes riches the property of the poor in order to convert them into

---

30. "And if there is one poor and needy among them, and they have no extra means, they fast two or three days to provide the necessary food for the one in need" (Aristides, *Ap.*, XV, Syriac version).

31. Cyprian, *De op. et eleem.*, XVI, XVII. He is referring to Matt. 10:37; Deut. 33:9 and 3 Kgs. 17:9 ff.

32. The *Protoevangelion of James* (second century) narrates that Joachim (the father of the Virgin Mary) was "very rich" and made twofold offerings saying: "That part of my offering which is in excess shall be for all the people; and that which I am bound to offer for the remission of my sins shall be the Lord's, that he may be merciful to me." But these were offerings made to the Temple.

33. Cyprian, *De op. et eleem.*, XVIII and XIX.

eternal wealth. This was not the way perhaps to economic progress, but certainly the poor were being fed.

As we have already said, there was fear of general impov-
ishment. But the bishop answered this objection with the
assurance that it is not possible to become poor by giving to
the poor; and he quotes the Bible: "He that giveth to the poor,
shall not want" (Prov. 28:27). In any case what is important
is not the fate of one's substance but the fate of one's soul.[34]

In short, Christian teaching was trying to detach man from
his money, property and wealth, in order to make him completely free before God — heroically free. And this explains
why the Fathers, following the example of Christ and the
Apostles, counseled honorable poverty as a condition of interior and exterior peace. Their detachment is in contrast to
the Roman concept of property, which considered it perpetual,
unlimited and absolute.

Assistance, then, is due to everyone. But for the reasons
mentioned in our treatment of the teaching of the Apostles,
widows and orphans are to receive it first. Among the precepts
of charity for the good Christian's daily life were this assistance
and service to the needy, and to widows and orphans first of
all, and this was the first care of the good bishop.[35] The Church
revenues, derived from the offerings of the faithful and usually
from the salary earned by heavy labor, belongs first of all to
them. And those deacons have been perfidious "who have mismanaged and have wasted the substance of the widows and
orphans, deriving from their ministry gain for themselves."[36]

Hence Ignatius, when he sketches the model bishop, places
among his first obligations that of giving temporal assistance
to all the needy, including the widows, whose care is entrusted
to him, next after the Lord.[37]

---

34. *Ib.*, IX and X.
35. Hermas, *Mand.*, VIII, 10, says: "to help the widows and care for the
orphans and the impoverished."
36. Id., *Sim.*, IX, 26, 2.
37. Ignatius, *Pol.*, IV, 1. Cf. Polycarp, IV, 3, and Tertullian, *Adv. Marc.*,
IV, 16.

Hospitals are unkown in this period; the condition of the sick is very bad and the assistance given them is rudimentary. But after the example of Jesus and the Apostles the holy Fathers remember the infirm in their moral instructions and make it especially obligatory to care for them all.[38]

At the end of the second century we find at Rome, Alexandria, Carthage and in the Orient definite traces of a philanthropic custom intended to help feed the poor. This was a dinner offered either by the Church from the common treasury or by some rich member. It was a concrete expression of social affection and had nothing whatever in common with the dinners offered client-parasites "aspiring to the glory of enslaving their liberty, to fill their bellies midst insults."[39] The Christian dinner was called *agape,* that is, love,[40] and so declared its character in its name.

Particular emphasis was placed on the virtue of hospitality, inculcated as one of the precepts of charity. Ancient society had always felt its need and had practiced it in varying degrees because of the difficulties of transportation, the conditions of the roads and the defective inn system. The inns, hospices, *cauponae* were places of ill-fame that openly competed with the houses of prostitution and were thrown open to the slum riffraff most liable to suspicion on the part of the police. Though there might be more luxurious and expensive lodgings here and there, the inns for the most part offered only wretched accommodations at a miserable price. Respectable people, with moral

---

38. Polycarp, VI, 1. Thecla cared for and cured many, with the help of divine grace, and made the doctors lose many patients (*Acts of Paul,* ed. Vouaux, pp. 233-4). The priest Dionysius, who died probably in the first half of the third century, was also a physician. The epigraphy of the catacombs records the names of bishops, priests and deacons who practiced medicine, especially in periods of persecution (De Rossi, *Roma sotterr.,* I, 342). The Christian Proculus was, until his death, the physician of Septimius Severus, since he had once cured him with oil. Among the martyrs of Lyons there was a Phrygian doctor, Alexander, who had been practicing in Gaul for many years (Eusebius, *H. E.,* V, 1, 49).

39. Tertullian, *Ap.,* XXIX, 16; see Batiffol, art. "Agapes" in *Dict. de théol. cath.*

40. Tert., *ib.,* renders it with the Latin *dilectio.*

standards like the Christians, must have been highly uncomfortable in them; hence for them the hospitality of private individuals was particularly recommended, and in any case everyone preferred it to the inns.

In the new Church, the orbit of hospitality is widened in theory to include all Christians of every nation and also the non-Christians. Ideally, each man's house is everybody's house. In practice, this has to be restricted because of the limited economic means of the host and the necessity for him to defend himself against parasites. Actually, however, the virtue of hospitality was practiced on a vast scale since every Christian traveling for business, necessity or relaxation immediately sought out the Christian community wherever he arrived; and in it he did not feel a stranger. And with these brothers who came from outside, the community realized that communion of life which the Apostolic writers had defined as an expression of the communion of saints.

The *Didache,* just as it regulates the most ordinary actions in the life of the Church, also gives very sensible norms for the practice of hospitality. Whoever comes in the name of the Lord is to be welcomed and helped as much as possible. However, he is not to remain more than two or three days at the host's expense. If he wishes to stay longer, then he is to be given work to do that he may earn his living and not become a lazy parasite.[41]

St. Clement of Rome cited the most famous examples of hospitality among the Hebrews. But it was Corinth, a busy harbor filled with the traffic between the Orient and the Occident, that was put to a severe test in matters of hospitality. And she passed it with honor, since the bishop of Rome, Clement, mentions "the splendid tradition of hospitality," known everywhere[42] as one of the chief claims of merit of the Corinthian church.

---

41. *Didache,* XII.
42. Clem. Rom., I, 2.

This virtue had taken on a universal quality among the Christians: "We who did not admit to our hearth anyone of another race and customs, now, since the coming of Christ, live together in community with them."[43] In the parable of the good Samaritan the Lord has given us this universal definition of our neighbor, "unlike the Jews, for whom he is only a kinsman, a fellow-countryman, a proselyte, or anyone else who is circumcised like them and follows the same law."[44]

Another bishop, Melito, even writes a treatise on the duties of hospitality; and Theophilus, bishop of Antioch, reinforces the Christian precepts with the Mosaic Law.[45] It is natural that the bishops should pay particular attention to this point. From his place of refuge during the persecution, Cyprian not only takes thought for the *lapsi* but also for the widows, the sick and every category of poor Christian, besides the pilgrims, asking that the sums they need be provided them from his own funds deposited with the presbyter Rogatianus.[46] The presbyters as well as the bishops were busy in this form of assistance. Tertullian thinks that hospitality is one of the things that marks the various churches as legitimate and apostolic in contrast to the heretical ones.[47]

Hermas too praises the hospitable Christians, "who always and gladly, without hypocrisy, received the servants of God into their houses";[48] for "in hospitality sometimes well-doing finds its outlet."[49] And among his reasons for disapproving

---

43. Justin, *I Ap.*, XIV, 3.
44. Clem. of Alex., *Quis dives salvetur?*, XXVIII.
45. He cites Exodus, 23:9. The Mishna forbade accepting hospitality from the ignorant (*Demai*, II, 2; cf. *The Talmud of Jerusalem*, ed. Schwab, t. II, p. 147).
46. *Ep.* XXXVI (*P. L.*, IV, 326-7).
47. "Receive our brother Heracles, *according to custom*," writes Sotas, perhaps a presbyter, to Peter (in a papyrus. Cf. Ghedini, *Lettere cristiane*, p. 129; compare *P. Oxy.*, VIII, 1162). *Appellatio fraternitatis et contesseratio hospitalitatis* (Tertullian, *De praescript.*, XX).
48. *Sim.*, IX, XXVIII, 2.
49. *Mand.*, VIII, 10. *Hospitalitatem sectantes* (Rom. 12:13) indicates that the guest must not only be received but sought out (Origen, *In ep. ad Rom.*, IX, 13). *Magna enim gratia in hospitalitatis officio non solum apud Deum, sed et apud homines invenitur* (*ib.*, X, 18).

marriages between a Christian woman and a pagan, Tertullian puts the fact that it will be impossible for her to receive pilgrims into her home.

Christian hosts must treat their foreign guests as Abraham treated the three unknown wayfarers at Mambre[50] and wash their feet and anoint them. This is a service in the interests of health and humility.

One community also helped other poor communities, considering itself a cell in one great organism. The church of Rome was for many reasons the richest as it was also the most important. It is enough to recall that Marcion on his arrival from Pontus donated to it the sum of two hundred thousand sesterces, and when it was discovered that he was a heretic it was able to give the entire amount back to him immediately. The Roman church considered it one of its ordinary functions to help the Christians in other communities.

Its readiness in giving this assistance was unlimited. While it had divided the population within the Urbs into seven districts under seven deacons, each of whom was assisted by seven subdeacons and six acolytes, taking care of no less than fifteen hundred poor, its help and its messengers with money, letters and sympathy were sent as far as Cappadocia and Arabia. It might be said the church of Rome was wherever there was grave need.

"There is extant," narrates Eusebius, that patient collector of documents, "a letter of the same Dionysius (bishop of Corinth) to the Romans, addressed to Soter, then bishop of Rome, a few passages of which it will not seem inopportune to quote. Praising the custom cherished by the Romans until the recent persecution, he writes: *'From the very beginning* this has been your custom, to come to the assistance of all the brethren in various ways and to send means of subsistence to numerous churches, in every city; relieving in such manner the needy in their distress, providing for the brethren con-

---

50. Origen, *In Gen.*, hom. IV, 1-2. Cf. Gen. 18:1 ff.

demned to the mines with the contributions you have sent
from the earliest times, cherishing as Romans a custom of your
Roman ancestors: a custom which your Bishop Soter has not
only preserved but developed, sending help in abundance to
the saints and consoling with pious exhortations our afflicted
brethren, as a loving father with his children'; Dionysius adds
that the letter of Soter, like that of his predecessor Clement,
is read periodically in the Corinthian church for edification and
as a remembrance of him."[51]

FROM ALMSGIVING TO THE COMMON SHARING OF GOODS

"Blessed is he who gives in obedience to the precept for
he is innocent. Woe to him who receives: if a man receives
who has need he will be innocent; but if a man receives who
has no need, he will have to render an account of his motive
and his purpose in taking; and having been put in prison, he
will be examined on his actions and he will not be let out until
he shall have restored what he has received even to the last
farthing." Thus the *Didache*[52] warns against giving aid blindly
and cites a *logion* of uncertain origin (probably rabbinic)
which says: "Let the alms sweat in your hand until you know
to whom you are giving."[53] This is repeated by St. Augustine,
St. Gregory, Cassiodorus and others. The *Didache* also warns
against parasites, who must have been many and invidious in
a period when employment was so scarce. If the person who
receives the alms has deceived the good faith of the giver,
then it is no longer considered an alms, but a loan, or better,
a theft. And the giver so tricked has the right to appeal to the
law to force the culprit, by imprisonment, to restore in their
entirety the goods thus stolen.

That such caution was necessary is proved by the incident
of Peregrinus Proteus, who, however exaggerated Lucian's
picture of him may be, seems nevertheless a highly probable

51. Eusebius, *H. E.*, IV, 23, 9-11.
52. I, 5-6. Cf. Resch, *Agrapha*, LXIX (L 12), p. 90.
53. Resch, *Agrapha*, LXX (L 35), p. 91.

individual in many respects. Among the varied adventures upon which the wily parasite embarked in his lively efforts to live by his wits, he even tried Christianity, having understood that because of the doctrines of immortality and brotherhood professed by the Christians, "if some cheat or impostor comes among them and knows how to conduct himself, he rapidly becomes very rich at the expense of the poor simpletons." And that is what he did: wormed his way into their ranks, learned their "marvelous wisdom," paraded himself as a teacher with great show, and became one of the rulers of the community, and so successfully that he ended in prison for the crime of Christianity. While he was there, his brothers in the faith tried every expedient to save him, and when they did not succeed they showered every care upon him. From early dawn, little old ladies, widows and orphans (the aristocracy of poverty in the new society) took up their posts near the prison, while the presbyters, by bribing the jailers, even succeeded in entering and spending the whole night with him to help him with their exhortations while they also brought him food, considering him a "new Socrates." . . . "Persons came even from the cities of Asia, in the name of the Christian communities there, to assist him, defend him during the trial, and comfort him. For they are of an incredible alacrity . . . and they do not spare themselves. So that in that emergency much money rained in upon Peregrinus. . . . "[54]

With all due allowance made for possible exaggeration in this sketch, it is certain that others tried the same thing, and so we can understand the diffidence expressed in the *Didache* even though it may seem excessive in comparison with the indulgent compassion of the Gospel, and more Jewish in nature than Christian. But the *Didache* also commands the Christians not to be greedy or rapacious, to love others more than their own persons; and it recommends generosity to the point of sharing their possessions in common with their brothers, re-

---

54. Lucian, *De morte Peregrini*, XI-XIII.

nouncing private ownership as an impediment to the complete realization of Christian brotherhood.

"Be not one who stretches out his hand to take, yet closes it against giving. If you have earnings, give a ransom for your sins. Do not hesitate to give nor grumble when you have given; for you will learn who it is that renders a goodly reward. Do not turn away the poor man but share everything in common with your brother, without saying that it is yours: for if you have in common what is undying, how much the more should you share what is but mortal" (IV, 5-8).

Then there is the tendency toward a community of goods characteristic of the mother Church. Pseudo-Barnabas keeps repeating it among the other precepts: "You shall share everything[55] with your neighbor and you shall not say that anything is your own: if, in fact, you hold in common the incorruptible, how much more (should you not hold in common) what is corruptible?" (XIX, 8).

Hermas insists repeatedly on the duty of giving to the needy; he knows very well that the poor man who lacks the necessities of life suffers cruelly. He must be saved from his distress and the one who saves him reaps great joy for himself. Poverty is a prison, and like the latter, it often leads to suicide. "He who knows the utter misery of the poor and does not save him, commits a great sin and becomes guilty of his blood."[56] These words assume even greater significance if they truly refer, as some believe, to the sufferings of the famine that raged under Antoninus Pius. Hermas belongs to the wealth-surrendering current of thought; but as we can see from the passage quoted, he does not aim at general impoverishment but rather at the elimination of the suffering of the poor, and this is the first thought of a religious spirit. Nor does he seem worried,

---

55. κοινωνήσεις. The *Didache* used συγκοινωνήσεις, an even more vivid expression of the idea, which, in words of the same origin, recurs in almost all the writers of the second century when they speak of almsgiving and social service. But gradually other words are added which in part explain and in part indicate a change in direction in the matter of sharing goods.

56.*Sim.*, X, 4, 2-3.

like the *Didache,* over the merit of the recipient of charity. He expresses a more generous feling, echoed later by Chrysostom, which considers almsgiving a beautiful thing in itself, as an act of giving, irrespective of the person who receives it.

"Do good, and, of the proceeds of your labors, granted you by God, give to all the needy, with a simple heart, without making distinctions between one person and another when you give: give to everyone, since God wills that all his gifts be distributed among all men."[57] Almsgiving is justified by a principle which brings the earnings of labor back to God, like all other goods of earth. Such earnings therefore belong not only to the one who labors but to all others as well — to the needy. And the good Hermas, who himself had put together a small fortune by his own labor (belonging as he did to the most industrious and active class, the freedmen) insists on this generosity in giving to the poor, on sharing with them the fruits of one's labor.[58] On the other hand (and on this point he follows the *Didache*) if the needy are not really so, they will pay the price of their hypocrisy to God.

It is the unerring judgment of God which justifies this moral and social practice, which, if it were carried out completely, would obliterate poverty because all would live from labor, both the workers and the infirm, both the strong and the weak, by virtue of the solidarity which binds them to one another as brothers. Then since their revenues would be held in common to a greater or less degree, their moral sensibilities would have to be kept awake and active in order to keep wandering impostors from insinuating themselves among them.

Thus conceived and practiced, almsgiving is something vaster and more complicated than what the term implies today. The word almsgiving, taken loosely as it is today, smacks a little of disparagement from any social point of view, for in common parlance it means the few pennies the richer man

57. Id., *Mand.,* II, 4.
58. Cf. *Sim.,* IX, 24, 2.

throws to the poor now and then. But it is clear that in the thought of the Fathers, as in that of the Apostles, the amount implied by alms is much greater indeed. It means a substantial and important transfer of one's own income, of one's own property, sufficient to enable the poor man to live without suffering any want or degradation. When the Fathers begin to complain that the charity of early times has grown lukewarm, this transfer is fixed at one-tenth of one's income, which is a handsome tithe; it is an agent in the redistribution of wealth, an effort toward the more equitable distribution of goods. In short, it is not alms or "charity" as these words are commonly used today, for it represents a substantial cut in the means of one man to compensate the indigence of another. It is a real and sizeable transfer of wealth from the former to the latter. It is a revolutionary phenomenon that takes place peacefully in a thousand little hidden ways, and the word itself (ἐλεημοσύνη: compassion) originally meant the feeling from which it sprang; for Christian compassion is what inspires this community of goods, the ordinary expression of which is almsgiving. Since the Christians are taught at the same time that it is their duty to labor, this transfer of means, intended to remedy the social injustices generated by original sin, by greed, the passions, violence, etc., does not mean impoverishment for the rich but rather enrichment for the poor. And it tends to put the latter in a position to surmount the depressing crisis of poverty so that they may be able to use their own energies again, to work harder and better and thus produce in their turn. The relative value assigned to wealth does not nullify it as such but causes it to circulate more easily and freely. And this is the more true the more the bourgeois, the freedman, the rich can be weaned from his habit of freezing his capital in precious objects or in his money-bags.

The Fathers of the Church will begin a long and persistent attack on wealth which is miserly — sterile — in an attempt to take from its earnings that fraction necessary to help the "have-nots" to live. And we find in their writings a pressure toward community of ownership, which means sharing in common the products of labor but not the means of production, for it never occurred to any one of them to entrust to the Church the management of any public or private enterprise whatever.

Thus almsgiving has led us to a discussion of that impulse of charity to put in common use the earnings of labor or the sum deriving from the sale of one's property in order to eliminate the miseries of the needy. We may recall the example of the church in Jerusalem. The member who so desires, sells what he has and gives the proceeds to the church; the members feel they are brothers and therefore take their meals in common or, if they are poor, they are fed from the common treasury. This remains the model and the aspiration of the Fathers.

— Do not say that there are private belongings: if you hold in common the immortal things, how much more logically must you hold in common the mortal? — asks the compiler of the *Didache* (IV, 8) and of the *Epistle of Barnabas* (XIX, 8). And in the modification of the *Didache* in the seventh book of the so-called *Apostolic Constitutions,* we still read (and it is about 400 A. D.): "Share everything with your brother and do not say thy goods are thine only."[59]

The *Epistle to Diognetus* says that the "Christians hold their table in common but not their bed" (V, 7). Tertullian says the same thing: "Among us everything is shared except our wives." It is the pagans, who, jealous guardians of property, begin to practice communism where Christians stop.[60]

It is a feature of the change wrought by conversion. First they practiced a shameful communism, now they practice a blessed one in the form of the most direct mutual assistance, such as sharing their food: "We who once abandoned ourselves to lasciviousness, now embrace only chastity . . . ; we who coveted most greedily the wealth and fortunes of others, now

---

59. VII, 12, 5: οὐκ ἐρεῖς ἴδια εἶναι; the same phrase occurs in the three different documents.

60. *Ap.,* XXXIX, 11-13.

place in common the goods we possess, dividing them with all the needy ... and we live in community."[61]

Philosophy defines the basic reasons for this use of one's resources, since, in the wake of Hebrew thought and because of its innate theological tendency, it goes back to God, the one and absolute Owner of all the goods of earth and their Creator. Men enjoy merely their usufruct. Now "God has directed the human race toward the community of goods, having first himself given and placed in common among all men his Son, his Word, and having created everything for the use of all. All things therefore are in common, nor must the rich appropriate to themselves the larger share. The formula therefore: — This is mine, and it is over and above my needs: why should I not enjoy it? — is neither human nor social.[62] More in accord with the spirit of charity is instead the formula: — It is mine; why do I not share it with the poor? ...

"The sums spent for vain pleasures deserve to be called waste and not expenditure: for God — I know it well — has given us the right of use, but only within the limits of necessity; and he has ordained that this use be in common. It is therefore wrong that one should be in luxury while the many are in distress. ... "[63] Without continuing the quotation, it is clear that the author aimed at a reorganization of the economic order in which serious inequalities would be resolved by the transfer of a part of one's possessions, the part that exceeds the purely necessary. The Church inaugurates an economic system of its own, founded on the communization of goods, or, as Clement of Alexandria terms it, mitigating the concept somewhat, the sharing or donation of a part of one's goods. This is realized in the least degree when the sums usually destined for luxuries (sumptuous homes, expensive furnishings, gems,

---

61. Justin, *I Ap.*, XIV, 2-3. Cf. Lucian, *Peregr.*, XIII, and Justin, *I Ap.*, LXVII, 1.

62. κοινωνικόν: communal, referable to the community.

63. Clem. of Alex., *Paed.*, II, 12. Cf. *Paed.*, III, 6, where it says that wealth must circulate: μεταληπτέον, that is, it must be shared with others, in common.

clothes, etc., voluptuous expenditures) devolve to the use of the community, and to the highest degree when one's entire revenues and property are donated to that use. The current concept of wealth is therefore radically modified. We have come a long way from the Quiritarian concept of property; we have arrived at the social concept of possessions as means given to us to use for something useful; so that if they are not so used, they are abused. This idea continues to evolve until the time of St. Augustine and it hinges on this principle: if the proprietor is God, we, his children, are all usufructuaries with equal rights. The usufruct belongs to all and no one may be deprived of it, "and no one can keep the human family from enjoying the bounty and munificence of God in equal measure (*aequaliter*)."[64]

---

64. Cyprian, *De opere et eleemosyna*, XXV.

CHAPTER XIII

HERETICAL DISTORTIONS
OF SOCIAL THOUGHT

THE COMPROMISE

THE Church, which is the visible image of the unity of God in a plurality of persons, desires to make of her members one single soul, in which they are all mystically united to Christ and behave in society as brothers one of the other. For the ecclesiastical bond does not end in "synaxis." It is forged in Baptism and strengthened by the Holy Eucharist, and so only sin can break it.

If the Christians all conducted themselves according to the law of the Church, there would be no injustices, no treachery and no conflicts among them. Varying in rank and scattered over the world, they would all yet tend toward a common goal, holding one another by the hand, sustaining one another in trial. But day by day sin wears away the efficacy of this solidarity; it clouds and deforms the law of charity and betrays it with hypocrisies. Hence day by day, the Church must lift the fallen, enlighten the erring and dissipate falsehood, endlessly reforging the links of brotherhood.

There is an activity of evil which tends constantly to disintegrate the spiritual unity expressed in the consciousness of the faithful through the feeling of solidarity; and there is an activity of the Church which tirelessly reconstructs this bond.

In the first three centuries, the Church as an institution spreads rapidly, invading every class of society. But as it spreads, the genuine spirit of the Gospel is weakened here and there and the control of the directing organs does not always reach the furthest members. Humanly speaking, solidarity becomes increasingly difficult to effectuate.

Every city has its church, with its bishop, assisted by presbyters and deacons. Its legitimacy is established by its derivation from the Apostles or from Apostolic churches; hence its teaching and its ecclesiastical function are understood to have come directly from the Apostles, and through them from Christ, and through Christ from God. In this chain of Apostolic authority the churches personally founded by the Apostles enjoy greater prestige, and the church of Rome, consecrated by the direction and martyrdom of the greatest Apostles, Peter and Paul, enjoys a preëminent prestige, preserving and transmitting the authority of Peter, the foundation stone of the Church. This authority in the first centuries is exercised gently and intermittently as circumstances permit and necessity requires. It becomes defined as the central authority principally under the pressure of secessionist movements, centrifugal impulses which set in motion centripetal energies.

These secessionist movements — schisms and heresies — split the social unity of Christendom. They divert the stream of charity into secondary channels that flow off at tangents. They create conflict within the Church, building walls against the tide of solidarity. Schisms and heresies rise from distortions of theology which necessarily result in social aberrations, weakening the original impulse of evangelical sociality.

They are the fruit of compromises, and from the ethical point of view they either deviate from the austerity of Christ's law or carry it to inhuman extremes. In the field of theology, they combine in some way with Judaism or with paganism and this inevitably influences the way of life of their adherents. In the course of this exposition we have mentioned various early heresies, and here we should like to point out their damaging effect on Christian social thought.

Along the edges of the first Christian preaching spreads the mold of Docetism. Its followers reduced the Incarnation of the Son of God, and hence also his Passion and Death, to a mere appearance, an optical illusion; they substituted a double for the suffering Christ or else maintained that his sufferings were merely "putative," apparent. They sowed the first seed of Gnosticism, or at least of the Gnostic current which divorced spirit from matter and made them two eternally conflicting principles deriving from two separate deities. In his own special form of Gnosticism, Marcion set the good God of the New Testament against the just but evil God of the Old Testament.[1]

These heresies, denying in one way or another the dogma of the Incarnation, pushed God infinitely far away from man and threw the latter back into an infinite helplessness. They anticipated other heresies, which in the effort to elevate the Creator, nullified the creature, destroying his liberty and his ability to lift himself from the effects of original sin. By separating matter and spirit in this way, they tended to emancipate the body from the moral law, maintaining that it was possible to preserve the soùl in purity even within a somatic and unclean vessel,[2] or else they condemned the body as a creation of evil and subjected it to inhuman rigorism. Social relations were placed in the category of meaningless or evil things so that men's supernatural solidarity was dissolved and nullified in practice.

These doctrines, which showed the influence of Persian dualism along with various elements of the Hellenic theogonies, confused men's minds and became crystallized in sects which were sometimes vehemently exclusive and usually bitterly hostile to the Mother Church. Thus they weakened her resistance to opposition and sowed the seeds of discouragement

---

1. In his controversy with the Marcionites, Clement of Alexandria declares that it is impossible to separate justice from goodness. If God is good then he is also just and vice versa; there is not a God and a Word distinct from him: they are both one and the same God. Justice is good because it wills the good of man even when it punishes him, for then it cuts from his soul the tumors of sin, guilt and pride, and make it new, "sound and true" (*Paed.,* I, 8).

2. This error is attributed to the followers of Nicolaus, who indulged in the pleasures of the flesh with the specious excuse of Aristippus of Cyrene. When the latter was rebuked for having a mistress, he answered, "I possess Lais, but I am not possessed by her" (Clem. of Alex., *Strom.,* II, 20).

and agnosticism in minds that were not equipped to face them. For the disciplined order and the harmonious hierarchy of offices in the Church, the heretics substituted the proud individualism of their own interpretations, and in the name of Christ they committed sins of insubordination and anti-social crimes that had nothing whatever to do with Christ.

Docetism was in substance the first great attempt to evade the social responsibilities deriving from the Incarnation and all the activity of the Son of God among men, an attempt to separate faith from works, the mystical from the social; and the Docetists did this on the pretense that they did not wish to dim the majesty of God with the trappings of man. And yet the Church exists precisely for this purpose, to transfuse the divine into the human, carrying on the work of the Incarnation, the Humanity and the Death of Christ, whose fullness she is.

The Judaizing heresies created dissension by making a cleavage between Peter and Paul, by lowering the nature and function of Jesus Christ and trying to circumscribe Christianity within the Temple, with Hebraism and circumcision; it might be said that they circumcised Catholic universality and first of all the impulse of charity toward all peoples without distinction.

THE RIGORISTS

Several apocryphal writings (Gospels, Acts, etc.) reveal rigorist tendencies; that is, they tend to resolve religion in asceticism. They are possessed with a kind of hatred for all that is matter; and while orthodox Christianity teaches that all that God has created is good in itself and only the use made of it by free men can render it evil, the rigorist heresies go so far as to identify evil with all of earthly creation and therefore even with man's food and with his body.

Gnosis, in fact "false gnosis," as Irenaeus calls the theories which presumed to make the new religion an esoteric phenomenon of superior knowledge, explains creation as the product of disorder in the heavenly life of the eons: the last result of a cycle of ignorance and passions. That is the way Valentinus explained it. The Gnostics who followed Saturninus did not eat anything that had ever been alive, and thus revived food restrictions like those of the Jews, which broke the Catholic synthesis of life.

The apocryphal *Acts of the Apostles* shared the obsessions of the Encratites and condemned the use of meat, wine and other foods. They went so far as to prescribe that the Consecration at Mass be of bread and water only. One sect was called for that reason the *Aquarii,* and among them we eventually find Tatian. The *Gospel of the Ebionites,* composed between 150 and 200 A. D., and the *Acts of Paul,* the *Acts of Thomas* and those of *Peter* and *Andrew* are born of analagous anxieties to reform Christianity in an ascetic sense.

Now the Catholic Church also accepted and taught sobriety and fasting, abstinence and continence as valid ascetic exercises, but at the same time she condemned any doctrinal rejection of any specific food. She considered that asceticism resided in the soul of the Christian; the heretics found it instead in elements in nature. The former mortified desire, the latter mortified things.

The orthodox Christians were sure they were in harmony with the spirit and the letter of the Gospel when they helped the poor; and a common way of doing this was the *agapes,* evening meals offered the poor and paid for with the church funds or with donations from rich members. Now when Tertullian became a Montanist, with that hypercritical judgment characteristic of those who fix their gaze on only one phase of the Christian system, he harshly rebuked the Catholics for "that charity in saucepans, that culinary faith, that hope in soup-bowls";[3] and this, as usual, is nothing but an attempt to separate faith from good works.

Thus the Church exalted celibacy, but she did not condemn

---

3. *De jeiuniis,* 17.

matrimony (quite the contrary!). Numerous Encratite and Gnostic sects, however, considered existence the receptacle of evil and like the Essenes abjured marriage and all sexual contact. They fled women as vessels of sin. A more or less crude and bizarre misogynist current runs through the heretical literature of the first centuries.[4] By an abnormal confusion of terms, it tended not so much to repress man's desires as to abolish woman altogether.

While some confined themselves to condemning second marriages as a kind of disguised adultery and a source of damnation, others saw the death of the soul in any nuptial embrace whatever.[5] The followers of Marcion and Valentinus and the Docetae of the sect of Cassianus called generation an evil; they wished human life to cease, possessed of a strange concupiscence for death, considered as the termination of guilt. Clement of Alexandria reminded them that the Redeemer, conceived in the womb of a Virgin, had entered this world by birth. And he used their very existence as an argument against their anti-social and anti-natural claims. Their hatred of the flesh he answered with the example of the human body in which the Lord had become Incarnate and of the physical cures he had wrought, healing bodies.[6]

Tatian also maintained that marriage was a form of degeneration[7] and thus allied himself with the Encratites and

---

4. In the *Apotelesmata Apollonii*, I, it is stated that a woman while menstruating can render a tree sterile merely by touching it.

5. Cf. Origen, *In Ierem.*, hom. XIX, 4.

6. *Strom.*, III, 17. He cites also and rejects a curious *logion* employed by Cassianus to bolster his teaching: "When Salome asked him, 'How long will death have its power?', the Lord answered, 'As long as you women bear children. In fact, I have come to end the work of women.' Then Salome said, 'I have therefore done well not to bear children?' And the Lord answered, 'Eat any herb whatever, but not that which is bitter.' Then when Salome asked him, 'When will the events take place that I have asked you of?' the Lord answered her, 'They will take place when you trample on the garment of shame, and when the two shall become one, and male and female shall become the same thing, and there shall no longer exist either male or female'" (*ib.*, III, 13 and *passim;* cf. Resch, *Agrapha,* Apokr. 34, pp. 252-4).

7. Cf. Hippolytus, *Philos.*, VIII, 16, who writes that those were innovations (καινά τινα).

Marcionites who demanded that the true Christian abjure marriage, and if he were married, that he divorce his wife. Hence they destroyed the indissolubility of the marriage bond, and they did so in the name of the Gospel!

Gnostic dualism stretched out into other social distortions as well. Not only did it separate its followers from the followers of orthodox Christianity, but it divided all the faithful (this is what the followers of Valentinus did, for example) into two categories: the *psychici* (*animales*) who are unshaken in their faith and good works; and the *pneumatici* (*spirituales*) who attain the gnosis that immunizes them from all contamination.[8] The ordinary people are below and the privileged class above: the Church and the sect. Man's evangelical equality of origin and end is destroyed. Marcion also deterministically excludes some men from salvation. To the two classes mentioned above some heretics added another, the *hylici* (material) who could not be saved in any way whatever. The Mystical Body was vivisected and the result was three bleeding stumps.

The distinction between these classes was consecrated even in the sacraments and the ritual. For instance, the usual baptism was considered sufficient for the ordinary faithful, but the *pneumatici* were baptized with perfumed oil (*apolytrosis* or redemption) in a nuptial chamber. Perfection was externalized in a kind of aristocracy with even a different standard of living.

Caius pointed out in this regard that the Gnostics based their theories more on human documents — on philosophy and in fact geometry — than on the Scriptures, more on Aristotle, Euclid and Galen than on Jesus, the prophets and the Apostles.[9]

SEXUAL COMMUNISM

Mention has already been made of the fact that some Gnostics erred in another direction, for while they did condemn marriage they did not condemn sexual intercourse. Ac-

---

8. Irenaeus, *Adv. haer.*, I, VI, 1-2.
9. Cited by Eusebius, *H. E.*, V, 28.

cording to St. Irenaeus the Valentinians pushed their dualism to paradoxical extremes, completely separating the things of the body from those of the spirit and denying that there was any communication or influence between the two. Consequently they not only went to obscene and savage spectacles and ate foods that had been sacrificed to idols but they also seduced women, committed adultery, and raped their sisters in the faith, maintaining that the orthodox who abstained from sin through fear of God were foolish and ignorant while they themselves were wise and perfect.[10] The Gnostic Marcus and his followers pursued women who were of higher social rank or wealthier, and on the pretext that they themselves were perfect they seduced a great number of them.[11]

There were heretics who preached public prostitution as a "mystical communion."[12] And consequently the pagan apologists who did not distinguish between the true Church and these spurious communities had grave reasons for attacking Christianity as an "unbridled superstition." These facts also explain why the Christian apologists are so anxious to defend their communion of goods, limited as it was to articles of consumption, meals, and having a voluntary and contingent character, from the charges that theirs was a more radical social communism and especially that it was communism in sexual matters achieved by violating the most revered civil laws. Evidently the amoral and immoral communitarian practices of some of the Gnostic sects threw dangerous suspicion on Christian gatherings. Tertullian as usual retorts with the same charge.[13] Clement of Alexandria is more practical and proceeds to condemn the Carpocratians who, under the name of Christ, circulated theories of revolting communism. This was also because the phenomenon had first appeared in Alexandria, where Carpocrates had taught between 130 and 150 A. D. with his

10. *Adv. haer.*, I, VI, 3.
11. *Ib.*, I, XIII.
12. Clem. of Alex., *Strom.*, III, 4.
13. So does Justin, *I Ap.*, 27, 5.

highly precocious son Epiphanes. The latter had written a work entitled *Justice* to demonstrate that divine Justice had originally created a community of goods, without any distinctions of class or sex, and that only human injustice had established the individual's right to appropriate them.

The work created a furore, and its author, who died at the age of seventeen, was considered by his followers a kind of god. This is a fanaticism which reminds us of the idolatrous admiration that has been showered on so many authors of revolutionary theories right down to Lenin. The theory of Carpocrates and Epiphanes implied also that women be held in common. In his book Epiphanes maintained that "the justice of God is a kind of common partaking of equality. An equal sky, extended in every direction, surrounds the entire earth; the night, in equal manner, displays all the stars; the sun, the author of day and the father of light, God bestows from on high in equal manner upon all on earth that are able to see — and all these see in common; for he does not distinguish between rich and poor, between the rulers and the people, the stupid and the wise, between male and female, free men and slaves. Nor does he act differently with respect to the irrational animals, shedding a common light from on high equally upon all animals, good and bad. He maintains justice, not permitting one to have more than another nor to take any away from his neighbor, in order to have a double share of light. The sun makes food grow in common for all living beings, according to a common justice bestowed on all in equal measure; and toward these goods, in equal manner, the oxen conduct themselves as oxen, the swine as swine, and the sheep as sheep and so forth; for even in them justice is manifest as participation in common. Then, too, all crops are sown, each in its kind, in common without distinction; and a common nourishment is offered on the earth to all the flocks that pasture, and to all in equal measure, outside the rule of any law, through a gift given by the command of its donor to all without distinction.

"Nor is generation subject to a written law; for it would already have been abrogated; they sow their seed and generate equally, having common participation ingrained in them by justice. To all and in equal measure the Creator and Father of the universe gave an eye to see, with a decree in conformity with his justice, without distinguishing between male and female, or between rational and irrational beings; bestowing it in common equality he has given a sight in equal measure to all with one single act of command. But human laws, not able to punish ignorance, taught men to act against right; and in fact, the individualism of the laws splintered and corroded the participation in common ordained by divine Law, without understanding the saying of the Apostle, 'Through the Law I have known sin.'[14] And through the laws entered the *mine* and the *yours* to take from common use the earth and its possessions and matrimony itself. And yet these things are common to all, for the Author gave the vines to all, which repulse neither the sparrow nor the thief, and also the grain and other products. It was the violation of the law of community and equality which created the thief of the flocks and fruits.[15]

"God, therefore, by creating everything in common for mankind, and joining the male with the female in common, and uniting all living beings in the same manner, has defined justice as the common partaking of equality. But some of the men born in this manner denied this community, which brings men closer together, repudiating their own birth.... [God] placed a more vigorous and vehement desire in the males, for the sake of the propagation of the species: and no law nor custom nor other force can suppress it: for it is the decree of God."[16]

---

14. Cf. Rom. 3:20; 7:7.
15. Hence the thief is the one who returns to the proper respect of divine Law; and the true thief would be the proprietor who has stolen from common use a part of the patrimony of all men. "Property is a theft"; the cry is an ancient one, we see.
16. Clem. of Alex., *Strom.*, III, 2.

According to teachings such as these, the banquets (not to be called *agape*) of the Carpocratians end in incestuous intercourse. Thus Clement of Alexandria says the same thing of them that the pagans were saying about the Christians.[17]

A similar aberration developed among the followers of Montanus, Priscilla, and Maximilla. During the anxious wait for the heavenly Jerusalem which was supposed to descend on the plain between Pepuza and Thymion in Phrygia, they broke all family and conjugal ties, sold their homes and flocks, and placed all their possessions and their women in common. Montanus is supposed to have given the towns of Pepuza and Thymion the name of heavenly Jerusalem in place of the Jerusalem which he and his co-prophets, Priscilla and Maximilla, had foretold would descend from heaven, but which failed to do so. In order for the community to live, he had to name an administrator, take up collections, invite donations and hire preachers capable of "bolstering their doctrine with gluttonies." The orthodox Christians rebuked the Montanists (whom Tertullian joined for a while) for these and other things, and they claimed that the communist leaders of the new Jerusalem, while they preached self-denial and fasting, led a merry life of it playing dice, frequenting the baths, loaning money at interest, and touching up their hair and eyes to seem more handsome.[18]

For this is the destiny of Christian virtues: if they are not perfectly balanced and fused in charity, there is danger that one will be atrophied in the exaggerated development of another, and this results in paradoxical excesses. Tertullian's case is proof of this. He went to extremes and then fell into rigorism and the rebellious hallucination of the Montanists, obsessed by the illusory idea that they were to inaugurate the regime of fire, of the Holy Spirit, midst that flare of psychopathic eccentricites.

---

17. *Ib.*, 2, 6.
18. Eusebius, *H. E.*, V, 18.

LABOR AND WEALTH

It is not surprising if, among these currents of thought that bordered on or fell into heresy, there also prospered theories that were anarchical from the political point of view and aimed to destroy all connections between Christian and non-Christian society.[19] The sects absorbed in the hope of an imminent eschatological palingenesis freed themselves of all civil obligations just as they dissolved all family ties. They deserted from the state and from society and lost themselves in a dreamy anarchy. It was not rare for confusion in theology to take the form of eschatological expectations, kindled by the eager desire for a social regeneration.

Among the pre-Gnostics, Cerinthus prophesied a new kingdom of Christ, supposedly revealed to him by the angels, which was to be realized in an earthly Jerusalem with a millennium of "nuptial feasts." We have already noted that some orthodox Christians also held millenarist beliefs. Mention is made of these here again to bring out the materialistic character of the chiliastic heresies.

Other aberrations derived from that decomposition of the vital factors in society. For example, while the orthodox Christians celebrated Christ also as a healer and reverenced in Luke the "physician friend" of St. Paul, the Marcionites and various Encratites, since they despised the body, also despised medicines and identified them with the work of the devil. And while the orthodox Christians received the rich into the Church, asking them to make good use of the mammon of iniquity, the Marcionites, repeating the distinctions of some of the Jewish schools of thought, considered the rich impious and the poor pious.

These and other anomalies show what decadence heresy represented, even from the social point of view. Whatever aspect it assumed it meant initially a diminution of the social efficacy of Christianity by the mere fact that it contracted a

---

19. Cf. Tertullian, *De oratione.*

number of the faithful into a sect, and certain theological elements into a particular system. By reducing faith either to rigorous asceticism (the Encratites) or to a phenomenon of knowledge (gnosis) it created unilateral and marginal unities to the detriment of the true basic unity, that in charity. Therefore it made room for minorities, closed groups and aristocracies. And Irenaeus, that great destroyer of heresies, quite rightly set as a corrective against the seductive phantasms of false gnosis the charitable activity of the great Church, bent over the miseries of mankind. The contemplation of these miseries would have effaced so much intellectual arrogance and cured the lunacy of so many visionaries.

For charity, like arterial blood, tirelessly rebuilds the health of the social body, which is the Church, in both the supernatural and the natural order. Hence the burning prayer for unity offered over the Eucharistic bread: "As this bread which is broken was scattered over the mountains and then being gathered has become one, so may thy Church be gathered from the ends of the earth into thy kingdom."[20]

And that is why the Roman bishop sorrowfully asked the Corinthians, tormented by internal dissensions: "Have we not one and the same God, one and the same Christ, and one and the same spirit of grace diffused in us, and the same vocation in Christ? And why then do we revolt against our own body? And why are we possessed by such madness as to forget that we are members one of another?"[21]

This heartsick query is repeated by almost all the Fathers of the Church as they contemplate the ruin wrought by heresy, that ally of persecution sent by Satan to work havoc from within.

---

20. *Didache*, IX, 4.
21. Clem. Rom., XLVI, 6-9.

CHRONOLOGICAL TABLE

POPES[1]

LINUS, 67-78
CLETUS, 78-90
CLEMENT, 90-100
ANACLETUS, 100-112
EVARISTUS, 112-121
ALEXANDER, 121-132
SIXTUS, 132-142
TELESPHORUS, 142-154
EUGENE, 154-158
PIUS, 158-167
ANICETUS, M. 175
SOTER, M. 182
ELEUTHERIUS, M. 193
VICTOR, 193-203
ZEPHYRINUS, 203-221
CALLIXTUS, 221-227
URBAN, 227-233
PONTIANUS, 233-238
ANTHERUS, 238-239
FABIANUS, 239-253
CORNELIUS, 253-255
LUCIUS, 255-257

EMPERORS

NERO, 54-68
GALBA, OTTO, VITELLIUS, 68-69
VESPASIAN, 69-79
TITUS, 79-81
DOMITIAN, 81-96
NERVA, 96-98
TRAJAN, 98-117
HADRIAN, 117-138
ANTONINUS PIUS, 138-161
MARCUS AURELIUS, 161-180
COMMODUS, 180-192
SEPTIMIUS SEVERUS, 193-211
CARACALLA, 211-217
MACRINUS, 217-218
HELIOGABALUS, 218-222
ALEXANDER SEVERUS, 222-235
MAXIMINUS, 235-238
GORDIANUS II, 238-244
PHILIP, 244-249
DECIUS, 249-251
GALLUS, 251-253
VALERIANUS, 253-260

---

1. Names and dates from the *Annuario pontificio* (1938).

BIBLIOGRAPHY[1]

GENERAL

Amatucci, A. G., *Storia della letteratura latina cristiana*, Bari, 1929.

Audollent, A. M. H., *Carthage romaine, 146 avant Jésus-Christ — 698 après Jésus-Christ*, Paris, 1901.

Bardenhewer, Otto, *Geschichte der altkirchlichen Literatur*, 2. Aufl., Freiburg i. B., 1913-32, 5 Bd.

—— *Patrologie . . .* , 3. Aufl., Freiburg i. B., 1910 (Engl. transl. by T. J. Shahan, St. Louis, 1908).

Bardy, Gustave, *Littérature latine chrétienne*, Paris, 1929.

Batiffol, Pierre, *La littérature grecque*, 4 éd., Paris, 1901.

Bell, H. I., *Jews and Christians in Egypt; the Jewish Troubles in Alexandria and the Athanasian Controversy*, illus. by texts from Greek papyri, Oxford, 1924.

Beiträge zur Geschichte des christlichen Altertums und der byzantinischen Literatur, hrsg. von A. M. Koeniger, Bonn and Leipzig, 1922.

Bevan, Edwin, *Sibyls and Seers, a Survey of Some Ancient Theories of Revelation and Inspiration*, London, 1928.

Bibliotheca hagiographica graeca, ed. hagiographi Bollandiani, Brussels, 1895.

Boulanger, André, . . . *Aelius Aristide et la sophistique dans la province d'Asie au II*e *siècle*, Paris, 1923.

Bullettino d'archeologia cristiana (Nuovo Bullettino . . .), Rome, 1863.

Buonaiuti, Ernesto, *Il cristianesimo nell'Africa romana*, Bari, 1928.

Carcopino, Jérôme, *La vie quotidienne à Rome*, Paris, 1938.

Case, S. J., *Bibliographical Guide to the History of Christianity*, Cambridge, 1931.

Chevalier, Ulysse, *Répertoire des sources historiques du moyen âge*, I. Bio-bibliographie, nouv. éd., Paris, 1905-07; II. Topo-bibliographie, Montbéliard, 1894-99.

Christ, W. and Staehlin, O., *Geschichte der griechischen Literatur*, 2. T. 6. Aufl., Munich, 1920-24.

Costa, Emilio, *Storia del diritto romano privato*, 3ª ed., Florence, 1921.

Delaunay, Ferdinand, *Moines et sibylles dans l'antiquité judéo-grecque*, 2e éd., Paris, 1874.

---

1. See also the bibliographies in the first two volumes of this series, *The Social Message of Jesus*, Paterson, 1943, and *The Social Message of the Apostles* (transl. in preparation).

335

Delehaye, Hippolyte, *Les légendes hagiographiques*, 2ᵉ éd., Brussels, 1906 (Engl. transl., *Legends of the Saints*, London, 1907).

De Rossi, G. B., *La Roma sotterranea cristiana descritta ed illustrata*, Rome, 1864-77, 3 vols.

Deutsches archäolog. Institut, *Jahrbuch, Bibliographie*, Berlin and Leipzig, 1924.

Drews, Arthur, *Die Entstehung des Christentums aus dem Gnostizismus*, Jena, 1924.

Dufourcq, Albert, *Etude sur les "Gesta martyrum" romains*, Paris, 1900.
────── *Histoire ancienne de l'Eglise*, Paris, 1924 (t. II. La révolution religieuse, 5ᵉ éd.; t. III. Le Christianisme primitif, 5ᵉ éd.; t. IV. Le Christianisme et l'empire, 4ᵉ éd., etc.).

Fabricius, J. A., *Bibliographia antiquaria, sive Introductio in notitiam scriptorum, qui antiquitates hebraicas, graecas, romanas et christianas scriptis illustraverunt*, editio 2, Hamburg and Leipzig, 1716.

Faye, E. de, *Gnostiques et gnosticisme*, 2ᵉ éd., Paris, 1924.

Friedländer, Ludwig, *Darstellung aus der Sittengeschichte Röms in der Zeit von August bis zum Ausgang der Antonine*, 11. Aufl., Leipzig, 1921.

Goldwitzer, F. W., *Bibliographie der Kirchenväter und Kirchenlehrer vom 1. bis zum 13. Jahrhundert*, Landshut, 1828.

Gregorovius, Ferdinand, *Glanz und Untergang Roms. Gemälde der römisch-hellenist. Welt zur Zeit der Kaisers Hadrian*, Berlin, 1932 (*L'imperatore Adriano*, vers. A. Tomei, Rome, 1910).

Grossi-Gondi, F., *I monumenti cristiani dei primi sei secoli*, Rome, 1920-23, 2 vols.
────── *Trattato di epigrafia cristiana*, Rome, 1920.

Harnack, Adolf von, *Dogmengeschichte ...5*. verb. Aufl., Tübingen, 1914.
────── *Geschichte der altchristlichen Literatur bis Eusebius*, Leipzig, 2 Teile, 1893-1904.
────── *Marcion: das Evangelium vom fremden Gott ...*, Leipzig, 1924 (*T. U.*).

Hefele, C. J. v., *Conciliengeschichte. Fortges. von F. Hergenröther*, Freiburg i. B., 1869-90. 9 Bd. (*Histoire des Conciles*, ed. Leclercq, H., Paris, 1907-1931).

Henderson, B. W., *The Life and Principate of the Emperor Hadrian*, London, 1923.

Herford, R. T., *Christianity in Talmud and Midrash*, London, 1903.

Jordan, Hermann, *Geschichte der altchristlichen Literatur ...*, Leipzig, 1911.

Kirsch, Conrad, *Enchiridion fontium historiae ecclesiasticae*, 2/3 ed., Freiburg, 1914.

Knopf, Rudolf, *Das nachapostolische Zeitalter*, Tübingen, 1905.

Kruger, Gustav, *Geschichte der altchristlichen Literatur in den ersten drei Jahrunderten*, Freiburg i. B., 1895.

Labriolle, Pierre de, *Histoire de la littérature chrétienne*, 2e éd., Paris, 1924.

La Piana, Giorgio, *Foreign Groups in Rome during the First Century of the Empire*, Harvard, 1928 (in It. in *Ricerche religiose*, II-IV, 1926-28).

Leclercq, Henri, *La vie chrétienne primitive*, Paris, 1928.

Leisegang, Hans, *Die Gnosis*, Leipzig, 1924.

Manitius, M., *Geschichte der christlich-lateinischen Poesie bis zur Mitte des 8. Jahrh.*, Stuttgart, 1891.

Mannucci, Ubaldo, *Istituzioni di patrologia . . .*, 2ª ed., Rome, 1920.

Marouzeau, Jules, *L'année philologique; bibliographie critique et analytique de l'antiquité gréco-latine*, Paris, 1928 —

Martigny, J. A., *Dictionnaire des antiquités chrétiennes*, 3e éd., Paris, 1889.

Mingana, A., *Woodbrooke Studies*, I-VII, Cambridge, 1927-35.

Monceaux, Paul, *Histoire de la littérature latine chrétienne*, Paris, 1924.

———— *Histoire littéraire de l'Afrique chrétienne, depuis les origines jusqu'à l'invasion arabe*, Paris, 1901-20, 5 vols.

Moricca, Umberto, *Storia della letteratura latina cristiana*, Turin (n.d.), 3 vols.

Paschini, Pio, *Lezioni di storia ecclesiastica*, Turin, 1930-32.

Pharmas, Phébus, *Sociologie du mariage chez les Romains*, Alexandria, 1938.

Richardson, E. C., *Bibliographical Synopsis to the Ante-Nicene Fathers*, Buffalo, 1887.

Rouet de Journel, M. J., *Enchiridion patristicum*, 8,9 ed., Freiburg, 1932.

Schanz, Martin, *Geschichte der römischen Litteratur*, 3. T. *Die Zeit von Hadrian 117 bis auf Constantin 324*, 3. Aufl., Munich, 1922.

Scholarios, Dorotheos, Κλεὶς πατρολογίας . . . , Athens, 1879.

———— Ταμεῖον τῆς πατρολογίας . . . , Athens, 1883-87, 2 vols.

Sinopoli di Giunta, *Storia letteraria della Chiesa*, Turin, 1919-22.

Sorel, Georges, *La ruine du monde antique . . .*, 2e éd., Paris, 1925.

Tillemont, Lenain de, *Mémoires pour servir à l'histoire ecclésiastique des six premiers siècles . . .*, Venice, 1732.

Tixeront, G., Raemers, *Handbook of Patrology*, St. Louis, 1923.

SOURCES, TEXTS, STUDIES

a. GENERAL

Acta apostolorum apocrypha, ed. R. A. Lipsius et M. Bonnet, Leipzig, 1891-1903.

Acta martyrum, P. Theodorici Ruinart opera ac studio coll., Ratisbon, 1859.

Acta martyrum selecta . . . , ed. O. L. Gebhardt, Berlin, 1902.

Acta sanctorum (Bollandists), Antwerp, 1643 (63 vols.).

Acta sanctorum, coll. F. Bollandus, etc., ed. noviss., Brussels, 1863-

Analecta Bollandiana, Paris-Brussels, 1882-

Anecdota Maredsolana, Maredsou, 1893-

Baronio, Cesare, *Annales ecclesiastici, denuo excusi* . . . , Bar-le-Duc, 1864-83, 37 vols.

Bibliotheca scriptorum graecorum et romanorum Teubneriana, Leipzig, 1850-. (Besides the texts of pagan Greek and Latin writers before and after Christ, this includes texts of Christian writers.)

Bibliotheca Ss. Patrum, ed. Vizzini, Rome, 1901.

Bibliothek der Kirchenväter. Eine Auswahl patristischer Werke in deutscher Übersetzung, Munich, 1911.

Cambridge Patristic Texts, Cambridge, 1899.

Classici cristiani, Siena, 1927.

Corona patrum salesiana, Series graeca [et] Series latina, Turin, 1934.

Corpus inscriptionum graecarum, Berlin, 1828-77, 4 vols. in 8. *Inscriptiones graecae*, ib., 1873.

Corpus inscriptionum latinarum, Berlin, 1862, 8 vols. in 11.

Corpus scriptorum ecclesiasticorum latinorum, ed. consilio et impensis Acad. litt. Vindobonensis, Vienna, 1866-

Delehaye, Hippolyte, *Les passions des martyrs et les genres littéraires*, Brussels, 1921.

De Rossi, G. B., *Inscriptiones christianae urbis Romae septimo saeculo antiquiores*, Rome, 1857; nova series, curante Angelo Silvagni, 1922.

Dessau, Hermann, *Inscriptiones latinae selectae*, Berlin, 1892-1916, 3 vols. in 5.

Epistola apostolorum. Gespräche Jesu mit seinen Jüngern nach der Auferstehung; ein katholisch-apostolisches Sendschreiben des 2. Jahrhunderts . . . , hrsg. von Carl Schmidt, Leipzig, 1919.

Evangelia apocrypha, ed. Constantinus Tischendorf . . . , Leipzig, 1876.

Florilegium patristicum . . . (nova series), Bonn, 1923 (begun in 1904).

Gibson, M. Dunlop, *Apocrypha sinaitica* . . . , London, 1896.

Gennadius of Marseilles, *De viris illustribus* (P. L., LVIII, 1059-1120).

Ghedini, G., *Lettere cristiane dai papiri greci del III° e IV° secolo*, Milan, 1923.

Goodspeed, E. I., *Index patristicus*, Leipzig, 1907.

Griechischen christlichen Schriftsteller der ersten drei Jahrhunderte, hrsg. von der Kirchenväter. Comm. der Preuss. Ad. der Wissenschaften, Leipzig, 1901.

Inscriptiones latinae christianae veteres, ed. E. Diehl, Berlin, 1925-27, 2 vols.

Jerome, St., *De viris illustribus* (P. L., XXIII, 601-720).

Kleine Texte für theologische und philologische Vorlesungen und Uebungen, ed. H. Lietzmann, Bonn, 1903-

Leclerq, Henri, *Les martyrs; recueil de pièces authentiques ...*, Paris, 1902-24, 15 vols.

Liber pontificalis, texte, intr. et comm. par L. Duchesne, Paris, 1886-92, 2 vols.

Migne, J. P., ed., *Patrologiae cursus completus ...*, Series graeca, Paris, 1857-86.

—— *Patrologiae cursus completus ...*, Series latina, Paris, 1844-64.

Münchener Beiträge zur Papyrusforschung, hrsg. von Leopold Wenger, Munich, 1915.

Oracula sibyllina, rec. Aloisius Rzach, Vienna, 1891.

—— *Die Oracula sibyllina*, Joh. Geffcken ..., Leipzig, 1902.

The Oxyrhynchus Papyri, ed. B. P. Grenfell and A. S. Hunt, London, 1898.

Papiri greco-egizi, pub. by the R. Accademia dei Lincei, under the direction of D. Comparetti e G. Vitelli, Milan, 1905-15, 3 vols.

Passio S. Perpetuae (The Passion of S. Perpetua, newly edited from the mss. with an introduction and notes, together with an appendix containing the original Latin text of the Scillitan Martyrdom, by J. Armitage Robinson), Cambridge, 1891 (*Texts and Studies*, I, 2).

Pitra, J. B., *Analecta sacra et classica*, Paris, 1888.

Pliny, *Epistolarum libri novem, Epistolarum ad Traianum liber, Panegyricus;* recensuit R. C. Kukula, ed. 2, Leipzig, 1912.

Sacrorum conciliorum nova et amplissima collectio, ed. F. D. Mansi, Florence (Venice), 1759; *contin.*, Paris, 1901.

Scrittori cristiani antichi, Rome, 1921-23.

Scrittori latini cristiani, antologia a cura di R. De Sanctis e V. Paronetto, Florence, 1938.

Studi e testi (Biblioteca Vaticana), Rome, 1900-

Testi cristiani, con versione italiana, dir. da G. Manacorda, Florence, 1930.

Texte und Untersuchungen zur Geschichte der altchristliche Literatur, hrsg. von Ov. Gebhardt, A. v. Harnack und C. Schmidt, Leipzig, 1887 (abbrev.: *T. U.*).

Textes et documents pour l'étude historique du christianisme, ed. H. Hemmer and Paul Lejay, Paris, 1904.

Texts and Studies, ed. by J. A. Robinson, Cambridge, 1891-1922.

b. THE APOSTOLIC FATHERS

Buccellato, Manlio, *Papias di Hierapoli*, Palermo, 1936.

Die Apostolischen Väter, Tübingen, 4 Teile, 1920-23.

Casamassa, Antonio, *I padri apostolici*, studio introduttivo, Rome, 1938.

Clement of Rome, *Das Schreiben der römischen Kirche an die korintische aus der Zeit Domitians* (1. Clemensbrief), hrsg. Ad. von Harnack, Leipzig, 1929.

——— (Igino Giordani), *S. Clemente Romano e la sua lettera ai Corinti,* Turin, 1925.

Connolly, R. H., "The *Didache* in Relation to the Epistle of Barnabas" (in *The Journal of Theological Studies,* 1932, no. 131, pp. 237-253).

Evangelium Petri. L'évangile de Pierre, par Léon Vaganay, Paris, 1930 (Etudes bibliques). This has a rich bibliography.

Funk, F. H., *Patres apostolici,* 3 ed., Tübingen, 1901-13, 2 vols. (ed. K. Bihlmeyer, 1924).

Gerke, M. F., *Die Stellung des ersten Clemensbriefes innerhalb der Entwicklung der altchristlichen Gemeindeverfassung und des Kirchenrechts,* Leipzig, 1931 (*T. U.*).

Hall, E. H., *Papias and His Contemporaries,* Boston and New York, 1899.

Lake, Kirsopp, *The Apostolic Fathers,* London, 1917, 1919, 2 vols.

Lightfoot, J. B., *The Apostolic Fathers,* London, 1885-90, 4 vols. in 5 (ed. minor, 1898) (2nd ed., 1912).

Moricca, Umberto, *Le lettere di Ignazio di Antiochia e di Policarpo. Il martirio di Policarpo,* Rome, 1923.

Patrum apostolicorum opera, textum . . . instr. O. de Gebhardt, A. de Harnack, Th. Zahn, ed. 3, Leipzig, 1876-78, 3 vols. in 4 (ed. V. minor, 1906).

Patrum apostolicorum opera graece, Turin, 1934 (another edition: *addita latina antiqua versione*).

Schlier, Heinrich, *Religionsgeschichtliche Untersuchungen zu den Ignatiusbriefen,* Giessen, 1929.

Zeller, Franz, *Die apostolischen Väter,* Kempten and Munich, 1918.

C. THE CHURCH FATHERS OF THE SECOND AND THIRD CENTURIES

Apollonius, *The Armenian Apology and Acts of Apollonius,* by F. C. Conybeare, 2nd ed., London, 1896.

——— *Der Process und die Acta S. Apollonii . . . ,* von E. T. Klette, Leipzig, 1897 (*T. U.*).

Aristides, *Die Apologie des Aristides. Aus dem Syrischen übersetzt . . . ,* von Richard Raabe, Leipzig, 1893 (*T. U.*).

——— *Die Apologie des Aristides,* Recension und Rekonstruktion des Textes von Edgar Hennecke, Leipzig, 1893 (*T. U.*).

——— *The Apology of Aristides on Behalf of the Christians, from a Syriac Manuscript Preserved on Mount Sinai,* ed. with an introduction and translation by J. Rendel Harris . . . , with an appendix containing the main portion of the original Greek text, by J. Armitage Robinson . . . , 2nd ed., Cambridge, 1893.

——— *Baralâm and Yĕwâsĕf,* being the Ethiopic Version of a Christianized recension of the Buddhist legend of the Buddha and the Bodhisattva, ed. E. A. W. Budge, Cambridge, 1923.

—— *St. John Damascene: Barlaam and Joasaph*, with an English translation by G. R. Woodward ... and H. Mattingly ..., London, 1914.

Athenagoras, *Libellus pro christianis. Oratio de resurrectione cadaverum*. Recensuit Edvardus Schwartz, Leipzig, 1891 (*T. U.*).

—— *La supplica per i cristiani*, testo critico e commento di Paolo Ubaldi, Turin, 1920.

Aube, Benjamin, *De l'apologétique chrétienne au IIe siècle. Saint Justin, philosophe et martyr*, Paris, 1861.

Bardy, Gustave, *Clément d'Alexandrie*, Paris, 1926 (*Moralistes chrétiens*).

—— *Origène*, Paris, 1931 (*Moralistes chrétiens*).

Bousset, Wilhelm, *Jüdisch-christlicher Schulbetrieb in Alexandria und Rom; literarische Untersuchungen zu Philo und Clemens von Alexandria, Justin und Irenäus* ..., Göttingen, 1915.

Buonaiuti, Ernesto, *Frammenti gnostici*, Rome, 1923.

Cadiou, René, *La jeunesse d'Origène*, Paris, 1925.

Clement of Alexandria, *Quis dives salvetur?*, hrsg. von Oberl. K. Köster, Freiburg i. B., 1893.

Clement of Alexandria, *Quis dives salvetur?*, re-ed. by P. Mordaunt Barnard, Cambridge, 1897 (*Texts and Studies*, V).

Corpus apologetarum christianorum saec. II, ed. I. C. Th. de Otto, Jena, 1847-72, 9 vols.

De Marchi, Attilio, *Apologisti cristiani, scelti e commentati*, Milan, 1907.

Donaldson, James, *A Critical History of Christian Literature and Doctrine from the Death of the Apostles to the Nicene Council*, vols. II-III, *The Apologists*, London, 1866.

Faye, Eugène de, *Clément d'Alexandrie. Etude sur les rapports du christianisme et de la philosophie grecque au IIe siècle* ..., Paris, 1898.

Franchi de' Cavalieri, Pio, *Gli atti di S. Giustino*, Rome, 1902 (*Studi e Testi*, 8).

Funk, F. X., "Clemens von Alexandrien über Familie und Eigentum," *Theol. Quartalschr.*, t. LIII, 1871, p. 427-449; reprinted in *Kirchegesch. Abhandl. m. Unters*, t. II, p. 45-60, Paderborn, 1899.

Geffcken, Johannes, *Zwei griechische Apologeten* (Aristides and Athenagoras), Leipzig, 1907 (*T. U.*).

Giordani, Igino, *La prima polemica cristiana. Gli apologisti greci del 2° secolo*, Turin, 1929.

Goodspeed, E. J., ed., *Die ältesten Apologeten*. Texte. Göttingen, 1914.

—— *Index apologeticus*, Leipzig, 1912.

Guignebert, Charles, *Tertullien; étude sur ses sentiments à l'égard de l'empire et de la société civile*, Paris, 1901.

Hagen, O. van der, *De Clementis Alexandrini sententiis oeconomicis, socialibus, politicis*, Utrecht, 1920.

Harnack, Adolf von, *Judentum und Judenschristentum in Justins Dialog mit Trypho, nebst einer Collation der Pariser Handschrift Ur. 450 . . .*, Leipzig, 1913.

——— *Die Ueberlieferung der griechischen Apologeten des zweiten Jahrh . . .*, Leipzig, 1882 (*T. U.*).

Hermas, "I filosofi pagani alla sbarra" (introd. and transl. of E. Buonaiuti, in *Ricerche religiose*, Rome, 1929, pp. 251 and ff.).

Herzog, R., *Die Wunderheilungen von Epidauros; ein Beitrag zur Geschichte der Medizin und der Religion*, Leipzig, 1931.

Irenaeus, *Libros quinque adversus haereses textu graeco*, versione latina, edidit W. W. Hervey, Cambridge, 1857.

Junius, F. J. J. A., *De Iustino martyre apologeta adversus ethnicos*, Leyden, 1836.

Justin, St., *Le Apologie e brani scelti dal "Dialogo con Trifone,"* ed. e tr. Igino Giordani, Florence, 1929.

——— *Le due apologie di S. Giustino martire con gli Atti del martirio*, tr. di Pietro Baldoncini, Rome, 1920.

——— *Dialogue avec Tryphon . . .*, par G. Archambault, 2 t., Paris, 1909 (*Textes et documents*).

Lagrange, M. J., *Saint Justin philosophe, martyr*, Paris, 1914.

Loofs, Friedrich, *Theophilus von Antiochien adversus Marcionem und die anderen theologischen Quellen bei Irenaeus*, Leipzig, 1930 (*T. U.*).

Lortz, Joseph, *Tertullian als Apologet*, Münster i. W., 1927-28, 2. Bde.

Massart, Guglielmo, *Società e Stato nel cristianesimo primitivo, la concezione di Origene*, Padua, 1932.

Mercati, Giovanni, "Un apologia antiellenica sotto forma di martirio" (*Studi e Testi*, 5, pp. 207-226), Rome, 1901.

Minucius Felix, *Octavius*, rec. Waltzing, Leipzig, 1912.

——— *Octavius*, rec. Aloisius Valmaggi, Turin, 1916.

Miura, Anna (Stange), *Celsus und Origenes; eine Studie zur Religions und Geistesgeschichte des 2. und 3. Jahrh.*, Giessen, 1926.

Natali, Giovanni, *Socrate nel giudizio dei padri apologisti*, Ascoli Piceno, 1902.

Neumann, K. J., *Hippolytus von Rom in seine Stellung zu Staat und Welt*, Leipzig, 1902.

Puèch, Aimé, *Les apologistes grecs du IIe siècle*, Paris, 1912.

——— *Recherches sur le discours aux Grecs de Tatien*, suivies d'une traduction française du discours avec notes . . ., Paris, 1903.

Rougier, L., *Celse, ou le conflit de la civilisation antique et du christianisme*, Paris, 1926.

Ruggieri, Emidio, *Vita e dottrina di S. Giustino filosofo e martire*, Rome, 1862.

Tatian, *Il discorso ai Greci*, ed. e tr. da Paolo Ubaldi, Turin, 1921.

―――― *Oratio ad Graecos*, ed. E. Schwartz, Leipzig, 1888 (*T. U.*).

Tertullian, *L' Apologetico*, ed. Sisto Colombo, Turin, 1916.

―――― *Apologétique*, texte établi et tr. par J. P. Waltzing, Paris, 1929.

―――― *Seme di sangue* (Apologetico e Prescrizione), cura di Igino Giordani, Brescia, 1935.

Vitton, Paolo, *I concetti giuridici nelle opere di Tertulliano*, Rome, 1924.

THE SOCIAL THOUGHT OF THE CHURCH

Augar, Friedrich, *Die Frau im römischen Christenprocess*, Leipzig, 1905 (*T. U.* n. Folge, 13, 14).

Baumgartner, Ephrem, *Eucharistie und Agape in Urchristentum*, Solothurn, 1909.

Beck, Alexander, *Römisches Recht bei Tertullian und Cyprian, Eine Studie zur frühen Kirchenrechtgeschichte*, Halle, 1930.

Campenhausen, Hans von, *Die asketische Heimatlosigkeit im altkirchlichen und frühmittelalterlichen Mönchtum*, Tübingen, 1930.

Chastel, E. L. *Études historiques sur l'influence de la charité durant les premiers siècles chrétiens*, Paris, 1853.

Costa, Giovanni, *Religione e politica nell'Impero romano*, Turin, 1923.

De Regibus, L., *Milizia e Cristianesimo nell'Impero romano* (*Didaskaleion*, 1924).

Dolger, Fr. J., *Sol salutis, Gebet und Gesang im christlichen Altertum*, 2 Aufl., Münster in W., 1925.

Goodenough, E. R., *The Church in the Roman Empire*, New York, 1931.

Harnack, Adolf von, *Militia Christi; Die Christliche Religion und der Soldatenstand in den ersten drei Jahrhunderten*, Tübingen, 1905.

―――― *Medicinisches aus der ältesten Kirchengeschichte*, Leipzig, 1892 (in *T. U.* VIII, 4, pp. (37), 152).

Homo, Léon, *Les empereurs romains et le christianisme*, Paris, 1931.

Liebenam, W., *Zur Geschichte und Organisation des römischen Vereinswesens*, Leipzig, 1890.

Larmann, Hans, *Christliche Wirtschaftsethik in der spätrömischen Antike*, Berlin, 1935.

Loening, Edgar, *Die Gemeindeverfassung des Urchristentums*, Halle, 1888.

Lohmeyer, Ernst, *Vom Begriff der religiösen Gemeinschaft*, Leipzig and Berlin, 1925.

Mayer, Josephine, *Monumenta de viduis, diaconissis virginibusque*, Bonn, 1938.

Möhler, J. A., *Die Einheit in der Kirche, oder das Prinzip des Katho-*

lizismus, dargestellt im Geiste der Kirchenväter der drei ersten Jahrhunderte, Mainz, 1925.

Mommsen, Theodor, *De collegiis et sodaliciis romanorum,* Kiel, 1843.

Monnier, Henri, *La notion de l'apostolat des origines à Irenée,* Paris, 1903.

Monti, G. M., *Lineamenti di storia delle corporazioni,* Bari, 1931.

Neubner, Joseph, *Die heiligen Handwerker in der Darstellung der Acta Sanctorum,* Münster i. W., 1929.

Poland, Franz, *Geschichte des griechischen Vereinswesens,* Leipzig, 1909.

Rademacher, Arnold, *Die Kirche als Gemeinschaft und Gesellschaft.* "Eine Studie zur Sociologie der Kirche. Kirche und Gesellschaft." Augsburg, 1931.

Salvatorelli, Luigi, "Il pensiero del cristianesimo antico intorno allo Stato, dagli apologeti ad Origene" (in *Bilychnis,* October, 1920).

Schepelern, W., *Der Montanismus und die phrygischen Kulte,* Tübingen, 1929.

Schmidt, C. G. A., *Essai historique sur la société civile dans le monde romain et sur la transformation par le christianisme,* Strasbourg-Paris, 1853.

Schweigmann, F. A., "De Kerkvaders en de theorie von het oorspronkelijk communisme" (in *Nederl. Kath. stemmen,* 1931, pp. 247 ff.).

Thomassin, Louis, *Vetus et nova Ecclesiae disciplina* (III, 1, 3, chap. 31-33 treat of hospitality, assistance to the needy etc. in the Church), Venice, 1752.

Vacandard, E. *Etudes de critique et d'histoire religieuse,* 2ᵉ série (L'institution formelle de l'Église par le Christ. Le service militaire et les premiers chrétiens), 2ᵉ éd., Paris, 1910.

Zeiller, Jacques, *L'Empire romain et l'Eglise,* Paris, 1928.

Zellinger, Johannes, *Bad und Bäder in der altchristlichen Kirche,* Munich, 1928.

CHRISTIAN THOUGHT, LITERATURE AND ART

Bardy, Gustave, "L'Eglise et l'enseignement pendant les trois premiers siècles," *Revue des sciences relig.,* 1932, t. XII and ff.

Cataudella, Quintino, *Critica ed estetica nella letteratura greca cristiana,* Turin, 1928.

Eynde, D. van den, *Les normes de l'enseignement chrétien dans la littérature patristique des trois premiers siècles,* Gembloux-Paris, 1933.

Lebreton, J., "La théorie de la connaissance religieuse chez Clément d'Alexandrie," in *Recherches de science religieuse,* October, 1928.

Neuss, Wilhelm, *Die Kunst der alten Christen,* Augsburg, 1926.

Pélagaud, Elysée, *Un conservateur au second siècle. Celse et les pre-*

mières luttes entre la philosophie antique et le christianisme naissant, Paris, 1879.

Quasten, Johannes, *Musik und Gesang in den Kulten der heidnischen Antike und christlichen Frühzeit*, Münster in W., 1930.

Revue de l'art chrétien, Amiens (etc.), 1857-1914.

Sauer, Joseph, *Symbolik des Kirchengebäudes*, Freiburg i. B., 1924 (with a rich bibliography).

INDEX

ALSO AVAILABLE
FROM ST. PAUL EDITIONS

BOOKS

THE CATECHISM OF MODERN MAN
Edited and compiled by a team of Daughters of St. Paul
Best Seller
—Over 9,000 topics—*The Catechism of Modern Man* is the only
complete source of the Council's new and profound expression of the Faith—all in the words of Vatican II and related
post-conciliar documents.
731 pages; plastic or cloth $6.95; paper $5.95

CHRIST, HOPE OF THE WORLD
Igino Giordani
A vibrant life of Christ, overflowing with timely and profound
insights into the teachings of the Divine Master. "Christ walked
with man, that man might walk with God." 32 striking full-color
illustrations.
480 pages; deluxe $10.00; cloth $8.00; paper $7.00

THE CHURCH AND THE CHANGE
Rev. Robert H. Howes
"We cannot find the image of the urban humanist on the
drafting board or in the slide rule or in the computer,
important as these tools are. We must seek him as the whole
man, the planner turned philosopher and humanist"
Charles A. Blessing. *The Church and the Change* recommends
itself to students of Church and students of change. Deals
heavily in events of major moment to all Americans: urban
renewal, suburbia, planning.
184 pages; cloth $3.00

DESIGN FOR A JUST SOCIETY

A brief, clear treatment of Catholic social teaching, including:
— the reasons why the Church speaks out on social issues;
— the dignity and rights of man;
— human solidarity and brotherhood;
— the vital importance of the family;
— the true role of the political community;
— the means of attaining and maintaining healthy and progressive economic life;
— guidelines for world development and peace.

Quotations from papal documents, Vatican II and Sacred Scripture give this volume a richness that may be increased still more by following up the abundant suggestions given for further reading. The discussion questions and project suggestions can lead to fruitful life applications. With teacher's manual.

250 pages; cloth $4.00; paper $3.00

THE LAWYER IN COMMUNISM

Dr. Lajos Kálman

Memoirs of a lawyer behind the Iron Curtain, with a foreword by Richard Cardinal Cushing.

196 pages; paper $2.00

THE LIFE OF CHRIST

Isidore O'Brien, OFM

"The life of Christ is of infinite significance to every human being. In every generation the Christian people have sought comfort and strength and inspiration from the Gospel story." Most Rev. Edwin V. O'Hara. Complete with full-color photographs of the Holy Land and discussion questions at the end of each chapter. Ideal for upper elementary and lower high school scripture courses.

615 pages; cloth $7.95; paper $6.95

MEDIEVAL TIES BETWEEN ITALY AND IRELAND

Rev. M. P. Harney, SJ

This book explores the ties uniting two great Catholic peoples — the bonds of religion and learning, Irish missions in Italy, Italian pilgrimages to St. Patrick's purgatory....

80 pages; cloth $1.50

ONE FAMILY UNDER GOD
Daughters of St. Paul
This timely, penetrating book contains general principles laid down by Vatican II, Pope John XXIII, Pope Paul VI, and the Bishops of the USA in order: to fashion the world more to man's surpassing dignity; to search for a brotherhood which is universal and more deeply rooted; and to meet the urgent needs of our age with a gallant and unified effort born of love.
104 pages; cloth $2.25; paper $1.25

PEACE — WHERE IS IT?
Annie Cagiati
This book takes up the ever current problem of peace. Is peace possible? Where can we find it? Is it something that comes from without or from within? Mr. John Q. Public, main character, pursues the problem of peace until he arrives at answers that satisfy. Its cartoon style makes it delightful for every age.
128 pages; plastic $2.95; paper $1.95

YES TO LIFE
An invaluable source-book bringing together the consistent teaching of the Church on the sacredness of human life from the early years of Christianity to our own days.
328 pages; cloth $5.95; paper $4.95

PAMPHLETS

APPEAL FOR PEACE
Pope Paul VI
Address given to the United Nations General Assembly in New York, October 4, 1965.
14 pages; 10c

A CALL TO A CONSISTENT ETHIC OF LIFE AND THE LAW
Humberto Cardinal Medeiros
"An ethic of life which will appeal to the consciences of men today must be constructed in a way that is both comprehensive in scope and consistent in substance."
22 pages; 15c

A CALL TO CATHOLIC WOMEN FOR THE APOSTOLATE OF WORKS OF LOVE

Richard Cardinal Cushing
Addressed to women whose charity at home overflows into the wider areas of the community.
16 pages; 15c

FOOD FOR THE TABLES OF THE WORLD

Humberto Cardinal Medeiros
World-hunger problem.
24 pages; 15c

FORMATION OF CON-SCIENCE (STATEMENT ON)

Issued by the Canadian Bishops
32 pages; 25c

HUMAN LIFE IN OUR DAY

U.S. Bishops
A joint pastoral letter commenting on Pope Paul's encyclical, "Of Human Life" —"Humanae Vitae."
70 pages; 35c

KILLING OR CARING? —YOU MUST CHOOSE

A joint statement by the Catholic Bishops of Massachusetts on abortion.
10 pages; 10c

DECLARATION ON PROCURED ABORTION

Sacred Congregation for the Doctrine of the Faith
"Life at all its levels comes from God, and bodily life is for man the indispensable beginning."
32 pages; 15c

INTER-RACIAL JUSTICE

Richard Cardinal Cushing
16 pages; 10c

THE HOME AND MENTAL HEALTH

Dr. Michael P. Penetar
How parents contribute to the mental health of their children.
36 pages; 25c

JUSTICE EXALTS...

John Cardinal Wright
"The Church exists to confront sin and communicate love."
28 pages; 10c

MAN'S CITIES AND GOD'S POOR

Humberto Cardinal Medeiros
"Life in its totality today is being cruelly strangled, especially in many of our cities."
80 pages; 50c

MORALITY IN OUR TIME

Humberto Cardinal Medeiros
"Man's problem today is not only that he has failed to adjust to his environment, but that he has also lost sight of his religious worth, his spiritual origins and his supernatural end."
16 pages; 10c

A SUMMONS TO RACIAL JUSTICE

Richard Cardinal Cushing
24 pages; 6c; special discount of 40% on orders of over 100 copies

RECONCILIATION WITHIN THE CHURCH

Pope Paul VI
"The duty of making peace extends personally to each and every member of the faithful."
32 pages; 15c

WE LONG TO BE PART OF YOUR LIFE

Daughters of St. Paul
The sacredness of all human life.
16 pages; 10c

VATICAN II, POST-CONCILIAR AND PAPAL DOCUMENTS

Decree on the Media of Social Communication *(Inter mirifica)* 15c
Dogmatic Constitution on the Church *(Lumen gentium)* 50c
Declaration on Religious Freedom *(Dignitatis humanae)* 20c
Pastoral Constitution on the Church in the Modern World
    (Gaudium et spes) 65c
Pastoral Instruction for the Application of the Decree of the
    Second Vatican Ecumenical Council on the Means of Social
    Communication *(Communio et progressio)* 50c
Synodal Document on Justice in the World 15c

POPE LEO XIII
Condition of Working Classes *(Rerum novarum)* 25c

POPE PIUS XI
Atheistic Communism *(Divini Redemptoris)* 25c
Social Reconstruction *(Quadragesimo anno)* 25c

POPE PIUS XII
Function of State in the Modern World 25c

POPE JOHN XXIII

Christianity and Social Progress *(Mater et magistra)* 25c
Peace on Earth *(Pacem in terris)* 25c

POPE PAUL VI

Apostolic Letter to Cardinal Maurice Roy, President of the
    Council of the Laity and of the Pontifical Commission
    on Justice and Peace, on the Occasion of the Eightieth
    Anniversary of the Encyclical Rerum novarum ("The
    Coming Eightieth") *(Octogesima adveniens)* 25c
The Development of Peoples *(Populorum progressio)* 25c
Of Human Life *(Humanae vitae)* 15c
Paths of the Church *(Ecclesiam Suam)* 25c

AUDIO-VISUALS

PEACE—WHERE IS IT?

Join John Q. Public's search for peace, from mental torture
of sleepless nights to unexpected meditation on table salt—
a quest agonizing yet delightful, realistic yet mysterious,
heart-warming yet thought-provoking. Touches many issues
vital to peace. A meaningful experience in reconciliation with
God and our fellow man. Discussion guide.
Jr. high/adult; 72 color frames; 15 min. cassette
_____SLIDE/SOUND PRESENTATION (Cassette recording.
Please check:
manual_____automatic_____), $26.95
_____FILMSTRIP/CASSETTE PROGRAM: $15.95

WHO IS JESUS?

An audio-visual encounter with Jesus today. Jesus—alive,
compelling, magnetic—mingles with the contemporary views
which challenge Him.
Jr. high/adult; 72 color frames; discussion guide; 15 min.
cassette
_____SLIDE/SOUND PRESENTATION (Cassette recording.
Please check: manual_____automatic_____), $26.95
_____FILMSTRIP/CASSETTE PROGRAM: $15.95

Please order from addresses on following page.

Daughters of St. Paul

IN MASSACHUSETTS
    50 St. Paul's Avenue, Boston, Ma. 02130
    172 Tremont Street, Boston, Ma. 02111
IN NEW YORK
    78 Fort Place, Staten Island, N.Y. 10301
    59 East 43rd St., New York, N.Y. 10017
    625 East 187th Street, Bronx, N.Y. 10458
    525 Main Street, Buffalo, N.Y. 14203
IN NEW JERSEY
    84 Washington Street, Bloomfield, N.J. 07003
IN CONNECTICUT
    202 Fairfield Avenue, Bridgeport, Ct. 06603
IN OHIO
    2105 Ontario St. (at Prospect Ave.), Cleveland, Oh. 44115
    25 E. Eighth Street, Cincinnati, Oh. 45202
IN PENNSYLVANIA
    1719 Chestnut St., Philadelphia, Pa. 19103
IN FLORIDA
    2700 Biscayne Blvd., Miami, Fl. 33137
IN LOUISIANA
    4403 Veterans Memorial Blvd.,
      Metairie, La. 70002
    86 Bolton Avenue, Alexandria, La. 71301
IN MISSOURI
    1001 Pine St. (at North 10th), St. Louis, Mo. 63101
IN TEXAS
    114 East Main Plaza, San Antonio, Tx. 78205
IN CALIFORNIA
    1570 Fifth Avenue, San Diego, Ca. 92101
    278 17th Street, Oakland, Ca. 94612
    46 Geary Street, San Francisco, Ca. 94108
IN HAWAII
    1184 Bishop St., Honolulu, Hi. 96813
IN ALASKA
    750 West 5th Avenue
    Anchorage, Ak. 99501
IN CANADA
    3022 Dufferin Street, Toronto 395, Ontario, Canada
IN ENGLAND
    57, Kensington Church Street, London W. 8, England
IN AUSTRALIA
    58, Abbotsford Rd., Homebush, N.S.W., Sydney 2140,
    Australia